LET ME TELL YOU THE REAL STORY OF MANKIND

J. Parnell McCarter

Adapted from Hendrick Van Loon's "The Story of Mankind"

SECOND EDITION

Copyright © 2019 McCarter Providential Enterprises LLC
All rights reserved. No part of this publication may be reproduced, stored in a retrieval system, or transmitted in any form or by any means, except for brief quotations in critical reviews or articles, without the prior written permission of the publisher.
Scripture references are from the Authorized Version.

ISBN-13: 9781708954369

"Remember now thy Creator in the days of thy youth, while the evil days come not, nor the years draw nigh, when thou shalt say, I have no pleasure in them." – Ecclesiastes 12:1

Dedicated to my two sons, D. Parnell and Calvin, that they may remember the Creator in the days of their youth and use their energies to promote Christ's kingdom.

Written and edited by J. Parnell McCarter
Illustrated by Caleb Nadeau, along with certain miscellaneous drawings

Part of the Puritans' Home School Curriculum
www.puritans.net

CONTENTS

FOREWORD v

CHAPTER 1: The First Man and Woman 1
CHAPTER 2: Mankind Judged with the Great Flood 5
CHAPTER 3: The Mesopotamians 11
CHAPTER 4: The Egyptians... 19
CHAPTER 5: The Canaanites, the Phoenicians, and the
    Hittites 29
CHAPTER 6: The Hebrews 35
CHAPTER 7: The Chinese 55
CHAPTER 8: The Indo-Europeans 63
CHAPTER 9: The Rise of the Greek Civilization 71
CHAPTER 10: The Persian Wars 85
CHAPTER 11: Athens *vs.* Sparta in the Peloponnesian Wars
    91
CHAPTER 12: Alexander the Great 93
CHAPTER 13: A Summary 97
CHAPTER 14: Rome and Carthage 99
CHAPTER 15: The Rise of Rome 113
CHAPTER 16: The Great Roman Empire 123
CHAPTER 17: The Everlasting Kingdom of Jesus Christ .. 127
CHAPTER 18: The Fall of Rome... 137
CHAPTER 19: The Spread of Christianity and the Rise of
    Anti-Christ.. 143
CHAPTER 20: Mohammed and Islam on the March 153
CHAPTER 21: Charlemagne and the Rise of the Holy
    Roman Empire in the West 161

CHAPTER 22: The Norsemen.. 167

CHAPTER 23: Feudalism 171

CHAPTER 24: Pope *vs.* Emporer.. 179

CHAPTER 25: The Crusades 185

CHAPTER 26: The Mediæval City 191

CHAPTER 27: The Mediæval World 203

CHAPTER 28: Mediæval Trade 211

CHAPTER 29: The Dawn of the Renaissance........................ 219

CHAPTER 30: The Morning Star of the Reformation......... 231

CHAPTER 31: The Response of Rome to the Renaissance
  and the Reformation... 243

CHAPTER 32: China and Marco Polo.................................... 249

CHAPTER 33: Great Discoveries by Sea 255

CHAPTER 34: India 269

CHAPTER 35: The Reformation.. 277

CHAPTER 36: The Further Spread of the Reformation in
  Continental Europe 289

CHAPTER 37: The Protestant Reformation Reaches
  England, Scotland and Beyond.. 301

CHAPTER 38: Rome's Counter-Reformation....................... 321

CHAPTER 39: England, Scotland, and the English Colonies
  in the 17th Century 329

CHAPTER 40: The Balance of Power 341

CHAPTER 41: The Rise of Russia.. 347

CHAPTER 42: Russia *vs.* Sweden 355

CHAPTER 43: The Rise of Prussia 359

CHAPTER 44: The Mercantile System 365

CHAPTER 45: The Enlightenment.. 369

CHAPTER 46: England, Scotland, and the English Colonies
  in the 18th Century 377

CHAPTER 47: The American Revolution 385

CHAPTER 48: The French Revolution 393

CHAPTER 49: Napoleon 409

CHAPTER 50: The (Un) Holy Alliance 419

CHAPTER 51: The Great Reaction 431

CHAPTER 52: National Independence 439

CHAPTER 53: The Age of the Engine and the Industrial Revolution 461

CHAPTER 54: The Social Revolution that Accompanied the Industrial Revolution 471

CHAPTER 55: Abolition of Slavery, States' Rights, ... 477
and the American Civil War 477

CHAPTER 56: Science and Pseudo-science 483

CHAPTER 57: Socialism and Marxism 487

CHAPTER 58: Art, Architecture, and Literature Through the Centuries 491

CHAPTER 59: Colonial Expansion and War 503

CHAPTER 60: World War I 509

CHAPTER 61: Communism, Fascism, World War II, and a Cold War 515

CHAPTER 62: Zionism and Islamic Resurgence 527

CHAPTER 63: Secular Humanism 533
and the Information Age 533

BIBLIOGRAPHY 541

INDEX 543

FOREWORD

Hendrik Van Loon's *Story of Mankind* recounted the history of mankind in a way characterized by a grandfather telling his grandchild a captivating story. In my history entitled *Let Me Tell You the Real Story of Mankind* I have sought to retain that engaging style and even much of Van Loon's detail. However, Hendrik Van Loon's original work leaned heavily upon materialistic evolution and a modernist interpretation of history, but my revised version of this history rests upon historic Biblical Christianity and seeks to offer an historical account conformable to it.

J. Parnell McCarter

Editor, Puritans' Home School Curriculum
Grand Rapids, Michigan, USA

CHAPTER 1: The First Man and Woman

Let me tell you the real story of mankind. I mean the story that looks to God and His infallible word the Bible as the ultimate foundation of truth, and not the ever-changing and faulty foundation of human theory. Let's start our story in the beginning of mankind, which was around six thousand years ago in a Paradise called Eden. There we meet with the first man that God created: Adam.

Setting the Stage

As he walked amidst the garden, he was awed by the beauty before his eyes. God had set him in the midst of such peace and splendor he could hardly imagine it. There was beautiful vegetation, remarkable animals, a marvelous climate, and delicious food to eat. He was honored by God to be ruler over all that he saw. And God had even honored him with a help meet for him- his wife, Eve.

While so engaged in wonder, Eve came running up to him. "Adam, come see what I have found." As he followed Eve and approached the tree to which she was leading him, Adam knew immediately which tree it was. "Not that tree, Eve. That is the one we have been warned about." As he gazed upon the tree and the fruit that Eve was now offering him, all the things God had told him were racing through Adam's mind. He remembered how God had said that he had created everything Adam could see. He remembered how God had given him the honor of naming these things. He remembered how God had responded to his loneliness and given him the woman. And most importantly at this particular time, he remembered how God had warned him not to eat the forbidden fruit of this tree. Adam was torn between two desires, one to abstain and one to eat, yet with a pure conscience which knew he ought not. In rebellion against the God who had bestowed upon him such kindness, Adam ate the forbidden fruit. Eve had eaten the forbidden fruit, being deceived by Satan in the form of a serpent, while Adam knew it was wrong and ate it nevertheless.

What I am going to tell you in this long story now begins with how Adam sinned against God. The story starts with man's sin and rebellion against God's perfect order but ends with God's redemption of man. It is the story of how God gloriously saves a people from their sins and redeems a world for his glory- a world which man scarred by his own rebellion against God.

God's Interview with the Man and the Woman

We left off with Adam and Eve eating the forbidden fruit. Well, having eaten the forbidden fruit, Adam and Eve thought their only safety was in hiding from God. Oh, how foolish man is! Can he really hide from the God who made and upholds the earth? Nevertheless, Adam and Eve tried then, and many men even still try today.

But, of course, God found them. "Where art thou?" he cried out to Adam. Adam sheepishly came forward. "I hid myself," he said. But God questioned him. Adam then blamed his present circumstances on Eve, who gave him the forbidden fruit, and on the God who made Eve. Eve in turn blamed the serpent, who had deceived Eve into eating the fruit.

God's anger surely was kindled at these three creatures he had made, yet that had rebelled against Him. To each He pronounced a certain judgment. Yet even in His judgment, God displayed His infinite mercy as well. He promised that the Seed of the woman should bruise the head of the serpent, the Devil. From the beginning of man's judgment there was also the Promise that God would raise up from the descendants of Eve a Christ who would save a people redeemed unto Himself. It is this Promise that the people of God clung onto for around four thousand years until the Seed came.

Nevertheless, Adam and Eve had to depart from the Paradise into which they originally had been planted, for God would not allow them to remain there. And so began man's existence under the curse of sin.

J. Parnell McCarter

LET ME TELL YOU THE REAL STORY OF MANKIND

CHAPTER 2: Mankind Judged with the Great Flood

God mercifully gave Eve sons, though they had to be borne by her with much pain and agony. Eve bore Abel, Cain, and Seth. Out of the line of Seth would come the Seed promised who would crush the Devil's head. But Cain gave his parents much grief.

Cain had offered God the fruits of the earth in his worship, but God was only pleased with Abel's offering of a lamb. God has ever been jealous for His worship, demanding what He has commanded. Cain, seeing God's favor towards Abel, became envious of his brother. When wicked Cain in his envy slew his brother Abel, he and his children were cast off by God.

This left Seth as the only living son who was not cast off by God. Seth had many descendants, some of whom were quite godly. But many of Seth's posterity over time joined themselves to the ungodly descendants of Cain. Such sin prevailed then that Enoch, the seventh from Adam who was descended from Seth, prophesied of judgment at hand. God rewarded Enoch's faithfulness by taking him up alive into Heaven.

There are many things we do not know about these peoples who lived before the Great Flood. How far did they disperse from the area that was the original Paradise? How many of the archeological artifacts which we find today are associated with these peoples that lived before the Flood? But we do know that some impressive technological development was made in this time. Indeed, in this time eight hundred and nine hundred years was the usual term of men's lives, and the race was in full strength and freshness, so there was time for mind and body to come to great force. We find that the chief inventions of man belong to the sons of Cain-the dwelling in tents, workmanship in brass and iron, and the use of musical instruments. On the other hand, the more holy of the line of Seth handed on from one to the other the history of the blessed days of Eden, and of God's promise, and lived upon hope and faith.

LET ME TELL YOU THE REAL STORY OF MANKIND

Noah, whose father had been alive in the latter years of Adam's life, was chosen by God from among the descendants of Seth. God had determined to judge man for the widespread wickedness, by sending a flood which would destroy it. But for Noah, God planned salvation. So, God commanded Noah to build an ark which could survive the flood. Noah warned his fellow man, even as he constructed the ark. But they only scoffed and mocked him.

When the time came for the flood, Noah's own family of eight persons were alone found faithful to be spared from the destruction, together with all the animals with them preserved in the ark. There were two of each kind of animal in the ark, and a sevenfold number of those milder and purer animals which part the hoof and chew the cud and were already marked out as fit for sacrifice.

It was around the year 2350 B.C. that Noah spent in floating upon the waste of waters while every living thing was perishing around him. But the flood waters returned to their beds in oceans, lakes, and rivers, which they shall never again overpass. The ark first came aground on the mountain of Ararat, in what is Armenia. It was here that God made His covenant with Noah. God also renewed His first blessing to Adam, permitting the use of animal food. God promised that the course of nature should never be disturbed again till the end of all things, and he made the glorious tints of the rainbow, which are produced by sunlight upon water, to stand as the pledge of this assurance. Of man He required abstinence from eating the blood of animals, and from shedding the blood of man. This put a mark of sacredness upon lifeblood, so as to lead the mind on to the Blood hereafter to be shed by the Lord and Savior Jesus Christ.

From Armenia the family of Noah began to spread as they multiplied. They gave rise in the course of time to three distinct people groups, from each of Noah's sons: Japheth, Ham, and Shem. These are most properly termed Japhethites, Hamites, and Shemites: the Caucasoid Japhethites (the root word of 'Japheth' meaning 'fair' [complexioned]), the darker skinned Hamites (the root word of 'Ham' meaning 'dark' [complexioned]), and the Semitic peoples. All of these began in the area of the Middle East, and so we find evidence even to this day that all lines of migration that are in any way still traceable are found to radiate from the Middle East.

Soon a choice was made among the sons of Noah by God. Ham mocked at his father's infirmity, while his two brothers veiled it. Noah was therefore inspired to prophesy that Canaan, the son of the undutiful Ham, should be accursed, and a servant of servants; that Shem should especially belong to the Lord God; and that Japheth's posterity should be enlarged, and should dwell in the tents of Shem. Shem was marked as the chosen, yet there was hope that the other people groups should eventually share in his gospel blessings.

LET ME TELL YOU THE REAL STORY OF MANKIND

It seems as if Ham had brought away some of the arts and habits of the giant sons of Cain, for in worldly prosperity his sons had the early advantage and were possibly more numerous as well. His sons had the power to control the choice regions of the time. The areas under their control included Mesopotamia, Egypt and beyond in Africa, much of Asia Minor (which today is the nation of Turkey), and Canaan. These areas were of mild climate and within closer proximity to where man had lived up until that time following the Flood. And these descendants of Ham shrewdly employed technology to harness the riches of the areas they controlled. They were many of the post-Flood world's political leaders, builders of cities, cultivators of the land, weavers and embroiderers, earnest after comfort and riches, but utterly forgetting, or grievously corrupting, the worship of God. Some of the most prominent descendants of Ham who would go on to form and lead nations of Hamites include Nimrod (who led the post-Flood world's first mighty empire headquartered in Babel), Mizraim (the father of the Egyptian nation), Canaan (the father of the Canaanite nation), and Heth (the father of the Hittite nation).

Shem's sons continued to live in tents and watch their cattle, scattered about in the same plains, called Mesopotamia, meaning 'the land of rivers'. Some travelled eastwards from present day Iran. Shem's posterity became a rich and wealthy people, but constantly losing more and more the recollection of the truth. Some of the most prominent descendants of Shem who would go on to form and lead nations of Shemites include Arphaxad (the father of the Chaldean nation), Eber and his descendant Abraham (the fathers of the Hebrew nation), Asshur (the father of the Assyrian nation), and Aram (the father of the Syrian nation).

Japheth's children seemed at first the least favored in living condition, for no place, save the cold dreary north, was found for most of them to be able to live and reign. Some few, the children of Javan, found a home in the fair isles of the Mediterranean, but the greater part were wild horsemen in Northern Asia and Europe. This was a dark and dismal training, but it braced them so that in future generations they proved to have more force and spirit than was to be found among the dwellers in milder climates. They were able to survive, thrive, and dominate large expanses of geographic territory, even as God had predestined and foretold.

These children are often called Indo-Europeans, because they eventually conquered and settled in the regions that extended from Europe in the west and down to India in the east. Sadly, these too departed from the true religion of their ancestor Noah and became corrupt in their religious worship. Some of the most prominent descendants of Japheth who would go on to form and lead nations of Japhethites include Javan (the father of the Greek/Ionian nation), Magog (the father of the Scythian nation, who would come to inhabit the territory north of the Black Sea and beyond), Madai (the father of the nation of the Medes), and Ashkenaz (the father of the Germanic nation).

LET ME TELL YOU THE REAL STORY OF MANKIND

CHAPTER 3: The Mesopotamians

The first great civilization and center of human empire established after the Flood was in the area geographically downriver from the original Paradise of Adam and Eve as well as from the mountains of Armenia. It was in a valley situated between two great rivers. It is the land of mystery and wonder which the Greeks called Mesopotamia – the "country between the rivers."

The names of the two rivers are the Euphrates (which the Babylonians called the Purattu) and the Tigris (which was known as the Diklat). The Tigris begins its course amidst the snows of the mountains of Armenia where Noah's Ark found a resting place, and slowly it flows through the southern plain until it reaches the muddy banks of the Persian Gulf, along with the Euphrates. They perform a very useful service. They turn the arid regions of western Asia into a fertile garden.

The "land between the rivers" was popular because it offered food to people upon fairly easy terms compared with many other places. It was a country full of promise. Consequently, both the inhabitants of the northern mountains and the tribes which roamed through the southern deserts tried to claim this territory as their own and most exclusive possession. The constant rivalry between the mountaineers and the desert-nomads led to endless warfare over the centuries. Only the strongest, most numerous and most crafty, willing to employ evil means when necessary, could hope to dominate. That will explain why Mesopotamia at first came under the rule of a strong tribe of men descended from Ham. The descendants of Ham in the centuries following the Flood dominated here as in other places like Egypt and Canaan.

The Sumerians and The Tower of Babel

Although dominated by Ham's descendants, there were peoples represented here from Shem and Japheth as well. The evidence now seems to indicate clearly the presence in Mesopotamia in very early times of these three distinct groups of people: the Hamitic peoples (such as the Sumerians), the Semitic peoples (such as the Chaldeans), and the Indo-European peoples (such as the Medes). People who study languages, called philologists, have found evidence of the presence of these three linguistic groups in the area. The presence of Japhethites is suggested only inferentially from a few place-names; the presence of the Semites is suggested by languages akin to Hebrew and Arabic; and the presence of the Hamites is found in the many artifacts of the dominant Sumerians.

One of Ham's descendants initiated a movement to prevent further dispersal by proposing the building of a monument as a visible rallying point on the flat plain. It was around 2250 B.C. when the sons of men banded themselves together to build the infamous Tower of Babel on the plain of Shinar, downriver from the hills of Armenia, where the two great rivers Euphrates and Tigris make the flats rich and fertile. Nimrod, the child of Cush and grandson of Ham, kept Babel, built the first city, and became the first king.

For their presumption, God confounded their speech, and the ethnic nations first were politically and linguistically divided. God's judgment led to an enforced and rapid scattering throughout the earth, each racial group and sub-group coming to dwell in its own geographic territory, even as God had planned.

The Writings of The Sumerians
The Hamitic Sumerian civilization wrote mysterious "cuneiform inscriptions" (so-called because the letters were wedge-shaped, and wedge is called "Cuneus" in Latin). Let me

now tell you how this mysterious writing was deciphered much later in history.

The fifteenth century A.D. was an age of great discoveries. Columbus tried to find a way to the island of Cathay and stumbled upon a new and unsuspected continent. An Austrian bishop equipped an expedition which was to travel eastward and find the home of the Grand Duke of Muscovy, a voyage which led to complete failure, for Moscow was not visited by western men until a generation later. Meanwhile a certain Venetian by the name of Barbero had explored the ruins of western Asia and had brought back reports of a most curious language which he had found carved in the rocks of the temples of Shiraz and engraved upon endless pieces of baked clay. It was later discovered that Barbero had discovered writings of the ancient Sumerians.

But Europe was busy with many other things and it was not until the end of the eighteenth century that the first "cuneiform inscriptions" were brought to Europe by a Danish surveyor, named Niebuhr. Then it took thirty years before a patient German schoolmaster by the name of Grotefend had deciphered the first four letters, the D, the A, the R and the SH, the name of the Persian King Darius. And another twenty years had to go by until a British officer, Henry Rawlinson, who found the famous inscription of Behistun, gave us a workable key to the nailwriting of western Asia. It was quite difficult, but these writings on tablets of clay were finally de-ciphered. The Sumerians kept many official records on these tablets of clay, so that we are able to learn about their society. It was from the Mesopotamian region dominated by Hamitic Sumerians, albeit inhabited by Semitic Chaldeans and others as well, that Abraham departed around 2000 B.C. And the cuneiform of Sumeria remained in use in the region for centuries past the time of Abraham.

Hammurabi's Reign in Babylon

Approximately 500 years after construction work on the Tower of Babel, a great king named Hammurabi reigned in the city. The city then was called Babylon, and it was not a mere city at this time, but an independent kingdom also.

King Hammurabi built himself a magnificent palace in the holy city of Babylon and gave his people a set of laws which made the Babylonian state the best administered empire of its time. The set of laws is called the Code of Hammurabi, and it was discovered on a seven-foot-high stone monument in 1901.

The Code of Hammurabi contained criminal law, outlawing false witness, sorcery, theft, and similar type crimes. It also contained commercial laws and property laws, governing business transactions and land ownership. It included marriage law, covering such issues as divorce and dowry settlements. It even included an appendix of slave laws, establishing rules for their purchase and sale.

But even the greatness of Babylon declined in years following the reign of Hammurabi. And in 1595 B.C. it was overrun, along with the rest of the Fertile Valley, by the Hittites, who we shall consider more fully later.

Nineveh of the Assyrians

They in turn were vanquished by the followers of the desert 'god', Ashur, the forefather who led them and who they in subsequent centuries deified. They called themselves Assyrians and made the city of Nineveh the center of a vast and terrible empire which conquered all of western Asia and Egypt and gathered taxes from countless subject races until the end of the seventh century before the birth of Christ.

Babylon

Around the end of the seventh century B.C. the Chaldeans re-established Babylon and made that city the most important capital of that day. It was the center of the then mighty Babylonian empire. Nebuchadnezzar, the best known of their kings, encouraged the study of science, and our modern knowledge of astronomy and mathematics is all based upon certain first principles which were discovered by the Chaldeans who ruled the Babylonian empire of that period.

The Persian Empire

In the year 538 B.C. a crude tribe of Medo-Persian shepherds invaded this old land and overthrew the empire of the Chaldeans. This was to mark a period when the descendants of Japheth ascended to imperial power, for the Medo-Persians, and later the Greeks and Romans, were all Indo-Europeans primarily descended from Japheth.

The Persian empire extended to Greece and Libya on the west and to India on the east.

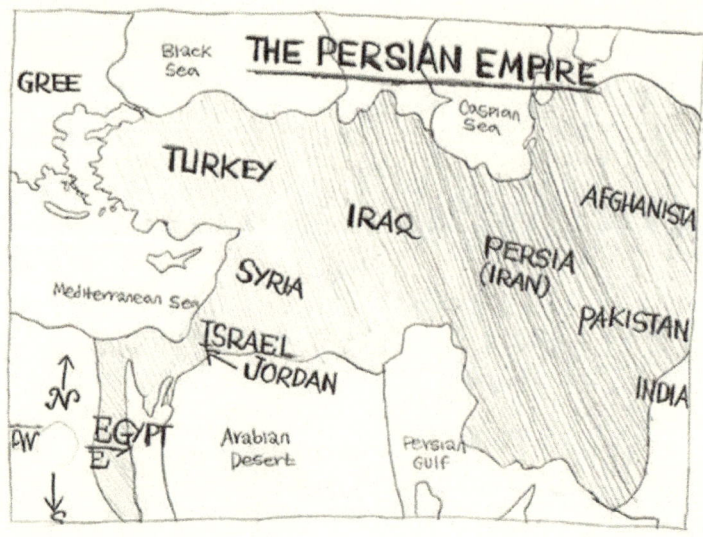

Two hundred years later, the Persians were overthrown by Alexander the Great, who turned the Fertile Valley, the old melting-pot of the three races, into a Greek province.

Next came the Romans and after the Romans, the Turks. Mesopotamia, the center of many of the world's early empires and its civilizations, became a vast wilderness where huge mounds of earth told a story of ancient glory.

CHAPTER 4: The Egyptians

Many of Ham's descendants dispersed to areas west of Mesopotamia, especially towards and in Africa. One son of Ham, Mizraim, settled in the land called Egypt. The name Mizraim literally means 'the two Egypts', likely referring to Lower Egypt and Upper Egypt. Many ancient cities and nations were named after their founder and leader, as Egypt was. Thus, Mizraim's children obtained the rich and beautiful valley of the Nile.

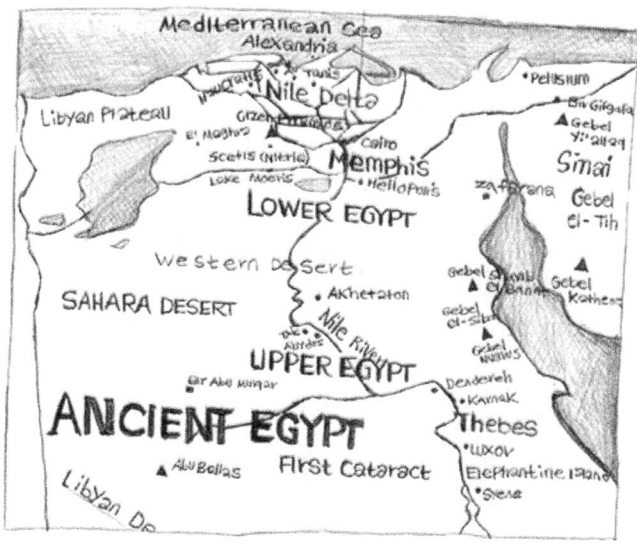

The people of the Nile valley developed a high stage of civilization thousands of years ago, like many of Ham's other descendants. The Egyptians were quite developed, but sadly pagan. They were excellent farmers. They knew all about irrigation. They built temples which were afterwards copied by the Greeks much later. They had a calendar which proved such a useful instrument for the purpose of measuring time that it has survived with a few changes until today. The Egyptians also had writing.

We are so accustomed to newspapers and books and magazines that we take for granted a world of reading and writing. But many societies in the course of human history have been without this ability, and it has greatly limited them. For more extensive learning and development to take place, writing is vital.

Hieroglyphics

In the first century before our era, when the Romans came to Egypt, they found the valley full of strange little pictures which seemed to have something to do with the history of the country. But the Romans were not interested in "anything foreign" and did not inquire into the origin of these queer figures which covered the walls of the temples and the walls of the palaces and endless reams of flat sheets made out of the papyrus reed. The last of the Egyptian priests who had understood the holy art of making such pictures had died several years before. Egypt deprived of its independence had become a storehouse filled with important historical documents which no one could decipher, and which were of no earthly use to either man or beast.

Seventeen centuries went by and these historical documents remained a mystery. But in the year 1798 a French general by the name of Bonaparte happened to visit eastern Africa to prepare for an attack upon the British Indian Colonies. He did not get beyond the Nile, and his campaign was a failure. But, quite accidentally, the famous French expedition solved the problem of the ancient Egyptian picture-language.

One day a young French officer, much bored by the dreary life of his little fortress on the Rosetta river (a mouth of the Nile) decided to spend a few idle hours rummaging among the ruins of the Nile Delta. And behold! he found a stone which greatly puzzled him. Like everything else in Egypt, it was covered with little figures. But this particular slab of black basalt was different from anything that had ever been discovered. It carried three inscriptions. One of these was in Greek. The Greek language was known. "All that is necessary," so he reasoned, "is to compare the Greek text with the Egyptian figures, and they will at once tell their secrets."

HIEROGLYPHIC   DEMOTIC   GREEK

The plan sounded simple enough but it took more than twenty years to solve the riddle. In the year 1802 a French professor by the name of Champollion began to compare the Greek and the Egyptian texts of the famous Rosetta stone. In the year 1823 he announced that he had discovered the meaning of fourteen little figures. A short time later he died from overwork, but the main principles of Egyptian writing had become known. Today the story of the valley of the Nile is better known to us than the story of the Mississippi River. We possess a written record which covers centuries of chronicled history.

As the ancient Egyptian hieroglyphics (the word means "sacred writing") have played such a very great role in history, (a few of them in modified form have even found their way into our own alphabet,) you ought to know something about the ingenious system which was used centuries ago to preserve the spoken word for the benefit of the coming generations.

Of course, you know what a sign language is. Every Indian story of our western plains has a chapter devoted to strange messages written in the form of little pictures which tell how many buffaloes were killed and how many hunters there were in a certain party. As a rule, it is not difficult to understand the meaning of such messages.

Ancient Egyptian, however, was not a sign language. Their pictures meant a great deal more than the object which they represented, as I shall try to explain to you now.

Suppose that you were Champollion, and that you were examining a stack of papyrus sheets, all covered with hieroglyphics. Suddenly you came across a picture of a man with a saw. "Very well," you would say, "that means of course that a farmer went out to cut down a tree." Then you take another papyrus. It tells the story of a queen who had died at the age of eighty-two. In the midst of a sentence appears the picture of the man with the saw. Queens of eighty-two do not handle saws. The picture therefore must mean something else. But what?

That is the riddle which the Frenchman finally solved. He discovered that the Egyptians used what we now call "phonetic writing" – a system of characters which reproduce the "sound" (or phone) of the spoken word and which make it possible for us to translate all our spoken words into a written form, with the help of only a few dots and dashes and pothooks.

Let us return for a moment to the little fellow with the saw. The word "saw" either means a certain tool which you will find in a carpenter's shop, or it means the past tense of the verb "to see."

This is what had happened to the word during the course of time. First of all, it had meant only the particular tool which it represented. Then that meaning had been lost and it had become the past participle of a verb. After more time elapsed, the Egyptians lost sight of both these meanings and the picture came to stand for a single letter, the letter S.

Having invented this system the Egyptians developed it over time until they could write anything they wanted, and they used these "canned words" to send messages to friends, to keep business accounts and to keep a record of the history of their country, that future generations might benefit by the mistakes of the past.

One real possibility is that it was the Hebrews, with their efficient Hebrew alphabet compared to the more cumbersome original Egyptian language, which prompted the Egyptians to convert their language.

Early Civilization Along the Nile Valley

Availability of food has always been a great factor in determining where men have settled. Wherever food was plentiful, thither man has travelled to make his home. The Valley of the Nile was indeed choice territory in providing food. In the summer of each year the Nile turned the valley into a shallow lake and when the waters receded all the grain fields and the pastures were covered with several inches of the most fertile clay.

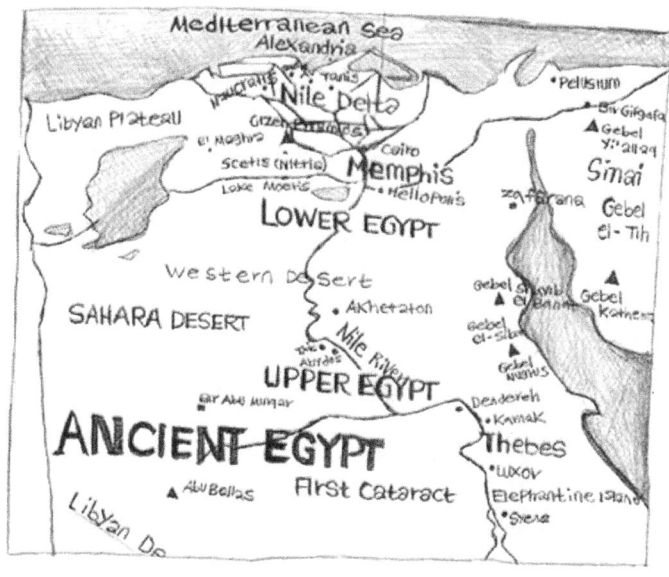

In Egypt a kindly river did the work of a million men and made it possible to feed the teeming population of the large cities which were to form there. It is true that all the arable land was not in the valley. But a complicated system of small canals and well-sweeps carried water from the river-level to the top of the highest banks and an even more intricate system of irrigation trenches spread it throughout the land. The abundance of the Nile Valley made the Egyptians capable of developing their civilization to an even greater extent.

Unlike subsistence farmers in other parts of the world, the Egyptian peasant or the inhabitant of the Egyptian city found himself possessed of a certain leisure. He used this spare time to make himself many things that were merely ornamental and not necessarily useful. Thus, the Egyptians developed more sophisticated artwork.

The Egyptians also devoted much of their time and resources to religion. Their religion was a mixture of truth which they had retained from their forefather Noah, but much falsehood which they invented from the vanity of their wicked hearts.

At the center of religious life in Egypt were its priests. The priests of Egypt had great respect in the community. They were highly learned men who were entrusted with the sacred task of keeping the written records. They understood that it is not good for man to think only of his immediate advantage in this world and they drew his attention to the days of the future when his soul would give an account.

Sadly, the 'god' of the Egyptians was a perversion of the true and living God. Their main 'god' was Osiris, who was the Ruler of the Living and the Dead and who judged the acts of men according to their merits. But alongside this 'god' there were many other gods in their religion, like Isis. They were what is called 'polytheistic', for their many gods. The priests sought to cultivate a culture in Egypt which prepared people for the afterlife and which honored these false gods.

In a strange way, the Egyptians had come to believe that no soul could enter the realm of Osiris without the possession of the body which had been its place of residence in this world. Therefore, as soon as a man was dead his relatives took his corpse and had it embalmed. For weeks it was soaked in a solution of natron and then it was filled with pitch. The Persian word for pitch was "Mumiai" and the embalmed body was called a "Mummy." It was wrapped in yards and yards of specially prepared linen and it was placed in a specially prepared coffin ready to be removed to its final home. But an Egyptian grave was a real home where the body was surrounded by pieces of furniture and musical instruments (to while away the dreary hours of waiting) and by little statues of cooks and bakers and barbers (that the occupant of this dark home might be decently provided with food and need not go about unshaven).

Building the Pyramids

For various reasons the Egyptians built mounds over the graves of their dead. The desert is full of wild animals and equally wild robbers and they broke into the graves and disturbed the mummy or stole the jewelry that had been buried with the body. To prevent such unholy desecration the Egyptians used to build small mounds of stones on top of the graves. These little mounds gradually grew in size, because the rich people built higher mounds than the poor and there was a good deal of competition to see who could make the highest hill of stones. The record was made by King Khufu, whom the Greeks called Cheops. His mound, which the Greeks called a pyramid (because the Egyptian word for high was pir-em-us), was over five hundred feet high. It covered more than thirteen acres of desert which is three times as much space as that occupied by the church of St. Peter, the largest edifice of the Christian world.

During twenty years, over a hundred thousand men were busy carrying the necessary stones from the other side of the river – ferrying them across the Nile (how they ever managed to do this, we do not understand), dragging them in many instances a long distance across the desert and finally hoisting them into their correct position. But so well did the King's architects and engineers perform their task that the narrow passage-way which leads to the royal tomb in the heart of the stone monster has never yet been pushed out of shape by the weight of those thousands of tons of stone which press upon it from all sides.

The Rise and Fall of Egypt

The river Nile was a kind friend but occasionally it was a hard taskmaster. It taught the people who lived along its banks the noble art of "team-work." They depended upon each other to build their irrigation trenches and keep their dikes in repair. They were organized under a leader who had virtually despotic authority, which was especially characteristic of the Hamitic cultures. In due course of time their King ruled all the land from the Mediterranean to the mountains of the west.

But these political adventures of the old Pharaohs (the word meant "the Man who lived in the Big House") rarely interested the patient and toiling peasant of the grain fields. Provided he was not obliged to pay more taxes to his King than he thought just, he accepted the rule of Pharaoh as he accepted the rule of Mighty Osiris.

It was different, however, when a foreign invader came and robbed him of his possessions in the eighteenth-century B.C. After centuries of independent life, a savage Semitic Arab tribe of shepherds, called the Hyksos, attacked Egypt and for a few centuries they were the masters of much of the valley of the Nile. They were highly unpopular.

Great hate also came to be felt for the Semitic Hebrews who came to the land of Goshen to find a shelter during the time of famine. During the beginning of the Hebrews' stay they had been welcomed, because of the service Joseph rendered to the Egyptians, while Egypt was under Hyksos rule. But a later generation arose which did not have the same feelings towards them, and they were made toil under Egyptian taskmasters.

Not long after the Hyksos arrived in Egypt the native Egyptian people of Thebes began a revolution and after a long struggle of many years the Hyksos were driven out of the country and Egypt was free once more of Hyksos rule. As we will discuss later, God also freed the Hebrews from their bondage in Egypt.

When Assyria conquered all of western Asia around 700 B.C., Egypt became part of the empire of Sardanapalus. In the seventh century B.C. it became once more an independent state which obeyed the rule of a king who lived in the city of Saïs in the Delta of the Nile. But in the year 525 B.C., Cambyses, the king of the Persians, took possession of Egypt and in the fourth century B.C., when Persia was conquered by Alexander the Great, Egypt too became a Macedonian province. It regained a semblance of independence when one of Alexander's generals set himself up as king of a new Egyptian state and founded the dynasty of the Ptolemies, who resided in the newly built city of Alexandria.

Finally, in the year 89 B.C., the Romans came. The last Egyptian queen, Cleopatra, tried her best to save the country. Her beauty and charm were more dangerous to the Roman generals than half a dozen Egyptian army corps. Twice she was successful in her attacks upon the hearts of her Roman conquerors.

But in the year 30 B.C., Augustus, the nephew and heir of Cæsar, landed in Alexandria. He did not share his late uncle's admiration for the lovely princess. He destroyed her armies but spared her life that he might make her march in his triumph as part of the spoils of war. When Cleopatra heard of this plan, she killed herself by taking poison. And Egypt became a Roman province.

So, the mighty Egyptian kingdom was brought to a low estate, from which it never has fully recovered. There is certainly a lesson for us here: no matter how powerful a wicked kingdom may appear at some time in history, we can be confident that God will bring it down, so that only Christ's kingdom, and the nations which honor Him, will be established and endure.

CHAPTER 5: The Canaanites, the Phoenicians, and the Hittites

We have previously seen how God cursed Canaan for Ham's sin. And we have seen how powerful the descendants of many of Ham's descendants were, creating strong civilizations in Sumeria and in Egypt. Most of Canaan's posterity settled in the territory which are now the nations of Israel and Lebanon. They became the Canaanites and the Phoenicians. This positioned them right in the midst of the Fertile Crescent stretching from Egypt to Babylon. But one of Canaan's sons, Heth, along with his family and descendants, settled primarily in the area now in the nation of Turkey. It became the great Hittite Empire.

The Canaanites

The curse on Canaan became inevitably reflected in the life of the Canaanites. Perhaps no people on the face of the earth has had such a wicked religion as these people. Their religion revolved around adultery and prostitution and idolatry. It would sometimes even degenerate into the sacrifice of people's own children in the fire, supposedly as part of worship to their 'gods'. The Canaanites were ensnared to a vile and dangerous religion.

Surely another element in the curse on Canaan and his postcrity was the very place God had them settle. They were located right in between very powerful neighbors- Egypt to the south and Syria, Assyria and Babylon to the north and west. While this location was very good for its business of trade- the name 'Canaan' itself meaning 'merchant' or 'trader'- it made these people quite often a pawn and a servant in the hands of much more powerful forces. Added to these factors was the fact that God had promised the land of Canaan to the Israelites. As we shall see later in our journey, God kept his promise to the Israelites, giving them power over their Promised Land. But in so doing, God also kept his promise regarding Canaan. Canaanite hegemony was diminished as the Hebrews waxed strong.

The Phoenicians
The Phoenicians settled along the shores of the Mediterranean north of the Canaanites' settlement. They had built themselves two well-fortified towns, Tyre and Sidon.

Like the Canaanites, they had a vile religion that revolved around adultery and idolatry. And also like the Canaanites, they were great traders, especially excelling in sea trade.

Within a short time, they had gained a monopoly of the trade of the western seas. Their ships went regularly to Greece and Italy and Spain and they even ventured beyond the straits of Gibraltar to visit the Scilly islands where they could buy tin. Wherever they went, they built themselves small trading stations, which they called colonies. Many of these were the origin of modern cities, such as Cadiz and Marseilles. Their greatest colonial settlement was Carthage.

They bought and sold whatever promised to bring them a good profit. They were not troubled by a conscience. If we are to believe all their neighbors, they did not know what the words honesty or integrity meant, which surely was all part of the curse upon them. They regarded a well-filled treasure chest the highest ideal of all good citizens. Indeed, they were very unpleasant people and did not have a single friend. Nevertheless, they have rendered all coming generations one service of great value: they brought us our alphabet.

The Phoenicians had been familiar with the art of writing from the Sumerians. But they regarded the pothooks as a clumsy waste of time, compared to the efficient Hebrew alphabet of their Hebrew neighbors. They were practical businessmen and could not spend hours engraving two or three letters. They likely adopted their new system of writing from the Hebrews, which was greatly superior to the old one. They also borrowed a few pictures from the Egyptians. They sacrificed the pretty looks of the older system for the advantage of speed and they reduced the thousands of different images to a short and handy alphabet of twenty-two letters.

In due course of time, this alphabet travelled across the Ægean Sea and entered Greece. The Greeks added a few letters of their own and carried the improved system to Italy. The Romans modified the figures somewhat and in turn taught them to the wild barbarians of western Europe. Those wild barbarians were our own ancestors, and that is the reason why this book is written in characters that came to us by way of the Phoenicians and not in the hieroglyphics of the Egyptians or in the nail-script of the Sumerians.

The Hittites

The Hittite Empire rose to power around 2000 B.C. This was approximately the same time as Abraham was departing Mesopotamia for the Promised Land. For more than a thousand years the Hittites ruled the region that is now Turkey and Syria. Its power rivaled that of Egypt and the Assyro-Babylonian empires of Mesopotamia.

The Hittite state was a military organization. Daily life was closely regulated by the laws of this state. Everything from the purchase price of land to the wages earned for labor was dictated by law.

The Hittites were perhaps the first people to use iron after the Flood, having perhaps passed down the knowledge of this craft through the generations from the time before the Flood. Their mines were along the Black Sea. And they were famous workers in metals. All of this was used to great advantage by the Hittites to enhance their military power. They had the best weapons and the best chariots during their period of military might.

It was not until the early twentieth century that archeological evidence of the Hittites came to light. Thousands of clay tablets, along with other artifacts, were discovered in archeological investigations in Turkey. For many years those who liked to consign the Bible to myth were wont to point out its allusions to the Hittites and the Hittite Empire. These Scripture critics argued that there were no such people as the

Hittites, because no archeological evidence had been found of this people until that time. But Scripture proved reliable once again, for now an immense amount of archeological evidence confirms the existence of the once Hittite Empire, and no one now denies its past existence.

Even though the Hittites avoided the precarious location of their brethren in Canaan; nevertheless, they did not avoid the curse of Canaan. The language of the Hittites was derived from the Indo-Europeans. It would seem certain Indo-Europeans early on conquered the Hittites and served as the rulers of their society. So, Japheth was enlarged at the expense of Canaan. Even later in history the Hittite Empire itself was over-run by Indo-Europeans, and ultimately disappeared from off the face of the earth. The very thing that had led Bible critics to deny the existence of the Hittites, was actually the fulfillment of the Scriptural sentence that Japheth was to be enlarged at Canaan's expense.

CHAPTER 6: The Hebrews

Abraham and His Seed

Among the sons of Shem (called Hebrews after Shem's descendant Heber, who dwelt in Mesopotamia, just as the term Semitic is derived from the name Shem) was Abram. Abram was a good and faithful man. He was chosen by God to be the father of the people in whom He was going to set His Light and be the father of many nations. In the year 1921 BC, God tried Abram's faith by calling on him to leave his home, and go into a land which he knew not, but which should belong to his children after him. This was at a time when Abram had no child at all. Yet he obeyed and believed and was led into the beautiful hilly land then held by the sons of Canaan, where he was a stranger, wandering with his flocks and herds and servants from one green pasture to another, without a foot of land to call his own.

For showing his faith by thus doing as he was commanded, Abram was rewarded by the covenant promise that in his Seed should all the families of the earth be blessed. Abram's name was changed to Abraham, which means a father of a great multitude. And as a sign of his covenant with God and his faith towards God, Abraham was to be circumcised. This sign of circumcision was also to be administered to his children, for an emblem of their separation to God as part of the visible church of God, along with Abraham. One son, Ishmael, had by this time been born to him of the bondmaid Hagar, so Abraham circumcised Ishmael according to God's command.

But the child of promise, Isaac, the son of his wife Sarah, was not given till he was a hundred years old. Ishmael was cast out for mocking at his half-brother, the heir of the promises. Nevertheless, in answer to his father's prayers, he too became the father of a great nation, namely the Arabs, many of whom still live in the desert, with their tents, their flocks, herds, and fine horses, much as Ishmael himself must have lived. They are still circumcised, and honor Abraham as their father. With them are joined the Midianites and other tribes descended from Abraham's last wife, Keturah, along with other people who assimilated into the Arab people.

Isaac alone was to inherit the promise. This promise was renewed to Isaac and to his father, when their faith had been proved by their submission to God's command, that Isaac should be offered as a burnt-offering upon Mount Moriah, a sign of the Great Sacrifice long afterwards, when God did indeed provide Himself a Lamb. Isaac's wife, Rebekah, was fetched from Abraham's former home, in Mesopotamia, that he might not be corrupted by marrying a Canaanite. Abraham's servant found Rebekah dutifully gathering water at a well and offering the servant water. The servant brought her back to Isaac with the consent and permission of her guardian.

Between Isaac's two sons, Esau and Jacob, there was again a choice. God had planned and foretold that the elder should serve the younger, making Jacob God's chosen seed. Esau and Jacob grew up to be very different young men, though they were twins.

In time Esau, the elder brother, did not value the birthright which would have made him heir to no lands that would enrich himself, and to a far-off honor that he did not understand. Despising the promises of God, he made his right over to his brother for a little food, when he was hungry, and though he repented with tears when it was too late, he could not win back what he had once thrown away. Jacob received all the blessings from his father Isaac.

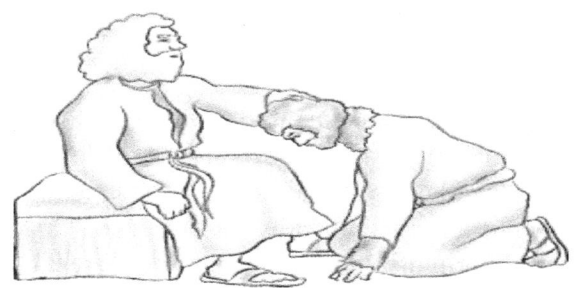

Esau's revengeful anger when he found how he had been supplanted, made Jacob flee to his mother's family in Mesopotamia, and there dwell for many years, before returning to Canaan with his large household. Jacob returned to live in the manner that had been ordained for the first heirs of the promise.

But Esau went away to Mount Seir, to the south of the Promised Land, and his descendants were called the Edomites, from his name, meaning the Red. And so, too, the sea which washed their shores, took the name of the Sea of Edom, or the Red Sea. They were also named Kenites from his son Kenaz. Their country, afterwards called Idumea, was full of rocks and precipices, and in these the Edomites hollowed out caves for themselves, making them most beautiful, with pillars supporting the roof within, and finely-carved entrances, cut with borders, flowers, and scrolls, so lasting that the cities of Bosra and Petra are still a wonder to travelers, though they have been empty and deserted for centuries past.

Jacob's name was changed to Israel, which meant a prince before God. And Jacob's whole family were taken into the covenant, though the three elder sons, for their crimes, forfeited the foremost places, which passed to Judah and Joseph. And Levi was afterwards chosen as the tribe set apart for the priesthood, the number twelve being made up by reckoning Ephraim and Manasseh, the sons of Joseph, as heads of tribes, like their uncles.

Long ago, Abraham had been told that his seed should sojourn in Egypt. This came to pass when the envious sons of Israel sold their innocent brother Joseph into slavery in Egypt. Although this was a wicked deed on the brothers' part, it was all designed by God to bring about His high purpose for the church.

In Egypt Joseph was inspired to interpret Pharaoh's dreams, which foretold the famine. Joseph was made a great leader in Egypt and saved many people since he had them prepare for the long years of famine. When by-and-by Joseph's brothers came to buy the corn that he had laid up in Egypt, Joseph made himself known to them. Joseph also forgave them with all his heart and sent them to fetch his father to see him once more. Then the whole family of Israel, seventy in number, besides their wives, came and settled in the land of Goshen, about the year 1700 B.C. The church in Egypt were there known by the name of Hebrews, after Heber, the great grandson of Shem. All of these events of the Israelites in Egypt occurred during the early years when the Hyksos reigned in Egypt.

Moses Leads the People out of Egypt

But a time came when the Hyksos no longer ruled in Egypt, and those that did rule felt no gratitude to the Hebrews. The king of Egypt, becoming afraid of having so numerous and rich a people settled in his dominions, tried to keep them down by hard bondage and heavy labor. He made them toil at his great buildings and oppressed them in every possible manner. When he found that they still throve and increased, he made the cruel decree, that every son who was born to them should be cast into the river. But man can do nothing against the will of God, and this murderous ordinance proved the very means of causing one of these persecuted Hebrew infants to be brought up in the palace of Pharaoh and instructed in all the wisdom of the Egyptians. This infant was Moses.

Moses' mother had him floated in the water near the Egyptian princess, and Moses was adopted by the princess and raised among Egyptian royalty. But even in his early life, Moses seems to have been aware that he was to be sent to put an end to the bondage of his people. Moses chose rather to suffer with them than to live in prosperity with their oppressors. He went out among them and tried to defend them, and to set them at peace with one another. But the time was not yet come, and they thrust him from them, so that he was forced to fly for shelter to the desert, among the Midianite descendants of Abraham.

After Moses had spent forty years there as a shepherd, God appeared to him in a burning bush. It was there that God first revealed Himself as JEHOVAH, the Name proclaiming His eternal self-existence, I AM THAT I AM.

Moses was then sent to Egypt to lead out the Israelites on their way back to the land so long promised to their forefathers. When Pharaoh obstinately refused to let them go, the dreadful plagues and wonders that were sent on the country were such as to show that their gods were no gods. Since their river, the glory of their land, became a loathsome stream of blood, creeping things came and went at the bidding of the Lord. Even their adored cattle perished before their eyes. At last, on the night of the Passover, in each of the houses unmarked by the blood of the Lamb, there was a great cry over the death of the first-born son. But where the sign of faith was seen, there was a mysterious obedient festival held by families prepared for a strange new journey.

Then the hard heart of the Egyptian Pharoah yielded to terror, and Israel went out of Egypt as a nation. They had come in around 1700 BC as seventy men; they went out in 1491 BC as six hundred thousand. Their Egyptian enemies, following after them, sank like lead in the mighty waters of that arm of the Red Sea, which had divided to let God's chosen church pass through.

When Moses had led the 600,000 men-with their wives, children, and cattle-beyond the reach of the Egyptians, they were in a small peninsula. The peninsula was between the arms of the Red Sea, with the wild desolate peaks of Mount Horeb towering in the midst, and all around grim stony crags, with hardly a spring of water. And though there were here and there slopes of grass, and bushes of hoary-leaved camelthorn, and long-spined shittim or acacia, there was nothing bearing fruit for human beings. There were strange howlings and crackings in the mountains, the sun glared back from the arid stones and rocks, and the change seemed frightful after the green meadows and broad river of Egypt. Frightened and faithless, the Israelites cried out reproachfully to Moses to ask how they should live in this desert place, forgetting that the Pillar of cloud and fire proved that they were under the care of Him who had brought them safely out of the hands of their enemies.

In His mercy God bore with their murmurs, fed them with manna from Heaven, and water out of the flinty rock. God also gave them the victory over the Edomite tribe of robber Amalekites at Rephidim, where Joshua fought, and Moses, upheld by Aaron and Hur, stretched forth his hands the whole day.

Then, fifty days after their coming out of Egypt, He called them round the peak of Sinai to hear His own Voice proclaim the terms of the Covenant. The Covenant with Abraham had circumcision for the token, faith as the condition, and the blessing to all nations in Christ as the promise. This Covenant remained in full force, but in the course of the last four hundred years, sin had grown so much that the old standard, handed down from the patriarchs, had been forgotten, and men would not have known what was right, nor how far they fell from it, without a written revelation and Law from God.

This Law, in Ten Commandments, all meeting together in teaching love to God and man, revealed the standard of God's perfection, without which no man could be fit to stand in the sight of God. He spoke it with His own mouth, from amid cloud, flame, thunder, and sounding trumpets, on Mount Sinai, while the Israelites watched around in awe and terror, unable to endure the dread of that Presence. The people were to realize from this Law how sinful they were, how much they depended upon the promised Savior to save them, and how they should serve God in grateful obedience. If they would heed this lesson, they should dwell prosperously in the Promised Land, and be a royal priesthood and peculiar treasure unto God. They answered with one voice, "All the words the Lord hath said will we do."

Moses then made a sacrifice, and sprinkled them with the blood, to consecrate them and confirm their oath. It was the blood of the Old Testament. Then he went up into the darkness of the cloud on the mountain top, there fasting, to talk with God, and to receive the two Tables of Stone written by the Finger of God, with its Ten Commandments. But man showed once again he could not obey God in his fallen state. The Israelites lost faith, and set up a golden calf, corrupting the right worship which God had not long before commanded them, and inventing worship of their own imagination.

When Moses discovered their sin, he destroyed the precious tables with the Ten Commandments, the token of God's covenant with His people. And God threatened to sweep them off in a moment and to fulfill His oaths to their forefathers in the children of Moses alone. Then Moses, having purified the camp by slaying the worst offenders, stood between the rest and the wrath of God, mediating for them until he obtained mercy for them, and a renewal of the Covenant.

Twice Moses spent forty days in God's Presence, where glorious visions were revealed to him. The Courts of Heaven itself were to be copied by him, by Divine guidance. It was the design for the Ark and Tabernacle. In the Tabernacle Moses' brother Aaron, and his seed after him, were to minister as priests, setting forth to the eye how there was a Holy Place, whence men were separated by sin, and how it could only be entered by a High Priest, after a sacrifice of atonement. Every ordinance of this service was a shadow of good things to come in Christ Jesus.

The ceremonial laws were strictly enjoined on Israel, as part of the conditions of the Covenant, guiding their faith onwards by this acted prophecy. God, as King of His people, put forth other commands, some relating to their daily habits, others to their government as a nation, all tending to keep them separate from other nations. While some of these ordinances were meant to be temporary until Christ should come, the Ten Commandments reflected God's moral character and were to be an abiding moral law for the people of God. The animal sacrifices and ceremonial law simply foreshadowed a day when there would be a fuller expiation for sin by a perfect and infinite sacrifice- God the Son, our Lord Jesus Christ.

Also, during this time, God providentially established civil and church governments for the people, and a weekly Sabbath assembly. It appears He established a civil council, or Sanhedrin, to adjudicate civil cases in the nation. And He established an ecclesiastical council of Levites to adjudicate church issues among all the visible church. This same model passed to the Christian church centuries later in the form of a Presbyterian synod of elders, and it has served as the political model for parliamentary government for generations. The assembly that met each Sabbath for worship came to be called the local synagogue or church, which endures to this day. *"For Moses of old time hath in every city them that preach Him, being read in the synagogues every sabbath day."* God's prescribed government, as well as His prescribed law, was a great mercy and blessing.

But despite God's mercies extended to the Israelites, they could not even be roused to look for the present temporal promise and hankered after the fine soil and rich fruits of Egypt, rather than the beautiful land of hill and valley that lay before them. When their spies reported the land where they were to dwell to be full of hill forts, held by Canaanites of giant stature, a cowardly cry of despair broke out. They complained that they should return to Egypt. Only two of the whole host, besides Moses, were ready to trust to Him who had delivered them from Pharaoh and had led them through the sea. Therefore, those two alone of the grown-up men were allowed to set foot in the Promised Land.

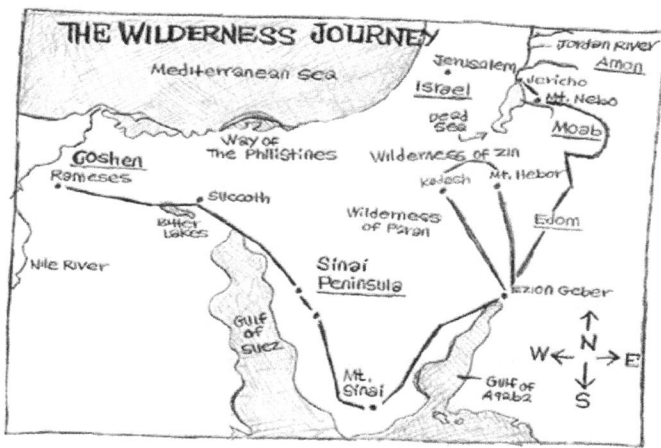

Till all the rest of Christ's visible church at that time should have fallen in the wilderness, and a better race have been trained up, God would not help them to take possession. In their willfulness they tried to advance, and were defeated, and thus were obliged to endure their forty years' desert wandering. Even

Moses had his patience worn out by their fretful faithlessness and committed an act of disobedience. Because of this he was sentenced not to enter the Promised Land, but to die on the borders after one sight of the promise of his fathers. Under him, however, began the work of conquest. The rich pasture lands of Gilead and Basan were subdued, and the tribes of Reuben and Gad, and half the tribe of Manasseh, were permitted to take these as their inheritance, though beyond the proper boundary, the Jordan River.

Moses was led by God to the top of Mount Nebo, whence he might see in its length and breadth, the pleasant land, the free hills, the green valleys watered by streams, the wooded banks of Jordan, the pale blue expanse of the Mediterranean Sea joining with the sky to the west. But God had better things for him in Heaven, and there upon the mountain top he died alone, and God buried him in the sepulcher whereof no man knows. None was like to him in the Old Covenant, who stood between God and the Israelites, but he left a promise that a Prophet should be raised up like unto himself. Moses had been a faithful servant and prophet of God in God's household, and a servant and prophet of such stature in the household was not to arise again until the Lord Jesus Christ. Before Moses had passed away, he prophesied of this coming even more excellent Prophet.

Joshua Leads the People into Israel
In the year 1451 BC Joshua led the tribes of Israel through the divided waters of the Jordan River, and received strength and skill to scatter the heathen before them, conquer the cities, and settle them in their inheritance. The Land of Canaan was very unlike Egypt, with its flat soil, dry climate, and single

river. Canaan was a narrow strip, enclosed between the Mediterranean Sea and the river Jordan. The Jordan River runs due south down a steep wooded cleft into the Dead Sea, the lowest water in the world, in a sort of pit of its own, with barren desolation all round it, so as to keep in memory the ruin of the cities of the plain. In the north, rise the high mountains of Lebanon, a spur from which goes the whole length of the land, and forms two slopes, whence the rivers flow, either westward into the Great Sea, or eastward into the Jordan. Many of these hills are too dry and stony to be cultivated; but the slopes of some have fine grassy pastures, and the soil of the valleys is exceedingly rich, bearing figs, vines, olive trees, and corn in plenty, wherever it is properly tilled. With such hills, rivers, valleys, and pastures, it was truly a goodly land, and when God's blessing was on it, it was the fairest spot where man could live. When the Israelites entered it, every hill was crowned by a strongly walled and fortified town, the abode of some little king of one of the seven Canaanite nations who were given into their hands to be utterly destroyed.

Though they were commanded to make a complete end of all the people in each place they took, they were forbidden to seize more than they could fill, lest the empty ruins should serve as a harbor for wild beasts. They had their several lots marked out where they might spread when their numbers should need room. As Jacob had promised to Joseph, Ephraim and half Manasseh had the richest portion, nearly in the middle. Also, Shiloh- where the Tabernacle was set up- was in their territory. Judah and Benjamin were in a very wild rocky part to the southwards, between the two seas, with only Simeon beyond them. Then came, north of Manasseh, the fine pasture lands of Issachar and Zebulon, and a small border for Asher between Lebanon and the sea. Reuben, Gad, and the rest of Manasseh were to the east of the Jordan, where they had begged to settle themselves in the meadows of Bashan and the balmy thickets of Gilead. Many a fortified town was still held by the Canaanites, especially Jebus, on Mount Moriah, between Judah and Benjamin.

Also, the Canaanites held the two great merchant cities of the Sidonians upon the seashore. These were called Tyre and Sidon, and their inhabitants were the Phoenicians, which we have already discussed.

As long as the generation lived who had been bred up in the wilderness, they obeyed, and felt themselves under the rule of God their King, Who made His Will known at Shiloh by the signs on the breastplate of the High Priest, while judges and elders governed in the cities. But afterwards they began to be tempted to make friends with their heathen neighbors, and thus learned to believe in their false deities, and to hanker after the service of some god who made no such laws of goodness as those by which the church of Israel was bound.

As certainly as they fell away, so surely the punishment came, and God stirred up some of these dangerous friends to attack them. Sometimes it was a Canaanite tribe with iron chariots who mightily oppressed them; sometimes the robber shepherds, tile Midianites, would burst in and carry off their cattle and their crops, until distress brought the Israelites back to a better mind, and they cried out to the Lord. Then He would raise up a mighty warrior, and give him the victory, so that he became ruler and judge over Israel. But no sooner was he dead, than they would fall back again into idolatry, and receive another chastisement, repent, and be again delivered.

This pattern went on for about 400 years, the Israelites growing constantly worse. In the latter part of this time, their chief enemies were the Philistines, in the borders of Simeon and Judah, near the sea. These were not Canaanites, but had once dwelt in Egypt, and then, after living for a time in Cyprus, had come and settled in Gaza and Ashkelon, and three other very strong cities on the coast, where they worshipped a fish-god, called Dagon. They had no king, but were ruled by lords of their five cities, and made terrible inroads upon all the country round.

At last the Israelites, in their self-will, fancied they could turn the Philistines to flight by causing the Ark to be carried out to battle by the two corrupt young priests, sons of Eli, whose doom had already been pronounced-that they should both die in one day. They were slain, when the Ark was taken by the enemies, and their aged father fell back and broke his neck in the shock of the tidings. The glory had departed; and though God proved His might by shattering Dagon's image before the Ark, and plaguing the Philistines wherever they carried it, till they were forced to send it home in a manner which again showed the Divine Hand, yet it never returned to Shiloh. God deserted the place where His Name had not been kept holy. The token of the Covenant seemed to be lost. The Philistines ruled over the broken and miserable Israelites, and there was only one promise to comfort them-that the Lord would raise up unto Himself a faithful Prophet, Priest, and King one day.

Already there was growing up at Shiloh the young Levite, Samuel, dedicated by his mother, and bred up by Eli. He is counted as first of the prophets, that long stream of inspired men, who constantly preached righteousness, and to whom occasionally future events were made known. He was also the last of the Judges, or heaven-sent deliverers. As soon as he grew up, he rallied the Israelites, restored the true worship, as far as could be with the Ark in concealment, and sent them out to battle. They defeated the Philistines, and under Samuel, again became a free nation.

When Samuel grew old, the Israelites would not trust to God to choose a fresh guardian for them but cried out for a king to keep them together and lead them to war like other nations. The Israelites manifested they were too wicked to be run simply by a council of judges and elders; they wanted the strong hand and rule of an earthly king. Their entreaty was granted, and in 1094 B.C. Saul the son of Kish, of the small but fierce tribe of Benjamin, was appointed by God. Saul was anointed by Samuel, on the understanding that he was not to rule by his own will, like the princes around, but as God's chief officer, to enforce His laws and carry out His bidding. Time would reveal though that Saul would not obey God and enforce His commands.

But the overall condition of the Israelites did gradually improve under Saul. Saul's son Jonathan and his uncle Abner were able generals, and they successfully fought back many of Israel's enemies. But Saul became proud, and he fancied he could go his own way. He took it upon himself to offer sacrifice to God, even though this role was reserved for the priests. God showed his hot displeasure with Saul over this, forever teaching God's people the lesson that the church and civil government are two separate institutions, and the officials in the one should not assume the functions of the other.

Saul disobeyed God yet more. One day when sent forth by God to destroy all belonging to the Amalekites, Saul spared the king and the choicest of the spoil. For this he was sentenced not to be the founder of a line of kings. The doom filled Saul with wrath against the priesthood, while an evil spirit was permitted to trouble his soul.

David, God's Anointed

Samuel's last great act was to anoint the youngest son of Jesse the Bethlehemite, the great grandchild of the loving Moabitess, Ruth, the same whom God had marked beside his sheepfolds as the man after His own Heart. This same David was to be the future father of the sceptered line of Judah, and of the " Root and Offspring of David, the bright and morning Star" for the church. He was, in other words, appointed the one from whom the future Messiah of the church would descend, even though this future Messiah was also to be "David's Lord", as David himself prophesied in song.

Fair and young, full of inspired song, and of gallant courage, the youth David was favored as the minstrel able to drive the evil spirit from Saul. He was also the champion who had slain the giant Goliath of Gath who had so distressed the Israelites. David killed the giant Philistine with no weapon but his sling.

David was the king's son-in-law by marriage to Saul's daughter, and the prince Jonathan's bosom friend. But as the hopes of Israel became set on him, Saul began to hate David as if he were a supplanter, though Jonathan submitted to the Will that deprived himself of a throne and loved his friend as faithfully as ever. At last, by Jonathan's counsel, David fled from court, and Saul in his rage at thinking him aided by the priests, slew all who fell into his hands, thus cutting off his own last link with Heaven.

A trusty band of brave men gathered round David, but he remained a loyal outlaw, and always abstained from any act against his sovereign, even though Saul twice lay at his mercy. Patiently he tarried the Lord's leisure, and the time came at last. The Philistines overran the country, and chased Saul even to the mountain fastnesses of Gilboa, where the miserable man, deserted by God, tried to learn his fate through evil spirits, and only met the certainty of his doom. In the next day's battle, his true-hearted son met a soldier's death. But Saul, when wounded by the archers, tried in vain to put an end to his own life, and was, after a reign of forty years, at last slain by an Amalekite, who brought his crown to David, and was executed by him for having profanely slain the Lord's anointed.

For seven years David reigned only in his own tribe of Judah, while the brave Abner kept the rest of the kingdom for Saul's son, Ishbosheth. But this condition ended when Abner- the skillful general so necessary to Ishbosheth's reign- took offence because Ishbosheth refused to give him one of Saul's widows to wife. Abner offered to come to terms with David, but in leaving the place of meeting, he was treacherously killed by David's overbearing nephew, Joab, in revenge for the death of a Joab's brother whom Abner had slain in single combat.

Ishbosheth was soon after murdered by two of his own servants, and David became sole king of all Israel. David ruled prudently with all his power, and with anxious heed to the will of his true King. He was a great conqueror and was the first to win for Israel her great city on Mount Moriah. It had once been called Salem, or peace, when the mysterious priest-king, Melchizedek, reigned there in Abraham's time. David was inspired to prophesy that the Messiah who was to descend from him would be a priest-king after the order of Melchizedek. It was there too that Abraham had sought to sacrifice Isaac at God's command, foreshadowing the day that God the Son would be sacrificed in Jerusalem. Great things were indeed planned for Jerusalem. But for many years up until the time of David it had been held by the Jebusites and called Jebus.

When David took Jebus, he named it Jerusalem, or 'the vision of peace'. David fortified Jerusalem, built a palace there, and fetched thither with songs and solemn dances, the longhidden Ark, so that it might be the place where God's Name was set, the center of worship. Well was the spot fitted for the purpose. It was a hill girdled round by other hills, and so strong by nature, that when built round with towers and walls, an enemy could hardly have taken it.

David longed to raise a solid home for the Ark, but this was not a work permitted to a man of war and bloodshed. David did collect materials though for the later construction of the Temple, and he restored the priests to their offices. He also gave the Priests his own glorious Book of Psalms, full of praise, prayer, and entreaty, to be sung before the Lord in the Temple by the Levites, accompanied by musical instruments. This Book of Psalms also became the 'hymn book' for the synagogues of the people's weekly Sabbath worship. These spiritual songs were sung in the synagogues and later the Christian churches without accompaniment of musical instruments or choirs, like they were in the Temple. And this same Book of Psalms remains today the church's hymn book of Spirit-inspired songs. God therefore provided a text for the scripture reading in His public worship as well as a hymn book for singing there.

David likewise made the Philistines, Moabites, Ammonites, and Edomites pay him tribute, and became the most powerful king in the East, receiving the fulfillment of the promises to Abraham.

But even David was far from guiltless. He was a man of strong passions, though of a tender heart, and erred greatly, both from hastiness and weakness, but never without repentance. And David's Psalms of contrition have ever since been the treasure of the penitent. Chastisement visited his sins, and was meekly borne, but bereavement and rebellion, care, sorrow, and disappointment, severely tried the Sweet Psalmist of Israel, shepherd, prophet, soldier, and king. In 1016 BC, in his seventieth year, David went to his rest, after having been king for forty years. He was assured that his seed should endure forever as kings, because he knew one Seed was to be none other than Christ the King.

All promises of temporal splendor were accomplished in David's peaceful son, Solomon. Solomon asked to be the wisest, and therefore was likewise made the richest, most prosperous, and most peaceful of kings.

No enemy rose against Solomon, but all the nations sought his friendship. Sidon for once had her merchandise hallowed by its being offered to build and adorn the Temple, Solomon's great work. The spot chosen for it was that of Isaac's sacrifice, where was the threshing-floor bought by David from Araunah. But to give more room, he leveled the head of the mountain, throwing it into the valley. He thus formed an even space where, silently built of huge stone, quarried at a distance, arose the courts, for strangers, women, men, and priests, surrounded by cloisters, supporting galleries of rooms for the lodging of the priests and Levites, many hundreds in number. The main building was of white marble, and the Holy of Holies was overlaid even to the roof outside with plates of gold, flashing back the sunshine. Even this was but a poor token of the Shechinah, that glorious light which descended at Solomon's prayer of consecration and filled the Sanctuary with the visible token of God's Presence on the Mercy Seat, to be seen by the High Priest once a year.

That consecration of the Temple was the happiest moment of the history of Israel, but what followed was mournful. Even David had been like the kings of other eastern nations in the multitude of his wives, and Solomon went far beyond him, bringing in heathen women, who won him into paying homage to their idols, and outraging God by building temples to Moloch and Ashtoreth. Though as a prophet he had been inspired to speak in his Proverbs, nevertheless he shamed himself in his conduct with foreign wives. A warning was sent that the power which had corrupted him should not continue in his family, and that the kingdom should be divided. Sadly, Solomon only grew more tyrannical. When the Ephraimite warrior, Jeroboam, was marked by the prophet Ahijah as the destined chief of the new kingdom, Solomon persecuted him, and drove him to take refuge with the great Shishak, King of Egypt, where he seems to have learned the idolatries from which Israel had been so slowly weaned.

Sick at heart, Solomon in his old age wrote the saddest book in the Bible; and though his first writing, the Canticles, had been a joyful prophetic song of the love between the Lord and His Church, his last was a mournful lamentation over the vanity and emptiness of the world, and full of scorn of all that earth can give. He discloses in the book of Ecclesiastes what he should have heeded throughout his life: life must be governed by the fear of God and obedience to His commandments. Any other life is full of vanity.

Reheboam, the son of Solomon, brought about, by his own harshness and folly, the punishment that God had decreed. By the advice of his hasty young counselors. He made so violent a reply to the petition brought to him by his subjects, that they took offence, and the ten northern tribes broke away from him, setting up as their king, Jeroboam, who had been already marked out by the prophet. So, the kingdom of Israel split into the Kingdom of Judah in the south and the Kingdom of Samaria (or sometimes called the Kingdom of Israel) in the north.

These two nations continued until the northern kingdom was conquered by the Assyrians and the southern kingdom by the Babylonians. Each fell because God judged it for its great wickedness and falling away from God's righteous law which He had graciously given the Hebrews on Mount Sinai years earlier. The populations of each were removed from the land and re-settled.

Even in their humbled condition in captivity, God held forth a mighty promise to His people, which He announced through His prophet Daniel. Daniel prophesied the four major kingdoms that were to arise in the coming centuries. Most importantly, Daniel proclaimed that during the fourth kingdom- which was to be the Roman Empire- would arise an everlasting kingdom of the promised Messiah. This Messiah, as we will later discover, was none other than Jesus Christ.

But before Messiah would come, many of the Jews captive in Babylon would have to first return to Jerusalem and to their ancient Promised Land in Canaan. It was to be only the inhabitants of the old southern kingdom which were thus one day to return and re-establish the Jewish nation in the Promised Land of their forefathers.

But we will return to this history of the Jews and God's special purpose for them later in our story. Now let's travel many miles to the east of the Promised Land and venture into the mysterious Chinese civilization.

LET ME TELL YOU THE REAL STORY OF MANKIND

CHAPTER 7: The Chinese

China, in the Far East of Asia, has a history that goes back almost to the time near the Great Flood of Noah's day. The Flood was as important in the ancient legends of the peoples of China, as it is in the Scriptures handed down to us from the Hebrews. We must call them legends, because there are inaccuracies not found in the account of the Bible. Nevertheless, there are many true features in these accounts. Many primitive peoples described the flood as a catastrophe of Biblical dimensions. The Miao Legend states that a single human couple escaped the deluge in a wooden drum, and then gave birth to the first members of post-Flood humanity. The Shu King, China's first "history", states: *"destructive in their overflow are the waters of the inundation. In their vast extent they embrace the hills and overtop the great heights, threatening the heavens with their floods."*

Yu, the Chinese "Noah", overcame the flood waters, but he and his immediate predecessors are of a lineage well known to world mythology and the true Biblical account. The Bible, the ancient Sumerians and the Chinese all cite a chronology of ten rulers whose last member was the hero of a Great Flood epoch. Similar legends are known from Greece and India. The Miao, another people that settled in the Far East, relate not only the Flood but also the confusion of tongues followed by migration to the East.

The Hsia Dynasty

After the Flood, some people began to migrate east of the Mesopotamian region at a very early date. Among these were the ancient Chinese. They began by just starting small villages. But within two hundred years after the Flood they had established China's first dynastic kingdom of the Hsia. This dynasty began around 2200 BC. It lasted to 1766 BC, in the same century when the Hebrews would settle in Egypt. These people, which migrated from Mesopotamia, brought with them the agricultural methods from their homeland to China, stimulating the growth of ancient Chinese civilization.

Like other ancient peoples, the Chinese developed unique attributes. Their form of writing was a complex system of picture writing using forms called ideograms, pictograms, and phonograms. We know about their writing today because of the archaeological discovery of their oracle bones, which were bones with writings inscribed on them. They were used for fortune-telling and record keeping in ancient China.

The Shang Dynasty

The Shang Dynasty replaced the Hsia dynasty in 1766 BC, and this dynastic kingdom has left us with the first documented era of ancient China. The highly developed hierarchy of the kingdom consisted of a king, nobles, commoners, and slaves. The capital city was Anyang, in north Henan Province. The people of this time were known for their use of jade, bronze, horse-drawn chariots, ancestor worship, and highly organized armies. The Shang Dynasty has left behind 'bone libraries', connected with their ancient palaces and temples. The records of the Shang dynasty were written on animal bones and tortoise shells. This dynasty lasted over 500 years.

The Chou Dynasty

The Shang Dynasty was replaced by the Chou Dynasty in 1122 BC. The Chou Dynasty saw the full flowering of ancient civilization in China. During this period the empire was unified, a middle class arose, and iron was introduced. The sage Confucius, who lived from 551 to 479 BC, developed the code of ethics that dominated Chinese culture for the next 25 centuries. The Chou conquest of the Shang was given an important meaning by later moralistic interpretations of the event. The Chou kings, whose chief deity was heaven, called themselves "Sons of Heaven," and their success in overcoming the Shang was seen as the "mandate of heaven." From this time on, Chinese rulers were called "Sons of Heaven" and the

Chinese Empire, the "Celestial Empire." The transfer of power from one dynasty to the next was based on the mandate of heaven.

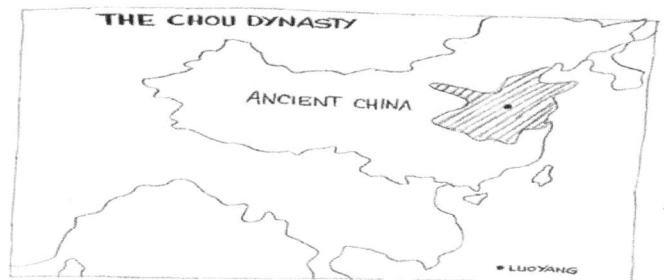

Chou rule in China continued for nearly nine centuries, from 1122 BC to 221 BC. During this time great cultural advances were made. The long period of the Chou Dynasty is commonly divided into two subperiods: The Western (Early) Chou and the Eastern (Later) Chou, named for the locations of the capitals.

The Western Chou rule lasted from 1122 to 771 BC. Its territory covered most of the North China Plain. It was divided into about 200 princely domains. The Chou political system was similar to the feudal system of medieval Europe. The Chou people combined hunting and agriculture for a living.

The people descended into gross errors in their religion, despite their great cultural advancements. They prayed to numerous nature gods for good harvests. One of the ruler's duties was to placate heaven and Earth for all people. Failure to do so deprived him of the right to rule. Ancestor worship also developed during the Chou period. All of these religious errors of the Chinese have persisted even until today.

The Chou were invaded in 771 BC by a less cultured, more militaristic people from the northwest. The capital was moved east to Luoyang. The manner in which the Western Chou fell followed a pattern that was repeated throughout Chinese history. People who led a nomadic, or wandering, life in the northern steppe land would invade settled agricultural communities to solve periodic food shortages. The conflict between the nomads and settled farmers has been a continuing feature of Chinese history. Settled Chinese called the nomads "barbarians," a term applied to all peoples of non-Chinese culture up to the 20th century.

During the Eastern Chou era iron replaced bronze for tools and weapons. The use of iron led to an increase in agricultural output, growth of the population, and warfare among the states. By the 4th century BC there were seven states that made up the dynastic kingdom. In 256 BC the princes of those states assumed the title of king, stopped paying homage to the Chou king, and continued to fight for supremacy. The strongest of the seven states was Ch'in.

The disruption caused by this prolonged warfare had a number of long-range consequences. One was the rise of a new social group, the scholars (shi). They were forerunners of the scholar-officials of the Chinese Empire, who became the most influential group in China. In the Later Chou period, however, they were a relatively small group of learned people. Often wandering from state to state in search of permanent employment, the shi worked as tutors to the children of feudal princes and as advisers to various state governments. The most famous of these scholarly shi was Confucius.

The Ch'in Dynasty

After nearly 900 years, the Chou Dynasty came to an end when the state of Ch'in, the strongest of the seven surviving states, unified China and established the first empire in 221 BC.

The Ch'in empire did not last long, but it left two enduring legacies: the name China and the idea and structure of the empire. This heritage outlasted the Ch'in Dynasty itself by more than 2,000 years.

The first Ch'in emperor was called Ch'in Shih Huang Ti. The title of emperor was used for the first time in Chinese history to set the Ch'in ruler apart–as the ruler of the unified land–from the kings, the heads of the earlier, smaller states. The construction of massive palaces and the ceremony of the court further enhanced the power of the emperor by inspiring awe in the people.

A centralized bureaucracy replaced the old feudal system. The empire was divided into provinces and counties, which were governed by centrally appointed governors and magistrates. The former ruling families who had inherited their places in the aristocracy were uprooted and forced to live in the capital of Xianyang. Other centralizing policies included census taking and standardization of the writing system and weights and measures.

The Ch'in army conducted massive military campaigns to complete the unification of the empire and expand its territory. The Ch'in empire stretched from the Mongolian plateau in the north to Vietnam in the south. As with rulers before and after him, the first emperor was preoccupied with defending his territory against northern nomads. After waging several successful campaigns, the emperor ordered the building of the wall of "ten thousand li" (a li is a Chinese unit of distance) to protect the empire. This task involved connecting the separate walls that were built by former northern states to form the famous Great Wall. The Ten Thousand Li Wall, as it is known in China, is 1,500 miles long, from 15 to 50 feet high, and from 15 to 25 feet wide. Although closely linked with the first ruler of the Ch'in Empire, the wall as it stands today dates mainly from the later Ming Dynasty.

Ch'in Shih Huang Ti's harsh rule provoked much opposition. The emperor feared the scholars most. He had them rounded up and put them to death or sent them into exile. Many went into hiding. Moreover, all books, except technical ones, were confiscated and burned. In the last years of his life, Ch'in Shih Huang Ti became fearful of threats on his life and lived in complete secrecy. He also became obsessed with obtaining immortality. He died in 210 BC in Shandong Province, far from the capital of Xianyang, during one of his long quests to find the elixir of life.

The Ch'in empire disintegrated rapidly after the death of the first emperor. The legitimate heir was killed in a palace intrigue, and a less able prince was put on the throne. Conditions worsened throughout the empire. In 209 BC, rebellions erupted all over China. Two men had the largest following. Hsiang Yu was a general of aristocratic background; Liu Pang was a minor official from a peasant family. By 206 BC rebels had subdued the Ch'in army and destroyed the capital. The struggle between Hsiang Yu and Liu Pang continued for the next four years, however, until Liu Pang emerged as the victor in 202 BC. Taking the title of Kao Tsu, High Progenitor, he established the Han Dynasty.

The Han Dynasty

The four-century-long Han rule preserved many features of the Ch'in imperial system, such as the administrative division of the country and the central bureaucracy. But the Han rulers lifted the Ch'in ban on philosophical and historical writings. Han Kao Tsu called for the services of men of talent, not only to restore the destroyed classics but to serve as officials in the government. From that time, the Chinese Empire was governed by a body of officials theoretically selected on merit. Such a practice has few parallels elsewhere at this early date in mankind's history.

In 124 BC, during the reign of Wu Ti, an imperial university was set up for the study of Confucian classics. The university recruited talented students, and the state supported them. Starting with 50 when the university first opened, the number of government-supported students reached 30,000 by the end of the Han Dynasty. Emperor Wu also established Confucianism as the official doctrine of the state. This designation lasted until the end of the Chinese Empire.

The Early Han faced two major difficulties: invasions by the barbarian Huns and the influence of the imperial consort families. In the Han Dynasty, the Huns (known as Hsiung-nu by the Chinese) threatened the expanding Chinese Empire from the north. Starting in Wu Ti's reign, costly, almost century-long campaigns had to be carried out to establish Chinese sovereignty along the northern and northwestern borders. Wu Ti also waged aggressive campaigns to incorporate northern Korea in 108 BC and northern Annam in 111 BC into the Han empire.

The Early Han's other difficulty started soon after the first emperor's death. The widowed Empress Lu dominated politics and almost succeeded in taking the throne for her family. Thereafter, families of the empresses exerted great political influence. In AD 9 Wang Mang, a nephew of the empress, seized the throne and founded a new dynasty of Hsin.

Wang Mang's overambitious reform program alienated him from the landlords. At the same time the peasants, disappointed with Wang's inability to push through the reform, rose in rebellion. In AD 17 a rebel group in Shandong painted their faces red (hence their name, Red Eyebrows) and adopted religious symbols, a practice later repeated by peasants who rebelled in times of extreme difficulty. Wang Mang's force was defeated, and he was killed in AD 23.

The new ruler who restored peace and order was a member of the house of Han, the original Liu family. His title was Kuang Wu Ti, "Shining Martial Emperor," from AD 25 to 57. During the Later Han, which lasted another 200 years, a concerted but unsuccessful effort was made to restore the glory of the former Han.

During all of this time- from the Hsia Dynasty to the Han Dynasty- the world of the Chinese and the Far East was almost completely separate from the world to its West. *"East is East, and West is West, and never the twain shall meet."* For much of human history that has been the case.

But centuries later a man by the name of Marco Polo would begin to dramatically change that relationship. But before we get to that, we first must resume our journey in the West.

CHAPTER 8: The Indo-Europeans

The Hamitic civilizations of Sumeria, Egypt, and Phoenicia had existed for centuries and the venerable races of the Fertile Valley were getting old and tired. Their doom was sealed when an energetic and motivated people confronted them with vigor. We call this people the Indo-Europeans, because it conquered not only Europe but also made itself the ruling class in the country which is now known as India. They were among the descendants of Noah's son Japhet, who had migrated north following the Great Flood.

The posterity of Japheth early on divided into two major bodies. One of these comprised the ancestors of the Indians and Persians, whereas the second was the aggregate of those tribes which afterwards composed the nations of Europe. The name Japheth is found in ancient literature as Iapetos, the legendary father of the Greeks, and Iyapeti, the reputed ancestor of the Aryans in India. In the Indian account of the Flood, Noah is known as Satyaurata, who had three sons, the eldest of whom was named Iyapeti. Thus, the word "Indo-European" well sums up most of the Japhethites. (Just as an aside, modernists must think it an incredible coincidence that these peoples from around the world all have an account of a Flood that destoyed almost all humanity- but that they think never took place! But back to our story.)

These Japhethites were white Caucasions, the very root word of 'Japheth' alluding to their fair complexion. They spoke a language which is regarded as the common ancestor of all European tongues with the exception of Hungarian and Finnish and the Basque dialects of Northern Spain.

A number of them had been living along the shores of the Caspian Sea for centuries. But one day they had packed their tents and they had wandered forth in search of a new home. Some of them had moved into the mountains of Central Asia and for centuries they had lived among the peaks which surround the plateau of Iran. That is why we call them Aryans. Others had followed the setting sun and they had taken possession of the plains of Europe as I shall tell you when I give you the story of Greece and Rome.

The Persian Conquest

For the moment we must follow the Aryans. Under the leadership of Zarathustra (or Zoroaster)- who was their great teacher- many of them had left their mountain homes to follow the swiftly flowing Indus river on its way to the sea.

Others had preferred to stay among the hills of western Asia and there they had founded the half-independent communities of the Medes and the Persians, two peoples whose names we have copied from the old Greek history-books. In the seventh century before the birth of Christ, the Medes had established a kingdom of their own called Media, but this perished when Cyrus, the chief of a clan known as the Anshan, made himself king of all the Persian tribes and started upon a career of conquest which soon made him and his children the undisputed masters of the whole of western Asia and of Egypt. Japheth truly was enlarged!

Indeed, with such energy did these Indo-European Persians push their triumphant campaigns in the west that they soon found themselves in serious difficulties with certain other Indo-European tribes which centuries before had moved into Europe and had taken possession of the Greek peninsula and the islands of the Ægean Sea.

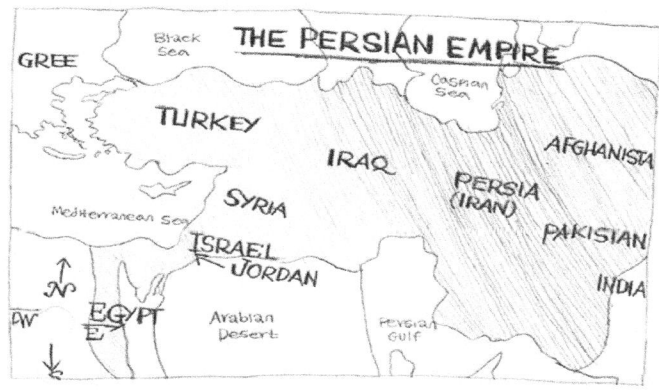

These difficulties led to the three famous wars between Greece and Persia during which King Darius and King Xerxes of Persia invaded the northern part of the peninsula. They ravaged the lands of the Greeks and tried very hard to get a foothold upon the European continent.

But in this they did not succeed. The navy of Athens proved unconquerable. By cutting off the lines of supplies of the Persian armies, the Greek sailors invariably forced the Asiatic rulers to return to their base.

It was the first encounter between Asia, the ancient teacher, and Europe, the young and eager pupil. A great many of the other chapters of this book will tell you how the struggle between east and west has continued until this very day.

The People of the Agean Sea

LET ME TELL YOU THE REAL STORY OF MANKIND

When Heinrich Schliemann was a little boy his father told him the story of Troy. He liked that story better than anything else he had ever heard and he made up his mind, that as soon as he was big enough to leave home, he would travel to Greece and "find Troy." That he was the son of a poor country parson in a Mecklenburg village did not bother him. He knew that he would need money, but he decided to gather a fortune first and do the digging afterwards. As a matter of fact, he managed to get a large fortune within a very short time, and as soon as he had enough money to equip an expedition, he went to the northwest corner of Asia Minor, where he supposed that Troy had been situated.

In that particular nook of old Asia Minor stood a high mound covered with grain fields. According to tradition it had been the home of Priamus the king of Troy. Schliemann, whose enthusiasm was somewhat greater than his knowledge, wasted no time in preliminary explorations. At once he began to dig. And he dug with such zeal and such speed that his trench went straight through the heart of the city for which he was looking and carried him to the ruins of another buried town which was at least a thousand years older than the Troy of which Homer had written. Then something very interesting occurred. If Schliemann had found a few polished stone hammers and perhaps a few pieces of crude pottery, no one would have been surprised. Instead of discovering such objects, which people had generally associated with the prehistoric men who had lived in these regions before the coming of the Greeks, Schliemann found beautiful statuettes and very costly jewelry and ornamented vases of a pattern that was unknown to the Greeks. He ventured the suggestion that fully ten centuries before the great Trojan war, the coast of the Ægean had been inhabited by a mysterious race of men who in many ways had been the superiors of the wild Greek tribes who had invaded their country and had destroyed their civilization or absorbed it until it had lost all trace of originality. And this proved to be the case.

In the 1870s, Schliemann visited the ruins of Mycenæ, ruins which were so old that Roman guidebooks marveled at their antiquity. There again, beneath the flat slabs of stone of a small round enclosure, Schliemann stumbled upon a wonderful treasure-trove, which had been left behind by those mysterious people who had covered the Greek coast with their cities and who had built walls, so big and so heavy and so strong, that the Greeks called them the work of the Titans, those god-like giants of Greek mythology who in very olden days had used to play ball with mountain peaks.

A very careful study of these many relics has done away with some of the romantic features of the story. The makers of these early works of art and the builders of these strong fortresses were no sorcerers, but simple sailors and traders. They had lived in Crete, and on the many small islands of the Ægean Sea. They had been hardy mariners and they had turned the Ægean into a center of commerce for the exchange of goods between the highly civilized east and the slowly developing wilderness of the European mainland.

For more than a thousand years they had maintained an island empire which had developed a very high form of art. Indeed, their most important city, Cnossus, on the northern coast of Crete, had been entirely modern in its insistence upon hygiene and comfort. The palace had been properly drained, and the houses had been provided with stoves and the Cnossians had perhaps been the first people to make a daily use of the hitherto unknown bathtub. The palace of their King had been famous for its winding staircases and its large banqueting hall. The cellars underneath this palace, where the wine and the grain and the olive-oil were stored, had been so vast and had so greatly impressed the first Greek visitors, that they had given rise to the story of the "labyrinth," the name which we give to a structure with so many complicated passages that it is almost impossible to find our way out, once the front door has closed upon our frightened selves.

But what finally became of this great Ægean Empire and what caused its sudden downfall, that I cannot tell.

The Cretans were familiar with the art of writing, but no one has yet been able to decipher their inscriptions. Their history therefore is unknown to us. We have to reconstruct the record of their adventures from the ruins which the Ægeans have left behind. These ruins make it clear that the Ægean world was suddenly conquered by a less civilized race which had recently come from the plains of northern Europe. Unless we are very much mistaken, the savages who were responsible for the destruction of the Cretan and the Ægean civilization were none other than certain tribes of wandering shepherds who had just taken possession of the rocky peninsula between the Adriatic and the Ægean seas and who are known to us as Greeks.

The Greeks

The Pyramids were centuries old and were beginning to show the first signs of decay, and Hammurabi, the wise king of Babylon, had been dead and buried several centuries as well, when a small tribe of shepherds left their homes along the banks of the River Danube and wandered southward in search of fresh pastures. They called themselves Hellenes, after Hellen, the son of Deucalion and Pyrrha. According to the accounts Greeks passed down from generation to generation, these were the only two human beings who had escaped the great flood, which countless years before had destroyed all the people of the world, when they had grown so wicked that they disgusted Zeus, the mighty 'god,' who lived on Mount Olympus. Of course, we know them as Noah and his wife, but in any case, it is but another confirmation of the worldwide Flood, which scattered peoples across the globe retain in their accounts of their histories.

Of these early Hellenes we know little. We do know that the Greeks trace themselves back to Japetos in their tradition, a name which without doubt is the same as Japheth. Significantly, 'Japetos' has no meaning in Greek. It does have a meaning, however, in Hebrew, in which it means 'fair', referring to the complexion of those so named. The Greeks were Indo-Europeans, just like their 'cousins' the Persians many miles away.

Thucydides, the historian of the fall of Athens, describing his earliest ancestors, said that they "did not amount to very much," and this was probably true. They were very ill-mannered. They lived like pigs and threw the bodies of their enemies to the wild dogs who guarded their sheep. They had very little respect for other people's rights, and they killed the natives of the Greek peninsula (who were called the Pelasgians) and stole their farms and took their cattle and made their wives and daughters slaves and wrote endless songs praising the courage of the clan of the Achæans, who had led the Hellenic advance-guard into the mountains of Thessaly and the Peloponnesus.

But here and there, on the tops of high rocks, they saw the castles of the Ægeans and those they did not attack for they feared the metal swords and the spears of the Ægean soldiers and knew that they could not hope to defeat them with their clumsy stone axes.

For many centuries they continued to wander from valley to valley and from mountain side to mountain side Then the whole of the land had been occupied and the migration had come to an end.

That moment was the beginning of Greek civilization. The Greek farmer, living within sight of the Ægean colonies, was finally driven by curiosity to visit his haughty neighbors. He discovered that he could learn many useful things from the men who dwelt behind the high stone walls of Mycenæ, and Tiryns.

He was a clever pupil. Within a short time, he mastered the art of handling those strange iron weapons which the Ægeans had brought from Babylon and from Thebes. He came to understand the mysteries of navigation. He began to build little

LET ME TELL YOU THE REAL STORY OF MANKIND

boats for his own use. In short order he would erect the great Greek civilization.

CHAPTER 9: The Rise of the Greek Civilization

And when he had learned everything the Ægeans could teach him he turned upon his teachers and drove them back to their islands. Soon afterwards he ventured forth upon the sea and conquered all the cities of the Ægean. Finally, in the fifteenth century before our era he plundered and ravaged Cnossus and became the undisputed rulers of Greece, of the Ægean and of the coastal regions of Asia Minor. Troy, the last great commercial stronghold of the older civilization, was destroyed in the eleventh century BC. European history was to begin in all seriousness.

We modern people love the sound of the word "big." We pride ourselves upon the fact that we belong to the "biggest" country in the world and possess the "biggest" navy and grow the "biggest" oranges and potatoes, and we love to live in cities of "millions" of inhabitants and when we are dead we are buried in the "biggest cemetery of the whole state."

A citizen of ancient Greece, could he have heard us talk, would not have known what we meant. "Moderation in all things" was the ideal of his life. Mere bulk did not impress him at all. And this love of moderation was not merely a hollow phrase used upon special occasions: it influenced the life of the Greeks from the day of their birth to the hour of their death. It was part of their literature and it made them build small but perfect temples. It found expression in the clothes which the men wore, and in the rings and the bracelets of their wives. It followed the crowds that went to the theater and made them hoot down any playwright who dared to sin against the iron law of good taste or good sense.

The Greeks even insisted upon this quality in their politicians and in their most popular athletes. When a powerful runner came to Sparta and boasted that he could stand longer on one foot than any other man in Hellas the people drove him from the city because he prided himself upon an accomplishment at which he could be beaten by any common goose. "That is all very well," you will say, "and no doubt it is a great virtue to care so much for moderation and perfection, but why should the Greeks have been the only people to develop this quality in olden times?" For an answer I shall point to the way in which the Greeks lived.

The people of Egypt or Mesopotamia had been the "subjects" of a mysterious political ruler who lived miles and miles away in a dark palace and who was rarely seen by the masses of the population. This was the general pattern of Hamitic cultures. The Greeks, on the other hand, were "free citizens" of a hundred independent little "cities", the largest of which counted fewer inhabitants than a large modern village. When a peasant who lived in Ur said that he was a Babylonian he meant that he was one of millions of other people who paid tribute to the king who at that particular moment happened to be master of western Asia. But when a Greek said proudly that he was an Athenian or a Theban he spoke of a small town, which was both his home and his country, and which recognized no master but the will of the people in the marketplace. This was the more general pattern of Japhetic cultures. And as we shall see, it does much to explain their success over the Hamitic cultures over time.

To the Greek, his fatherland was the place where he was born; where he had spent his earliest years playing hide and seek amidst the forbidden rocks of the Acropolis; where he had grown into manhood with a thousand other boys and girls, whose nicknames were as familiar to him as those of your own schoolmates. His Fatherland was the holy soil where his father and mother lay buried. It was the small house within the high city-walls where his wife and children lived in safety. It was a complete world which covered no more than four or five acres of rocky land. Don't you see how these surroundings must have influenced a man in everything he did and said and thought? The people of Babylon and Assyria and Egypt had been part of a vast mob. They had been lost in the multitude. The Greek on the other hand had never lost touch with his immediate surroundings. He never ceased to be part of a little town where everybody knew everyone else. He felt that his intelligent neighbors were watching him. Whatever he did, whether he wrote plays or made statues out of marble or composed songs, he remembered that his efforts were going to be judged by all the free-born citizens of his hometown who knew about such things. This knowledge forced him to strive after perfection, and perfection, as he had been taught from childhood, was not possible without moderation.

In this hard school, the Greeks learned to excel in many things. They created new forms of government and new forms of literature and new ideals in art. They performed these miracles in little villages that covered less ground than four or five modern city blocks.

And look, what finally happened!

In the fourth century before our era, Alexander of Macedonia conquered the world. As soon as he had done with fighting, Alexander decided that he must bestow the benefits of the true Greek genius upon all mankind. He took it away from the little cities and the little villages and tried to make it blossom and bear fruit amidst the vast royal residences of his newly acquired Empire. But the Greeks, removed from the familiar sight of their own temples, removed from the well-known sounds and smells of their own crooked streets, at once lost the cheerful joy and the marvelous sense of moderation which had inspired the work of their hands and brains while they labored for the glory of their old city-states. They became cheap artisans, content with second-rate work. The day the little city-states of old Hellas lost their independence and were forced to become part of a big nation, the old Greek spirit died. And to a great extent it has been dead ever since.

Greek Self-Government

In the beginning, all the Greeks had been equally rich and equally poor. Every man had owned a certain number of cows and sheep. His mud-hut had been his castle. He had been free to come and go as he wished. Whenever it was necessary to discuss matters of public importance, all the citizens had gathered in the marketplace. One of the older men of the village was elected chairman and it was his duty to see that everybody had a chance to express his views. In case of war, a particularly energetic and self-confident villager was chosen commander-in-chief, but the same people who had voluntarily given this man the right to be their leader, claimed an equal right to deprive him of his job, once the danger had been averted.

But gradually the village had grown into a city. Some people had worked hard and others had been lazy. A few had been through difficult times and still others had been just plain dishonest in dealing with their neighbors and had gathered wealth. As a result, the city no longer consisted of a number of men who were equally well-off. On the contrary it was inhabited by a small class of very rich people and a large class of very poor ones.

There had been another change. The old commander-in-chief who had been willingly recognized as "headman" or "King" because he knew how to lead his men to victory, had disappeared from the scene. His place had been taken by the nobles – a class of rich people who during the course of time had got hold of a large share of the farms and estates.

These nobles enjoyed many advantages over the common crowd of freemen. They were able to buy the best weapons which were to be found on the market of the eastern Mediterranean. They had much spare time in which they could practice the art of fighting. They lived in strongly built houses and they could hire soldiers to fight for them. They were constantly quarrelling among each other to decide who should rule the city. The victorious nobleman then assumed a sort of Kingship over all his neighbors and governed the town until he in turn was killed or driven away by still another ambitious nobleman.

Such a King, by the grace of his soldiers, was called a "Tyrant" and during the seventh and sixth centuries before Christ's advent every Greek city was for a time ruled by such Tyrants, many of whom, by the way, happened to be exceedingly capable men. But in the long run, this state of affairs became unbearable. Then attempts were made to bring about reforms and out of these reforms grew a democratic government.

It was early in the seventh century that the people of Athens decided to do some housecleaning and give the large number of freemen once more a voice in the government as they were supposed to have had in the days of their Achæan ancestors. They asked a man by the name of Draco to provide them with a set of laws that would protect the poor against the aggressions of the rich. Draco set to work. Unfortunately, he was a professional lawyer and very much out of touch with ordinary life. In his eyes a crime was a crime and when he had finished his code, the people of Athens discovered that these Draconian laws were so severe that they could not possibly be put into effect. There would not have been rope enough to hang all the criminals under their new system of jurisprudence which made the stealing of an apple a capital offence.

The Athenians looked about for a more humane reformer. At last they found someone who could do that sort of thing better than anybody else. His name was Solon. He belonged to a noble family and he had travelled all over the world and had studied the forms of government of many other countries. After a careful study of the subject, Solon gave Athens a set of laws which bore testimony to that principle of moderation which was part of the Greek character. He tried to improve the condition of the peasant without however destroying the prosperity of the nobles who were (or rather who could be) of such great service to the state as soldiers. To protect the poorer classes against abuse on the part of the judges (who were always elected from the class of the nobles because they received no salary) Solon made a provision whereby a citizen with a grievance had the right to state his case before a jury of thirty of his fellow Athenians.

Most important of all, Solon forced the average freeman to take a direct and personal interest in the affairs of the city. No longer could he stay at home and say "oh, I am too busy today" or "it is raining and I had better stay indoors." He was expected to do his share; to be at the meeting of the town council; and carry part of the responsibility for the safety and the prosperity of the state.

This government by the "demos," the people, was often far from successful. There was too much idle talk. There were too many hateful and spiteful scenes between rivals for official honor. But it taught the Greek people self-government and that was a very good thing. And this very practice of allowing some degree of self-government, and dispersing power among more people, has been one key to the success of Japhetic societies over the earlier civilized Hamitic societies. By allowing more self-government of territories conquered, and dispersing power to more people, conquered peoples were more willing to remain part of an umbrella empire. It was far more humane and fairer than having one man- often autocratic and despotic- rule a vast territory with little accountability.

Greek Life

But how, you will ask, did the ancient Greeks have time to look after their families and their business if they were forever running to the marketplace to discuss affairs of state? In this chapter I shall tell you.

In all matters of government, the Greek democracy recognized only one class of citizens – the freemen. Every Greek city was composed of a small number of free born citizens, a large number of slaves, and a sprinkling of foreigners.

At rare intervals (usually during a war, when men were needed for the army) the Greeks showed themselves willing to confer the rights of citizenship upon the "barbarians" as they called the foreigners. But this was an exception. Citizenship was a matter of birth. You were an Athenian because your father and your grandfather had been Athenians before you. But however great your merits as a trader or a soldier, if you were born of non-Athenian parents, you remained a "foreigner" until the end of time.

The Greek city, therefore, whenever it was not ruled by a king or a tyrant, was run by and for the freemen, and this would not have been possible without a large army of slaves who outnumbered the free citizens at the rate of six or five to one and who performed those tasks to which we modern people must devote most of our time and energy if we wish to provide for our families and pay the rent of our apartments. The slaves did all the cooking and baking and candlestick making of the entire city. They were the tailors and the carpenters and the jewelers and the school-teachers and the bookkeepers and they tended the store and looked after the factory while the master went to the public meeting to discuss questions of war and peace or visited the theater to see the latest play of Æschylus or hear a discussion of the revolutionary ideas of Euripides, who had dared to express certain doubts upon the omnipotence of the great 'god' Zeus.

Indeed, ancient Athens resembled a modern club. All the freeborn citizens were hereditary members and all the slaves were hereditary servants and waited upon the needs of their masters. It was very pleasant to be a member of the organization.

But when we talk about slaves. we do not mean the sort of people about whom you have read in the pages of "Uncle Tom's Cabin." It is true that the position of those slaves who tilled the fields was a very unpleasant one, but the average freeman who had come down in the world and who had been obliged to hire himself out as a farm hand led just as miserable a life. In the cities, furthermore, many of the slaves were more prosperous than the poorer classes of the freemen. For the Greeks, who loved moderation in all things, did not like to treat their slaves after the fashion which afterward was so common in Rome, where a slave had as few rights as an engine in a modern factory and could be thrown to the wild animals upon the smallest pretext.

The Greeks accepted slavery as a necessary institution, without which no city could possibly become the home of a truly civilized people they thought.

The slaves also took care of those tasks which nowadays are performed by the businessmen and the professional men. As for those household duties which take up so much of the time of your mother and which worry your father when he comes home from his office, the Greeks had reduced such duties to the smallest possible minimum by living amidst surroundings of extreme simplicity.

To begin with, their homes were very plain. Even the rich nobles spent their lives in a sort of adobe barn, which lacked all the comforts which a modern workman expects as his natural right. A Greek home consisted of four walls and a roof. There was a door which led into the street but there were no windows. The kitchen, the living rooms and the sleeping quarters were built around an open courtyard in which there was a small fountain, or a statue and a few plants to make it look bright. Within this courtyard the family lived when it did not rain or when it was not too cold. In one corner of the yard the cook (who was a slave) prepared the meal and in another corner, the teacher (who was also a slave) taught the children the alpha beta gamma and the tables of multiplication. And in still another corner the lady of the house, who rarely left her domain (since it was not considered good form for a married woman to be seen on the street too often) was repairing her husband's coat with her seamstresses (who were slaves,) and in the little office, right off the door, the master was inspecting the accounts which the overseer of his farm (who was a slave) had just brought to him.

When dinner was ready the family came together but the meal was a very simple one and did not take much time. The Greeks seem to have regarded eating as an unavoidable evil and not a pastime, which kills many dreary hours and eventually kills many dreary people. They lived on bread and on wine, with a little meat and some green vegetables. They drank water only when nothing else was available because they did not think it very healthy. They loved to call on each other for dinner, but our idea of a festive meal, where everybody is supposed to eat much more than is good for him, would have disgusted them. They came together at the table for the purpose of a good talk and a good glass of wine and water, but as they were moderate people, they despised those who drank too much.

The same simplicity which prevailed in the dining room also dominated their choice of clothes. They liked to be clean and well groomed, to have their hair and beards neatly cut, to feel their bodies strong with the exercise and the swimming of the gymnasium, but they never followed the Asiatic fashion which prescribed loud colors and strange patterns. They wore a long white coat and they managed to look as smart as a modern Italian officer in his long blue cape.

They loved to see their wives wear ornaments, but they thought it very vulgar to display their wealth (or their wives) in public and whenever the women left their home they were as inconspicuous as possible.

In short, the story of Greek life is a story not only of moderation but also of simplicity. "Things," chairs and tables and books and houses and carriages, are apt to take up a great deal of their owner's time. In the end they invariably make him their slave and his hours are spent looking after their wants, keeping them polished and brushed and painted. The Greeks, before everything else, wanted to be "free," both in mind and in body. That they might maintain their liberty, and be truly free in spirit, they reduced their daily needs to the lowest possible point.

The Greek Theater

At a very early stage of their history the Greeks had begun to collect the poems, which had been written in honor of their brave ancestors who had driven the Pelasgians out of Hellas and had destroyed the power of Troy. These poems were recited in public and everybody came to listen to them. But the theater did not grow out of these recited heroic tales. It had such a curious origin that I must tell you something about it.

The Greeks had always been fond of parades. Every year they held solemn processions in honor of Dionysos the 'god' of the wine. As everybody in Greece drank wine (the Greeks thought water only useful for the purpose of swimming and sailing) this particular divinity was quite popular.

And because the false wine-god was supposed to live in the vineyards, amidst a merry mob of Satyrs (strange creatures who were half man and half goat), the crowd that joined the procession used to wear goat-skins and to hee-haw like real billy-goats. The Greek word for goat is "tragos" and the Greek word for singer is "oidos." The singer who meh-mehed like a goat therefore was called a "tragos-oidos" or goat singer, and it is this strange name which developed into the modern word "Tragedy," which means in the theatrical sense a piece with an unhappy ending, just as Comedy (which really means the singing of something "comos" or gay) is the name given to a play which ends happily.

But how, you will ask, did this noisy chorus of masqueraders, stamping around like wild goats, ever develop into the tragedies which have filled the theaters of the world for almost two thousand years?

The connecting link between the goat-singer and Shakespeare's Hamlet is really very simple as I shall show you in a moment.

The singing chorus attracted large crowds of spectators who stood along the side of the road and laughed. But soon this business of tree-hawing grew tiresome and the Greeks thought dullness an evil only comparable to ugliness or sickness. They asked for something more entertaining. Then an inventive young poet from the village of Icaria in Attica hit upon a new idea which proved a tremendous success. He made one of the members of the goat-chorus step forward and engage in conversation with the leader of the musicians who marched at the head of the parade playing upon their pipes of Pan. This individual was allowed to step out of line. He waved his arms and gesticulated while he spoke (that is to say he "acted" while the others merely stood by and sang) and he asked a lot of questions, which the bandmaster answered according to the roll of papyrus upon which the poet had written down these answers before the show began.

LET ME TELL YOU THE REAL STORY OF MANKIND

This rough and ready conversation – the dialogue – which told the story of Dionysos or one of the other false gods of Greek myth, became at once popular with the crowd. Henceforth every Dionysian procession had an "acted scene" and very soon the "acting" was considered more important than the procession and the meh-mehing.

Æschylus, the most successful of all "tragedians" who wrote no less than eighty plays during his long life (from 526 to 455 B.C.) made a bold step when he introduced two "actors" instead of one. A generation later Sophocles increased the number of actors to three. When Euripides began to write his terrible tragedies in the middle of the fifth century, B.C., he was allowed as many actors as he liked and when Aristophanes wrote those comedies in which he poked fun at everybody and everything, including the false gods of Mount Olympus, the chorus had been reduced to the rôle of mere by-standers who were lined up behind the principal performers and who sang "this is a terrible world" while the hero in the foreground committed a crime against the will of the 'gods.'

To accommodate this new form of dramatic entertainment, soon every Greek city owned a theater, cut out of the rock of a nearby hill. The spectators sat upon wooden benches and faced a wide circle. Upon this half-circle, which was the stage, the actors and the chorus took their stand. Behind them there was a tent where they made up with large clay masks which hid their faces, and which showed the spectators whether the actors were supposed to be happy and smiling or unhappy and weeping. The Greek word for tent is "skene" and that is the reason why we talk of the "scenery" of the stage.

When once the tragedy had become part of Greek life, a new play became as important an event as an election and a successful playwright was received with greater honors than those bestowed upon a general who had just returned from a famous victory. But God in His wisdom did not provide or approve of this form of entertainment for His people, which typically degenerated into immorality and promoted lies, so the early Christian Church which came into contact with Greek culture condemned the Greek dramas.

LET ME TELL YOU THE REAL STORY OF MANKIND

CHAPTER 10: The Persian Wars

The Greeks had learned the art of trading from the Ægeans, who had been the pupils of the Phoenicians. They had founded colonies after the Phoenician pattern. They had even improved upon the Phoenician methods by a more general use of money in dealing with foreign customers. In the sixth century B.C. they had established themselves firmly along the coast of Asia Minor and they were taking away trade from the Phoenicians at a fast rate. This the Phoenicians of course did not like but they were not strong enough to risk a war with their Greek competitors. They sat and waited, nor did they wait in vain.

In a former chapter, I have told you how a humble tribe of Persian shepherds had suddenly gone upon the warpath and had conquered the greater part of western Asia. The Persians were too civilized to plunder their new subjects. They contented themselves with a yearly tribute, allowing more self-government of their territories- the pattern of Japhetic conquest, as we have already noted. When they reached the coast of Asia Minor, they insisted that the Greek colonies of Lydia recognize the Persian Kings as their over-lords and pay them a stipulated tax. The Greek colonies objected. The Persians insisted. Then the Greek colonies appealed to the home country and the stage was set for a quarrel.

For if the truth be told, the Persian Kings regarded the Greek city-states as very dangerous political institutions and bad examples for all other people who were supposed to be the patient slaves of the mighty Persian Kings.

Of course, the Greeks enjoyed a certain degree of safety because their country lay hidden beyond the deep waters of the Ægean.

The Persian Fleet is Destroyed Near Mount Athos

But here their old enemies, the Phoenicians, stepped forward with offers of help and advice to the Persians. If the Persian King would provide the soldiers, the Phoenicians would guarantee to deliver the necessary ships to carry them to Europe. It was the year 492 before the birth of Christ, and Asia made ready to destroy the rising power of Europe.

As a final warning the King of Persia sent messengers to the Greeks asking for "earth and water" as a token of their submission. The Greeks promptly threw the messengers into the nearest well where they would find both "earth and water" in large abundance. Thereafter, of course, peace was impossible.

But when the Phoenician fleet carrying the Persian troops was near Mount Athos, the fleet was destroyed by a terrible hurricane and the Persians were all drowned.

The Battle of Marathon

Two years later they returned. This time they sailed straight across the Ægean Sea and landed near the village of Marathon. As soon as the Athenians heard this, they sent their army of ten thousand men to guard the hills that surrounded the Marathonian plain. At the same time, they dispatched a fast runner to Sparta to ask for help. But Sparta was envious of the fame of Athens and refused to come to her assistance. The other Greek cities followed her example with the exception of tiny Plataea which sent a thousand men. On the twelfth of September of the year 490 B.C., Miltiades, the Athenian commander, threw this little army against the hordes of the Persians. The Greeks broke through the Persian barrage of arrows and their spears caused terrible havoc among the disorganized Asiatic troops who had never been called upon to resist such an enemy.

That night the people of Athens watched the sky grow red with the flames of burning ships. Anxiously they waited for news. At last a little cloud of dust appeared upon the road that led to the North. It was Pheidippides, the runner. He stumbled and gasped for his end was near. Only a few days before had he returned from his errand to Sparta. He had hastened to join Miltiades. That morning he had taken part in the attack and later he had volunteered to carry the news of victory to his beloved city. The people saw him fall and they rushed forward to support him. "We have won," he whispered and then he died, a glorious death which made him envied of all men.

As for the Persians, they tried, after this defeat, to land near Athens but they found the coast guarded and disappeared, and once more the land of Hellas was at peace.

Eight years they waited and during this time the Greeks were not idle. They knew that a final attack was to be expected but they did not agree upon the best way to avert the danger. Some people wanted to increase the army. Others said that a strong fleet was necessary for success. The two parties led by Aristides (for the army) and Themistocles (the leader of the bigger-navy men) fought each other bitterly and nothing was done until Aristides was exiled. Then Themistocles had his chance and he built all the ships he could and turned the Piræus into a strong naval base.

In the year 481 B.C. a tremendous Persian army appeared in Thessaly, a province of northern Greece. In this hour of danger, Sparta, the great military city of Greece, was elected commander-in-chief. But the Spartans cared little what happened to northern Greece provided their own country was not invaded. They neglected to fortify the passes that led into Greece.

Thermopylae

A small detachment of Spartans under Leonidas had been told to guard the narrow road between the high mountains and the sea which connected Thessaly with the southern provinces. Leonidas obeyed his orders. He fought and held the pass with unequalled bravery. But a traitor by the name of Ephialtes who knew the little byways of Malis guided a regiment of Persians through the hills and made it possible for them to attack Leonidas in the rear. Near the Warm Wells – the Thermopylae – a terrible battle was fought. When night came Leonidas and his faithful soldiers lay dead under the corpses of their enemies.

But the pass had been lost and the greater part of Greece fell into the hands of the Persians. They marched upon Athens, threw the garrison from the rocks of the Acropolis and burned the city. The people fled to the Island of Salamis. All seemed lost. But on the 20th of September of the year 480 Themistocles forced the Persian fleet to give battle within the narrow straits which separated the Island of Salamis from the mainland and within a few hours he destroyed three quarters of the Persian ships.

In this way the victory of Thermopylae came to naught.

The Persians Burn Athens

Xerxes was forced to retire. The next year, so he decreed, would bring a final decision. He took his troops to Thessaly and there he waited for spring.

But this time the Spartans understood the seriousness of the hour. They left the safe shelter of the wall which they had built across the isthmus of Corinth and under the leadership of Pausanias they marched against Mardonius the Persian general. The united Greeks (some one hundred thousand men from a dozen different cities) attacked the three hundred thousand men of the enemy near Plataea. Once more the heavy Greek infantry broke through the Persian barrage of arrows. The Persians were defeated, as they had been at Marathon, and this time they left for good. By a strange providence, the same day that the Greek armies won their victory near Plataea, the Athenian ships destroyed the enemy's fleet near Cape Mycale in Asia Minor.

Thus did the first encounter between Asia and Europe end. Athens had covered herself with glory and Sparta had fought bravely and well. If these two cities had been able to come to an agreement, if they had been willing to forget their little jealousies, they might have become the leaders of a strong and united Hellas.

But alas, they allowed the hour of victory and enthusiasm to slip by, and the same opportunity never returned.

LET ME TELL YOU THE REAL STORY OF MANKIND

CHAPTER 11: Athens *vs.* Sparta in the Peloponnesian Wars

Athens and Sparta were both Greek cities and their people spoke a common language. In every other respect they were different. Athens rose high from the plain. It was a city exposed to the fresh breezes from the sea, willing to look at the world with the eyes of a happy child. Sparta, on the other hand, was built at the bottom of a deep valley, and used the surrounding mountains as a barrier against foreign thought. Athens was a city of busy trade. Sparta was an armed camp where people were soldiers for the sake of being soldiers. The people of Athens loved to sit in the sun and discuss poetry or listen to the words of a philosopher. The Spartans, on the other hand, never wrote a single line that was considered literature, but they knew how to fight, they liked to fight, and they sacrificed all human emotions to their ideal of military preparedness.

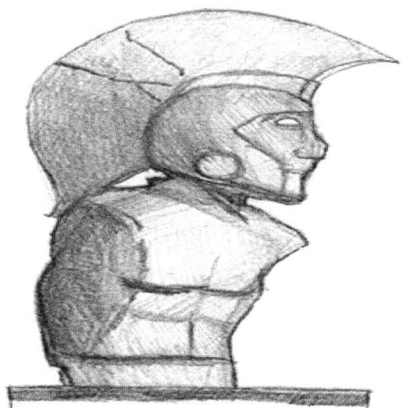

No wonder that these somber Spartans viewed the success of Athens with malicious hate. The energy which the defence of the common home had developed in Athens was now used for purposes of a more peaceful nature. The Acropolis was rebuilt and was made into a marble shrine to the false goddess Athena. Pericles, the leader of the Athenian democracy, sent far and wide to find famous sculptors and painters and scientists to make the city more beautiful and the young Athenians more worthy of their home. At the same time, he kept a watchful eye on Sparta and built high walls which connected Athens with the sea and made her the strongest fortress of that day.

An insignificant quarrel between two little Greek cities led to the final conflict. For thirty years the war between Athens and Sparta continued. It ended in a terrible disaster for Athens.

During the third year of the war the plague had entered the city. More than half of the people and Pericles, the great leader, had been killed. The plague was followed by a period of bad and untrustworthy leadership. A brilliant young fellow by the name of Alcibiades had gained the favor of the popular assembly. He suggested a raid upon the Spartan colony of Syracuse in Sicily. An expedition was equipped, and everything was ready. But Alcibiades got mixed up in a street brawl and was forced to flee. The general who succeeded him was a bungler. First, he lost his ships, and then he lost his army, and the few surviving Athenians were thrown into the stone-quarries of Syracuse, where they died from hunger and thirst. The expedition had killed all the young men of Athens. The city was doomed. After a long siege the town surrendered in April of the year 404. The high walls were demolished. The navy was taken away by the Spartans.

Athens ceased to exist as the center of the great colonial empire which it had conquered during the days of its prosperity. But that wonderful desire to learn and to know and to investigate which had distinguished her free citizens during the days of greatness and prosperity did not perish with the walls and the ships. It continued to live. It became even more brilliant, albeit pagan and darkened without the revelation of God. Athens no longer shaped the destinies of the land of Greece. But now, as the home of the first great university the city began to influence the minds of intelligent people far beyond the narrow frontiers of Hellas.

CHAPTER 12: Alexander the Great

When the Achæans had left their homes along the banks of the Danube to look for pastures new, they had spent some time among the mountains of Macedonia. Ever since, the Greeks had maintained certain more or less formal relations with the people of this northern country. The Macedonians from their side had kept themselves well informed about conditions in Greece.

Now it happened, just when Sparta and Athens had finished their disastrous war for the leadership of Hellas, that Macedonia was ruled by an extraordinarily clever man by the name of Philip. He admired the Greek spirit in letters and art but he despised the Greek lack of self-control in political affairs. It irritated him to see a perfectly good people waste its men and money upon fruitless quarrels. So he settled the difficulty by making himself the master of all Greece and then he asked his new subjects to join him on a voyage which he meant to pay to Persia in return for the visit which Xerxes had paid the Greeks one hundred and fifty years before.

Unfortunately, Philip was murdered before he could start upon this well-prepared expedition. The task of avenging the destruction of Athens was left to Philip's son Alexander, the beloved pupil of Aristotle, wisest (in pagan terms) of all Greek teachers.

Alexander bade farewell to Europe in the spring of the year 334 B.C. Seven years later he reached India. In the meantime, he had destroyed Phoenicia, the old rival of the Greek merchants. He had conquered Egypt and had been worshipped by the people of the Nile valley as the son and heir of the Pharaohs. He had defeated the last Persian king – he had overthrown the Persian empire and he had given orders to rebuild Babylon – he had led his troops into the heart of the Himalayan mountains and had made the entire world a Macedonian province and dependency. Then he stopped and announced even more ambitious plans.

The newly formed Empire must be brought under the influence of the Greek mind. The people must be taught the Greek language – they must live in cities built after a Greek model. The Alexandrian soldier now turned schoolmaster. The military camps of yesterday became the peaceful centers of the newly imported Greek civilization. Higher and higher did the flood of Greek manners and Greek customs rise, when suddenly Alexander was stricken with a fever and died in the old palace of King Hammurabi of Babylon in the year 323 B.C.

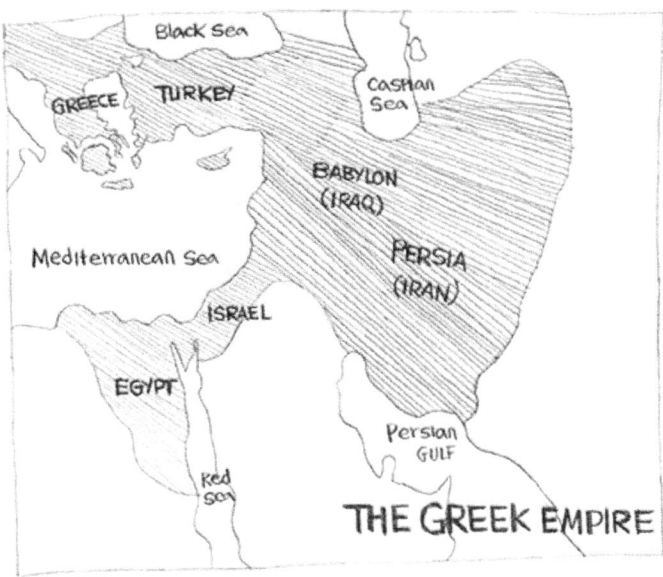

Then the waters receded. But they left behind the fertile clay of a higher civilization and Alexander, with all his childish ambitions and his silly vanities, had performed a most valuable service. His Empire did not long survive him. A number of ambitious generals divided the territory among themselves. But they too remained faithful to the dream of a great world brotherhood of Greek and Asiatic ideas and knowledge.

They maintained their independence until the Romans added western Asia and Egypt to their other domains. The strange inheritance of this Hellenistic civilization (part Greek, part Persian, part Egyptian and Babylonian) fell to the Roman conquerors. During the following centuries, it got such a firm hold upon the Roman world, that we feel its influence in our own lives this very day. Furthermore, God used all of this to prepare a more universal language – Greek – by which His gospel could be more readily spread several hundred years later.

LET ME TELL YOU THE REAL STORY OF MANKIND

CHAPTER 13: A Summary

Thus far, from the top of our high tower we have been looking primarily eastward. But from this time on, I must take you to study primarily the western landscape.

Before we do this though, let us stop a moment and make clear to ourselves what we have seen.

First of all, I showed you Adam, who rebelled against God and plunged all his posterity into sin and death. Yet there was the promise of a coming Christ who would save men from this misery and redeem a people and ultimately the world to Himself.

Then came the period before the Flood lasting a few thousand years when most men disobeyed God to an increasing extent. But we saw that there remained a faithful few like Enoch and Noah who trusted and obeyed Him.

Then I told you about the Flood, and how God destroyed all mankind in it, except Noah and his family.

I then rehearsed the great civilizations like Mesopotamia and Egypt and Phoenicia that came from some of Noah's posterity, especially descended from Ham. I explained how they were exceedingly rich and powerful but also exceedingly immoral.

Then I showed you God's covenant promise to Abraham, and how through him blessings were to flow to all humanity, especially through the promised Christ who would descend from him. We considered the time of the Hebrews in Egypt and their deliverance from bondage under Moses. We looked at the period when the Hebrews were ruled by judges and then by great kings like David and Solomon. We saw how Israel sinned and was humbled through captivity. But we saw how the prophet Daniel prophesied that in a fourth kingdom of iron would arise the eternal kingdom of the Christ.

Then I explained how people and civilizations radiated ever further outward, both to China in the Far East and to Greece in the West. I showed how knowledge and science came to Greece by way of the little island bridges of the Ægean Sea.

Next I told you of an Indo-European tribe, called the Hellenes, who years before had left the heart of Asia and who had in the eleventh century B.C. pushed their way into the rocky peninsula of Greece and who, since then, have been known to us as the Greeks. And I told you the story of the little Greek cities that were really states, where the civilization of old Egypt and Asia was transfigured (that is a big word, but you can "figure out" what it means) into something quite new.

When you look at the map, you will see how by this time civilization has moved. It begins in Mesopotamia. From there it has radiated westward to Egypt, and by way of the Ægean Islands it moves further west until it reaches the European continent. Also, from Mesopotamia it has radiated eastward to China and other Eastern civilizations.

From its movement westward ultimately arises the victorious Roman Empire. During the Roman Empire arises a kingdom which shall never end. Though humble in its beginnings, the kingdom of Christ overpowers even the mighty pagan Roman Empire. This Roman Empire is Christianized, and Christ's gospel of redemption spreads throughout the world, just as Jesus Christ had promised. Although it is to meet with much opposition along the way, yet its ultimate triumph is assured.

I know all this sounds very complicated, but if you get hold of these few principles, the rest of our history will become a great deal simpler. The maps will make clear what the words fail to tell. And after this short intermission, we go back to our story and give you an account of the famous war between Carthage and Rome.

CHAPTER 14: Rome and Carthage

The little Phoenician trading post of Carthage stood on a low hill which overlooked the African Sea, a stretch of water ninety miles wide which separates Africa from Europe. It was an ideal spot for a commercial center. Almost too ideal. It grew too fast and became too rich. When, in the sixth century before our era, Nebuchadnezzar of Babylon destroyed Tyre, Carthage broke off all further relations with the Mother Country and became an independent state – the great western advance-post of the Hamitic race.

Unfortunately, the city had inherited many of the traits which for a thousand years had been characteristic of the Phoenicians. It was a vast business-house, protected by a strong navy, indifferent to most of the finer aspects of life. The city and the surrounding country and the distant colonies were all ruled by a small but exceedingly powerful group of rich men, typical of most Hamitic rule up to this time. The Greek word for rich is "ploutos" and the Greeks called such a government by "rich men" a "Plutocracy." Carthage was a plutocracy and the real power of the state lay in the hands of a dozen big ship-owners and mine-owners and merchants who met in the back room of an office and regarded their common Fatherland as a business enterprise which ought to yield them a decent profit. They were however wide awake and full of energy and worked very hard.

LET ME TELL YOU THE REAL STORY OF MANKIND

Carthage

As the years went by the influence of Carthage upon her neighbors increased until the greater part of the African coast, Spain and certain regions of France were Carthaginian possessions, and paid tribute, taxes and dividends to the mighty city on the African Sea.

Of course, such a "plutocracy" was forever at the mercy of the crowd. As long as there was plenty of work and wages were high, the majority of the citizens were quite contented, allowed their "betters" to rule them and asked no embarrassing questions. But when no ships left the harbor, when no ore was brought to the smelting-ovens, when dockworkers and stevedores were thrown out of employment, then there were grumblings and there was a demand that the popular assembly be called together as in the olden days when Carthage had been a self-governing republic with somewhat less autocratic tendencies.

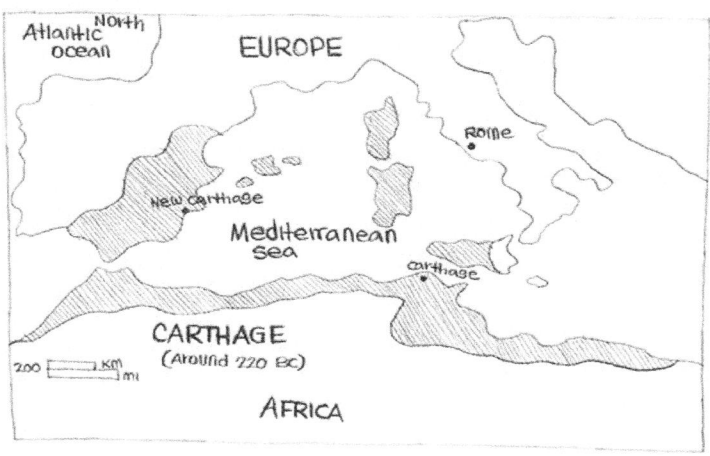

Spheres of Influence

To prevent such an occurrence the plutocracy was obliged to keep the business of the town going at full speed. They had managed to do this very successfully for almost five hundred years when they were greatly disturbed by certain rumors which reached them from the western coast of Italy. It was said that a little village on the banks of the Tiber had suddenly risen to great power and was making itself the acknowledged leader of all the Latin tribes who inhabited central Italy. It was also said that this village, which by the way was called Rome, intended to build ships and go after the commerce of Sicily and the southern coast of France.

Carthage could not possibly tolerate such competition. The young rival must be destroyed lest the Carthaginian rulers lose their prestige as the absolute rulers of the western Mediterranean. The rumors were duly investigated and in a general way these were the facts that came to light.

The west coast of Italy had long been neglected by civilization. Whereas in Greece all the good harbors faced eastward and enjoyed a full view of the busy islands of the Ægean, the west coast of Italy contemplated nothing more exciting than the desolate waves of the Mediterranean. The country was poor. It was therefore rarely visited by foreign merchants and the natives were allowed to live in undisturbed possession of their hills and their marshy plains.

How the City of Rome Happened

The first serious invasion of this land came from the north. At an unknown date, certain Indo-European tribes had managed to find their way through the passes of the Alps and had pushed southward until they had filled the heel and the toe of the famous Italian boot with their villages and their flocks. Of these early conquerors we know nothing. No Homer sang their glory. Their own accounts of the foundation of Rome (written eight hundred years later when the little city had become the center of an Empire) are fairy stories and do not belong in a history. Romulus and Remus jumping across each other's walls (I always forget who jumped across whose wall) make entertaining reading, but the foundation of the City of Rome was a much more prosaic affair. Rome began as a thousand American cities have done, by being a convenient place for barter and horse-trading. It lay in the heart of the plains of central Italy. The Tiber provided direct access to the sea. The land-road from north to south found here a convenient ford which could be used all the year around. And seven little hills along the banks of the river offered the inhabitants a safe shelter against their enemies who lived in the mountains and those who lived beyond the horizon of the nearby sea.

The mountaineers were called the Sabines. They were a rough crowd with an unholy desire for easy plunder. But they were very backward. They used stone axes and wooden shields and were no match for the Romans with their steel swords. The sea-people on the other hand were dangerous foes. They were called the Etruscans and they were (and still are) one of the great mysteries of history. Nobody knew (or knows) whence they came; who they were; what had driven them away from their original homes. We have found the remains of their cities and their cemeteries and their waterworks all along the Italian coast. We are familiar with their inscriptions. But as no one has ever been able to decipher the Etruscan alphabet, these written messages are, so far, merely annoying and not at all useful.

Our best guess is that the Etruscans came originally from Asia Minor and that a great war or a pestilence in that country had forced them to go away and seek a new home elsewhere. Whatever the reason for their coming, the Etruscans played a great rôle in history. They carried the pollen of the ancient civilization from the east to the west and they taught the Romans who, as we know, came from the north, the first principles of architecture and street-building and fighting and art and cookery and medicine and astronomy.

But just as the Greeks had not loved their Ægean teachers, in this same way did the Romans hate their Etruscan masters. They got rid of them as soon as they could, and the opportunity offered itself when Greek merchants discovered the commercial possibilities of Italy and when the first Greek vessels reached Rome. The Greeks came to trade, but they stayed to instruct. They found the tribes who inhabited the Roman countryside (and who were called the Latins) quite willing to learn such things as might be of practical use. At once they understood the great benefit that could be derived from a written alphabet and they copied that of the Greeks. They also understood the commercial advantages of a well-regulated system of coins and measures and weights. Eventually the Romans swallowed Greek civilization hook, line and sinker.

They even welcomed the false gods and pagan religion of the Greeks to their country. Zeus was taken to Rome where he became known as Jupiter and the other divinities followed him. The Roman 'gods' however never were quite like their cheerful cousins who had accompanied the Greeks on their road through life and through history. The Roman 'gods' were state functionaries. Each one managed his own department with great prudence and a deep sense of justice, but in turn he was exact in demanding the obedience of his worshippers. This obedience the Romans rendered with scrupulous care. But they never established the cordial personal relations which had existed between the old Hellenes and the mighty residents of the high Olympian peak.

The Romans did not imitate the Greek form of government but, being of the same Indo-European stock as the people of

Hellas, the early history of Rome resembles that of Athens and the other Greek cities. They did not find it difficult to get rid of their kings, the descendants of the ancient tribal chieftains. But once the kings had been driven from the city, the Romans were forced to bridle the power of the nobles, and it took many centuries before they managed to establish a system which gave every free citizen of Rome a chance to take a personal interest in the affairs of his town.

Thereafter the Romans enjoyed one great advantage over the Greeks. They managed the affairs of their country without making too many speeches. They were less imaginative than the Greeks and they preferred an ounce of action to a pound of words. They understood the tendency of the multitude (the "plebe," as the assemblage of free citizens was called) only too well to waste valuable time upon mere talk. They therefore placed the actual business of running the city into the hands of two "consuls" who were assisted by a council of Elders, called the Senate (because the word "senex" means an old man). As a matter of custom and practical advantage the senators were elected from the nobility. But their power had been strictly defined.

Rome at one time had passed through the same sort of struggle between the poor and the rich which had forced Athens to adopt the laws of Draco and Solon. In Rome this conflict had occurred in the fifth century B. C. As a result, the freemen had obtained a written code of laws which protected them against the despotism of the aristocratic judges by the institution of the "Tribune." These Tribunes were city-magistrates, elected by the freemen. They had the right to protect any citizen against those actions of the government officials which were thought to be unjust. A consul had the right to condemn a man to death, but if the case had not been absolutely proved the Tribune could interfere and save the poor fellow's life.

But when I use the word Rome, I seem to refer to a little city of a few thousand inhabitants. And the real strength of Rome lay in the country districts outside her walls. And it was in the government of these outlying provinces that Rome at an early age showed her wonderful gift as a colonizing power.

In very early times Rome had been the only strongly fortified city in central Italy, but it had always offered a hospitable refuge to other Latin tribes who happened to be in danger of attack. The Latin neighbors had recognized the advantages of a close union with such a powerful friend and they had tried to find a basis for some sort of defensive and offensive alliance. Other nations, Egyptians, Babylonians, Phoenicians, even Greeks, would have insisted upon a treaty of submission on the part of the "barbarians," but the Romans did nothing of the sort. They gave the "outsider" a chance to become partners in a common "res publica" – or commonwealth.

"You want to join us," they said. "Very well, go ahead and join. We shall treat you as if you were full-fledged citizens of Rome. In return for this privilege we expect you to fight for our city, the mother of us all, whenever it shall be necessary." The "outsider" appreciated this generosity and he showed his gratitude by his unswerving loyalty. It was a brilliant and successful way in which to expand, and as we have noted a number of times before, it is due in large measure to this method of governance that Japhetic peoples like the Romans ended up overcoming and conquering the civilizations of the Hamitic peoples.

Whenever a Greek city had been attacked, the foreign residents had moved out as quickly as they could. Why defend something which meant nothing to them but a temporary boarding house in which they were tolerated as long as they paid their bills? But when the enemy was before the gates of Rome, all the Latins rushed to her defence. It was their Mother who was in danger. It was their true "home" even if they lived a hundred miles away and had never seen the walls of the 'sacred hills'.

No defeat and no disaster could change this sentiment. In the beginning of the fourth century B.C. the wild Gauls forced their way into Italy. They had defeated the Roman army near the River Allia and had marched upon the city. They had taken Rome and then they expected that the people would come and sue for peace. They waited, but nothing happened. After a short time, the Gauls found themselves surrounded by a hostile population which made it impossible for them to obtain supplies. After seven months, hunger forced them to withdraw. The policy of Rome to treat the "foreigner" on equal terms had proved a great success and Rome stood stronger than ever before.

This short account of the early history of Rome shows you the enormous difference between the Roman ideal of a healthy state, and that of the ancient world which was embodied in the town of Carthage. The Romans counted upon the cheerful and hearty co-operation between a number of "equal citizens." The Carthaginians, following the example of Egypt and western Asia, insisted upon the unreasoning (and therefore unwilling) obedience of "Subjects" and when these failed, they hired professional soldiers to do their fighting for them.

You will now understand why Carthage was bound to fear such a clever and powerful enemy and why the plutocracy of Carthage was only too willing to pick a quarrel that they might destroy the dangerous rival before it was too late.

But the Carthaginians, being good businessmen, knew that it never pays to rush matters. They proposed to the Romans that their respective cities draw two circles on the map and that each town claim one of these circles as her own "sphere of influence" and promise to keep out of the other fellow's circle. The agreement was promptly made and was broken just as promptly when both sides thought it wise to send their armies to Sicily where a rich soil and a bad government invited foreign interference.

The war which followed (the so-called first Punic War) lasted twenty-four years. It was fought out on the high seas and, in the beginning, it seemed that the experienced Carthaginian navy would defeat the newly created Roman fleet. Following their ancient tactics, the Carthaginian ships would either ram the enemy vessels or by a bold attack from the side they would break their oars and would then kill the sailors of the helpless vessel with their arrows and with fire balls. But Roman engineers invented a new craft which carried a boarding bridge across which the Roman infantrymen stormed the hostile ship. Then there was a sudden end to Carthaginian victories. At the battle of Mylae their fleet was badly defeated. Carthage was obliged to sue for peace, and Sicily became part of the Roman domains.

Twenty-three years later new trouble arose. Rome (in quest of copper) had taken the island of Sardinia. Carthage (in quest of silver) thereupon occupied all of southern Spain. This made Carthage a direct neighbor of the Romans. The latter did not like this at all and they ordered their troops to cross the Pyrenees and watch the Carthaginian army of occupation.

The stage was set for the second outbreak between the two rivals. Once more a Greek colony was the pretext for a war. The Carthaginians were besieging Saguntum on the east coast of Spain. The Saguntians appealed to Rome and Rome, as usual, was willing to help. The Senate promised the help of the Latin armies, but the preparation for this expedition took some time, and meanwhile Saguntum had been taken and had been destroyed. This had been done in direct opposition to the will of Rome. The Senate decided upon war. One Roman army was to cross the African sea and make a landing on Carthaginian soil. A second division was to keep the Carthaginian armies occupied in Spain to prevent them from rushing to the aid of the hometown. It was an excellent plan, and everybody expected a great victory. But God had decided otherwise.

Hannibal Crosses the Alps

It was the fall of the year 218 before the birth of Christ and the Roman army which was to attack the Carthaginians in Spain had left Italy. People were eagerly waiting for news of an easy and complete victory when a terrible rumor began to spread through the plain of the Po. Wild mountaineers, their lips trembling with fear, told of hundreds of thousands of brown men accompanied by strange beasts "each one as big as a house," who had suddenly emerged from the clouds of snow which surrounded the old Graian pass. Soon an endless stream of bedraggled refugees appeared before the gates of Rome, with more complete details.

Hannibal, the son of Hamilcar, with fifty thousand soldiers, nine thousand horsemen and thirty-seven fighting elephants, had crossed the Pyrenees. He had defeated the Roman army of Scipio on the banks of the Rhone and he had guided his army safely across the mountain passes of the Alps although it was October and the roads were thickly covered with snow and ice. Then he had joined forces with the Gauls and together they had defeated a second Roman army just before they crossed the Trebia and laid siege to Placentia, the northern terminus of the road which connected Rome with the province of the Alpine districts.

The Senate, surprised but calm and energetic as usual, hushed up the news of these many defeats and sent two fresh armies to stop the invader. Hannibal managed to surprise these troops on a narrow road along the shores of the Trasimene Lake and there he killed all the Roman officers and most of their men. This time there was a panic among the people of Rome, but the Senate kept its nerve. A third army was organized, and the command was given to Quintus Fabius Maximus with full power to act "as was necessary to save the state."

Fabius knew that he must be very careful lest all be lost. His raw and untrained men, the last available soldiers, were no match for Hannibal's veterans. He refused to accept battle but forever he followed Hannibal, destroyed everything eatable, destroyed the roads, attacked small detachments and generally weakened the morale of the Carthaginian troops by a most distressing and annoying form of guerilla warfare.

Hannibal and the C. E. F.
Such methods however did not satisfy the fearsome crowds who had found safety behind the walls of Rome. They wanted "action." Something must be done and must be done quickly. A popular hero by the name of Varro, the sort of man who went about the city telling everybody how much better he could do

things than slow old Fabius, the "Delayer," was made commander-in-chief by popular acclamation. At the battle of Cannae (216) he suffered the most terrible defeat of Roman history. More than seventy thousand men were killed. Hannibal was master of all Italy.

He marched from one end of the peninsula to the other, proclaiming himself the "deliverer from the yoke of Rome" and asking the different provinces to join him in warfare upon the mother city. Then once more the wisdom of Rome bore noble fruit. With the exceptions of Capua and Syracuse, all Roman cities remained loyal. Hannibal, the deliverer, found himself opposed by the people whose friend he pretended to be. He was far away from home and did not like the situation. He sent messengers to Carthage to ask for fresh supplies and new men. Alas, Carthage could not send him either.

The Romans with their boarding-bridges, were the masters of the sea. Hannibal must help himself as best he could. He continued to defeat the Roman armies that were sent out against him, but his own numbers were decreasing rapidly, and the Italian peasants held aloof from this self-appointed "deliverer."

After many years of uninterrupted victories, Hannibal found himself besieged in the country which he had just conquered. For a moment, the situation seemed to turn. Hasdrubal, his brother, had defeated the Roman armies in Spain. He had crossed the Alps to come to Hannibal's assistance. He sent messengers to the south to tell of his arrival and ask the other army to meet him in the plain of the Tiber. Unfortunately, the messengers fell into the hands of the Romans and Hannibal waited in vain for further news until his brother's head, neatly packed in a basket, came rolling into his camp and told him of the fate of the last of the Carthaginian troops.

With Hasdrubal out of the way, young Publius Scipio easily reconquered Spain and four years later the Romans were ready for a final attack upon Carthage. Hannibal was called back. He crossed the African Sea and tried to organize the defences of his home-city. In the year 202 at the battle of Zama, the Carthaginians were defeated. Hannibal fled to Tyre. From there he went to Asia Minor to stir up the Syrians and the Macedonians against Rome. He accomplished very little but his activities among these Asiatic powers gave the Romans an excuse to carry their warfare into the territory of the east and annex the greater part of the Ægean world.

The Death of Hannibal

Driven from one city to another, a fugitive without a home, Hannibal at last knew that the end of his ambitious dream had come. His beloved city of Carthage had been ruined by the war. She had been forced to sign a terrible peace. Her navy had been sunk. She had been forbidden to make war without Roman permission. She had been condemned to pay the Romans millions of dollars for endless less years to come. Life "under the sun" offered no hope of a better future, or so he thought. In the year 190 B.C. Hannibal took poison and killed himself. And so we have the lesson re-enforced that our hope must ultimately reside in Christ and not in the things of this world.

Forty years later, the Romans forced their last war upon Carthage. Three long years the inhabitants of the old Phoenician colony held out against the power of the new republic. Hunger forced them to surrender. The few men and women who had survived the siege were sold as slaves. The city was set on fire. For two whole weeks the storehouses and the palaces and the great arsenal burned. Then a terrible curse was pronounced upon the blackened ruins and the Roman legions returned to Italy to enjoy their victory.

For the next thousand years, the Mediterranean remained a European sea. But as soon as the Roman Empire had been destroyed, Asia made another attempt to dominate this great inland sea, as you will learn when I tell you about Mohammed.

LET ME TELL YOU THE REAL STORY OF MANKIND

CHAPTER 15: The Rise of Rome

God had planned the Roman Empire from all eternity, especially as a vehicle to spread the gospel of Jesus Christ throughout much of the world. The Roman Empire prepared the excellent roads and the safe sea lines by which this gospel was so readily and widely transported.

But in sheer human terms, the Roman Empire was an accident. It just "happened." No famous general or statesman or cut-throat ever got up and said "Friends, Romans, Citizens, we must found an Empire. Follow me and together we shall conquer all the land from the Gates of Hercules to Mount Taurus."

Rome produced famous generals and equally distinguished statesmen and cut-throats, and Roman armies fought all over the world. But the Roman empire-making was done without a human preconceived plan. The average Roman was a very matter-of-fact citizen. He disliked theories about government. When someone began to recite "eastward the course of Roman

Empire, etc., etc.," he hastily left the forum. He just continued to take more and more land because circumstances forced him to do so. He was not driven by ambition or by greed. Both by nature and inclination he was a farmer and wanted to stay at home. But when he was attacked he was obliged to defend himself and when the enemy happened to cross the sea to ask for aid in a distant country then the patient Roman marched many dreary miles to defeat this dangerous foe and when this had been accomplished, he stayed behind to administer his newly conquered provinces lest they fall into the hands of wandering Barbarians and become themselves a menace to Roman safety. It sounds rather complicated and yet to the contemporaries it was so very simple, as you shall see in a moment.

In the year 203 B.C. Scipio had crossed the African Sea and had carried the war into Africa. Carthage had called Hannibal back. Badly supported by his mercenaries, Hannibal had been defeated near Zama. The Romans had asked for his surrender and Hannibal had fled to get aid from the kings of Macedonia and Syria, as I told you in my last chapter.

The rulers of these two countries (remnants of the Empire of Alexander the Great) just then were contemplating an expedition against Egypt. They hoped to divide the rich Nile valley between themselves. The king of Egypt had heard of this and he had asked Rome to come to his support. The stage was set for a number of highly interesting plots and counterplots. But the Romans, with their lack of imagination, rang the curtain down before the play had been fairly started. Their legions completely defeated the heavy Greek phalanx which was still used by the Macedonians as their battle formation. That happened in the year 197 B.C. at the battle in the plains of Cynoscephalæ, or "Dogs' Heads," in central Thessaly.

The Romans then marched southward to Attica and informed the Greeks that they had come to "deliver the Hellenes from the Macedonian yoke." The Greeks, having learned nothing in their years of semi-slavery, used their new freedom in a most unfortunate way. All the little city-states once more began to quarrel with each other as they had done in the good old days.

The Romans, who had little understanding and less love for these silly bickerings of a race which they rather despised, showed great forbearance. But tiring of these endless dissensions they lost patience, invaded Greece, burned down Corinth (to "encourage the other Greeks") and sent a Roman governor to Athens to rule this turbulent province. In this way, Macedonia and Greece became buffer states which protected Rome's eastern frontier.

Meanwhile, right across the Hellespont lay the Kingdom of Syria, and Antiochus III, who ruled that vast land. Antiochus had shown great eagerness when his distinguished guest, General Hannibal, explained to him how easy it would be to invade Italy and sack the city of Rome.

Lucius Scipio, a brother of Scipio the African fighter who had defeated Hannibal and his Carthaginians at Zama, was sent to Asia Minor. He destroyed the armies of the Syrian king near Magnesia (in the year 190 B.C.) Shortly afterwards, Antiochus was lynched by his own people. Asia Minor became a Roman protectorate and the small City-Republic of Rome was mistress of most of the lands which bordered upon the Mediterranean.

When the Roman armies returned from these many victorious campaigns, they were received with great jubilation. Alas and alack! this sudden glory did not make the country any happier. On the contrary. The endless campaigns had ruined the farmers who had been obliged to do the hard work of Empire making. It had placed too much power in the hands of the successful generals (and their private friends) who had used the war as an excuse for wholesale robbery.

The old Roman Republic had been proud of the simplicity which had characterized the lives of her famous men. The new Republic felt ashamed of the shabby coats and the high principles which had been fashionable in the days of its grandfathers. It became a land of rich people ruled by rich people for the benefit of rich people. As such it was doomed to disastrous failure, as I shall now tell you.

LET ME TELL YOU THE REAL STORY OF MANKIND

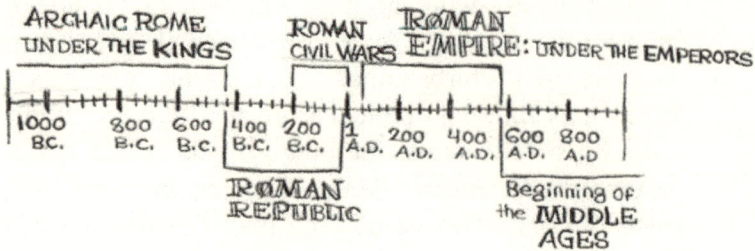

Within less than a century and a half, Rome had become the mistress of practically all the land around the Mediterranean. In those early days of history, a prisoner of war lost his freedom and became a slave. The Roman regarded war as a very serious business and he showed no mercy to a conquered foe. After the fall of Carthage, the Carthaginian women and children were sold into bondage together with their own slaves. And a like fate awaited the obstinate inhabitants of Greece and Macedonia and Spain and Syria when they dared to revolt against the Roman power.

Two thousand years ago a slave was merely a piece of machinery. Nowadays a rich man invests his money in factories. The rich people of Rome (senators, generals and war-profiteers) invested theirs in land and in slaves. The land they bought or took in the newly acquired provinces. The slaves they bought in open market wherever they happened to be cheapest. During most of the third and second centuries before Christ there was a plentiful supply, and as a result the landowners worked their slaves until they dropped dead in their tracks, when they bought new ones at the nearest bargain-counter of Corinthian or Carthaginian captives.

And now behold the situation of the freeborn farmer!

He had done his duty toward Rome and he had fought her battles without complaint. But when he came home after ten, fifteen or twenty years, his lands were covered with weeds and his family had been ruined. But he was a strong man and willing to begin life anew. He sowed and planted and waited for the harvest. He carried his grain to the market together with his cattle and his poultry, to find that the large landowners who worked their estates with slaves could underbid him all along the line. For a couple of years, he tried to hold his own. Then he gave up in despair. He left the country and he went to the nearest city. In the city he was as hungry as he had been before on the land. But he shared his misery with thousands of other disinherited beings. They crouched together in filthy hovels in the suburbs of the large cities. They were apt to get sick and die from terrible epidemics. They were all profoundly discontented. They had fought for their country and this was their reward. They were always willing to listen to those plausible spellbinders who gather around a public grievance like so many hungry vultures, and soon they became a grave menace to the safety of the state.

But the class of the newly rich shrugged its shoulders. "We have our army and our policemen," they argued, "they will keep the mob in order." And they hid themselves behind the high walls of their pleasant villas and cultivated their gardens and read the poems of a certain Homer which a Greek slave had just translated into very pleasing Latin hexameters.

In a few families however the old tradition of unselfish service to the Commonwealth continued. Cornelia, the daughter of Scipio Africanus, had been married to a Roman by the name of Gracchus. She had two sons, Tiberius and Gaius. When the boys grew up, they entered politics and tried to bring about certain much-needed reforms. A census had shown that most of the land of the Italian peninsula was owned by two thousand noble families. Tiberius Gracchus, having been elected a Tribune, tried to help the freemen. He revived two ancient laws which restricted the number of acres which a single owner might possess. In this way he hoped to revive the valuable old class of small and independent freeholders. The newly rich called him a robber and an enemy of the state. There were street riots. A party of thugs was hired to kill the popular Tribune. Tiberius Gracchus was attacked when he entered the assembly and was beaten to death. Ten years later his brother Gaius tried the experiment of reforming a nation against the expressed wishes of a strong privileged class. He passed a "poor law" which was meant to help the destitute farmers. Eventually it made the greater part of the Roman citizens into professional beggars.

He established colonies of destitute people in distant parts of the empire, but these settlements failed to attract the right sort of people. Before Gaius Gracchus could do more harm he too was murdered, and his followers were either killed or exiled. The first two reformers had been gentlemen. The two who came after were of a very different stamp. They were professional soldiers. One was called Marius. The name of the other was Sulla. Both enjoyed a large personal following.

Sulla was the leader of the landowners. Marius, the victor in a great battle at the foot of the Alps when the Teutons and the Cimbri had been annihilated, was the popular hero of the disinherited freemen.

Now it happened in the year 88 B.C. that the Senate of Rome was greatly disturbed by rumors that came from Asia. Mithridates, king of a country along the shores of the Black Sea, and a Greek on his mother's side, had seen the possibility of establishing a second Alexandrian Empire. He began his campaign for world-domination with the murder of all Roman citizens who happened to be in Asia Minor- men, women and children. Such an act, of course, meant war. The Senate equipped an army to march against the King of Pontus and punish him for his crime. But who was to be commander-in-chief? "Sulla," said the Senate, "because he is Consul." "Marius," said the mob, "because he has been Consul five times and because he is the champion of our rights."

Possession is nine points of the law. Sulla happened to be in actual command of the army. He went west to defeat Mithridates and Marius fled to Africa. There he waited until he heard that Sulla had crossed into Asia. He then returned to Italy, gathered a motley crew of malcontents, marched on Rome and entered the city with his professional highwaymen, spent five days and five nights, slaughtering the enemies of the Senatorial party, got himself elected Consul and promptly died from the excitement of the last fortnight.

There followed four years of disorder. Then Sulla, having defeated Mithridates, announced that he was ready to return to Rome and settle a few old scores of his own. He was as good as his word. For weeks his soldiers were busy executing those of their fellow citizens who were suspected of democratic sympathies. One day they got hold of a young fellow who had been often seen in the company of Marius. They were going to hang him when someone interfered. "The boy is too young," he said, and they let him go. His name was Julius Cæsar. You shall meet him again very shortly.

As for Sulla, he became "Dictator," which meant sole and supreme ruler of all the Roman possessions. He ruled Rome for four years, and he died quietly in his bed, having spent the last year of his life tenderly raising his cabbages, as was the custom of so many Romans who had spent a lifetime killing their fellowmen.

But conditions did not grow better. On the contrary, they grew worse. Another general, Gnæus Pompeius, or Pompey, a close friend of Sulla, went east to renew the war against the ever troublesome Mithridates. He drove that energetic potentate into the mountains where Mithridates took poison and killed himself, well knowing what fate awaited him as a Roman captive. Next he re-established the authority of Rome over Syria, destroyed Jerusalem, roamed through western Asia, trying to revive the myth of Alexander the Great, and at last (in the year 62 BC) returned to Rome with a dozen ship-loads of defeated Kings and Princes and Generals, all of whom were forced to march in the triumphal procession of this enormously popular Roman who presented his city with the sum of forty million dollars in plunder.

It was necessary that the government of Rome be placed in the hands of a strong man. Only a few months before, the town had almost fallen into the hands of a good-for-nothing young aristocrat by the name of Catiline, who had gambled away his money and hoped to reimburse himself for his losses by a little plundering. Cicero, a public-spirited lawyer, had discovered the plot, had warned the Senate, and had forced Catiline to flee. But there were other young men with similar ambitions, and it was no time for idle talk.

Pompey organized a triumvirate which was to take charge of affairs. He became the leader of this Vigilante Committee. Gaius Julius Cæsar, who had made a reputation for himself as governor of Spain, was the second in command. The third was an indifferent sort of person by the name of Crassus. He had been elected because he was incredibly rich, having been a successful contractor of war supplies. He soon went upon an expedition against the Parthians and was killed.

As for Cæsar, who was by far the ablest of the three, he decided that he needed a little more military glory to become a popular hero. He crossed the Alps and conquered that part of the world which is now called France. Then he hammered a solid wooden bridge across the Rhine and invaded the land of the wild Teutons. Finally, he took ship and visited England. Who knows where he might have ended if he had not been forced to return to Italy? Pompey, so he was informed, had been appointed dictator for life. This of course meant that Cæsar was to be placed on the list of the "retired officers," and the idea did not appeal to him. He remembered that he had begun life as a follower of Marius. He decided to teach the Senators and their "dictator" another lesson. He crossed the Rubicon River which separated the province of Cisalpine Gaul from Italy.

Everywhere he was received as the "friend of the people." Without difficulty Cæsar entered Rome and Pompey fled to Greece. Cæsar followed him and defeated his followers near Pharsalus. Pompey sailed across the Mediterranean and escaped to Egypt. When he landed, he was murdered by order of young king Ptolemy. A few days later Cæsar arrived. He found himself caught in a trap. Both the Egyptians and the Roman garrison which had remained faithful to Pompey, attacked his camp.

But Providence was on Cæsar's side. He succeeded in setting fire to the Egyptian fleet. Incidentally the sparks of the burning vessels fell on the roof of the famous library of Alexandria, which was just off the waterfront, and destroyed it. Next, he attacked the Egyptian army, drove the soldiers into the Nile, drowned Ptolemy, and established a new government under Cleopatra, the sister of the late king. Just then word reached him that Pharnaces, the son and heir of Mithridates, had gone on the warpath. Cæsar marched northward, defeated Pharnaces in a war which lasted five days, sent word of his victory to Rome in the famous sentence "veni, vidi, vici," which is Latin for "I came, I saw, I conquered," and returned to Egypt where he fell desperately in love with Cleopatra, who followed him to Rome when he returned to take charge of the government, in the year 46 BC. He marched at the head of not less than four different victory-parades, having won four different campaigns.

Then Cæsar appeared in the Senate to report upon his adventures, and the grateful Senate made him "dictator" for ten years. It was a fatal step.

The new dictator made serious attempts to reform the Roman state. He made it possible for freemen to become members of the Senate. He conferred the rights of citizenship upon distant communities as had been done in the early days of Roman history. He permitted "foreigners" to exercise influence upon the government. He reformed the administration of the distant provinces which certain aristocratic families had come to regard as their private possessions. In short, he did many things for the good of the majority of the people, but which made him thoroughly unpopular with the most powerful men in the state. Half a hundred young aristocrats formed a plot "to save the

Republic." On the Ides of March (the fifteenth of March, according to that new calendar which Cæsar had brought with him from Egypt) Cæsar was murdered when he entered the Senate. Once more Rome was without a master.

CHAPTER 16: The Great Roman Empire

There were two men who tried to continue the tradition of Cæsar's glory. One was Antony, his former secretary. The other was Octavian, Cæsar's grand-nephew and heir to his estate. Octavian remained in Rome, but Antony went to Egypt to be near Cleopatra with whom he too had fallen in love, as seems to have been the habit of Roman generals.

A war broke out between the two. In the battle of Actium, Octavian defeated Antony. Antony killed himself and Cleopatra was left alone to face the enemy. She tried very hard to make Octavian her third Roman conquest. When she saw that she could make no impression upon this very proud aristocrat, she killed herself, and Egypt became a Roman province.

As for Octavian, he was a very wise young man and he did not repeat the mistake of his famous uncle. He knew how people will shy at words. He was very modest in his demands when he returned to Rome. He did not want to be a "dictator." He would be entirely satisfied with the title of "the Honorable." But when the Senate, a few years later, addressed him as Augustus – the Illustrious – he did not object and a few years later the man in the street called him Cæsar, or Kaiser, while the soldiers, accustomed to regard Octavian as their Commander-in-chief referred to him as the Chief, the Imperator or Emperor. The Republic had become an Empire, but the average Roman was hardly aware of the fact.

In 14 AD his position as the Absolute Ruler of the Roman people had become so well established that he was made an object of that divine worship which hitherto had been reserved for their false gods. And his successors were true "Emperors" – the absolute rulers of the greatest empire the world had ever seen.

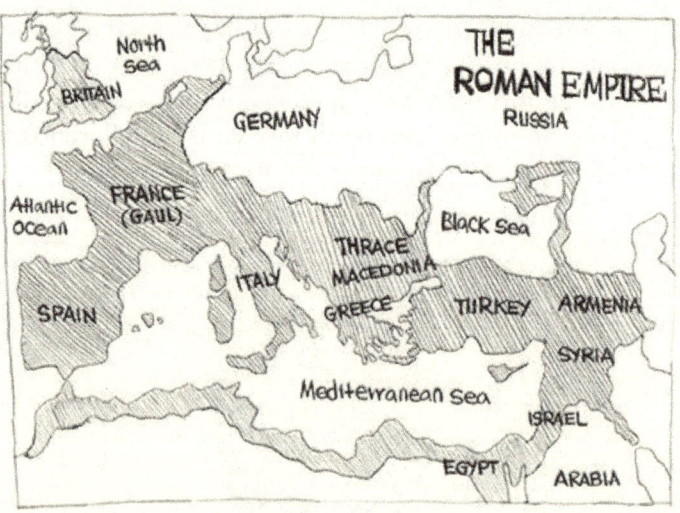

If the truth be told, the average citizen was sick and tired of anarchy and disorder. He did not care who ruled him provided the new master gave him a chance to live quietly and without the noise of eternal street riots. Octavian assured his subjects forty years of peace. He had no desire to extend the frontiers of his domains. In the year 9 AD he had contemplated an invasion of the northwestern wilderness which was inhabited by the Teutons. But Varrus, his general, had been killed with all his men in the Teutoburg Woods, and after that the Romans made no further attempts to civilize these wild people.

They concentrated their efforts upon the gigantic problem of internal reform. But it was too late to do much good. Two centuries of revolution and foreign war had repeatedly killed the best men among the younger generations. It had ruined the class of the free farmers. It had introduced slave labor, against which no freeman could hope to compete. It had turned the cities into beehives inhabited by pauperized and unhealthy mobs of runaway peasants. It had created a large bureaucracy – petty officials who were underpaid and who were enticed to take graft in order to buy bread and clothing for their families. Worst of all, it had accustomed people to violence, to bloodshed, to a barbarous pleasure in the pain and suffering of others.

Outwardly, the Roman state during the first century of our era was a magnificent political structure, so large that Alexander's empire became one of its minor provinces. Underneath this glory there lived millions upon millions of poor and tired human beings, toiling like ants who have built a nest underneath a heavy stone. They worked for the benefit of someone else. They shared their food with the animals of the fields. They lived in stables. They died without hope.

It was the seven hundred and fifty-third year since the founding of Rome. Gaius Julius Cæsar Octavianus Augustus was living in the palace of the Palatine Hill, busily engaged upon the task of ruling his empire.

In a little village of distant Syria, Mary, the wife of Joseph the Carpenter, was tending her little boy, born in a stable of Bethlehem. This is a world where God works miracles that human wisdom could not predict. Before long, the palace and the stable were to meet in open combat. And the stable was to emerge victorious.

LET ME TELL YOU THE REAL STORY OF MANKIND

CHAPTER 17: The Everlasting Kingdom of Jesus Christ

Approximately 4,000 years since the creation of the world and man's fall into sin had passed. The world was groaning under the weight of its sin, but God's chosen people yet maintained their hope in a Christ- a Messiah- to rescue them. The Old Testament prophets had declared that the Christ would descend from King David. He was to be born in Bethlehem.

During the intervening centuries before Christ came, the Jews had endured many difficult times, often owing to their own sin. Under men like Ezra and Nehemiah, the Jews had returned to Canaan from Babylon. They-built Jerusalem. They were always under the rule and authority of other, greater political powers. But they were allowed some measure of self-government, depending upon the regime which controlled them. They had passed through subjection to Persian, Greek, Syrian, and finally Roman rule.

Many empires and civilizations indeed had risen and fallen since Adam had sinned and been forced to leave Paradise. But all during that time the really important event- the event that had been promised by God that He would have Satan's head crushed through the Seed of the woman- had not yet occurred. But just as had been prophesied by the prophet Daniel many years before, during the Roman Empire an even greater kingdom was to arise. This kingdom of the Christ would be an everlasting kingdom. And now the time had arrived for its establishment.

It was during the reign of Caesar Augustus in Rome and Herod the Edomite in the region where Jesus Christ was born, that Augustus, wishing to know the number of his subjects, so as to regulate the taxes paid by the conquered countries, to provide corn for the poorer Roman citizens, sent out an edict that each person should enroll his name at his native place, and there pay a piece of money. Thus, the Divine Power brought it to pass, that Mary, who was about to bring forth a son, should travel with her betrothed husband to the home of their fathers, Rachel's burial place, Bethlehem. This was the little city where David had once been called away from the sheepfolds. There the stable of the ox and ass received the Master of Heaven and earth- Jesus Christ- when His people considered Him not and shut their doors. But "unto us a Child was born, unto us a Son was given." The very years of our calendar are marked by the approximate year of His birth. From the Birth of our Lord, time is counted onwards, and the years marked as A.D., Anno Domini, Year of the Lord.

The shepherds on the hills heard the angels sing their song of peace on earth, good will to men. On the eighth day of His Life on earth, that Child was circumcised, and received the Greek form of the Divine name, Jehovah the Savior. This was the same name of Joshua who had been borne before by the Captain and by the Priest, who had led His people to their inheritance. Thence the Desire of all nations was carried to His presentation in the Temple. He was truly the first-born of all creation, but He was only known to the aged Simeon and devout Anna, as the messenger of the covenant, the Lord for whom they had waited. To Bethlehem came the mysterious wise men from the east. They had been led by the star to Jerusalem, and were there directed on by the scribes, learned in the prophecies.

But the wise men's inquiries had alarmed the jealousy of Herod- the king the Roman Empire had installed in this region. Herod sent forth the savage order, that the babes of Bethlehem should all be murdered, in hopes of cutting off the new-born King of the Jews. But while the mothers wept for the children who should come again to them in a better inheritance, the Holy One was safe in Egypt, where Joseph had carried Him, by the warning of God.

Augustus died in 17 A.D., leaving his power to his stepson, Tiberius, whom he had adopted as his own son, and thus given him the name of Caesar. Tiberius had not been kindly treated in his youth, and he was gloomy and harsh, and exceedingly disliked by the Romans. Under him, Pontius Pilate was made Procurator of Judea. Pilate took up his abode in Caesarea, a city built by Herod and his son Philip, on the coast, and named after the emperors. Pilate set up shields with idolatrous inscriptions in Jerusalem. But the Jews petitioned Tiberius, who ordered them to be removed, and there was much hatred between the Procurator and the Jews.

The thirty years of silent bearing of the common lot of man were now nearly over. Six months before the Messiah began to make Himself known, His messenger, John, the Desert Priest, began to prepare His way by preaching repentance in the spirit and power of the great Elijah, and then baptizing in the Jordan unto repentance.

The great purpose of the Old Covenant was accomplished when John, having made his followers feel all the weight of their sins against the Commandments, pointed out Him whom he had already baptized, and said, "Behold the Lamb of God, which taketh away the sin of the world!" A few faithful Galileans followed and believed, and miracles began to testify that here was indeed the Christ, the Prophet like to Moses, giving bread to the hungry, eyes to the blind, feet to the lame.

Meanwhile, the Pharisees and Sadducees, their heads full of the prophecies of greatness and deliverance, they grew more and more enraged at every token that the lowly Nazarene was indeed the Savior, the Hope of the whole world. Each token of perfection, each saying too pure for them, each undoubted miracle, only made them more furious, and for once they made common cause together. The Passover came. Herod Antipas came to Jerusalem to observe the feast. Jerusalem saw her King coming, meek, and riding on an ass. Amid the Hosannas of the children, Jesus wept at the vengeance that He foresaw for the favored city where He had been despised and rejected, and where He was Himself about to become the true Passover, which should purchase everlasting Redemption for His elect people.

The traitor – Judas Iscariot – sold Him to the Sanhedrin, or council, in which the last words of the prophecy through the Priesthood had declared that one man must die for the people. A band of Roman soldiers was obtained from Pilate to apprehend Jesus. Meanwhile, our blessed Lord instituted the new Passover- the Lord's Supper. In this Communion the faithful disciples of Jesus Christ remember His sacrifice on their behalf and look forward to His Second Coming and Day of Judgment. Then Jesus went out to the garden, among the grey olives which still stand beside the brook Kedron, and there, after His night of Agony, He was betrayed by a kiss of Judas Iscariot.

Jesus was then dragged before the High Priest by the Roman soldiers under an accusation of blasphemy. As the Sanhedrin had not power of life and death, and such a charge would have mattered little to a Roman, a political offence was invented to bring before Pilate. The procurator perceived the innocence of the Holy One but feared to befriend Him because of the raging multitude. After vainly trying to shift the responsibility on Herod Antipas, he washed his hands, to show that it was no affair of his own and gave the Victim up to the murderers. They chose the most shameful death of Roman slaves, that they might show their hatred and contempt, unwitting that each act and each word had been foretold and foreshown in their own Law and Prophets.

For six hours He hung on His Cross at a place called Golgotha (which means 'the place of the skull'), while the sun was dark, and awe crept on the most ignorant hearts. Then came the cry, "It is finished", and the work was done. The sinless, once-for-all-time Sacrifice had died. The price of sin was paid on behalf God's chosen people. The veil of the Temple was rent in twain, to show that the way to the true Mercy-Seat was opened and the old ceremonial worship and laws were coming to an end. The rich man buried Him while the women watched.

And when the Sabbath was over, the Tomb was broken through, and the First-fruits of them that slept arose. Jesus Christ rose from the dead on the first day of the week.

Jesus Christ wondrously visited His followers for forty days, gave them His last charges, and then ascended into Heaven, carrying manhood to the bosom of the Father, and Himself being glorified sitting at the right hand of God the Father. There Jesus Christ – the very Son of God – intercedes continually on behalf of His people. God's people can thus come directly to the Father in prayer, in the Name of His Son.

Jesus Christ's other great gift for the church came soon after His ascension. On a first day of the week, on Pentecost, while His disciples were gathered to worship, Christ gave His people a special outpouring of the Holy Spirit, just as He had previously promised. This same gift of the Holy Spirit was to be a blessing for His church from then on. And on that special occasion He revealed it would be a blessing for men of many nations by allowing his disciples to speak and understand the languages of many nations.

The Christian Church

The beginning of the Christian Church is reckoned from the great day on which the Holy Ghost came down, according as our Lord had promised to His Apostles. At that time, "Jews, devout men, out of every nation under heaven," were gathered together at Jerusalem, to keep the Feast of Pentecost (or Feast of Weeks), which was one of the three holy seasons at which God required His people to appear before Him in the place which He had chosen (Deuteronomy xvi. 16). Many of these devout men there converted by what they then saw and heard, to believe the Gospel; and, when they returned to their own countries, they carried back with them the news of the wonderful things which had taken place at Jerusalem. And so was the Christian Church founded, covenanted to Christ in a Covenant of Grace newly administered and newly ordered.

By the coming of Jesus Christ who had been so long promised, in His human Body, and the completion of His sacrifice, and then the Pentecostal outpouring of the Holy Spirit, all the objects of the old ceremonial Law were fulfilled. The shadows passed away and the substance took their place. The Passover was replaced by the New Passover- the Lord's Supper. In addition, circumcision was replaced by baptism in the Name of the Father, Son, and Holy Spirit. Both circumcision and baptism were defined by God as symbols of the new birth and regeneration, just as the Passover and the Lord's Supper are symbols of conversion and remembrance of redemption in Christ. But baptism and the Lord's Supper more clearly point to the substance of spiritual realities in Christ, inasmuch as they signify Holy Spirit baptism and redemption accomplished through Christ's sacrifice on the Cross. Another change for the church was that regarding the Sabbath. God's church on earth was now to keep the first day of the week, commonly called the Lord's Day, as its weekly Sabbath. Since the time of the original Creation the seventh day had been designated by God as the Sabbath, but in the New Creation ushered in by Christ's resurrection and the Pentecostal gift of the Holy Spirit on the first day of the week, the first day of each week was designated as His weekly day of Sabbath worship.

With the Christian Church now established and its ordinances set, it was time for it to fulfill its Great Commission mandate. This mandate was to preach the gospel to all men of all nations, so that men of all nations might be saved, and the nations of the world redeemed in Christ.

So, the Apostles went forth "into all the world," as their Master had ordered them, to "preach the Gospel to every creature" (St Mark xvi. 15). The Book of Acts tells us something of what they did, and we may learn something more about it from the Epistles. And, although this be but a small part of the whole, it will give us a notion of the rest, if we consider that, while St. Paul was preaching in Asia Minor, Greece, and at Rome, the other Apostles were busily doing the same work in other countries.

We must remember, too, the constant coming and going which in those days took place throughout the world, how Jews from all quarters went up to keep Britain as far as Persia and Ethiopia, and people from all parts of it were continually going to Rome and returning. We must consider how merchants traveled from country to country on account of their trade; how soldiers were sent into all quarters of the empire and were moved about from one country to another. And from these things we may get some understanding of the way in which the knowledge of the Gospel would be spread, when once it had taken root in the great cities of Jerusalem and Rome. Thus it came to pass, that, by the end of the first hundred years after our Savior's birth something was known of the Christian faith throughout all the Roman empire, and even in countries beyond it; and if in many cases, only a very little was known, still even that was a gain, and served as a preparation for more.

The last chapter of the Acts leaves the Apostle Paul at Rome, waiting for his trial on account of the things which the Jews had laid to his charge. We find from the Epistles that he afterwards got his liberty and returned into the East. There is reason to suppose that he also visited Spain, as he had spoken of doing in his Epistle to the Romans (ch. xv. 28); and it has been thought by some that he even preached in Britain; but this does not seem likely. He was at last imprisoned again at Rome, where the wicked Emperor Nero persecuted the Christians very cruelly; and it is believed that both the Apostles Peter and Paul were put to death there in the year of our Lord 68 AD.

The bishops of Rome (the Popes, or Papacy) afterwards set up claims to great power and honor, because they said that Peter was the first bishop of their church, and that they were his successors. But although we may reasonably believe that the Apostle was martyred at Rome, there does not appear to be any good ground for thinking that he had been settled there as bishop of the city. The claim is simply a deceitful means for the Papacy to obtain power which she has not been given by God.

All the Apostles, except John, are supposed to have been martyred (or put to death for the sake of the Gospel). James the Less, who was an elder (sometimes called a 'bishop' in scripture as well) in Jerusalem, was killed by the Jews in an uproar, about the year 62 AD. By 70 AD most of the Jews had still not repented and received Christ as their Lord and Savior. God's seventy weeks of years prophesied in Daniel were at end, and judgment was nigh. The Romans sent their armies into Judea, and, after a bloody war, they took the city of Jerusalem, and destroyed the Temple. Since that day the Temple has never been re-established, and the records as to who could be lawful Levitical priests for the Temple have been lost. God therefore utterly and completely closed the door on the Old Testament dispensation of His church.

Thirty years after Herod's time another cruel emperor, Domitian, raised a fresh persecution against the Christians (AD 95). Among those who suffered were some of his own near relations; for the Gospel had now made its way among the great people of the earth, as well as among the poor, who were the first to listen to it. It is generally believed (but this is not certain) that it was during Domitian's persecution that the Apostle John was banished to the island of Patmos and wrote his "Revelation."

John, in his old age, was much troubled by false teachers, who had begun to corrupt the Gospel. These persons are called "heretics", and their doctrines are called "heresy" from a Greek word which means "to choose", because they chose to follow their own fancies, instead of receiving the Gospel as the Apostles and the Church taught it. Simon the sorcerer, who is mentioned in the eighth chapter of the Acts, is counted as the first heretic, and even in the time of the Apostles a number of others arose, such as Hymenaeus, Philetus, and Alexander, who are mentioned by St. Paul (1 Tim. i. 19f; 2 Tim. ii. 17f). These earliest heretics were mostly of the kind called Gnostics, a word which means that they pretended to be more knowing than ordinary Christians. Perhaps the Apostle. Paul may have alluded especially to them when he warned Timothy against "science" (or knowledge) "falsely so called" (1 Tim. vi. 20). Their doctrines were a strange mixture of Jewish and heathen notions with Christianity; and it is curious that some of the very strangest of their opinions have been brought up again from time to time by people who fancied that they had found out something new, while they had only fallen into old errors, which had been condemned by the Church hundreds of years before.

But despite its humble beginnings and the opposition against it, the kingdom of Jesus Christ was firmly established. Jesus Christ had crushed Satan's head when He died on the Cross for sins and rose again on the first day of the week. He took His seat of authority at the right hand of God the Father, from whence He reigns even as He is redeeming the nations to Himself. His Apostles spread the gospel message of redemption in Jesus Christ throughout the Roman Empire and beyond. Many kings and kingdoms on earth would have their day, as we have seen and will see more in the chapters that follow, but this kingdom of God the Son is forever.

CHAPTER 18: The Fall of Rome

The textbooks of ancient history give the date 476 as the year in which Rome fell, because in that year the last emperor was driven off his throne. But Rome, which was not built in a day, took a long time falling. The process was so slow and so gradual that most Romans did not realize how their old world was coming to an end. They complained about the unrest of the times – they grumbled about the high prices of food and about the low wages of the workmen - they cursed the profiteers who had a monopoly of the grain and the wool and the gold coin. Occasionally they rebelled against an unusually rapacious governor. But the majority of the people during the first four centuries after Christ's advent ate and drank (whatever their purse allowed them to buy) and hated or loved (according to their nature) and went to the theater (whenever there was a free show of fighting gladiators) or starved in the slums of the big cities, utterly ignorant of the fact that God had appointed a date for it to collapse.

How could they realize the threatened danger? Rome made a fine showing of outward glory. Well-paved roads connected the different provinces, the imperial police were active and showed little tenderness for highwaymen. The frontier was closely guarded against the savage tribes who seemed to be occupying the waste lands of northern Europe. The whole world was paying tribute to the mighty city of Rome, and a score of able men were working day and night to undo the mistakes of the past and bring about a return to the happier conditions of the early Republic.

But the underlying causes of the decay of the State, of which I have told you in a former chapter, had not been removed and reform therefore was impossible.

Rome was, first and last and all the time, a city-state as Athens and Corinth had been city states in ancient Hellas. It had been able to dominate the Italian peninsula. But Rome as the ruler of the entire civilized world was a political impossibility and could not endure. Her young men were killed in her endless wars. Her farmers were ruined by long military service and by taxation. They either became professional beggars or hired themselves out to rich landowners who gave them board and lodging in exchange for their services and made them "serfs."

The Empire, the State, had become everything. The common citizen had dwindled down to less than nothing. As for many of the slaves, they had heard the gospel of Jesus Christ and embraced it. They did not rebel against their masters. On the contrary, they had been taught to be meek and they obeyed their superiors. But they were less than enthusiastic to engage in warfare for the benefit of an ambitious emperor who aspired to glory by way of a foreign campaign in the land of the Parthians or the Numidians or the Scots.

And so, conditions grew worse as the centuries went by. The first Emperors had continued the tradition of "leadership" which had given the old tribal chieftains such a hold upon their subjects. But the Emperors of the second and third centuries were Barrack-Emperors, professional soldiers, who existed by the grace of their bodyguards, the so-called Prætorians. They succeeded each other with terrifying rapidity, murdering their way into the palace and being murdered out of it as soon as their successors had become rich enough to bribe the guards into a new rebellion.

When the Barbarians Got Through with a Roman City

Meanwhile, the barbarians were hammering at the gates of the northern frontier. As there were no longer any native Roman armies to stop their progress, foreign mercenaries had to be hired to fight the invader. As the foreign soldier happened to be of the same blood as his supposed enemy, he was apt to be quite lenient when he engaged in battle. Finally, by way of experiment, a few tribes were allowed to settle within the confines of the Empire. Others followed. Soon these tribes complained bitterly of the greedy Roman tax-gatherers, who took away their last penny. When they got no redress; they marched to Rome and loudly demanded that they be heard.

This made Rome very uncomfortable as an Imperial residence. Constantine (who ruled from 323 to 337 A.D.) looked for a new capital. He chose Byzantium, the gateway for the commerce between Europe and Asia. The city was renamed Constantinople, and the court moved eastward. When Constantine died, his two sons, for the sake of a more efficient administration, divided the Empire between them. The elder lived in Rome and ruled in the west. The younger stayed in Constantinople and was master of the east.

Then came the fourth century and the terrible visitation of the Huns, those mysterious Asiatic horsemen who for more than two centuries maintained themselves in Northern Europe and continued their career of bloodshed until they were defeated near Chalons-sur-Marne in France in the year 451. As soon as the Huns had reached the Danube, they had begun to press hard upon the Goths. The Goths, in order to save themselves, were thereupon obliged to invade Rome. The Emperor Valens tried to stop them but was killed near Adrianople in the year 378 AD. Twenty-two years later, under their king, Alaric, these same West Goths marched westward and attacked Rome. They did not plunder and destroyed only a few palaces. Next came the Vandals and showed less respect for the venerable traditions of the city. Then the Burgundians. Then the East Goths. Then the Alemanni. Then the Franks. There was no end to the invasions. Rome at last was at the mercy of every ambitious highway robber who could gather a few followers.

In the year 402 the Emperor fled to Ravenna, which was a sea-port and strongly fortified, and there, in the year 475, Odoacer, commander of a regiment of the German mercenaries, who wanted the farms of Italy to be divided among themselves, gently but effectively pushed Romulus Augustulus, the last of the emperors who ruled the western division, from his throne, and proclaimed himself Patriarch or ruler of Rome. The eastern Emperor, who was very busy with his own affairs, recognized him, and for ten years Odoacer ruled what was left of the western provinces.

The Invasions of the Barbarians

A few years later, Theodoric, King of the East Goths, invaded the newly formed Patriciat, took Ravenna, murdered Odoacer at his own dinner table, and established a Gothic Kingdom amidst the ruins of the western part of the Empire. This Patriciate state did not last long. In the sixth century a motley crowd of Lombards and Saxons and Slavs and Avars invaded Italy, destroyed the Gothic kingdom, and established a new state of which Pavia became the capital.

Then, at last, the imperial city sank into a state of utter neglect and despair. The ancient palaces had been plundered time and again. The schools had been burned down. The teachers had been starved to death. The rich people had been thrown out of their villas which were now inhabited by barbarians. The roads had fallen into decay. The old bridges were gone and commerce had come to a standstill. Civilization – the product of thousands of years of patient labor on the part of Egyptians and Babylonians and Greeks and Romans, threatened to perish from the western continent.

It is true that in the far east, Constantinople continued to be the center of an Empire for another thousand years. But it hardly counted as a part of the European continent. Its interests lay in the east. It began to forget its western origin. Gradually the Roman language was given up for the Greek. The Roman alphabet was discarded, and Roman law was written in Greek characters and explained by Greek judges. The Emperor became an Asiatic despot. When missionaries of the Byzantine church looked for fresh fields of activity, they went eastward and carried the civilization of Byzantium into the vast wilderness of Russia.

As for the west, it was left to the mercies of the Barbarians. For twelve generations, murder, war, arson, and plundering were the order of the day. One thing – and one thing alone – saved Europe from complete anarchy and destruction: Christianity.

LET ME TELL YOU THE REAL STORY OF MANKIND

CHAPTER 19: The Spread of Christianity and the Rise of Anti-Christ

The average intelligent Roman who lived under the Empire had taken very little interest in the gods of his fathers. A few times a year he went to the temple, but merely as a matter of custom. He looked on patiently when the people celebrated a religious festival with a solemn procession. But he regarded the worship of Jupiter and Minerva and Neptune as something rather childish, a survival from the crude days of the early republic and not a fit subject of study for a man who had mastered the works of the Stoics and the Epicureans and the other great philosophers of Athens.

This attitude made the Roman a very "tolerant", pluralist man. The government insisted that all people, Romans, foreigners, Greeks, Babylonians, Jews, should pay a certain outward respect to the image of the Emperor which was supposed to stand in every temple, just as a picture of the President of the United States is apt to hang in an American Post Office. But this was a formality without any deeper meaning. Generally speaking, everybody could honor, revere and adore whatever gods he pleased, and as a result, Rome was filled with all sorts of queer little temples, dedicated to the worship of Egyptian and African and Asiatic divinities.

When the first disciples of Jesus Christ reached Rome and began to preach the gospel, nobody objected. The man in the street stopped and listened. Rome, the capital of the world, had always been full of wandering preachers, each proclaiming his own "mystery." Most of the self-appointed priests appealed to the senses – promised golden rewards and endless pleasure to the followers of their own particular 'god.' Soon the crowd in the street noticed that the so-called Christians (the followers of the Christ or "anointed one") spoke a very different language. They did not appear to be impressed by great riches or a noble position. They extolled the beauties of humility and meekness. These were not exactly the virtues which had made Rome the mistress of the world. It was rather interesting to listen to a "mystery'" which told people in the hey-day of their glory that their worldly success could not possibly bring them lasting happiness and eternal life.

Besides, the preachers of Christianity told the truth about what awaited those who died in their sins, uncleansed by the righteousness of Christ imputed to their account. The preachers proclaimed the gospel of how Jesus Christ died on the Cross to pay for His people's sins, and how men may only be saved through faith in Him. It was not wise to reject such a gospel and face God on the Day of Judgement.

Furthermore, the preachers informed the people of their superstitions and false gods. People began to have doubts about them. They returned to listen to further explanations of the new creed. After a while they began to meet the men and women who preached the words of Jesus. They found them very different from the average Roman priests. They were morally upright and willing to die for Christ.

All of these factors, but most fundamentally the working of the Holy Spirit, led many Romans to forsake the old religion. They joined the small communities of Christians who met in the back rooms of private houses or somewhere in an open field or even in the underground catacombs in Rome, and the temples were deserted.

This went on year after year and the number of Christians continued to increase. Presbyters or priests (the original Greek meant "elder") were elected to guard the interests of the small churches in each town. As time passed, the authority given to certain elders in the larger cities increased. Over the course of time, the teaching elder, or bishop, in a larger city was made the head of all the communities within a single province. (A few centuries after the fall of the Roman Empire, this increasing concentration of power led the bishop of Rome even to assert himself Pope over the entire church, as we shall speak of later.)

The church became a powerful institution within the Empire. The Christian doctrines were embraced by increasing multitudes. At last the state was obliged to take notice. The Roman Empire (I have said this before) was 'tolerant' through indifference. It allowed everybody to seek salvation after his or her own fashion. But it insisted that the different sects keep the peace among themselves and obey the wise rule of "live and let live."

The Christian communities however, refused to practice any sort of such wicked 'tolerance' and pluralism. They publicly declared that the God of the Bible, and Him alone, was the true ruler of Heaven and Earth, and that all other gods were imposters. This seemed unfair to the other sects and the police discouraged such utterances. The Christians persisted.

Soon there were further difficulties. The Christians refused to go through the formalities of paying homage to the emperor. They refused to appear when they were called upon to join the army upon the conditions required by the pagan Empire, with the taking of oaths that would have been lies. The Roman magistrates threatened to punish them. The Christians answered that this miserable world was only the anteroom to Heaven and that they were more than willing to suffer death for their principles. The Romans killed many such offenders or persecuted them. There was a certain amount of lynching during the earliest years of the church, but this was the work of that part of the mob which accused their meek Christian neighbors of every conceivable crime, (such as slaughtering and eating babies, bringing about sickness and pestilence, betraying the country in times of danger) because it was a harmless sport and devoid of danger, as the Christians refused to fight back.

Meanwhile, Rome continued to be invaded by the Barbarians and when her armies failed, Christian missionaries went forth to preach their gospel of peace to the wild Teutons. They were strong men without fear of death. They spoke a language which left no doubt as to the future of unrepentant sinners. The Teutons were deeply impressed. They still had a deep respect for the wisdom of the ancient city of Rome. Those men were Romans. They spoke the truth. Soon the Christian missionary became a power in the savage regions of the Teutons and the Franks. Half a dozen missionaries were as valuable as a whole regiment of soldiers. The Emperors began to understand that the Christian might be of great use to them. In some of the provinces they were given equal rights with those who remained faithful to the old gods. The great change however came during the last half of the fourth century.

Constantine was emperor. During a long career, Constantine had experienced many ups and downs. In one battle Constantine promised that he too would become a Christian if he were successful in it. He won the victory and thereafter he was convinced of the power of the Christian God and allowed himself to be baptized.

From that moment on, the Christian church was officially recognized, and this greatly strengthened the position of the new faith. Constantine did a number of services to enhance the vitality of the Church, in accordance with the scriptural principle that civil rulers are to be nursing mothers to God's church. He enacted laws to move the society towards an appropriate sanctification of the Lord's Day, as well as to conform the laws in general to scriptural moral law. He encouraged the Church to be united in a sound faith. There was a controversy in the church of his day splitting it apart. Heretics led by Arius were advancing the position that Jesus Christ was not God the Son, but merely an exalted creature of God. However, Athanasius and others were defending the Biblical stance that Jesus Christ was and is God the Son. Constantine called an assembly or synod of bishops (also called elders) from all over the Christian Church to resolve the dispute. The meeting was at Nicaea in Asia Minor in 325 A.D. The council condemned the Arian heresy and drew up the Nicene Creed, which we still have today. Constantine then worked to suppress this heresy using the powers of the State. Generally speaking, Constantine served as a good example of how a Christian civil ruler can support the Christian Church and protect Christ's interests in the nation (which we call the 'establishment principle').

But the Christians still formed a very small minority of all the people, (not more than five or six percent,) and in order to win, they were forced to refuse all compromise. The old pagan gods must be destroyed, for God has commanded in his word the duty of Christian magistrates to extirpate false religion and false worship. For a short spell the emperor Julian, a lover of Greek wisdom, managed to save the pagan 'gods' from further destruction. But Julian died of his wounds during a campaign in Persia and his successor Jovian re-established the church in all its glory. One after the other the doors of the ancient temples were then closed. Then came the emperor Justinian (who built the church of Saint Sophia in Constantinople), who discontinued the school of philosophy at Athens which had been founded by Plato. These Christian rulers suppressed false religion and false worship, in accordance with Biblical command.

During an age when nothing was certain, the church stood like a rock and never receded from those principles which it held to be true and sacred. This steadfast courage gained the admiration of the multitudes and carried the church safely through the difficulties which destroyed the Roman state.

It was at just this time that God provided a great gift to the church: Augustine. Augustine was the son of a Christian mother and a wealthy, pagan father. As a young man he rejected Christianity and embraced an immoral way of life. But God honored the prayers of his mother and the preaching of Ambrose of Milan. God saved Augustine, and he was baptized into the Christian faith. For thirty-five years Augustine served as a bishop of Hippo in Roman controlled northern Africa. He wrote the account of his spiritual journey through life in his book entitled *Confessions*. This book has blessed generations of readers, illustrating to us how God saves sinners through Jesus Christ.

Augustine explained the great doctrines of the Christian faith, and he is generally regarded as the greatest theologian of early church history. He championed the importance of the visible unity of the Christian Church, refuting the separatism of the Donatists. He championed God's complete grace in the salvation of sinners and the doctrine of predestination, refuting the heresy of the Pelagians. He championed the duty of the Christian civil ruler to enforce the Ten Commandments, and he upheld the glorious vision of ultimate Christian triumph in his work *The City of God*. Yet even Augustine did not see through some of the rising errors of the Church of the Middle Ages. Augustine, who died in 430 A.D. during the waning days of the Roman Empire, explained the faith of the Christian Church to his generation and generations to come.

Nevertheless, there was a dark cloud forming on the horizon of the Christian Church. After the disappearance of Theodoric's Roman-Gothic kingdom, in the fifth century, Italy was comparatively free from foreign invasion. The Lombards and Saxons and Slavs who succeeded the Goths were weak and backward tribes. Under those circumstances it was possible for the bishops of Rome to maintain the independence of their city. Soon the remnants of the empire, scattered throughout the peninsula, recognized the Dukes of Rome (or bishops) as their political and spiritual rulers. The Bishop of Rome was amassing more and more power, contrary to scriptural principle.

Accordingly, the stage was set for a strong man to rule in an office of the Church which Christ had retained for Himself. In the year 590 Gregory began to rule as the Bishop of Rome. He belonged to the ruling classes of ancient Rome, and he had been prefect or mayor of the city. Then he had become a monk and a bishop, and finally he was made Pope. He ruled only fourteen years but when he died the Christian world of western Europe had officially recognized the bishops of Rome, the Popes, as the head of the entire church. The Papacy, the office of the 'man of sin' which was warned about by the Apostle Paul, was thus more fully formed and developed. It was an office within Christ's Church or Temple, but it was anathema to Christ's true interests and the true gospel. As future years would pass, this Anti-Christian Papacy would undermine the true faith from within the visible Christian Church, and the errors of the Church of Rome would multiply.

This power, however, did not extend to the east. The Eastern Church did not recognize the supremacy of the Pope, and for a time avoided certain of his heretical idolatries. God blessed the Eastern Church and the Eastern Roman Empire (which became known as the Byzantine Empire) during a time when the

Western Roman Empire was destroyed and divided, and the Roman Catholic Church was rising in its place.

One notable Byzantine Emperor was Leo III. From the beginning centuries the Christian Church had taken a strong stand against all forms of idolatry, including images (also called icons) of God the Son- Jesus Christ. This they did because the Second Commandment forbids use of such graven images in worship. But as time passed more and more Christians fell into the sin of using icons as parts of their religious worship. The greatest defender of this idolatry was the Roman Pope himself, who was thus undermining the Biblical Christian faith. But the more godly Emperor of the Byzantine Empire, Leo III, took a stand against icons. In 730 their use was officially prohibited. This caused a rift with the Roman Pope and his church. But God blessed Leo's faithfulness. He successful thwarted the efforts of the Muslim Arab enemies to his east. And he also issued a legal handbook called the *Ecloga,* which was an important influence on Byzantine and Slavic law for centuries.

Those emperors which followed in Leo's footsteps of suppressing false worship in the use of icons were called 'iconoclasts', a word we retain in our language even to this day. In 754 a Council or Synod of bishops (or elders) of the eastern Christian churches met to define iconoclastic doctrine, in the Council of Hieria. God continued to bless the Byzantine Empire as it defended a more Biblical form of worship.

But later, a wicked empress named Irene arose who was opposed to iconoclasm. She loved icons more than Christ and Christ's law. She convoked a Council of churches to rubberstamp her opposition to iconoclasm in 787. The use of icons was promoted by the Empire, and false worship waxed strong. God punished the Byzantine Empire for this unfaithfulness. Enemies from the east and west made great inroads into the Empire, and its power in most of what had been the western Roman Empire virtually collapsed.

Although some later Byzantine emperors tried to restore iconoclasm, during the period when another woman was in control of the Empire icon veneration was permanently established in the eastern churches and in the eastern empire, starting in 843 A.D. The Eastern Orthodox Church still celebrates this event in its so called 'Feast of Orthodoxy', because the Eastern Orthodox Church adheres to icon veneration and rejects iconoclasm. But for this disobedience God was slowly but surely destroying the Byzantine Empire by an enemy to its east, an enemy which however wicked, did not use icons in its worship. (I'll tell you about Mohammed and his followers, and their wars against the Byzantine Empire, shortly.)

In the year 1453 the eastern Roman Empire was finally and utterly vanquished by the Turks. Constantinople was taken, and Constantine Paleologue, the last Roman Emperor, was killed on the steps of the Church of the Holy Sophia.

A few years before, Zoë, the daughter of his brother Thomas, had married Ivan III of Russia. In this way did the grand dukes of Moscow fall heir to the traditions of Constantinople. The double-eagle of old Byzantium (reminiscent of the days when Rome had been divided into an eastern and a western part) became the coat of arms of modern Russia. The Tsar who had been merely the first of the Russian nobles, assumed the aloofness and the dignity of a Roman emperor before whom all subjects, both high and low, were inconsiderable slaves.

The court was refashioned after the oriental pattern which the eastern Emperors had imported from Asia and from Egypt and which (so they flattered themselves) resembled the court of

Alexander the Great. This strange inheritance which the dying Byzantine Empire bequeathed to an unsuspecting world continued to live with great vigor for six more centuries, amidst the vast plains of Russia. The last man to wear the crown with the double eagle of Constantinople, Tsar Nicholas, was murdered in the early twentieth century. His body was thrown into a well. His son and his daughters were all killed. All his ancient rights and prerogatives were abolished, and the church was reduced to the position which it had held in Rome before the days of Constantine. (But we shall discuss the rise of Communism later.)

The eastern church however fared very differently, as we shall see in the next chapter when the whole Christian world is going to be threatened with destruction by the rival creed of an Arab camel-driver.

CHAPTER 20: Mohammed and Islam on the March

We have spent a great deal of time discussing the Indo-Europeans, but God was raising up a people to the east who would challenge and afflict them for their unfaithfulness to Christ and His commandments. These challengers were the Arabs, shepherds who had roamed through the deserts of Arabia since the time Abraham had conceived Ishmael and sent him and Hagar away into the desert.

These nomadic Arabs listened to one of their own named Mohammed, mounted their horses, and in less than a century they had pushed to the heart of Europe and proclaimed the glories of Allah, "the only God," and Mohammed, "the prophet of the only God," to the frightened peasants of France.

The story of Ahmed, the son of Abdallah and Aminah, usually known as Mohammed (or 'he who will be praised') reads like a chapter in the "Thousand and One Nights." He was a camel-driver, born in Mecca. His work as a caravan leader carried him all over Arabia and he was constantly falling in with Jewish merchants and with Christian traders, and he came to see that the worship of a single God was a very excellent thing. He also gathered other tidbits from the Christian religion, but his understanding of it was surely lacking, perhaps because he could not even read or write. He seems to have been an epileptic and he suffered from spells of unconsciousness when he dreamed strange dreams and when he thought he heard the voice of the angel Gabriel. His words telling what he thought and dreamed were later written down in a book called the Koran. His own people, the Arabs, still revered queer stones and trunks of trees as their ancestors had done for centuries. In Mecca, their holy city, stood a little square building, the Kaaba, full of idols and strange odds and ends of Hoo-doo worship.

The Flight of Mohammed

Mohammed decided to be the Moses of the Arab people. He could not well be a prophet and a camel-driver at the same time. So, he made himself independent by marrying his employer, the rich widow Chadija. Then he told his neighbors in Mecca that he was the long-expected prophet sent by Allah to save the world. The neighbors laughed most heartily and when Mohammed continued to annoy them with his speeches, they decided to kill him. They regarded him as a lunatic and a public bore who deserved no mercy. Mohammed heard of the plot and in the dark of night he fled to Medina together with Abu Bekr, his trusted pupil. This happened in the year 622. It is the most important date in Mohammedan history and is known as the Hegira – the year of the Great Flight.

In Medina, Mohammed, who was a stranger, found it easier to proclaim himself a prophet than in his home city, where everyone had known him as a simple camel-driver. Soon he was surrounded by an increasing number of followers, or Moslems (or Muslims), who accepted the Islam, "the submission to the will of God," which Mohammed praised as the highest of all virtues. For seven years he preached to the people of Medina. Then he believed himself strong enough to begin a campaign against his former neighbors who had dared to sneer at him and his Holy Mission in his old camel-driving days. At the head of an army of Medinese he marched across the desert. His followers took Mecca without great difficulty, and having slaughtered a number of the inhabitants, they found it quite easy to convince the others that Mohammed was really a great prophet.

From that time on until the year of his death, Mohammed's power was on the rise.

There are several reasons for the success of Islam. In the first place, the creed which Mohammed taught to his followers had a great deal of truth in it- certainly more than these poor Arabs possessed in their paganism. God has endowed humans with a conscience to know that there is only one God of the Universe, who is spiritual, and not a mere stone or tree. And He has endowed man to know that all men and institutions of men should obey this God. And he has given them a conscience to know they should not worship material idols or icons, and that they must honor and obey their parents, and not steal, but be just to the poor and sick. And he has given them a conscience to know they will one day be judged according to God's rules. All of these things were aspects of Mohammed's teachings, which he had borrowed from Christianity. He even acknowledged much of the history of the Bible (although Mohammed got some of the facts of the Bible mixed up), from the blessing of Abraham to the fact that Jesus was a great prophet. So, all of this made Islam quite compelling and believable.

In fact, in certain respects Muslim worship was even closer to the Biblical pattern than the form of corrupted worship practiced by many Christians at the time. Muslim worship rejected icon veneration. The Mohammedan churches or mosques were merely large stone halls without benches or pictures, where the faithful could gather to hear the preached word and pray. (Such simple worship was a rebuke to Christians who were wanting to add invention upon invention to their religious worship.)

A second reason for Islamic success lies in its ease. Islam did not require its followers to do spiritual battle with the sinful flesh in the way Christianity demands, nor to take great strides to bring glory to God on earth. So long as the Muslim observed his set of rituals, he was promised Heaven. Five times a day he turned his face towards Mecca, the Holy City, and said a simple prayer. For the rest of the time he let Allah rule the world as he saw fit and accepted whatever fate brought him with patient resignation.

Of course, such an attitude towards life did not encourage the 'faithful' to go forth and invent electrical machinery or bother about railroads and steamship lines. Nor did it encourage him to fight against sinful tendencies, but rather let him indulge himself with sins like polygamy. But it gave every Mohammedan a certain amount of contentment. It bade him be at peace with himself, which is something most men want to do anyway- religion or no religion.

The third reason which explains the success of the Muslims in their warfare upon the Christians, had to do with the conduct of those Mohammedan soldiers who went forth to do battle for their faith. The Prophet promised that those who fell, facing the enemy, would go directly to Heaven. This made sudden death in the field preferable to a long but dreary existence upon this earth. Incidentally it explains why even to-day Moslem soldiers will charge into the fire of European machine guns quite indifferent to the fate that awaits them and why they are such dangerous and persistent enemies. They are taught the glories of 'holy war' (called jihad) to conquer the world for Islam by military force.

The fourth reason, which we have suggested earlier, is that God wanted to punish Christians for their own religious backsliding. Christians were embracing the lies of the Pope and the false worship of icon veneration. He raised up a people who did neither, although they had terrible and wicked sins of their own.

Having put his religious house in order, Mohammed now began to enjoy his power as the undisputed ruler of a large number of Arab tribes. But success has been the undoing of a large number of men who were great in the days of adversity. He tried to gain the good will of the rich people by a number of regulations which could appeal to those of wealth. He allowed the faithful to have four wives. As one wife was a costly investment in those olden days when brides were bought directly from the parents, four wives became a positive luxury except to those who possessed camels and dromedaries and date orchards beyond the dreams of avarice. A religion which at first had been meant for the hardy hunters of the high skied desert was gradually transformed to suit the needs of the smug merchants who lived in the bazaars of the cities. As for the prophet himself, he went on preaching, accumulating wives and concubines, and proclaiming new rules of conduct until he died, quite suddenly, of a fever on June the seventh of the year 632.

His successor as Caliph (or leader) of the Moslems was his father-in-law, Abu-Bekr, who had shared the early dangers of the prophet's life. Two years later, Abu-Bekr died and Omar ibn Al-Khattab followed him. In less than ten years he conquered Egypt, Persia, Phoenicia, Syria and Palestine and made Damascus the capital of the first Mohammedan world empire.

Omar was succeeded by Ali, the husband of Mohammed's daughter, Fatima, but a quarrel broke out upon a point of Moslem doctrine and Ali was murdered. The major division within Islam resulted at this point. Those who thought the family of Ali should retain the caliphate are called the Shi'ites, but the majority who thought otherwise are called the Sunnites.

Even to this day there are differences between these two factions of Islam.

After Ali's death, the caliphate was made hereditary and the leaders of the faithful who had begun their career as the spiritual head of a religious sect became the rulers of a vast empire. They built a new city on the shores of the Euphrates, near the ruins of Babylon and called it Bagdad, and organizing the Arab horsemen into regiments of cavalry, they set forth to bring their Moslem faith to all unbelievers. In the year 700 A.D. a Mohammedan general by the name of Tarik crossed the old gates of Hercules and reached the high rock on the European side which he called the Gibel-al-tarik, the Hill of Tarik or Gibraltar.

Eleven years later, in the battle of Xeres de la Frontera, he defeated the king of the Visigoths and then the Moslem army moved northward and following the route of Hannibal, they crossed the passes of the Pyrenees. They defeated the Duke of Aquitania, who tried to halt them near Bordeaux, and marched upon Paris. But in the year 732 (one hundred years after the death of Mohammed) they were beaten in a battle between Tours and Poitiers. On that day, Charles Martel (Charles with the Hammer) the Frankish chieftain, saved Europe from a Mohammedan conquest. He drove the Moslems out of France, but they maintained themselves in Spain where Abd-ar-Rahman founded the Caliphate of Cordova, which became the greatest center of science and art of mediæval Europe.

This Moorish kingdom, so-called because the people came from Mauretania in Morocco, lasted seven centuries. It was only after the capture of Granada, the last Moslem stronghold, in the year 1492, that Columbus received the royal grant which allowed him to go upon a voyage of discovery. The Mohammedans soon regained their strength in the new conquests which they made in Asia and Africa and to-day there are almost as many followers of Mohammed as there are of Christ.

J. Parnell McCarter

LET ME TELL YOU THE REAL STORY OF MANKIND

CHAPTER 21: Charlemagne and the Rise of the Holy Roman Empire in the West

The battle of Poitiers had saved Europe from the Mohammedans. But the enemy within – the Anti-Christian Papacy – was a far more subtle threat and foe. It was ever-amassing power to itself, and increasingly espousing false doctrine and false worship. Yet even many true Christians believers were deceived by the Papacy, for the ancient and sound creeds of the faith (like the Apostles' Creed and the Nicene Creed) were in place in the Western churches, and the error came in only slowly and gradually.

The Papacy connived for political as well as spiritual power. As we have already mentioned, it could not look to the Byzantine Emperor for political power, for in the early years of the Papacy the Byzantine Emperor rejected the veneration of icons promoted by the Pope as well as the authority which the Pope assumed to himself. Even though later Byzantine Emperors shifted their position on the former issue, they did not on the latter. So, the Pope looked elsewhere for political power and military force.

It cast its eye on the Germanic tribes who had occupied north-western Europe after the fall of Rome. They were called the Franks. One of their earliest kings, called Merovech, had helped the Romans in the battle of the Catalaunian fields in the year 451 when they defeated the Huns. His descendants, the Merovingians, had continued to take little bits of imperial territory until the year 486 when king Clovis (the old French word for "Louis") felt himself strong enough to beat the Romans in the open. But his descendants were weak men who left the affairs of state to their Prime minister, the "Major Domus" or Master of the Palace.

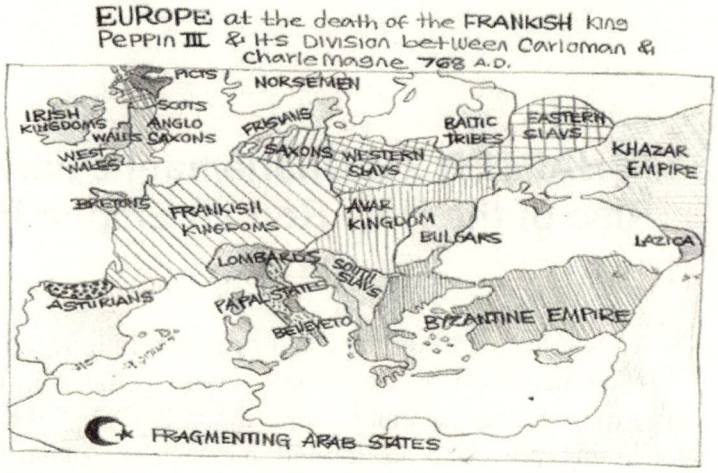

Pepin the Short, the son of the famous Charles Martel, who succeeded his father as Master of the Palace, hardly knew how to handle the situation. His royal master was a theologian, without any interest in politics. Pepin asked the Pope for advice. The Pope answered that the "power in the state belonged to him who was actually possessed of it." Pepin took the hint. He persuaded Childeric, the last of the Merovingians, to become a monk and then made himself king with the approval of the other Germanic chieftains. But this did not satisfy the shrewd Pepin. He wanted to be something more than a barbarian chieftain. He staged an elaborate ceremony at which Boniface, the missionary of the European northwest born in England, anointed him and made him a "King by the grace of God." It was easy to slip those words, "Del gratia," into the coronation service. It took almost fifteen hundred years to get them out again.

Pepin was sincerely grateful for this kindness on the part of the Roman Catholic Church. He made two expeditions to Italy to defend the Pope against his enemies. He took Ravenna and several other cities away from the Longobards and presented them to the Pope, who incorporated these new domains into the so-called Papal State, which remained an independent country until the nineteenth century. (Only Vatican City remains until today as an independent nation of the Papacy.)

After Pepin's death, the relations between Rome and Aix-la-Chapelle or Nymwegen or Ingelheim, (the Frankish Kings did not have one official residence but travelled from place to place with all their ministers and court officers,) became more and more cordial. Finally, the Pope and the King took a step which was to influence the history of Europe in a most profound way.

Charles, commonly known as Carolus Magnus or Charlemagne, succeeded Pepin in the year 768. He had conquered the land of the Saxons in eastern Germany and had built towns and monasteries all over the greater part of northern Europe. At the request of certain enemies of Abd-arRahman, he had invaded Spain to fight the Moors. But in the Pyrenees, he had been attacked by the wild Basques and had been forced to retire. It was upon this occasion that Roland, the great Margrave of Breton, showed what a Frankish chieftain of those early days meant when he promised to be faithful to his King, and gave his life and that of his trusted followers to safeguard the retreat of the royal army.

During the last ten years of the eighth century, however, Charles was obliged to devote himself exclusively to affairs of the South. The Pope, Leo III, had been attacked by a band of Roman rowdies and had been left for dead in the street. Some people had bandaged his wounds and had helped him to escape to the camp of Charles, where he asked for help. An army of Franks soon restored quiet and carried Leo back to the Lateran Palace which ever since the days of Constantine, had been the home of the Pope. That was in December of the year 799. On Christmas day of the next year, Charlemagne, who was staying in Rome, attended the service in the ancient church of St. Peter. When he arose from prayer, the Pope placed a crown upon his head, called him Emperor of the Romans and hailed him once more with the title of "Augustus" which had not been heard for hundreds of years. This act was to be claimed by the Papacy as evidence of its authority over the state as well as the church.

LET ME TELL YOU THE REAL STORY OF MANKIND

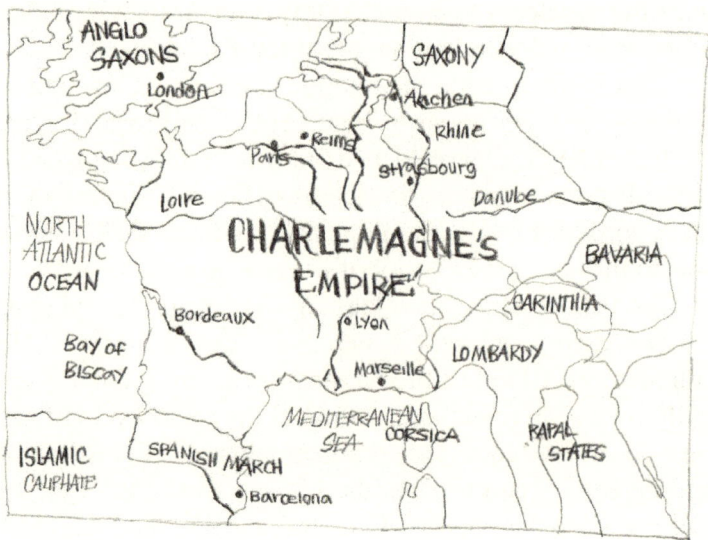

Once more, Northern Europe was part of a Roman Empire, but the dignity was held by a German chieftain who could read just a little and never learned to write. But he could fight and for a short while there was order and even the rival emperor in Constantinople sent a letter of approval to his "dear Brother."

But Charlemagne died in the year 814. His sons and his grandsons at once began to fight for the largest share of the imperial inheritance. Twice the Carolingian lands were divided, by the treaties of Verdun in the year 843 and by the treaty of Mersen-on-the-Meuse in the year 870. The latter treaty divided the entire Frankish Kingdom into two parts. Charles the Bold received the western half. It contained the old Roman province called Gaul where the language of the people had become thoroughly Romanized. The Franks soon learned to speak this language, and this accounts for the strange fact that a purely Germanic land like France should speak a Latin tongue.

The other grandson got the eastern part, the land which the Romans had called Germania. Those inhospitable regions had never been part of the old Empire. Augustus had tried to conquer this "far east," but his legions had been annihilated in the Teutoburg Wood in the year 9 and the people had never been influenced by the higher Roman civilization. They spoke the popular Germanic tongue. The Teuton word for "people" was "thiot." The Christian missionaries therefore called the German language the "lingua theotisca" or the "lingua teutisca," the "popular dialect", and this word "teutisca" was changed into "Deutsch" which accounts for the name "Deutschland."

As for the famous Imperial Crown, it very soon slipped off the heads of the Carolingian successors and rolled back onto the Italian plain, where it became a sort of plaything of a number of little potentates who stole the crown from each other amidst much bloodshed and wore it until it was the turn of some more ambitious neighbor. The Pope, once more sorely beset by his enemies, sent north for help. He did not appeal to the ruler of the west-Frankish kingdom, this time. His messengers crossed the Alps and addressed themselves to Otto, a Saxon Prince who was recognized as the greatest chieftain of the different Germanic tribes.

Otto, who shared his people's affection for the blue skies and the people of the Italian peninsula, hastened to the rescue. In return for his services, the Pope, Leo VIII, made Otto "Emperor," and the eastern half of Charles' old kingdom was henceforth known as the "Holy Roman Empire of the German Nation."

This strange political creation managed to live to the ripe old age of eight hundred and thirty-nine years. In the year 1801, (during the American presidency of Thomas Jefferson,) it was most unceremoniously relegated to the historical scrapheap. The brutal fellow who destroyed the old Germanic Empire was the son of a Corsican notary-public who had made a brilliant career in the service of the French Republic. He was ruler of Europe by the grace of his famous Guard Regiments, but he desired to be something more. He sent to Rome for the Pope and the Pope came and stood by while General Napoleon placed the imperial crown upon his own head and proclaimed himself heir to the tradition of Charlemagne. For history is like life.

The more things change, the more they remain the same.

LET ME TELL YOU THE REAL STORY OF MANKIND

CHAPTER 22: The Norsemen

In the third and fourth centuries, the Germanic tribes of central Europe had broken through the defenses of the Empire that they might plunder Rome and live on the fat of the land. In the eighth century it became the turn of the Germans to be the "plundered-ones." They did not like this at all, even if their enemies were their first cousins, the Norsemen, who lived in Denmark and Sweden and Norway.

What forced these hardy sailors to turn pirate we do not know, but once they had discovered the advantages and pleasures of a buccaneering career there was no one who could stop them. They would suddenly descend upon a peaceful

Frankish or Frisian village, situated on the mouth of a river. They would kill all the men and steal all the women. Then they would sail away in their fast-sailing ships and when the soldiers of the king or emperor arrived upon the scene, the robbers were gone, and nothing remained but a few smoldering ruins.

During the days of disorder which followed the death of Charlemagne, the Northmen developed great activity. Their fleets made raids upon every country and their sailors established small independent kingdoms along the coast of Holland and France and England and Germany, and they even found their way into Italy. The Northmen were very intelligent. They soon learned to speak the language of their subjects and gave up the uncivilized ways of the early Vikings (or Sea-Kings) who had been very picturesque but also very unwashed and terribly cruel.

Early in the tenth century a Viking by the name of Rollo had repeatedly attacked the coast of France. The king of France, too weak to resist these northern robbers, tried to bribe them into "being good." He offered them the province of Normandy, if they would promise to stop bothering the rest of his domains. Rollo accepted this bargain and became "Duke of Normandy."

But the passion of conquest was strong in the blood of his children. Across the channel, only a few hours away from the

European mainland, they could see the white cliffs and the green fields of England. Poor England had passed through difficult days. For two hundred years it had been a Roman colony. After the Romans left, it had been conquered by the Angles and the Saxons, two German tribes from Schleswig, despite the best efforts of the native Britons to stop them. Next the Danes had taken the greater part of the country and had established the kingdom of Cnut. The Danes had been driven away and now (it was early in the eleventh century) another Saxon king, Edward the Confessor, was on the throne. But Edward was not expected to live long and he had no children. The circumstances favored the ambitious dukes of Normandy.

In 1066 Edward died. Immediately, William the Conqueror of Normandy crossed the channel, defeated and killed Harold of Wessex (who had taken the crown) at the battle of Hastings, and proclaimed himself king of England.

In another chapter I have told you how in the year 800 a German chieftain had become a Roman Emperor. Now in the year 1066 the grandson of a Norse pirate was recognized as King of England. Why should we ever read fairy stories, when the truth of history is so much more interesting?

CHAPTER 23: Feudalism

The following, then, is the state of Europe in the year one thousand.

At an unknown date, the Germanic tribes had left their old home in Asia and had moved westward into Europe, along with the other Indo-Europeans who came west. By sheer pressure of numbers, they had forced their way into the Roman Empire. They had destroyed the great western empire, but the eastern part, being off the main route of the great migrations, and by God's Providence secured until a later date, had managed to survive and feebly continued the traditions of Rome's ancient glory.

During the days of disorder which had followed in the sixth and seventh centuries A.D. the German tribes had been persuaded to accept the Christian religion and had recognized the Bishop of Rome as the Pope or spiritual head of the world. In the ninth century, the organizing genius of Charlemagne had revived the Roman Empire and had united the greater part of western Europe into a single state. During the tenth century this empire had gone to pieces. The western part had become a separate kingdom, France. The eastern half was known as the Holy Roman Empire of the German nation, and the rulers of this federation of states then pretended that they were the direct heirs of Cæsar and Augustus.

But the power of the kings of France did not stretch beyond the moat of their royal residence, while the Holy Roman Emperor was openly defied by his powerful subjects whenever it suited their fancy or their profit.

To increase the misery of the masses of the people, the triangle of western Europe was forever exposed to attacks from three sides. On the south lived the ever-dangerous Mohammedans. The western coast was ravaged by the Northmen. The eastern frontier (defenseless except for the short stretch of the Carpathian Mountains) was at the mercy of hordes of Huns, Hungarians, Slavs and Tartars.

The peace of Rome was a thing of the remote past, a dream of the "Good Old Days" that were gone forever. It was a question of "fight or die," and quite naturally people preferred to fight. Forced by circumstances, Europe became an armed camp and there was a demand for strong leadership. Both King and Emperor were far away. The frontiersmen (and most of Europe in the year 1000 was "frontier") must help themselves. They willingly submitted to the representatives of the king who were sent to administer the outlying districts, provided they could protect them against their enemies.

Soon central Europe was dotted with small principalities, each one ruled by a duke or a count or a baron or a bishop, as the case might be, and organized as a fighting unit. These dukes and counts and barons had sworn to be faithful to the king who had given them their "feudum" (hence our word "feudal,") in return for their loyal services and a certain amount of taxes. But travel in those days was slow and the means of communication were exceedingly poor. The royal or imperial administrators therefore enjoyed great independence, and within the boundaries of their own province they assumed most of the rights which in truth belonged to the king.

But you would make a mistake if you supposed that the people of the eleventh century objected to this form of government. They supported Feudalism because it was a very practical and necessary institution. Their lord and master usually lived in a big stone house erected on the top of a steep rock or built between deep moats, but within sight of his subjects. In case of danger the subjects found shelter behind the walls of the baronial stronghold. That is why they tried to live as near the castle as possible and it accounts for the many European cities which began their career around a feudal fortress.

But the knight of the early middle ages was much more than a professional soldier. He was the civil servant of that day. He was the judge of his community and he was the chief of police. He caught the highwaymen and protected the wandering peddlers who were the merchants of the eleventh century. He looked after the dikes so that the countryside should not be flooded (just as the first noblemen had done in the valley of the

Nile four thousand years before). He encouraged the Troubadours who wandered from place to place telling the stories of the ancient heroes who had fought in the great wars of the migrations. Besides, he protected the churches and the monasteries within his territory, and although he could neither read nor write, (it was considered unmanly to know such things,) he employed a number of priests who kept his accounts and who registered the marriages and the births and the deaths which occurred within the baronial or ducal domains.

In the fifteenth century the kings once more became strong enough to exercise those powers. Then the feudal knights lost their former independence. Reduced to the rank of country squires, they no longer filled a need and soon they became a nuisance. But Europe would have perished without the "feudal system" of the dark ages. There were many bad knights as there are many bad people today. But generally speaking, the rough-fisted barons of the twelfth and thirteenth century were hard-working administrators who rendered a most useful service to the cause of progress. During that era the noble torch of learning and art which had illuminated the world of the Egyptians and the Greeks and the Romans was burning very low. Without the knights and their good friends, the monks, civilization would have been extinguished almost entirely in much of Europe.

It was quite natural that the professional fighting-men of the Middle Ages should try to establish some sort of organization for their mutual benefit and protection. Out of this need for close organization, Knighthood or Chivalry was born.

LET ME TELL YOU THE REAL STORY OF MANKIND

We know very little about the origins of Knighthood. But as the system developed, it gave the world something which it needed very badly – a definite rule of conduct which softened the barbarous customs of that day and made life more livable than it had been during the five hundred years of the Dark Ages. It was not an easy task to civilize the rough frontiersmen who had spent most of their time fighting Mohammedans and Huns and Norsemen. Often, they were guilty of backsliding, and having vowed all sorts of oaths about mercy and charity in the morning, they would murder all their prisoners before evening. But progress is ever the result of slow and ceaseless labor, and finally the most unscrupulous of knights was forced to obey the rules of his "class" or suffer the consequences.

These rules were different in the various parts of Europe, but they all made much of "service" and "loyalty to duty." The

Middle Ages regarded service as something very noble and beautiful. It was no disgrace to be a servant (for Jesus Christ Himself was a servant), provided you were a good servant and did not slacken on the job. As for loyalty, at a time when life depended upon the faithful performance of many unpleasant duties, it was the chief virtue of the fighting man.

A young knight therefore was asked to swear that he would be faithful as a servant to God and as a servant to his King. Furthermore, he promised to be generous to those whose need was greater than his own. He pledged his word that he would be humble in his personal behavior and would never boast of his own accomplishments and that he would be a friend of all those who suffered, (with the exception of the Mohammedans, whom he was expected to kill on sight).

Around these vows, which were merely the Ten Commandments expressed in terms which the people of the Middle Ages could understand, there developed a complicated system of manners and outward behavior. The knights tried to model their own lives after the example of those heroes of Arthur's Round Table and Charlemagne's court of whom the Troubadours had told them and of whom you may read in many delightful books. They hoped that they might prove as brave as Lancelot and as faithful as Roland. They carried themselves with dignity and they spoke careful and gracious words that they might be known as True Knights, however humble the cut of their coat or the size of their purse.

In this way the order of Knighthood became a school of those good manners which are the oil of the social machinery. Chivalry came to mean courtesy and the feudal castle showed the rest of the world what clothes to wear, how to eat, and the thousand and one little things of every-day behavior which help to make life interesting and agreeable.

Like all human institutions, Knighthood was doomed to perish as soon as it had outlived its usefulness.

The crusades, about which one of the next chapters tells, were followed by a great revival of trade. Cities grew overnight. The townspeople became rich, hired good schoolteachers and soon were the equals of the knights. The invention of gunpowder deprived the heavily armed "Chevalier" of his former advantage and the use of mercenaries made it impossible to conduct a battle with the delicate niceties of a chess tournament. The knight became superfluous. Soon he became a ridiculous figure. It was said that the noble Don Quixote de la Mancha had been the last of the true knights. After his death, his trusted sword and his armor were sold to pay his debts.

But somehow or other that sword seems to have fallen into the hands of a number of men.

Washington carried it during the hopeless days of Valley Forge. It was the only defense of Gordon, when he had refused to desert the people who had been entrusted to his care and stayed to meet his death in the besieged fortress of Khartoum.

And I am not quite sure but that it proved of invaluable strength in winning the Great War.

LET ME TELL YOU THE REAL STORY OF MANKIND

CHAPTER 24: Pope *vs.* Emporer

The average man of the Middle Ages lived a very simple and uneventful life. Even if he was a free citizen, able to come and go at will, he rarely left his own neighborhood. There were no printed books and only a few manuscripts. Here and there, a small band of industrious monks taught reading and writing and some arithmetic. But science and history and geography lay buried beneath the ruins of Greece and Rome.

Whatever most people knew about the past they had learned by listening to stories and legends. Such information, which goes from father to son, is often slightly incorrect in details, but it will preserve the main facts of history with astonishing accuracy. After more than two thousand years, the mothers of India still frighten their naughty children by telling them that "Iskander will get them," and Iskander is none other than Alexander the Great, who visited India in the year 330 before the birth of Christ, but whose story has lived through all these ages.

Most people of the early Middle Ages never saw a textbook of Roman history. They were ignorant of many things which every schoolboy to-day knows before he has entered the third grade. But the Roman Empire, which is merely a name to you, was to them something very much alive. They felt it. They willingly recognized the Pope as their spiritual leader because he lived in Rome and represented the idea of the Roman super-power. And they were profoundly grateful when Charlemagne, and afterwards Otto the Great, revived the idea of a world-empire and created the Holy Roman Empire, that the world might again be as it had been.

But the fact that there were two different heirs to the Roman tradition placed the faithful burghers of the Middle Ages in a difficult position. The Pope alleged that since the spiritual superseded the secular, that his ultimate authority was above the Emperor's in everything. But some Emperors rejected such an arrangement, and some tried to use political and military means to control the Papacy.

Under those circumstances, what were the people to do? Some rightly began to realize that the Pope was an imposter and Anti-Christ within the Church, but most did not. So most tried to obey both the Pope and his King. But the Pope and the Emperor were sometimes enemies. Which side should a dutiful subject and an equally dutiful Christian take?

It was a hard question for most people at the time to answer. When the Emperor happened to be a man of energy and was sufficiently well provided with money to organize an army, he was very apt to cross the Alps and march on Rome, besiege the Pope in his own palace if need be, and force him to obey the imperial instructions or suffer the consequences.

But more frequently the Pope was the stronger. Then the Emperor or the King together with all his subjects was excommunicated. This meant that all churches were closed, that no one could be baptized, that no dying man could be given absolution – in short, that half of the functions of mediæval government came to an end.

More than that, the people were absolved from their oath of loyalty to their sovereign and were urged to rebel against their master. But if they followed this advice of the distant Pope and were caught, they were hanged by their near-by Lege Lord and that too was very unpleasant.

Indeed, the poor fellows were in a difficult position and none fared worse than those who lived during the latter half of the eleventh century, when the Emperor Henry IV of Germany and Pope Gregory VII fought a two-round battle which decided nothing and upset the peace of Europe for almost fifty years. Sadly, these were wicked men, neither of which knew Christ nor were serving Christ's interests.

In the middle of the eleventh century there had been a strong movement for change in the church. The election of the Popes, thus far, had been a most irregular affair. It was to the advantage of the Holy Roman Emperors to have a well-disposed priest elected to the Holy See. They frequently came to Rome at the time of election and used their influence for the benefit of one of their friends.

In the year 1059 this had been changed. By a decree of Pope Nicholas II, the principal priests and deacons of the churches in and around Rome were organized into the so-called College of Cardinals, and this gathering of prominent churchmen (the word "Cardinal" meant principal) was given the exclusive power of electing the future Popes. This greatly enhanced their power.

In the year 1073, the College of Cardinals elected a priest by the name of Hildebrand, the son of very simple parents in Tuscany, as Pope, and he took the name of Gregory VII. His energy was unbounded. His belief in the supreme powers of the Papacy was unequivocal. In the mind of Gregory, the Pope was not only the absolute head of the Christian church, but also the highest Court of Appeal in all worldly matters. The Pope who had elevated simple German princes to the dignity of Emperor could depose them at will. He could veto any law passed by duke or king or emperor, but whosoever should question a papal decree, let him beware, for the punishment would be swift and merciless. No such power was conferred upon him in the word of God, but he usurped Christ's authority in the office of the Man of Sin and Anti-Christ.

Gregory sent ambassadors to all the European courts to inform the potentates of Europe of his new laws and asked them to take due notice of their contents. William the Conqueror promised to be good, but Henry IV, who since the age of six had been fighting with his subjects, had no intention of submitting to the Papal will. He called together a college of German bishops, accused Gregory of every crime under the sun and then had him deposed by the council of Worms.

The Pope answered with excommunication and a demand that the German princes rid themselves of their unworthy ruler. The German princes, only too happy to be rid of Henry, asked the Pope to come to Augsburg and help them elect a new Emperor.

Gregory left Rome and travelled northward. Henry, who was no fool, appreciated the danger of his position. At all costs he must make peace with the Pope, and he must do it at once. In the midst of winter, he crossed the Alps and hastened to Canossa where the Pope had stopped for a short rest. Three long days, from the 25th to the 28th of January of the year 1077, Henry, dressed as a penitent pilgrim (but with a warm sweater underneath his monkish garb), waited outside the gates of the castle of Canossa. Then he was allowed to enter and was pardoned for his sins. But the repentance did not last long. As soon as Henry had returned to Germany, he behaved exactly as before. Again, he was excommunicated.

For the second time a council of German bishops deposed Gregory, but this time, when Henry crossed the Alps he was at the head of a large army, besieged Rome and forced Gregory to retire to Salerno, where he died in exile. This first violent outbreak decided nothing. As soon as Henry was back in Germany, the struggle between Pope and Emperor was continued.

The Hohenstaufen family which got hold of the Imperial German Throne shortly afterwards, were even more independent than their predecessors. Gregory had claimed that the Popes were superior to all kings because they (the Popes) at the Day of Judgement would be responsible for the behavior of all the sheep of their flock, and in the eyes of God, a king was one of that faithful herd.

Frederick of Hohenstaufen, commonly known as Barbarossa or Red Beard, set up the counter-claim that the Empire had been bestowed upon his predecessor "by God himself" and as the Empire included Italy and Rome, he began a campaign which was to add these "lost provinces" to the northern country. Barbarossa accidentally drowned in Asia Minor during the second Crusade, but his son Frederick II, a brilliant young man who in his youth had been exposed to the civilization of the Mohammedans of Sicily, continued the war. The Popes accused him of heresy. It is true that Frederick seems to have felt a deep and serious contempt for the rough Christian world of the North, for the boorish German Knights and the intriguing Italian priests. But he held his tongue, went on a Crusade and took Jerusalem from the infidel and was duly crowned as King of the Holy City. Even this act did not placate the Popes. They deposed Frederick and gave his Italian possessions to Charles of Anjou, the brother of that King Louis of France who became famous as Saint Louis.

This led to more warfare. Conrad V, the son of Conrad IV, and the last of the Hohenstaufens, tried to regain the kingdom, and was defeated and decapitated at Naples. But twenty years later, the French who had made themselves thoroughly unpopular in Sicily were all murdered during the so-called Sicilian Vespers, and so it went.

The quarrel between the Popes and the Emperors was never settled, but the shameful infighting subsided to some degree.

In the year 1278, Rudolph of Hapsburg was elected Emperor. He did not take the trouble to go to Rome to be crowned. The Popes did not object, but neither did they capitulate. Indeed, neither side admitted error, but both were weary of war, at least for a time.

It is an ill wind, however, that bloweth no good to someone. The little cities of Italy, by a process of careful balancing, had managed to increase their power and their independence at the expense of both Emperors and Popes. When the rush for the Holy Land began, they were able to handle the transportation problem of the thousands of eager pilgrims who were clamoring for passage, and at the end of the Crusades they had built themselves such strong defenses of brick and of gold that they could to some degree defy Pope and Emperor.

Nevertheless, most of Christendom remained mesmerized by Romanism and the Papacy, which each century seemed to add some false doctrine or false worship practice into the churches, taking the Church further away from the Christianity ordained in the word of God.

CHAPTER 25: The Crusades

During three centuries there had been relative peace between Christians and Moslems except in Spain and in the eastern Roman Empire, the two states defending the gateways of Europe. The Mohammedans, having conquered Syria in the seventh century, were in possession of the Holy Land and by sword they had conquered North Africa and the Middle East as well. The Moslems would like to have conquered the world for Islam by sword, but God in His Providence kept these horrible infidels at bay and from subjugating all the peoples under their ignorant errors.

Nevertheless, the Arab Moslems, having subjugated vast territories under Islam, did allow some freedoms to Christians, albeit still oppressing them. For Moslems regarded Jesus as a great prophet (though not quite as great as Mohammed), and so maintained some limited respect for Christianity. So, they did not interfere with the Christian pilgrims who wished to pray in the church which Helena, the mother of the Emperor Constantine, had built on the spot thought to be Christ's grave. But early in the eleventh century, a Tartar tribe from the wilds of Asia, called the Seljuks or Turks, became masters of the Mohammedan state in western Asia and then the period of even limited tolerance came to an end. The Turks took all of Asia Minor away from the eastern Roman Emperors and they made an end to the trade between east and west.

Alexis, the Emperor, who rarely saw anything of his Christian neighbors of the west, appealed for help and pointed to the danger which threatened Europe should the Turks take Constantinople. The Italian cities which had established colonies along the coast of Asia Minor and Palestine, in fear for their possessions, reported terrible stories of Turkish atrocities and Christian suffering. All Europe got excited.

Pope Urban II, a Frenchman from Reims, who had been educated at the same famous cloister of Cluny which had trained Gregory VII, thought that the time had come for action. The general state of Europe was far from satisfactory. The primitive agricultural methods of that day (unchanged since Roman times) caused a constant scarcity of food. There was unemployment and hunger, and these are apt to lead to discontent and riots. Western Asia in older days had fed millions. It was an excellent field for the purpose of immigration.

Therefore, at the council of Clermont, in France, in the year 1095, the Pope arose, described the terrible horrors which the infidels had inflicted upon the Holy Land, gave a glowing description of this country which ever since the days of Moses had been overflowing with milk and honey, and exhorted the knights of France and the people of Europe in general to leave wife and child and deliver Palestine from the Turks.

A wave of religious hysteria swept across the continent. All reason stopped. Men would drop their hammer and saw, walk out of their shop and take the nearest road to the east to go and kill Turks. Children would leave their homes to "go to Palestine" and bring the terrible Turks to their knees by the mere appeal of their youthful zeal and Christian piety. Fully ninety percent of those enthusiasts never got within sight of the Holy Land. They had no money. They were forced to beg or steal to keep alive. They became a danger to the safety of the highroads, and they were killed by the angry country people.

The first Crusade, a wild mob of sincere but deluded Christians, defaulting bankrupts, penniless noblemen and fugitives from justice, following the lead of half-crazy Peter the Hermit and Walter-without-a-Cent, began their campaign against the Infidels by murdering all the Jews whom they met by the way. They got as far as Hungary and then they were all killed.

This experience taught the Church a lesson. Enthusiasm alone would not set the Holy Land free. Organization was as necessary as good-will and courage. A year was spent in training and equipping an army of 200,000 men. They were placed under command of Godfrey of Bouillon, Robert, duke of Normandy, Robert, count of Flanders, and a number of other noblemen, all experienced in the art of war.

In the year 1096, this second crusade started upon its long voyage. At Constantinople the knights did homage to the Emperor. (For as I have told you, traditions die hard, and a Roman Emperor, however poor and powerless, was still held in great respect). Then they crossed into Asia, killed all the Moslems who fell into their hands, stormed Jerusalem, massacred the Mohammedan population, and marched to the Holy Sepulcher to give praise and thanks amidst tears of piety and gratitude. But soon the Turks were strengthened by the arrival of fresh troops. Then they retook Jerusalem and in turn killed the faithful followers of the Cross.

During the next two centuries, seven other crusades took place. Gradually the Crusaders learned the technique of the trip. The land voyage was too tedious and too dangerous. They preferred to cross the Alps and go to Genoa or Venice where they took ship for the east. The Genoese and the Venetians made this trans-Mediterranean passenger service a very profitable business. They charged exorbitant rates, and when the Crusaders (most of whom had very little money) could not pay the price, these Italian "profiteers" kindly allowed them to "work their way across." In return for a fare from Venice to Acre, the Crusader undertook to do a stated amount of fighting for the owners of his vessel. In this way, Venice greatly increased her territory along the coast of the Adriatic and in Greece, where Athens became a Venetian colony, and in the islands of Cyprus and Crete and Rhodes.

All this, however, helped little in settling the question of the Holy Land. After the first enthusiasm had worn off, a short crusading trip became part of the liberal education of every well-bred young man, and there never was any lack of candidates for service in Palestine. But the old zeal was gone. And it was becoming apparent the whole mis-guided and poorly planned enterprise would come to nothing. From a military and political point of view the Crusades were a failure. Jerusalem and a number of cities were taken and lost. A dozen little kingdoms were established in Syria and Palestine and Asia Minor, but they were re-conquered by the Turks and after the year 1244 (when Jerusalem became definitely Turkish) the status of the Holy Land was the same as it had been before 1095.

The Crusades actually weakened the old Byzantine Empire (formerly the Eastern Roman Empire). It had survived for centuries after the Western Roman Empire had fallen. But following the Crusades Turkish Moslems were mobilized to conquer what remained of it, finally conquering its glorious capital of Constantinople itself, as I had explained to you in a previous chapter. Constantinople was renamed Istanbul, and later became the capital of the Moslem Ottoman Empire.

The Crusader did carry away some positive things from his expeditions though. He brought home with him several new foodstuffs, such as peaches and spinach which he planted in his garden and grew for his own benefit. He gave up the custom of wearing a load of heavy armor and appeared in the flowing robes of silk or cotton which were the traditional habit of the followers of Muhammed and were originally worn by the Turks. And he acquired knowledge of civilization which he would never have learned if he had stayed home.

Europe had undergone a great change during the Crusades. The people of the west had been allowed a glimpse of the wider world and the civilization of the east. Their horizon was greatly expanded. And they re-discovered in places like Constantinople many things which had been lost to them for centuries.

CHAPTER 26: The Mediæval City

The early part of the Middle Ages had been an era of pioneering and of settlement. A new people, who thus far had lived outside the wild range of forest, mountains and marshes which protected the north-eastern frontier of the Roman Empire, had forced its way into the plains of western Europe and had taken possession of most of the land. They were restless, as all pioneers have been since the beginning of time. They liked to be "on the go." They cut down the forests and they cut each other's throats with equal energy. Few of them wanted to live in cities. They insisted upon being "free," they loved to feel the fresh air of the hillsides fill their lungs while they drove their herds across the wind-swept pastures. When they no longer liked their old homes, they pulled up stakes and went away in search of fresh adventures.

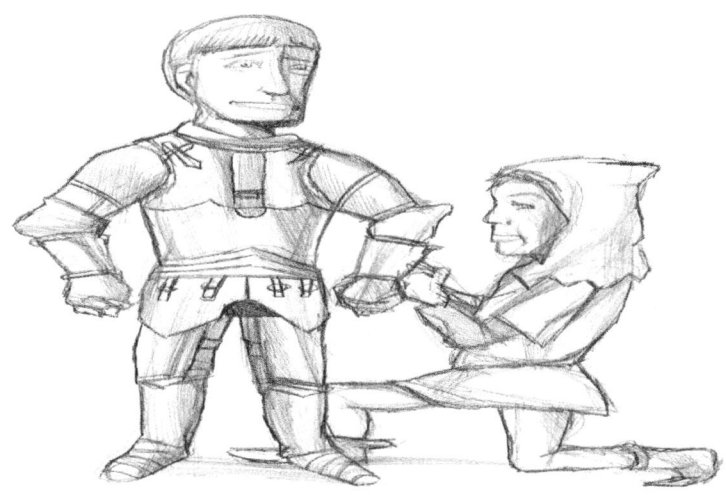

The weaker ones died. The hardy fighters and the courageous women who had followed their men into the wilderness survived. In this way, they developed a strong race of men. They cared little for the graces of life. They were too busy to play the fiddle or write pieces of poetry. They had little love for discussions. The priest, "the learned man" of the village (and before the middle of the thirteenth century, a layman who could read and write was regarded as a "sissy") was looked to answer religious questions. Meanwhile the German chieftain, the Frankish Baron, the Northman Duke (or whatever their names and titles) occupied their share of the territory which once had been part of the great Roman Empire and among the ruins of past glory, they built a world of their own which pleased them mightily and which they considered quite perfect.

They managed the affairs of their castle and the surrounding country to the best of their ability. They generally were loyal to the Church. They were sufficiently loyal to their king or emperor to keep on good terms with those distant but always dangerous potentates. In short, they tried to do right and to be fair to their neighbors without being exactly unfair to their own interests.

It was not an ideal world in which they found themselves. The greater part of the people were serfs or "villains," farmhands who were as much a part of the soil upon which they lived as the cows and sheep whose stables they shared. The serfs did not complain but when they were too hard driven, they would die off like cattle which are not fed and stabled in the right way, and then something would be hastily done to better their condition. So, do not be too sentimental about the "good old days."

Many people who only see the beautiful churches and the great works of art which the Middle Ages have left behind grow quite eloquent when they compare our own ugly civilization with its hurry and its noise and the evil smells of back-firing motor trucks with the cities of a thousand years ago. But these mediæval churches were invariably surrounded by miserable hovels compared to which a modern tenement house stands forth as a luxurious palace. It is true that the noble Lancelot and the equally noble Parsifal, the young hero who went in search of the Holy Grail, were not bothered by the odor of gasoline. But there were other smells of the barnyard variety – odors of decaying refuse which had been thrown into the street – of pigsties surrounding the Bishop's palace – of unwashed people who had inherited their coats and hats from their grandfathers and who had never learned the blessing of soap. I do not want to paint too unpleasant a picture. But when you read in the ancient chronicles that the King of France, looking out of the windows of his palace, fainted at the stench caused by the pigs rooting in the streets of Paris, when an ancient manuscript recounts a few details of an epidemic of the plague or of small-pox, then you begin to understand that "progress" is something more than a catchword used by modern advertising men.

No, there has been progress in the last seven hundred years, and God often used the institutions in the cities to accomplish it. Jerusalem was the heart of life and society of God's visible church during many centuries of the Old Testament dispensation. Egypt and Babylonia and Assyria had been a world of cities. Greece had been a country of City-States. The history of Phoenicia was the history of two cities called Sidon and Tyre. The Roman Empire was the "hinterland" of a single town. For centuries cities had been a major facet of the civilizations. Then came the great migrations. The Roman Empire was destroyed. The cities were burned down and Europe once more became a land of pastures and little agricultural villages. During the Middle Ages a significant portion of the fields of civilization had lain fallow, especially in much of western Europe.

The Crusades had prepared the soil for a new crop. It was time for the harvest, but the fruit was plucked by the burghers of the free cities.

I have told you the story of the castles and the monasteries, with their heavy stone enclosures – the homes of the knights and the monks, who guarded men's bodies and their souls. You have seen how a few artisans (butchers and bakers and an occasional candle-stick maker) came to live near the castle to tend to the wants of their masters and to find protection in case of danger. Sometimes the feudal lord allowed these people to surround their houses with a stockade. But they were dependent for their living upon the good-will of the mighty Seigneur of the castle. When he went about, they knelt before him and kissed his hand.

Then came the Crusades and many things changed. The migrations had driven people from the north-east to the west. The Crusades made millions of people travel from the west to the highly civilized regions of the south-east. They discovered that the world was not bounded by the four walls of their little settlement. They came to appreciate better clothes, more comfortable houses, new dishes, products of the mysterious Orient. After their return to their old homes, they insisted that they be supplied with those articles. The peddler with his pack upon his back – the only merchant of the Dark Ages – added these goods to his old merchandise, bought a cart, hired a few ex-crusaders to protect him against the crime wave which followed this great international war, and went forth to do business upon a more modern and larger scale. His career was not an easy one. Every time he entered the domains of another lord, he had to pay tolls and taxes. But the business was profitable all the same and the peddler continued to make his rounds.

Soon, certain energetic merchants discovered that the goods which they had always imported from afar could be made at home. They turned part of their homes into a workshop. They ceased to be merchants and became manufacturers. They sold their products not only to the lord of the castle and to the abbot in his monastery, but they exported them to nearby towns. The lord and the abbot paid them with products of their farms, eggs and wines, and with honey, which in those early days was used as sugar. But the citizens of distant towns were obliged to pay in cash, and the manufacturer and the merchant began to own little pieces of gold, which entirely changed their position in the society of the early Middle Ages.

It is difficult for you to imagine a world without money. In a modern city one cannot possible live without money. All day long you carry a pocket full of small disks of metal and paper to "pay your way." You need a quarter for the toll booth, several dollars for a dinner, and several dimes for a newspaper. But many people of the early Middle Ages never saw a piece of coined money from the time they were born to the day of their death. The gold and silver of Greece and Rome lay buried beneath the ruins of their cities. The world of the migrations, which had succeeded the Empire, was an agricultural world. Every farmer raised enough grain and enough sheep and enough cows for his own use.

The mediæval knight was a country squire and was rarely forced to pay for materials in money. His estates produced everything that he and his family ate and drank and wore on their backs. The bricks for his house were made along the banks of the nearest river. Wood for the rafters of the hall was cut from the baronial forest. The few articles that had to come from abroad were paid for in goods – in honey – in eggs – in fagots.

But the Crusades upset the routine of the old agricultural life in a very drastic fashion. Suppose that the Duke of Hildesheim was going to the Holy Land. He must travel thousands of miles and he must pay his passage and his hotel-bills. At home he could pay with products of his farm. But he could not well take a hundred dozen eggs and a cartload of hams with him to satisfy the greed of the shipping agent of Venice or the innkeeper of the Brenner Pass. These gentlemen insisted upon cash. His lordship therefore was obliged to take a small quantity of gold with him upon his voyage. Where could he find this gold? He could borrow it from the Lombards, the descendants of the old Longobards, who had turned professional money-lenders, who seated behind their exchange-table (commonly known as "banco" or bank) were glad to let his grace have a few hundred gold pieces in exchange for a mortgage upon his estates, that they might be repaid in case his lordship should die at the hands of the Turks.

That was dangerous business for the borrower. In the end, the Lombards invariably owned the estates and the Knight became a bankrupt, who hired himself out as a fighting man to a more powerful and more careful neighbor.

His grace could also go to that part of the town where the Jews were forced to live. There he could borrow money at a rate of fifty or sixty percent interest. That, too, was bad business. But was there a way out? Some of the people of the little city which surrounded the castle were said to have money. They had known the young lord all his life. His father and their fathers had been good friends. They would not be unreasonable in their demands. Very well. His lordship's clerk, a monk who could write and keep accounts, sent a note to the best-known merchants and asked for a small loan. The townspeople met in the workroom of the jeweler who made chalices for the nearby churches and discussed this demand. They could not well refuse. It would serve no purpose to ask for "interest." In the first place, it was against the religious principles of the Roman Catholic Church. (The Protestant Reformers corrected this error, but more about them later.) In the second place, it would never be paid except in agricultural products and of these the people had enough and to spare.

"But," suggested the tailor who spent his days quietly sitting upon his table and who was somewhat of a philosopher, "suppose that we ask some favor in return for our money. We are all fond of fishing. But his lordship won't let us fish in his brook. Suppose that we let him have a hundred ducats and that he give us in return a written guarantee allowing us to fish all we want in all of his rivers. Then he gets the hundred which he needs, but we get the fish and it will be good business all around."

The day his lordship accepted this proposition (it seemed such an easy way of getting a hundred gold pieces) he signed the death-warrant of his own power. His clerk drew up the agreement. His lordship made his mark (for he could not sign his name) and departed for the East. Two years later he came back, dead broke. The townspeople were fishing in the castle pond. The sight of this silent row of anglers annoyed his lordship. He told his equerry to go and chase the crowd away. They went, but that night a delegation of merchants visited the castle. They were very polite. They congratulated his lordship upon his safe return. They were sorry his lordship had been annoyed by the fishermen, but as his lordship might perhaps remember he had given them permission to do so himself, and the tailor produced the Charter which had been kept in the safe of the jeweler ever since the master had gone to the Holy Land.

His lordship was much annoyed. But once more he was in dire need of some money. In Italy he had signed his name to certain documents which were now in the possession of Salvestro dei Medici, the well-known banker. These documents were "promissory notes" and they were due two months from date. Their total amount came to three hundred and forty pounds, Flemish gold. Under these circumstances, the noble knight could not well show the rage which filled his heart and his proud soul. Instead, he suggested another little loan. The merchants retired to discuss the matter.

After three days they came back and said "yes." They were only too happy to be able to help their master in his difficulties, but in return for the 345 golden pounds would he give them another written promise (another charter) that they, the townspeople, might establish a council of their own to be elected by all the merchants and free citizens of the city, said council to manage civic affairs without interference from the side of the castle?

His lordship was confoundedly angry. But again, he needed the money. He said yes and signed the charter. Next week, he repented. He called his soldiers and went to the house of the jeweler and asked for the documents which his crafty subjects had cajoled out of him under the pressure of circumstances. He took them away and burned them. The townspeople stood by and said nothing. But when next his lordship needed money to pay for the dowry of his daughter. he was unable to get a single penny. After that little affair at the jeweler's his credit was not considered good. He was forced to eat humble-pie and offer to make certain reparations. Before his lordship got the first installment of the stipulated sum, the townspeople were once more in possession of all their old charters and a brand new one which permitted them to build a "city hall" and a strong tower where all the charters might be kept protected against fire and theft, which really meant protected against future violence on the part of the lord and his armed followers.

This, in a very general way, is what happened during the centuries which followed the Crusades. It was a slow process, this gradual shifting of power from the castle to the city. There was some fighting. A few tailors and jewelers were killed, and a few castles went up in smoke. But such occurrences were not common. Almost imperceptibly the towns grew richer and the feudal lords grew poorer. To maintain themselves they were forever forced to exchange charters of civic liberty in return for ready cash. The cities grew. They offered an asylum to runaway serfs who gained their liberty after they had lived a number of years behind the city walls. They came to be the home of the more energetic elements of the surrounding country districts. They were proud of their new importance and expressed their power in the churches and public buildings which they erected around the old marketplace, where centuries before the barter of eggs and sheep and honey and salt had taken place. They wanted their children to have a better chance in life than they had enjoyed themselves. They hired monks to come to their city and be schoolteachers. When they heard of a man who could paint pictures upon boards of wood, they offered him a pension if he would come and cover the walls of their chapels and their town hall with scenes from the Holy Scriptures. (This too was before the Protestant Reformation, when men again realized- like the iconoclasts and early Christians- that we should not make images of God, and churches and worship should be simple.)

Meanwhile his lordship, in the dreary and drafty halls of his castle, saw all this up-start splendor and regretted the day when first he had signed away a single one of his sovereign rights and prerogatives. But he was helpless. The townspeople with their well-filled strongboxes snapped their fingers at him. They were free men, fully prepared to hold what they had gained by the sweat of their brow and after a struggle which had lasted for more than ten generations.

CHAPTER 27: The Mediæval World

Dates are a very useful invention. We could not do without them but unless we are very careful, they will play tricks with us. They are apt to make history too precise. For example, when I talk of the point-of-view of medieval man, I do not mean that on the 31st of December of the year 476, suddenly all the people of Europe said, "Ah, now the Roman Empire has come to an end and we are living in the Middle Ages. How interesting!"

You could have found men at the Frankish court of Charlemagne who were Romans in their habits, in their manners, in their out-look upon life. On the other hand, when you grow up you will discover that some of the people in this world have never passed beyond the pre-Christian era. Times and ages can overlap, and the ideas of succeeding generations play tag with each other. But it is possible to study the minds of a good many true representatives of the Middle Ages and then give you an idea of the average man's attitude toward life and the many difficult problems of living.

First of all, remember that the people of the Middle Ages did not generally think of themselves as free-born citizens, who could come and go at will and shape their future. There was far less of what we know of today as 'social mobility' (a big term that just means your occupation can be other than what your parent was) and 'geographic mobility' (mobility just means change, so you can guess what geographic mobility means). People generally were of the same station as their parents and remained in the same area. If one's father was a knight, then it was expected the son would be a knight. And if one's father were a serf, then it was expected the son would be a serf.

Furthermore, like the God-fearing Christians of all eras, they were cognizant of the coming Day of Judgment, Heaven, and Hell. They recognized the brevity of this life, and so they wisely prepared for the life hereafter. Unlike the foolish atheists, they realized there was a God and that He would judge the world in righteousness.

But sadly, in this era before the Protestant Reformation many people had a poor understanding of what the Bible teaches. Few could read and write. And so many had to depend solely upon what the leaders of the Church told them, for they could not read the Bible themselves. Sadly, however, as the power of the Pope and His Romish Church grew, so grew the level of superstition and false doctrine. There were many who heard the pure gospel of free grace in Christ, but there were far more who heard the lies of the Pope that men could be saved based upon their supposedly 'good works'. And these 'good works' increasingly meant doing things like making certain pilgrimages or observing Lent that had no basis in scripture, but were simply invented by men. Such lies kept men in terror, lest their works were not enough to be saved. Sometimes, their fear of the future filled their souls with humility and piety, but often it influenced them the other way and made them cruel and sentimental. They would first of all murder all the women and children of a captured city and then they would devoutly march to a holy spot and with their hands gory with the blood of innocent victims, they would pray to a saint or to Mary to plead their forgiveness before God.

Of course, the Crusaders were Knights and obeyed a somewhat different code of manners from the common men. But in such respects the common man was just the same as his master. He, too, resembled a shy horse, easily frightened by a shadow or a silly piece of paper, capable of excellent and faithful service but liable to run away and do terrible damage when his feverish imagination saw a ghost.

In judging these people, however, it is wise to remember the terrible disadvantages under which they lived. Many had just come out of paganism where they had thought every tree and stump was a god. Many had never been taught to read or write, and it was hardly in the interest of the Pope or his minions to teach them either. Many were fighting for sheer survival against the diseases that plagued human societies, the crimes and wars that permeated these societies, and the requirement to provide the basic necessities of life. And they lacked most of our advantages which were ushered in with the Protestant Reformation. Even for those who could read their own language, the Bible was not in their own language, but in the languages of Latin, Greek, and Hebrew. With all of these disadvantages, it is by the grace of God that there were yet those like the Waldenses that knew the gospel truth.

While the Romish Church officially recognized the authority of the Bible, all too often it kept its teachings from the people. It added to the teachings of the Bible its own invented traditions and the pronouncements of the Popes. Often though these were not consistent. In the twelfth century, another authoritative source of information was added. It was the great encyclopædia of useful knowledge, compiled by Aristotle, the Greek philosopher of the fourth century before Christ. Why the Romish church should have been willing to accord such high honors to the teacher of Alexander the Great, whereas they condemned all other Greek philosophers on account of their heathenish doctrines, I really do not know. But Aristotle was recognized as the only reliable teacher among the heathen philosophers whose ideas could be safely taught and believed.

His works had reached Europe in a somewhat roundabout way. They had gone from Greece to Alexandria. They had then been translated from the Greek into the Arabic language by the Mohammedans who conquered Egypt in the seventh century. They had followed the Moslem armies into Spain and the philosophy of the great Stagirite (Aristotle was a native of Stagira in Macedonia) was taught in the Moorish universities of Cordova. The Arabic text was then translated into Latin by the Christian students who had crossed the Pyrenees to get a liberal education and this much traveled version of the famous books was at last taught at the different schools of northwestern Europe. It was not very clear, but that made it all the more interesting.

With the help of an odd combination of the Bible, the Romish traditions, and Aristotle, many of the most brilliant men of the Middle Ages now set to work to explain all things between Heaven and Earth. These brilliant men, the so-called Scholastics or Schoolmen, were really very intelligent, but they started from erroneous presuppositions (this is another big word, but it simply means what are our underlying beliefs which we put our faith in and build our knowledge upon). The great Christian theologian Augustine, who had lived near the end of the Roman Empire, had noted what scripture itself teaches: "I believe in order that I may know." We must first place our faith in God and God's word (the only proper presupposition), and build our knowledge upon that base, or we will fly off into all sorts of errors and vain speculations. Flying off into all sorts of errors and vain speculations is exactly what the Schoolmen did, for their faith was in false assumptions. They created an edifice of knowledge upon a very shaky foundation. And in time it would be obvious to all that this building was collapsing in mid-construction.

Even such famous scholars as Albertus Magnus and Thomas Aquinas fell into the Schoolmen's folly. The Schoolmen would 'deduce' things that were contrary to God's revelation in scripture and nature. When a Roger Bacon or later a John Wycliffe appeared in the council of the learned and began to contradict their deductions with evidence from nature or scripture, the Schoolmen shook their dignified heads. They are going too far. So the scholastics, with the help of the leaders of the Romish Church, went to the police and said, "Such men are dangers to the safety of the state." The leaders of the Romish Church would put pressure on the government authorities to clamp down, for the Romish Church had much invested in the lies of the Schoolmen.

And so well did the Romish Church plead its cause that in most cases it managed to silence those who dared to say, "the emperor has no clothes." These frightened guardians of the false peace forbade Bacon to write a single word for more than ten years. When he resumed his studies, he had learned a lesson. He wrote his books in a queer cipher which made it impossible for his contemporaries to read them, a trick which became common as the Romish Church became more desperate in its attempts to prevent people from asking questions which would lead to doubts and infidelity in their false doctrines.

Such was the Romish method of keeping many people in ignorance and in subjection to the Anti-Christ during the greater part of the Middles Ages. This accomplished a false peace and security. For one day all men will appear before the Judgment Seat of Christ, and the false gospel of Rome will surely do the sinner no good. He needs the true gospel of salvation by grace alone through faith alone to enter Heaven.

Indeed, Rome's method did not do him even a whole lot of good on this earth. The Romish Church kept man from pursuing what the word of God allows and even encourages him to do. The word of God encourages men to learn to read, so they can study God's written word and learn about the nature God has created. It encourages men to master his trade and craft and to have dominion over the earth and to prosper. But all of these things Rome discouraged, for its power was based upon keeping men in ignorance.

Rome created a form of safety' that was appealing to many. It allowed the wicked to remain in their wicked defiance of the Ten Commandments and march into Heaven by their church-invented rites. And Rome protected the slacker who wanted to live a lazy life begging off of others in the name of religion, like the mendicant friars. It also protected slackers within certain of the guilds.

LET ME TELL YOU THE REAL STORY OF MANKIND

Let me take a moment to explain the guilds, which were an important feature of the Medieval period. In the towns the merchants and the artisans established trade groups, called guilds, which assured every member of a steady income. It did not encourage the ambitious to do better than their neighbors. Often the guilds gave protection to the "slacker" who managed to "get by." But they established a general feeling of content and assurance among the laboring classes which no longer exists in our day of general competition. The Middle Ages were familiar with the dangers of what we modern people call "corners," when a single rich man gets hold of all the available grain or soap or pickled herring, and then forces the world to buy from him at his own price. The authorities, therefore, discouraged wholesale trading and regulated the price at which merchants were allowed to sell their goods. The Middle Ages disliked competition. And the guilds greatly regulated competition.

In short, the people of the Middle Ages were asked by the Roman Catholic Church to surrender the truth and true godliness in order to preserve a false peace and security, that kept men enslaved. But the Christ whose kingdom is eternal would not forever let this Anti-Christ so abuse His Church and People.

CHAPTER 28: Mediæval Trade

There were three good reasons why the Italian cities should have been the first to regain a position of great importance during the late Middle Ages. The Italian peninsula had been settled by Rome at a very early date. There had been more roads and more towns and more schools than anywhere else in Europe.

The barbarians had burned as lustily in Italy as elsewhere, but there had been so much to destroy that more had been able to survive. In the second place, the Pope lived in Italy and as the head of a vast political machine, which owned land and serfs and buildings and forests and rivers and conducted courts of law, he was in constant receipt of a great deal of money. The Papal authorities had to be paid in gold and silver as did the merchants and ship-owners of Venice and Genoa. The cows and the eggs and the horses and all the other agricultural products of the north and the west must be changed into actual cash before the debt could be paid in the distant city of Rome. This made Italy the one country where there was a comparative abundance of gold and silver. Finally, during the Crusades, the Italian cities had become the point of embarkation for the Crusaders and had profiteered to an almost unbelievable extent.

And after the Crusades had come to an end, these same Italian cities remained the distributing centers for those Oriental goods upon which the people of Europe had come to depend during the time they had spent in the near east.

LET ME TELL YOU THE REAL STORY OF MANKIND

Of these towns, few were as famous as Venice. Venice was a republic built upon a mud bank. Thither people from the mainland had fled during the invasions of the barbarians in the fourth century. Surrounded on all sides by the sea they had engaged in the business of salt making. Salt had been very scarce during the Middle Ages, and the price had been high. For hundreds of years Venice had enjoyed a monopoly of this indispensable table commodity (I say indispensable, because people, like sheep, fall ill unless they get a certain amount of salt in their food). The people had used this monopoly to increase the power of their city. At times they had even dared to defy the power of the Popes. The town had grown rich and had begun to build ships, which engaged in trade with the Orient. During the Crusades, these ships were used to carry passengers to the Holy Land, and when the passengers could not pay for their tickets in cash, they were obliged to help the Venetians who were for ever increasing their colonies in the Ægean Sea, in Asia Minor and in Egypt.

By the end of the fourteenth century, the population had grown to two hundred thousand, which made Venice the biggest city of the Middle Ages. The people were without influence upon the government which was the private affair of a small number of rich merchant families. They elected a senate and a Doge (or Duke), but the actual rulers of the city were the members of the famous Council of Ten, – who maintained themselves with the help of a highly organized system of secret service men and professional murderers, who kept watch upon all citizens and quietly removed those who might be dangerous to the safety of their high-handed and unscrupulous Committee of Public Safety.

The other extreme of government, a democracy of very turbulent habits, was to be found in Florence. This city controlled the main road from northern Europe to Rome and used the money which it had derived from this fortunate economic position to engage in manufacturing. The Florentines tried to follow the example of Athens. Noblemen, priests and members of the guilds all took part in the discussions of civic affairs. This led to great civic upheaval. People were forever being divided into political parties and these parties fought each other with intense bitterness and exiled their enemies and confiscated their possessions as soon as they had gained a victory in the council.

After several centuries of this rule by organized mobs, the inevitable happened. A powerful family made itself master of the city and governed the town and the surrounding country after the fashion of the old Greek "tyrants." They were called the Medici. The earliest Medici had been physicians (medicus is Latin for physician, hence their name), but later they had turned banker. Their banks and their pawnshops were to be found in all the more important centers of trade. Even today our American pawnshops display the three golden balls which were part of the coat of arms of the mighty house of the Medici, who became rulers of Florence and married their daughters to the kings of France and were buried in graves worthy of a Roman Cæsar.

Then there was Genoa, the great rival of Venice, where the merchants specialized in trade with Tunis in Africa and the grain depots of the Black Sea. Then there were more than two hundred other cities, some large and some small, each a perfect commercial unit, all of them fighting their neighbors and rivals with the undying hatred of neighbors who are depriving each other of their profits.

Once the products of the Orient and Africa had been brought to these distributing centers, they must be prepared for the voyage to the west and the north.

Genoa carried her goods by water to Marseilles, from where they were reshipped to the cities along the Rhone, which in turn served as the marketplaces of northern and western France.

Venice used the land route to northern Europe. This ancient road led across the Brenner pass, the old gateway for the barbarians who had invaded Italy. Past Innsbruck, the merchandise was carried to Basel. From there it drifted down the Rhine to the North Sea and England, or it was taken to Augsburg where the Fugger family (who were both bankers and manufacturers and who prospered greatly by "shaving" the coins with which they paid their workmen), looked after the further distribution to Nuremberg and Leipzig and the cities of the Baltic and to Wisby (on the Island of Gotland) which looked after the needs of the Northern Baltic and dealt directly with the Republic of Novgorod, the old commercial center of Russia which was destroyed by Ivan the Terrible in the middle of the sixteenth century.

The little cities on the coast of north-western Europe had an interesting story of their own. The mediæval world ate a great deal of fish. There were many fast days and then people were not permitted to eat meat. For those who lived away from the coast and from the rivers, this meant a diet of eggs or nothing at all. But early in the thirteenth century a Dutch fisherman had discovered a way of curing herring, so that it could be transported to distant points. The herring fisheries of the North

Sea then became of great importance. But some time during the thirteenth century, this useful little fish (for reasons of its own) moved from the North Sea to the Baltic and the cities of that inland sea began to make money. All the world now sailed to the Baltic to catch herring and as that fish could only be caught during a few months each year (the rest of the time it spends in deep water, raising large families of little herrings) the ships would have been idle during the rest of the time unless they had found another occupation. They were then used to carry the wheat of northern and central Russia to southern and western Europe. On the return voyage they brought spices and silks and carpets and Oriental rugs from Venice and Genoa to Bruges and Hamburg and Bremen.

Out of such simple beginnings there developed an important system of international trade which reached from the manufacturing cities of Bruges and Ghent (where the almighty guilds fought pitched battles with the kings of France and England and established a labor tyranny which completely ruined both the employers and the workmen) to the Republic of Novgorod in northern Russia, which was a mighty city until Tsar Ivan, who distrusted all merchants, took the town and killed sixty thousand people in less than a month's time and reduced the survivors to beggary.

That they might protect themselves against pirates and excessive tolls and annoying legislation, the merchants of the north founded a protective league which was called the "Hansa." The Hansa, which had its headquarters in Lübeck, was a voluntary association of more than one hundred cities. The association maintained a navy of its own which patrolled the seas and fought and defeated the Kings of England and Denmark when they dared to interfere with the rights and the privileges of the mighty Hanseatic merchants.

I wish that I had more space to tell you some of the wonderful stories of this strange commerce which was carried on across the high mountains and across the deep seas amidst such dangers that every voyage became a glorious adventure. But it would take several volumes and it cannot be done here. Besides, I hope that I have told you enough about the Middle

Ages to make you curious to read more books about this fascinating time in man's history.

The Middle Ages, as I have tried to show you, had been a period of very slow progress. The people who were in power believed that "progress" was very undesirable and ought to be discouraged, and as they happened to occupy the seats of the mighty, it was easy to enforce their will upon the patient serfs and the illiterate knights. Here and there a few brave souls sometimes ventured forth into the forbidden region of real Biblical scholarship or science, but they fared badly and were considered blessed when they escaped with their lives and a jail sentence of twenty years.

In the twelfth and thirteenth centuries the flood of international commerce swept over western Europe as the Nile had swept across the valley of ancient Egypt. It left behind a fertile sediment of prosperity. Prosperity meant hours to engage in activities beyond bare necessities. And these hours gave both men and women a chance to buy manuscripts and take an interest in literature and art and music. Most importantly, men were beginning to read for themselves what the Bible taught, unfiltered through the Romish Church. God sovereignly used the conditions of the times to work a great change in the world.

Just as the experience during the Crusades had widened the horizon of Europeans, so did this too, but even more so. The Middle Ages were drawing to an end and a new era was dawning. We call that time of change the Renaissance and Reformation.

CHAPTER 29: The Dawn of the Renaissance

The Renaissance and the Reformation occurred at roughly the same time, and each contributed to the other. But each had its own unique focus. "Renaissance," French for "rebirth," describes the renewed interest in classical learning, literature, music, art, architecture, and culture. It was a period of investigation and expression of the civilization and culture that had existed during the ancient Roman and Greek Empires. The Reformation describes the change that occurred as scholars, and then society in general, began to read the scriptures in their original languages, and then translated them into the 'vulgar' (which just means commonly used) languages of the people. People began to see that the religion of the Pope was not the religion of Christ, and to demand that Biblical Christianity be restored. So, both the Renaissance and the Reformation looked back in history to derive ideas and inspiration for how we should now live. (And who says history does not matter?)

In this chapter, let me tell you about the beginnings of the Renaissance, and in the next the beginnings of the Reformation.

I have quite often warned you against the danger that lies in historical dates. People take them too literally. They think of the Middle Ages as a period of darkness and ignorance. "Click," says the clock, and the Renaissance begins, and cities and palaces are flooded with the Renaissance.

As a matter of fact, it is quite impossible to draw such sharp lines. The thirteenth century belonged most decidedly to the Middle Ages. All historians agree upon that. But was it a time of darkness and stagnation merely? By no means. People were tremendously alive. Great states were being founded. Large centers of commerce were being developed. High above the turreted towers of the castle and the peaked roof of the town-hall, rose the slender spire of the newly built Gothic cathedral. Everywhere the world was in motion. The high and mighty gentlemen of the city-hall, who had just become conscious of their own strength (by way of their recently acquired riches) were struggling for more power with their feudal masters. The members of the guilds who had just become aware of the important fact that "numbers count" were fighting the high and mighty gentlemen of the city-hall. The king and his shrewd advisers went fishing in these troubled waters and caught many a shining bass of profit which they proceeded to cook and eat before the noses of the surprised and disappointed councilors and guild brethren.

To enliven the scenery during the long hours of evening when the badly lighted streets did not invite further political and economic dispute, the Troubadours and Minnesingers told their stories and sang their songs of romance and adventure and heroism and loyalty to all fair women. Meanwhile youth flocked to the universities, and thereby hangs a story.

The Middle Ages were "internationally minded." That sounds difficult but wait until I explain it to you. We modern people are "nationally minded." We are Americans or Englishmen or Frenchmen or Italians and speak English or French or Italian and go to English and French and Italian universities, unless we want to specialize in some particular branch of learning which is only taught elsewhere, and then we learn another language and go to Munich or Madrid or Moscow. But the people of the thirteenth or fourteenth century rarely talked of themselves as Englishmen or Frenchmen or Italians. They said, "I am a citizen of Sheffield or Bordeaux or Genoa." Because they all belonged to one and the same church, they felt a certain bond of brotherhood. (We should look forward to the day there is again one visible church around the world, but this time Protestant, Biblical, and ruled by a worldwide reformed council of elders instead of a Pope.) And as all educated men could speak Latin, they possessed an international language which removed the language barriers which have grown up in modern Europe and which place the small nations at such an enormous disadvantage. Just as an example, take the case of Erasmus, who wrote his books in the sixteenth century. He was the native of a small Dutch village. He wrote in Latin and all the world was his audience. If he were alive today, he would write in Dutch. Then only the Dutch would be able to read him. To be understood by the rest of Europe and America, his publishers would be obliged to translate his books into twenty different languages. That would cost a lot of money and most likely the publishers would never take the trouble or the risk.

Seven hundred years ago that could not happen. The greater part of the people was still very ignorant and could not read or write at all. But those who had mastered the difficult art of handling the goosequill belonged to an international republic of letters which spread across the entire continent and which knew of no boundaries and respected no limitations of language or nationality. The universities were the strongholds of this republic. Unlike modern fortifications, they did not follow the frontier. They were to be found wherever a teacher and a few pupils happened to find themselves together. There again the Middle Ages and the Renaissance differed from our own time. Nowadays, when a new university is built, the process (almost invariably) is as follows: Some rich man wants to do something for the community in which he lives or a particular religious sect wants to build a school to keep its faithful children under decent supervision, or a state needs doctors and lawyers and teachers. The university begins as a large sum of money which is deposited in a bank. This money is then used to construct buildings and laboratories and dormitories. Finally, professional teachers are hired, entrance examinations are held, and the university is on the way.

But in the Middle Ages things were done differently. A wise man said to himself, "I have discovered a great truth. I must impart my knowledge to others." And he began to preach his wisdom wherever and whenever he could get a few people to listen to him, like a modern soapbox orator. If he was an interesting speaker, the crowd came and stayed. If he was dull, they shrugged their shoulders and continued their way. By and by certain young men began to come regularly to hear the words of wisdom of this great teacher. They brought copybooks with them and a little bottle of ink and a goose quill and wrote down what seemed to be important. One day it rained. The teacher and his pupils retired to an empty basement or the room of the "Professor." The learned man sat in his chair and the boys sat on the floor. That was the beginning of the University, the "universitas," a corporation of professors and students during the Middle Ages, when the "teacher" counted for everything and the building in which he taught counted for very little.

As an example, let me tell you of something that happened in the ninth century. In the town of Salerno near Naples there were a number of excellent physicians. They attracted people desirous of learning the medical profession and for almost a thousand years (until 1817) there was a university of Salerno which taught the wisdom of Hippocrates, the great Greek doctor who had practiced his art in ancient Hellas in the fifth century before the birth of Christ.

Then there was Abelard, the young priest from Brittany, who early in the twelfth century began to lecture on theology and logic in Paris. Thousands of eager young men flocked to the French city to hear him. Other priests who disagreed with him stepped forward to explain their point of view. Paris was soon filled with a clamoring multitude of Englishmen and Germans and Italians and students from Sweden and Hungary and around the old cathedral which stood on a little island in the Seine there grew the famous University of Paris.

In Bologna, in Italy, a monk by the name of Gratian had compiled a textbook for those whose business it was to know the laws of the church. Young priests and many laymen then came from all over Europe to hear Gratian explain his ideas. To protect themselves against the landlords and the innkeepers and the boarding-house ladies of the city, they formed a corporation (or University) and behold the beginning of the university of Bologna.

Next, there was a quarrel in the University of Paris. We do not know what caused it, but a number of disgruntled teachers together with their pupils crossed the channel and found a hospitable home in n little village on the Thames called Oxford, and in this way the famous University of Oxford came into being. In the same way, in the year 1222, there had been a split in the University of Bologna. The discontented teachers (again followed by their pupils) had moved to Padua and their proud city thenceforward boasted of a university of its own. And so it went from Valladolid in Spain to Cracow in distant Poland and from Poitiers in France to Rostock in Germany.

The point which I want to make is this – the Middle Ages were not a time when the world stood still and in total darkness. There was education and learning. One can say in commendation of these Middle Age scholars that they realized all learning should be Christian. But they lacked some of the resources and tools that put the Reformation in a great advantage.

But just before the curtain went down upon the last scene of the Medieval world, a solitary figure crossed the stage, of whom you ought to know more than his mere name. This man was called Dante. He was the son of a Florentine lawyer who belonged to the Alighieri family and he saw the light of day in the year 1265. He grew up in the city of his ancestors while Giotto was painting his stories of the life of St. Francis of Assisi upon the walls of the Church of the Holy Cross, but often when he went to school, his frightened eyes would see the puddles of blood which told of the terrible and endless warfare that raged forever between the Guelphs and the Ghibellines, the followers of the Pope and the adherents of the Emperors.

When he grew up, he became a Guelph, because his father had been one before him, just as an American boy might become a Democrat or a Republican, simply because his father had happened to be a Democrat or a Republican. But after a few years, Dante saw that Italy, unless united under a single head, threatened to perish as a victim of the disordered jealousies of a thousand little cities. Then he became a Ghilbeiline.

He looked for help beyond the Alps. He hoped that a mighty emperor might come and reestablish unity and order. Alas! he hoped in vain. The Ghibellines were driven out of Florence in the year 1302. From that time on until the day of his death amidst the dreary ruins of Ravenna, in the year 1321, Dante was a homeless wanderer, eating the bread of charity at the table of rich patrons whose names would have sunk into the deepest pit of oblivion but for this single fact, that they had been kind to a poet in his misery. During the many years of exile, Dante felt compelled to justify himself and his actions when he had been a political leader in his home-town, and when he had spent his days walking along the banks of the Arno that he might catch a glimpse of the lovely Beatrice Portinari, who died the wife of another man, a dozen years before the Ghibelline disaster.

He had failed in the ambitions of his career. He had faithfully served the town of his birth and before a corrupt court he had been accused of stealing the public funds and had been condemned to be burned alive should he venture back within the realm of the city of Florence. To clear himself before his own conscience and before his contemporaries, Dante then created an Imaginary World and with great detail he described the circumstances which had led to his defeat and depicted the hopeless condition of greed and lust and hatred which had turned his fair and beloved Italy into a battlefield for the pitiless mercenaries of wicked and selfish tyrants. He tells us how on the Thursday before Easter of the year 1300 he had lost his way in a dense forest and how he found his path barred by a leopard and a lion and a wolf. He gave himself up for lost when a white figure appeared amidst the trees. It was Virgil, the Roman poet and philosopher, sent upon his errand of mercy by the "Blessed Virgin" and by Beatrice, who from high Heaven watched over the fate of her true lover. Virgil then takes Dante through Purgatory and through Hell. Deeper and deeper the path leads them until they reach the lowest pit where Lucifer himself stands frozen into the eternal ice surrounded by the most terrible of sinners, traitors and liars and those who have achieved fame and success by lies and by deceit. But before the two wanderers have reached this terrible spot, Dante has met all those who in some way or other have played a role in the history of his beloved city. Emperors and Popes, dashing knights and whining usurers, they are all there, doomed to eternal punishment or awaiting the day of deliverance, when they shall leave Purgatory for Heaven. (Remember, Dante was steeped in Roman Catholic teaching.)

It is a curious story. It is a handbook of many things the people of the thirteenth century did and felt and feared and prayed for. Through it all moves the figure of the lonely Florentine exile, forever followed by the shadow of his own despair.

And behold! when the gates of death were closing upon the sad poet of the Middle Ages, the portals of life swung open to the child who was to be the first of the men of the Renaissance. That was Francesco Petrarca, the son of the notary public of the little town of Arezzo.

Francesco's father had belonged to the same political party as Dante. He too had been exiled and thus it happened that Petrarca (or Petrarch, as we call him) was born away from Florence. At the age of fifteen he was sent to Montpellier in France that he might become a lawyer like his father. But the boy did not want to be a jurist. He hated the law. He wanted to be a scholar and a poet – and because he wanted to be a scholar and a poet beyond everything else, he became one, as people of a strong will are apt to do. He made long voyages, copying manuscripts in Flanders and in the cloisters along the Rhine and in Paris and Liège and finally in Rome. Then he went to live in a lonely valley of the wild mountains of Vaucluse, and there he studied and wrote and soon he had become so famous for his verse and for his learning that both the University of Paris and the king of Naples invited him to come and teach their students and subjects. On the way to his new job, he was obliged to pass through Rome. The people had heard of his fame as an editor of half-forgotten Roman authors. They decided to honor him and in the ancient forum of the Imperial City, Petrarch was crowned with the laurel wreath of the Poet.

From that moment on, his life was an endless career of honor and appreciation. He wrote the things which people wanted most to hear. They were tired of the disputations of the Schoolmen. But Petrarch wrote of love and of nature and the sun. And when Petrarch came to a city, all the people flocked out to meet him and he was received like a conquering hero. If he happened to bring his young friend Boccaccio, the storyteller, with him, so much the better. They were both men of their time, full of curiosity, willing to read everything once, digging in forgotten and musty libraries that they might find still another manuscript of Virgil or Ovid or Lucrece or any of the other old Latin poets.

The people quickly became enamored and intrigued with the products of the great old Roman and Greek civilizations. Take a spade and dig into the soil. What did you find? Beautiful old statues. Beautiful old vases. Ruins of ancient buildings. All these things were made by the people of the great Roman Empire. They ruled much of the world for centuries. They were strong and rich and handsome (just look at that bust of the Emperor Augustus!). Such, in short, was the spirit that had begun to fill the narrow and crooked streets of the many little Italian cities.

You know what we mean by the "bicycle craze" or the "automobile craze." Someone invents a bicycle. People who for hundreds of years have moved slowly and painfully from one place to another go "crazy" over the prospect of rolling rapidly and easily over hill and dale. Then a clever mechanic makes the first automobile. No longer is it necessary to pedal and pedal and pedal. You just sit and let little drops of gasoline do the work for you. Then everybody wants an automobile. Everybody talks about Rolls-Royces and Flivvers and carburetors and mileage and oil. Explorers penetrate into the hearts of unknown countries that they may find new supplies of gas. Forests arise in Sumatra and in the Congo to supply us with rubber. Rubber and oil become so valuable that people fight wars for their possession. The whole world is "automobile mad" and little children can say "car" before they learn to whisper "papa" and "mamma."

In the fourteenth century, the Italian people went crazy about the newly discovered beauties of the buried world of Rome. Soon their enthusiasm was shared by most of the people of western Europe. The finding of an unknown manuscript became the excuse for a civic holiday. The man who wrote a grammar became as popular as the fellow who nowadays invents a new spark plug. The humanist, the scholar who devoted his time and his energies to a study of "homo" or mankind, that man was regarded with greater honor and a deeper respect than was ever bestowed upon a hero who had just conquered all the Cannibal Islands.

In the midst of this intellectual upheaval, an event occurred which greatly favored the study of the ancient philosophers and authors. The Turks were renewing their attacks upon Europe. Constantinople, capital of the last remnant of the original Roman Empire, was hard pressed. In the year 1393 the Emperor, Manuel Paleologue, sent Emmanuel Chrysoloras to western Europe to explain the desperate state of old Byzantium and to ask for aid. This aid never came. The Roman Catholic Church leadership was more than willing to see the Greek Catholic world go to the punishment that awaited those that would challenge its authority. But however indifferent western Europe might be to the fate of the Byzantines, they were greatly interested in the ancient Greeks whose colonists had founded the city on the Bosphorus ten centuries after the Trojan war. They wanted to learn Greek that they might read Aristotle and Homer and Plato. They wanted to learn it very badly, but they had no books and no grammars and no teachers.

The magistrates of Florence heard of the visit of Chrysoloras. The people of their city were "crazy to learn Greek." Would he please come and teach them? He would, and behold! the first professor of Greek teaching alpha, beta, gamma to hundreds of eager young men, begging their way to the city of the Arno, living in stables and in dingy attics that they night learn how to decline the verb and enter into the companionship of Sophocles and Homer and ultimately the Greek New Testament.

God used even the humanist Renaissance to achieve His Reformation ends. For amidst the ancient Roman Empire, which so many now wanted to study, there came forth the everlasting kingdom of Christ, proclaimed by Apostles and Prophets in the Greek language New Testament.

LET ME TELL YOU THE REAL STORY OF MANKIND

CHAPTER 30: The Morning Star of the Reformation

He is called the "Morning Star of the Reformation." John Wycliffe was to set in motion, by God's grace, what a later monk in Germany set flying. He was born about the year 1330 AD, in the reign of Edward II of England, terminating the 1,260 years following the destruction of Jerusalem by the Romans in 70 AD. It was the terminus of the High Middle Ages. Wycliffe's parents designed him for an occupation in the Church, sent him to Queen's College, Oxford, about that period founded by Robert Eaglesfield. But not meeting with the advantages for study in that newly established house which he expected, he removed to Merton College, which was then esteemed one of the most learned societies in Europe.

The first thing which drew Wycliffe into public notice was his defense of the university against the begging friars. The friars, since their settlement in Oxford in 1230, had been troublesome neighbors to the university. Feuds were continually fomented. The friars would appeal to the Pope, while the scholars to the civil power. Sometimes one party, and sometimes the other, prevailed. The friars became very fond of a notion that Christ was a common beggar; that his disciples were beggars also; and that begging was of Gospel institution. This doctrine they urged from the pulpit and wherever they had access.

Wycliffe had long held these religious friars in contempt for the laziness of their lives and had now a fair opportunity of exposing them. He published a treatise against able beggary, in which he lashed the friars, and proved that they were not only a reproach to religion, but also to human society. The university began to consider him one of their first champions. He was soon promoted to the mastership of Baliol College.

About this time, Archbishop Islip founded Canterbury Hall, in Oxford, where he established a warden and eleven scholars. To this wardenship Wickliffe was elected by the archbishop. But upon the demise of Islip, Wycliffe was displaced by his successor, Stephen Langham, bishop of Ely. As there was a degree of flagrant injustice in the affair, Wycliffe appealed to the Pope. But the Pope ruled against Wycliffe for very political reasons.

Here is why we say it was for political reasons that Wycliffe was refused the position by the Pope. At around this same time Edward III, then king of England, had withdrawn paying a special tax to the Pope, which from the time of King John had been paid to the pope. The Pope was outraged. In response, King Edward called a parliament. The English parliament resolved that King John had done an illegal thing in ever paying the Pope. So, the parliament advised the king not to submit to the Pope in this matter. The clergy now began to write in favor of the Pope, and a learned monk published a spirited and plausible treatise, which had many advocates. Wycliffe, irritated at seeing so bad a cause so well defended, opposed the monk, and did it in so masterly a way that he was considered no longer as unanswerable. Wycliffe's own personal suit at Rome was immediately determined against him; and nobody doubted but his opposition to the Pope, at so critical a period, was the true cause of his being non-suited at Rome.

Wycliffe was afterward elected to the chair of divinity professor. He had also become fully convinced of the errors of the Romish Church, and the vileness of its monastic agents. He determined to expose them. In public lectures he lashed out at their vices and opposed their follies. He unfolded a variety of abuses covered by the darkness of superstition. Wycliffe not only demonstrated the corruptions of the Romish Church, but he also began to proclaim the true Biblical doctrines which for so long the Papacy had undermined. This soon procured him the clamor of the clergy, who, with the archbishop of Canterbury, deprived him of his office.

The duke of Lancaster, well known by the name of John of Gaunt, then began to rule England as King Edward III was infirm. The duke returned Wycliffe to his ecclesiastical position. Wycliffe used the occasion to further deride the Romish Church for its corruptions and greed. Having recovered his former situation, he inveighed, in his lectures, against the Pope-his usurpation-his infallibility-his pride-his avarice- and his tyranny. He termed the pope Antichrist. From the Pope, he would turn to the pomp, the luxury, and trappings of the bishops, and compared them with the simplicity of bishops of the early Church. Their superstitions and deceptions were topics that he urged with energy of mind and logical precision.

After the death of Edward III his grandson Richard II succeeded, in the eleventh year of his age. The duke of Lancaster not obtaining to be the sole regent, as he expected, his power began to decline, and the enemies of Wycliffe, taking advantage of the circumstance, renewed their articles of accusation against him. Five bulls were dispatched in consequence by the Pope to the king and certain bishops, but the regency and the people manifested a spirit of contempt at the haughty proceedings of the Pope, and the former at that time wanting money to oppose an expected invasion of the French, proposed to apply a large sum, collected for the use of the Pope, to that purpose. The question was submitted to the decision of Wycliffe. The bishops, however, supported by the papal authority, insisted upon bringing Wycliffe to trial, and he was actually undergoing examination at Lambeth, when, from the riotous behavior of the populace without, and awed by the command of Sir Lewis Clifford, a gentleman of the court, that they should not proceed to any definitive sentence, they terminated the whole affair in a prohibition to Wickliffe, not to preach those doctrines which were obnoxious to the Pope. But this was laughed at by our reformer, who, going about barefoot, and in a long frieze gown, preached more vehemently than before.

In the year 1378, a contest arose between two popes, Urban VI and Clement VII, over which was the lawful Pope, and true vicegerent of God. This was a favorable period for the exertion of Wycliffe's talents. He soon produced a tract against Popery, which was eagerly read by all sorts of people.

About the end of the year, Wycliffe was seized with a violent disorder, which it was feared might prove fatal. The begging friars, accompanied by four of the most eminent citizens of Oxford, gained admittance to his bed chamber, and begged of him to retract, for his soul's sake, the unjust things he had asserted of their order. Wycliffe, surprised at the solemn message, raised himself in his bed, and with a stern countenance replied, "I shall not die, but live to declare the evil deeds of the friars."

When Wycliffe recovered, he set about a most important work, the translation of the Bible into English. Before this work appeared, he published a tract in which he showed the necessity of it. The zeal of the bishops to suppress the Scriptures greatly promoted its sale, and they who were not able to purchase copies, procured transcripts of particular Gospels or Epistles.

About this time those who were followers of Wycliffe and agreed with his religious views began to be called Lollards by their opponents. This was not a very flattering term because in Dutch 'lollaerd' means 'a mumbler' or 'mutterer.' But the opponents of the Lollards did more to them than just call them bad names. The Lollards began to be persecuted by church and state. As Lollardy increased, and the flames kindled wherein the Lollards were put to death, it was a common practice to fasten about the neck of the condemned heretic such of these scraps of Scripture as were found in his possession, which generally shared his fate.

Immediately after this transaction, Wycliffe ventured a step further, and attacked the Romish doctrine of 'transubstantiation.' (Transubstantiation is a big word. It means that in the Lord's Supper Roman Catholics believe the bread is actually Jesus' body, and not simply a sign of His body. And they believe the wine is actually Jesus' blood, and not simply a sign of His blood. Roman Catholics believe that in every Lord's Supper Jesus Christ is being re-sacrificed, whereas the Bible teaches that the Lord's Supper is a remembrance of Christ's once-for-all-time sacrifice on the Cross.) This strange opinion of Rome was invented by Paschade Radbert and asserted with amazing boldness. Wycliffe, in his lecture before the University of Oxford, 1381, attacked this doctrine, and published a treatise on the subject. Dr. Barton, at this time vice-chancellor of Oxford, calling together the heads of the university, condemned Wycliffe's doctrines as heretical, and threatened their author with excommunication.

Wycliffe could now derive no support from the duke of Lancaster, and being cited to appear before his former adversary, William Courteney, now made archbishop of Canterbury, he sheltered himself under the plea, that, as a member of the university, he was exempt from episcopal jurisdiction. This plea was admitted, as the university was determined to support its member.

The court met at the appointed time, determined, at least to sit in judgment upon his opinions, and some they condemned as erroneous, others as heretical. The publication on this subject was immediately answered by Wycliffe, who had become a subject of the archbishop's determined malice. The king, solicited by the archbishop, granted a license to imprison the teacher of heresy, but the commons made the king revoke this act as illegal. The primate, however, obtained letters from the king, directing the head of the University of Oxford to search for all heresies and books published by Wycliffe. Due to this order, the university became a scene of tumult. Wycliffe is supposed to have retired from the storm, into an obscure part of the kingdom. The seeds, however, were scattered, and Wycliffe's opinions were so prevalent that it was said if you met two persons upon the road, you might be sure that one was a Lollard.

At this period, the disputes between the two Popes continued. Urban published a bull, in which he earnestly called upon all who had any regard for religion, to exert themselves in its cause; and to take up arms against Clement and his adherents in defense of the Holy See. God used this feud within the Roman Catholic Church to protect Wycliffe's movement. The Church was so distracted by its internal battles that it did not have time to focus as much attention on exterminating Wycliffe and his Lollards. So Wycliffe continued to write and accuse the Papacy of great crimes against the true Christian religion.

These attacks of Wycliffe upon the Romish Church drew their ire even more, but it seems God always preserved and protected Wycliffe, just as He would over a century later a certain German monk. Wycliffe died in 1384, having lived a long life, his enemies remarkably never able to have him put to death.

Forty-one years later, the Romish Church thought they would teach Wycliffe's dead remains a lesson. So they ungraved him, and turned him from earth to ashes; which ashes they also took and threw into the river. And so was he resolved into three elements, earth, fire, and water, thinking thereby utterly to extinguish and abolish both the name and doctrine of Wycliffe forever. Not much unlike the example of the old Pharisees and sepulcher knights, who, when they had brought the Lord unto the grave, thought to make him sure never to rise again. But these and all others must know that, as there is no counsel against the Lord, so there is no keeping down of truth. Truth will spring up and come out of dust and ashes, as appeared right well in this man; for though they dug up his body, burned his bones, and drowned his ashes, yet the Word of God and the truth of his doctrine, with the fruit and success thereof, they could not burn. Lollardy continued right down to time of the full-blown Reformation.

Nor was its influence confined to England. It spread throughout the British Isles. And, strangely enough, it spread to Bohemia, deep in continental Europe. There, a scholar at the University of Prague was deeply impressed by what Wycliffe wrote. John Huss not only discussed his agreement with fellow faculty members, but also publicly preached the reformist doctrines in a chapel attended by many Czechs. He even had the audacity to preach in the Czech language so the people could understand what he was saying, instead of in Latin like most of the priests of the time!

Meantime, the two Popes just kept right on quarreling about which one was the real Pope. And to add to the confusion, a Council elected yet a third Pope.

Huss was charged with heresy for what he preached. This included his preaching against transubstantiation (which we have already explained) and for predestination (which we need to explain). Predestination is a Biblical doctrine that simply says everything that happens happens because God has willed it to happen. This includes who is saved and who is not saved. You may remember that we had said Augustine defended this same doctrine against the Pelagians of his day. But as the centuries passed the Roman Church abandoned it, though still admiring Augustine. Men like Wycliffe and Huss defended predestination and the doctrines of grace, which put them in direct conflict with official Roman Catholic dogma.

The wrath of Romanism fell especially hard when Huss preached against indulgences and for the authority of scripture over Papal authority. Huss' critics would have no more of this fellow. Huss was summoned to the town of Constance in Switzerland where he was to be given a fair hearing by a Council consisting of the Pope, the Emperor, twenty-three cardinals, thirty-three archbishops and bishops, one hundred and fifty abbots and more than a hundred princes and dukes who had gathered together. Huss had even been promised 'safe conduct', which meant that he was guaranteed not to be harmed. But it was all a trick. Huss was given a quick trial in Constance, and then burned at the stake. But like the Lollards in England, Huss' followers - called Hussites - succeeded him in proclaiming the Biblical gospel and doctrines to the time of the Reformation and beyond.

Even as the dawn of the Reformation was breaking, many other events were gripping the world.

France had been fighting for a hundred years that she might drive the English from her territories and just then was saved from utter defeat by the appearance of Joan of Arc. And no sooner had this struggle come to an end than France and Burgundy were at each other's throats, engaged upon a struggle of life and death for the supremacy of western Europe. In the south, a Pope at Rome was calling the curses of Heaven down upon a second Pope who resided at Avignon, in southern France, and who retaliated in kind. In the far east the Turks were destroying the last remnants of the Roman Empire and the Russians had started upon a final crusade to crush the power of their Tartar masters. But in terms of Christ's kingdom, and in the broad scope of eternity, all these events were eclipsed by the awakening Reformation.

Neither the gates of hell nor Rome's one, two, or three Popes could stop what God has from all eternity promised for His true church.

LET ME TELL YOU THE REAL STORY OF MANKIND

CHAPTER 31: The Response of Rome to the Renaissance and the Reformation

The Church of Rome has never been totally certain how to most effectively arrest Biblical Reformation. Of course, we have already seen one way it has tried: persecution and execution. The Papacy tried with all the means in its power to kill the Waldensians, the Lollards, the Hussites, and anyone else who dared proclaim the Biblical gospel and defend Biblical worship. But as we have already seen as well, this method has met with limited success. For every martyr killed, it seems like two rise in his place. So, Rome has had to expand its arsenal of attack.

One weapon that the Church of Rome has employed is an appeal to people's humanist yearnings for eloquence and grandeur and beauty. This was especially compelling during a period of Renaissance.

In the Renaissance many Europeans became intrigued by humanist possibilities. The Florentine historian, Niccolò Macchiavelli, authored books describing the ideal humanist state. Giotto, Fra Angelico, Rafael and many others produced magnificent humanist paintings. Leonardo da Vinci revealed humanist possibilities in his many inventions, as well as his prose, his painting, and his sculptures. One of da Vinci's most famous paintings is of Mona Lisa.

The Romish Church capitalized on these humanist yearnings. She hired the great humanist artists and architects of the day to build grand cathedrals and produce religious paintings and sculptures. Michael Angelo, for example, was hired to draw the plans for the Church of St. Peter in Rome and then to work on its construction. Never mind that this was not what God commanded for His church nor its worship. It attracted many to Rome and away from simple scriptural worship and church life.

Those who actively opposed this humanist intrusion into the life of the Romish Church found themselves in a precarious position. Listen to what happened to one who tried.

Savonarola was born in Ferrara, Italy in 1452. Even as a young man God laid it upon his heart to detest the humanistic paganism which had corrupted life and religion in Italy. He entered the Dominican order in Bologna and returned to Ferrara four years later to teach the Scriptures. In 1490 he arrived in Florence to preach how there must be reform.

An unusual series of providential circumstances, combined with the convicting preaching of Savonarola, resulted in Savonarola's actually becoming the leader of Florence. He quickly established a democratic republic in Florence and removed the corruption which had been legend there. But the forces of Rome were all against him. The Pope invited Savonarola to Rome to congratulate him. This was but a clever ploy to kill Savonarola, and he saw through it. Next the Pope ordered Savonarola to Rome, to which Savonarola refused. Next the Pope ordered him to stop preaching.

SAVONAROLA

But Savonarola continued to preach against the scandalous court life of Rome. Next the Pope sought to bribe him with a high cardinal's position. But Savonarola only replied, 'A red hat? I want a hat of blood.' Finally, the Pope threatened the city with an interdict and instigated a mob to take Savonarola. After apprehension and a perfunctory trial, Savonarola was hanged and burned. Such was the life of one who dared stand in the way of Rome's pomp.

Another weapon the Romish Church has employed to arrest Biblical reformation, besides persecution and the lure of worldly splendor, is pseudo-reform in the place of real reform. It is like the white-washed sepulcher that our Savior inveighed against. It presents to people the appearance of improvement and holiness but underneath there remains the same old corruptions. Over the course of its history some of these have been tried, and many have succeeded in their deceit. As we will see later in our story, the Counter-Reformation spearheaded by the Jesuits was just such an enterprise. And there were other, though less notable, efforts of similar kind.

But having said all this, we must not assume all that did not strongly protest the Church of Rome were necessarily un-Christian. There were certainly those in its ranks that quietly went about their business, having a simple, Biblical faith. These were not after the worldly gain and advantage of Rome, but the heavenly kingdom which centuries of Christians even within the Roman Catholic Church had desired. On certain issues we could indeed find fault in these quiet citizens of the Roman Catholic Church, yet the spiritual heart of the matter was there. Let me relate the story of one such example.

In the year 1471, there died a pious old man who had spent seventy-two of his ninety-one years behind the sheltering walls of the cloister of Mount St. Agnes near the good town of Zwolle, the old Dutch Hanseatic city on the river Ysel. He was known as Brother Thomas and because he had been born in the village of Kempen, he was called Thomas à Kempis. At the age of twelve he had been sent to Deventer, where Gerhard Groot, a brilliant graduate of the universities of Paris, Cologne and Prague, and famous as a wandering preacher, had founded the Society of the Brothers of the Common Life. The brothers were humble laymen who tried to live the simple life of the early Apostles of Christ while working at their regular jobs as carpenters and housepainters and stone masons. They maintained an excellent school, that deserving boys of poor parents might be taught the wisdom of the Fathers of the church. At this school, little Thomas had learned how to conjugate Latin verbs and how to copy manuscripts. Then he had taken his vows, had put his little bundle of books upon his back, had wandered to Zwolle and poured his love of God into a little volume. He called it the Imitation of Christ. It has since been translated into more languages than any other book save the Bible. It has been read by almost as many people as ever studied the Holy Scriptures. And it has influenced the lives of countless millions.

Sadly, the Romish Church as a whole was not moving in the way of simple scriptural faith, but away from it. And more thorough reformation in Christ's visible church was on its way. But before we explore that reformation, let's first explore the mysterious Far East with Marco Polo.

LET ME TELL YOU THE REAL STORY OF MANKIND

CHAPTER 32: China and Marco Polo

Marco Polo

The Crusades had been a lesson in the liberal art of travelling. But very few people had ever ventured beyond the well-known beaten track which led from Venice to Jaffe. In the thirteenth century the Polo brothers, merchants of Venice, had wandered across the great Mongolian desert and after climbing mountains as high as the moon, they had found their way to the court of the great Khan of Cathay, the mighty emperor of China. The son of one of the Polos, by the name of Marco, had written a book about their adventures, which covered a period of more than twenty years. The astonished world had gaped at his descriptions of the golden towers of the strange island of Zipangu, which was his Italian way of spelling Japan. Many people had wanted to go east, that they might find this gold-land and grow rich. But the trip was too far and too dangerous and so they stayed at home. Marco Polo's revelations excited centuries of efforts to explore this region of the world so mysterious to Europeans.

China

Marco Polo discovered a civilization in China which had lasted for thousands of years.

I have already told you about the history of China up to the time around the days of the Apostles of Jesus Christ. As you may recall, this was the time when China was under control of the Han dynasty. Now let's resume our journey through its history.

The Han had some slight contact with the Roman Empire. Sent to befriend the tribes on the northwestern frontier in AD 73, a great diplomat-general, Pan Ch'ao, led an army of 70,000 almost to the borders of eastern Europe. Pan Ch'ao returned to China in 101 and brought back information about the Roman Empire. The Romans also knew about China, but they thought of it only as the land where silk was produced.

The latter years of the Han dynasty were plagued with evils caused by eunuchs, castrated males recruited from the lower classes to serve as bodyguards for the imperial harem. Coming from uneducated and poor backgrounds, they were ruthlessly ambitious once they were placed within reach of power. Toward the end of the Later Han, power struggles between the eunuchs and the landlord-officials were prolonged and destructive. Peasant rebellions of the Taoist-leaning Yellow Turbans in 184 and the Five Pecks of Rice in 190 led to the rise of generals who massacred over 2,000 eunuchs, destroyed the capital, and one after another became dictators. By 207 General Ts'ao Ts'ao had emerged as dictator in the north. When he died in 220 his son removed the powerless emperor and established the kingdom of Wei. The Eastern Han came to an end, and the empire was divided into the three kingdoms of Wei, Shu Han, and Wu. The pattern of the rise and fall of Han was to be repeated in later periods with other dynasties. This came to be known as the dynastic cycle.

The Chinese show their pride in Han accomplishments by calling themselves the Han people. Philosophies and institutions that began in the Chou and Ch'in periods reached maturity under the Han. During Han times, the Chinese distinguished themselves in making scientific discoveries, many of which were not known to Westerners until centuries later. The Chinese were most advanced in astronomy. They invented sundials and water clocks, divided the day equally into ten and then into 12 periods, devised the lunar calendar that continued to be used until 1912, and recorded sunspots regularly. In mathematics, the Chinese were the first to use the place value system, whereby the value of a component of a number is indicated by its placement. Other innovations were of a more practical nature: wheelbarrows, locks to control water levels in streams and canals, and compasses.

The Han Chinese were especially distinguished in the field of art and history. The famous sculpture of the "Han flying horse" and the carving of the jade burial suit found in Han period tombs are only two examples. The technique of making lacquer ware was also highly developed. The Chinese are noted for their historical writing that began in the Han period.

But the Chinese remained by and large under the darkness of religious heathenism, even though the gospel of Jesus Christ was first preached in China during the Han dynasty. The Chinese philosophy of nature tried to explain the workings of the universe by the alternating forces of yin and yang–dark and light–and the five elements: earth, wood, metal, fire, and water. The Han period was marked by combining different, inconsistent religions into one broad philosophy. Many Han emperors favored Taoism, especially the Taoist idea of immortality. But Taoism was more mystical and incoherent than anything else.

The Han dynasty came to an end, resulting in an extended period of disunity. The period lasted several hundred years. During this period of disunity Buddhism (which I will tell you about in a later chapter) became quite popular in China.

A general from the northwest of China put an end to this period of disunity in 581 AD. He united China under an empire, creating a dynasty that lasted but a short time. It was soon replaced by the T'ang dynasty, which lasted until 907 A.D. During the T'ang dynasty, and the Sung dynasty which succeeded it, great technological advancements were made by the Chinese, in printing, papermaking, shipbuilding, and firearms.

Confucianism – mixed with teachings from Taoism and Buddhism – was the official state religion of China during these dynasties. But there were even then Christian churches and Muslim mosques in China.

And finally, we come to the period when our friend Marco Polo arrived in China. It was a period when despised Mongol barbarians from the north invaded and conquered all of China. When Marco Polo visited them, this Mongol regime controlling China was led by the great Kublai Khan.

Marco Polo's descriptions of the riches of China enticed centuries of Europeans, including one by the name of Christopher Columbus, to desire an easier way to this haven of wealth. They did not want to have to make the slow dangerous trip by land that Marco Polo had made. But how else to get into there? That was the challenge for Europeans looking with longing eyes through the window glass into the candy store.

Despite its material riches, China and the rest of the Far East were deep in the throes of superstitious and vain religions. They were desperately in need of more light of Christ, and God was providentially paving its way through a rising tide of exploration originating far to its west.

LET ME TELL YOU THE REAL STORY OF MANKIND

CHAPTER 33: Great Discoveries by Sea

The Europeans desperately wanted to travel to China and the Far East, as I have said. Some wanted the adventure, some the trade, and others wanted to bring the people of this region the gospel of Jesus Christ, and some desired a combination of all these things. But how to readily get there- a land so far away from Europe?

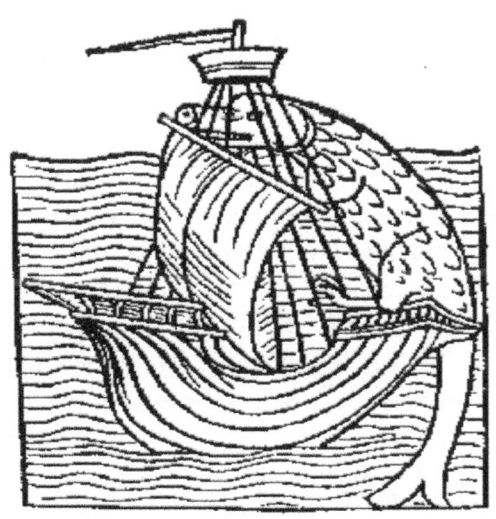

Of course, there was always the possibility of making the voyage by sea. But the sea was very unpopular in the Middle Ages and for many very good reasons. In the first place, ships were very small. The vessels on which Magellan made his famous trip around the world, which lasted many years, were not as large as a modern ferryboat. They carried from twenty to fifty men, who lived in dingy quarters (too low to allow any of them to stand up straight) and the sailors were obliged to eat poorly cooked food as the kitchen arrangements were very bad and no fire could be made whenever the weather was the least bit rough.

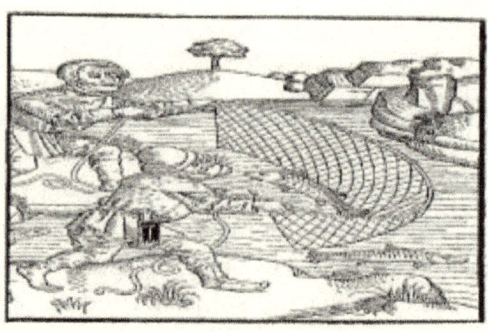

The mediæval world knew how to pickle herring and how to dry fish. But there were no canned goods and fresh vegetables were never seen on the bill of fare as soon as the coast had been left behind. Water was carried in small barrels. It soon became stale and then tasted of rotten wood and iron rust and was full of slimy growing things. As the people of the Middle Ages knew nothing about microbes (Roger Bacon, the learned monk of the thirteenth century seems to have suspected their existence, but he wisely kept his discovery to himself) they often drank unclean water and sometimes the whole crew died of typhoid fever. Indeed, the mortality on board the ships of the earliest navigators was terrible. Of the two hundred sailors who in the year 1519 left Seville to accompany Magellan on his famous voyage around the world, only eighteen returned. As late as the seventeenth century when there was a brisk trade between western Europe and the Indies, a mortality of 40 percent was nothing unusual for a trip from Amsterdam to Batavia and back. The greater part of these victims died of scurvy, a disease which is caused by lack of fresh vegetables and which affects the gums and poisons the blood until the patient dies of sheer exhaustion.

Under those circumstances you will understand that the sea did not attract the best elements of the population. Famous discoverers like Magellan and Columbus and Vasco da Gama travelled at the head of crews that were almost entirely composed of ex-jailbirds, future murderers and pickpockets out of a Job.

These navigators certainly deserve our admiration for the courage and the pluck with which they accomplished their hopeless tasks in the face of difficulties of which the people of our own comfortable world can have no conception. Their ships were leaky. The rigging was clumsy. Since the middle of the thirteenth century they had possessed some sort of a compass (which had come to Europe from China by way of Arabia and the Crusades) but they had very bad and incorrect maps. They set their course by God and by guess. If providence was with them, they returned after one or two or three years. In the other case, their bleached bones remained behind on some lonely beach. But they were true pioneers. They took the gamble. Life to them was a glorious adventure. And all the suffering, the thirst and the hunger and the pain were forgotten when their eyes beheld the dim outlines of a new coast or the placid waters of an ocean that had lain forgotten since the beginning of time. Again, I wish that I could make this book a thousand pages long. The subject of the early discoveries is so fascinating. But history, to give you a true idea of past times, should be like those etchings which Rembrandt used to make. It should cast a vivid light on certain important causes, on those which are best and greatest. All the rest should be left in the shadow or should be indicated by a few lines. And in this chapter, I can only give you a short list of the most important discoveries.

Keep in mind that all during the fourteenth and fifteenth centuries the navigators were trying to accomplish just *one thing* – they wanted to find a comfortable and safe road to the empire of Cathay (China), to the island of Zipangu (Japan) and to those mysterious islands, where grew the spices which the mediæval world had come to like since the days of the Crusades, and which people needed in those days before the introduction of cold storage, when meat and fish spoiled very quickly and could only be eaten after a liberal sprinkling of pepper or nutmeg.

The Venetians and the Genoese had been the great navigators of the Mediterranean, but the honor for exploring the coast of the Atlantic goes to the Portuguese. Spain and Portugal were full of that patriotic energy which their age-old struggle against the Moorish invaders had developed. Such energy, once it exists, can easily be forced into new channels. In the thirteenth century, King Alphonso III had conquered the kingdom of Algarve in the southwestern corner of the Spanish peninsula and had added it to his dominions. In the next century, the Portuguese had turned the tables on the Mohammedans, had crossed the straits of Gibraltar and had taken possession of Ceuta, opposite the Arabic city of Ta'Rifa (a word which in Arabic means "inventory" and which by way of the Spanish language has come down to us as "tariff,") and Tangiers, which became the capital of an African addition to Algarve.

They were ready to begin their career as explorers.

In the year 1415, Prince Henry, known as Henry the Navigator, the son of John I of Portugal and Philippa, the daughter of John of Gaunt (about whom you can read in Richard II, a play by William Shakespeare), began to make preparations for the systematic exploration of northwestern Africa. Before this, that hot and sandy coast had been visited by the Phoenicians and by the Norsemen, who remembered it as the home of the hairy "wild man" whom we have come to know as the gorilla. One after another, Prince Henry and his captains discovered the Canary Islands – re-discovered the island of Madeira which a century before had been visited by a Genoese ship, carefully charted the Azores which had been vaguely known to both the Portuguese and the Spaniards, and caught a glimpse of the mouth of the Senegal River on the west coast of Africa, which they supposed to be the western mouth of the Nile. At last, by the middle of the fifteenth century, they saw Cape Verde, or the Green Cape, and the Cape Verde Islands, which lie almost halfway between the coast of Africa and Brazil.

But Henry did not restrict himself in his investigations to the waters of the ocean. He was Grand Master of the Order of Christ. This was a Portuguese continuation of the crusading order of the Templars which had been abolished by Pope Clement V in the year 1312 at the request of King Philip the Fair of France, who had improved the occasion by burning his own Templars at the stake and stealing all their possessions. Prince Henry used the revenues of the domains of his religious order to equip several expeditions which explored the hinterland of the Sahara and of the coast of Guinea.

But he was still very much a son of the Middle Ages and spent a great deal of time and wasted a lot of money upon a search for the mysterious "Presser John," the mythical Christian Priest who was said to be the Emperor of a vast empire "situated somewhere in the east." The story of this strange potentate had first been told in Europe in the middle of the twelfth century. For three hundred years people had tried to find "Presser John" and his descendants. Henry took part in the search. Thirty years after his death, the riddle was solved.

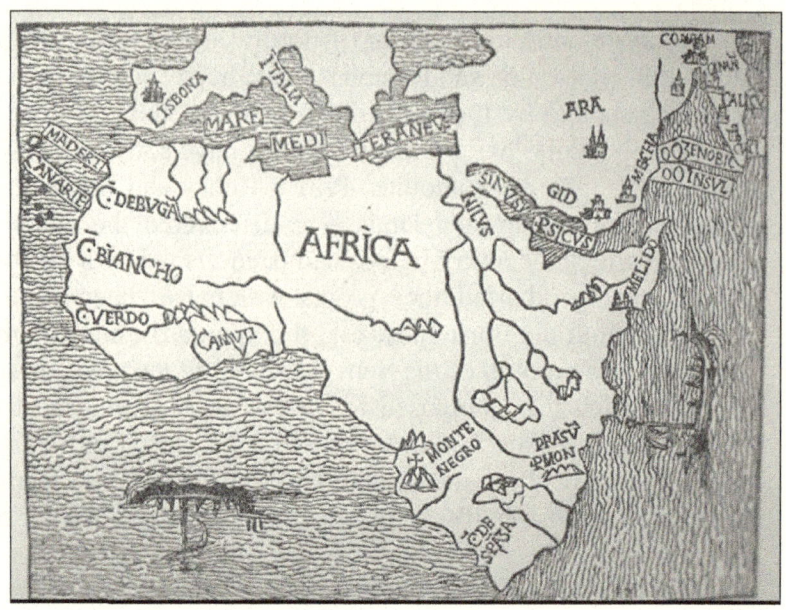

In the year 1486, Bartholomew Diaz, trying to find the land of Presser John by sea, had reached the southernmost point of Africa. At first he called it the Storm Cape, on account of the strong winds which had prevented him from continuing his voyage toward the east, but the Lisbon pilots who understood the importance of this discovery in their quest for the India water route, changed the name into that of the Cape of Good Hope.

One year later, Pedro de Covilham, provided with letters of credit on the house of Medici, started upon a similar mission by land. He crossed the Mediterranean, and after leaving Egypt, he travelled southward. He reached Aden, and from there, travelling through the waters of the Persian Gulf which few white men had seen since the days of Alexander the Great, eighteen centuries before. He visited Goa and Calicut on the coast of India where he got a great deal of news about the island of the Moon (Madagascar) which was supposed to lie halfway between Africa and India. Then he returned, paid a secret visit to Mecca and to Medina, crossed the Red Sea once more and in the year 1490 he discovered the realm of Presser John, who was no one less than the Black Negus (or King) of Abyssinia, whose ancestors had adopted Christianity in the fourth century, seven hundred years before the Christian missionaries had found their way to Scandinavia.

These many voyages had convinced the Portuguese geographers and cartographers that while the voyage to the Indies by an eastern sea-route was possible, it was by no means easy. Then there arose a great debate. Some people wanted to continue the explorations east of the Cape of Good Hope. Others said, "No, we must sail west across the Atlantic and then we shall reach Cathay."

Let us state right here that most intelligent people of that day were firmly convinced that the earth was not as flat as a pancake but was round. The belief in the roundness of the earth was common among the nautical experts and, as I said, they were now debating the respective advantages of the eastern and the western routes.

Among the advocates of the western route was a Genoese mariner by the name of Cristoforo Colombo. He was the son of a wool merchant. He seems to have been a student at the University of Pavia where he specialized in mathematics and geometry. Then he took up his father's trade but soon we find him in Chios in the eastern Mediterranean travelling on business. Thereafter we hear of voyages to England but whether he went north in search of wool or as the captain of a ship we do not know. In February of the year 1477, Colombo (if we are to believe his own words) visited Iceland, but very likely he only got as far as the Faröe Islands which are cold enough in February to be mistaken for Iceland by anyone. Here Colombo met the descendants of those brave Norsemen who in the tenth century had settled in Greenland and who had visited America in the eleventh century, when Leif's vessel had been blown to the coast of Vineland, or Labrador.

What had become of those far western colonies, no one knew. The American colony of Thorfinn Karlsefne, the husband of the widow of Leif's brother Thorstein, founded in the year 1003, had been discontinued three years later on account of the hostility of the Esquimaux. As for Greenland, not a word had been heard from the settlers since the year 1440.

Very likely the Greenlanders had all died of the Black Death. which had just killed half the people of Norway. However, that might be, the tradition of a "vast land in the distant west" still survived among the people of the Faröe and Iceland, and Colombo must have heard of it. He gathered further information among the fishermen of the northern Scottish islands and then went to Portugal where he married the daughter of one of the captains who had served under Prince Henry the Navigator.

From that moment on (the year 1478) he devoted himself to the quest of the western route to the Indies. He sent his plans for such a voyage to the courts of Portugal and Spain. The Portuguese, who felt certain that they possessed a monopoly of the eastern route, would not listen to his plans. In Spain, Ferdinand of Aragon and Isabella of Castile, whose marriage in 1469 had made Spain into a single kingdom, were busy driving the Moors from their last stronghold, Granada. They had no money for risky expeditions. They needed every peseta for their soldiers.

Few people were ever forced to fight as desperately for their ideas as this brave Italian. But the story of Colombo (or Colon or Columbus, as we call him,) is too well known to bear repeating.

The Moors surrendered Granada on the second of January of the year 1492. In the month of April of the same year, Columbus signed a contract with the King and Queen of Spain. On Friday, the 3rd of August, he left Palos with three little ships and a crew of 88 men, many of whom were criminals who had been offered indemnity of punishment if they joined the expedition. At two o'clock in the morning of Friday, the 12th of October, Columbus discovered land. On the fourth of January of the year 1493, Columbus waved farewell to the 44 men of the little fortress of La Navidad (none of whom was ever again seen alive) and returned homeward. By the middle of February, he reached the Azores where the Portuguese threatened to throw him into gaol. On the fifteenth of March, 1493, the admiral reached Palos and together with his Indians (for he was convinced that he had discovered some outlying islands of the Indies and called the natives red Indians) he hastened to Barcelona to tell his faithful patrons that he had been successful and that the road to the gold and the silver of Cathay and Zipangu was at the disposal of their most Catholic Majesties.

Alas, Columbus never knew the truth. Towards the end of his life, on his fourth voyage, when he had touched the mainland of South America, he may have suspected that all was not well with his discovery. But he died in the firm belief that there was no solid continent between Europe and Asia and that he had found the direct route to China.

Meanwhile, the Portuguese, sticking to their eastern route, had been more fortunate. In the year 1498, Vasco da Gama had been able to reach the coast of Malabar and return safely to Lisbon with a cargo of spice. In the year 1502 he had repeated the visit. But along the western route, the work of exploration had been most disappointing. In 1497 and 1498 John and Sebastian Cabot had tried to find a passage to Japan but they had seen nothing but the snowbound coasts and the rocks of Newfoundland, which had first been sighted by the Northmen, five centuries before. Amerigo Vespucci, a Florentine who became the Pilot Major of Spain, and who gave his name to our continent, had explored the coast of Brazil, but had found not a trace of the Indies.

In the year 1513, seven years after the death of Columbus, the truth at last began to dawn upon the geographers of Europe. Vasco Nuñez de Balboa had crossed the Isthmus of Panama, had climbed the famous peak in Darien, and had looked down upon a vast expanse of water which seemed to suggest the existence of another ocean.

Finally, in the year 1519, a fleet of five small Spanish ships under command of the Portuguese navigator, Ferdinand de Magellan, sailed westward (and not eastward since that route was absolutely in the hands of the Portuguese who allowed no competition) in search of the Spice Islands. Magellan crossed the Atlantic between Africa and Brazil and sailed southward. He reached a narrow channel between the southernmost point of Patagonia, the "land of the people with the big feet," and the Fire Island (so named on account of a fire, the only sign of the existence of natives, which the sailors watched one night). For almost five weeks the ships of Magellan were at the mercy of the terrible storms and blizzards which swept through the straits. A mutiny broke out among the sailors. Magellan suppressed it with terrible severity and sent two of his men on shore where they were left to repent of their sins at leisure. At last the storms quieted down, the channel broadened, and Magellan entered a new ocean. Its waves were quiet and placid.

He called it the Peaceful Sea, the Mare Pacifico. Then he continued in a western direction. He sailed for ninety-eight days without seeing land. His people almost perished from hunger and thirst and ate the rats that infested the ships, and when these were all gone, they chewed pieces of sail to still their gnawing hunger.

In March of the year 1521, they saw land. Magellan called it the land of the Ladrones (which means robbers) because the natives stole everything they could lay hands on. Then further westward to the Spice Islands!

Again, land was sighted. A group of lonely islands. Magellan called them the Philippines, after Philip, the son of his master Charles V, the Philip II of unpleasant historical memory. At first Magellan was well received, but when he used the guns of his ships to make Christian converts, he was killed by the aborigines, together with a number of his captains and sailors. The survivors burned one of the three remaining ships and continued their voyage. They found the Moluccas, the famous Spice Islands; they sighted Borneo and reached Tidor. There, one of the two ships, too leaky to be of further use, remained behind with her crew. The "Vittoria," under Sebastian del Cano, crossed the Indian Ocean, missed seeing the northern coast of Australia (which was not discovered until the first half of the seventeenth century when ships of the Dutch East India Company explored this flat and inhospitable land), and after great hardships reached Spain.

This was the most notable of all voyages. It had taken three years. It had been accomplished at a great cost both of men and money. But it had established the fact that the earth was round and that the new lands discovered by Columbus were not a part of the Indies but a separate continent. From that time on Spain and Portugal devoted all their energies to the development of their Indian and American trade. To prevent an armed conflict between the rivals, Pope Alexander VI (the most avowed heathen to ever occupy that infamous office) had obligingly divided the world into two equal parts by a line of demarcation which followed the 50th degree of longitude west of Greenwich, the so-called division of Tordesillas of 1494. The Portuguese were to establish their colonies to the east of this line, the Spaniards were to have theirs to the west. This accounts for the fact that the entire American continent with the exception of Brazil became Spanish and that all of the Indies and most of Africa became Portuguese until the English and the Dutch colonists (who had no respect for Papal decisions) took these possessions away in the seventeenth and eighteenth centuries.

When news of the discovery of Columbus reached the Rialto of Venice, the Wall street of the Middle Ages, there was a terrible panic. Stocks and bonds went down 40 and 50 percent. After a short while, when it appeared that Columbus had failed to find the road to Cathay, the Venetian merchants recovered from their fright. But the voyages of da Gama and Magellan proved the practical possibilities of an eastern water-route to the Indies. Then the rulers of Genoa and Venice, the two great commercial centers of the Middle Ages and the Renaissance, began to be sorry that they had refused to listen to Columbus. But it was too late. Their Mediterranean became an inland sea. The overland trade to the Indies and China dwindled to insignificant proportions. The old days of Italian glory were gone. The Atlantic became the new center of commerce and therefore the center of civilization. It has remained so ever since.

See how strangely civilization has progressed since those early days. From Mesopotamia it spread to Egypt. And from Egypt to Canaan and Phoenicia. And from Phoenicia to Crete and Greece and Rome. In the sixteenth century it moved westward once more and made the countries that border upon the Atlantic become the most powerful worldly masters. But throughout all of this time the real power was with Christ in heaven. He looked down and blessed His saints and mocked His enemies.

The westward trip was accompanied by a steady increase in the size of ships and a broadening of the knowledge of the navigators. The flat-bottomed vessels of the Nile and the Euphrates were replaced by the sailing vessels of the Phoenicians, the Ægeans, the Greeks, the Carthaginians and the Romans. These in turn were discarded for the square-rigged vessels of the Portuguese and the Spaniards. And the latter were driven from the ocean by the full-rigged craft of the English and the Dutch.

LET ME TELL YOU THE REAL STORY OF MANKIND

CHAPTER 34: India

The discoveries of the Portuguese and the Spaniards had brought the Christians of western Europe into close contact with the people of India and of China. I have already told you something of the history of China; now let me tell you something of the history of India.

The people that now make up India are the result of wave-after-wave of immigration over the centuries, not so unlike the waves of immigration into America. The earliest waves seem to have been more dark-skinned peoples, descendants of Ham perhaps along with some descendants of Shem. Very early after the Great Flood they settled in India, forming the Indus Valley civilization. These were a very sophisticated people. They had drainage systems, household utensils, and copper weapons. These early inhabitants spread out over most of India.

But their world was turned upside down when a new wave of immigrants arrived around 1400 BC (about the same time Moses was leading the Israelites out of Egypt). These new immigrants were the Aryans. They were a warrior people, and they easily conquered the native Indians. The Aryans were distant cousins of the Europeans, and they had traveled from north of Mesopotamia before finally arriving in India. (In other words, they were the Indo-European descendants of Japhet I have told you about before.) The Aryans became the rulers and masters of tens of millions of docile little brown men. To maintain themselves in the seat of the mighty, they had divided the population into different classes and gradually a system of "caste" of the most rigid sort had been enforced upon the natives. The descendants of the Indo-European conquerors belonged to the highest "caste," the class of warriors and nobles. Next came the caste of the priests. Below these followed the peasants and the businessmen. The ancient natives, however, who were called Pariahs, formed a class of despised and miserable slaves and never could hope to be anything else. (It is interesting to note that the Indo-Europeans that moved into Europe did not create so equally a rigid caste system, probably because in Europe there were no other peoples for the most part but the Indo-Europeans, so it was not as easy to distinguish different groups of people by appearance.)

Even the religion of the people was a matter of caste. The old Indo-Europeans, during their years of wandering, had met with many strange adventures. These had been collected in a book of hymns called the Vedas. The language of this book was called Sanskrit, and it was closely related to the different languages of the European continent, to Greek and Latin and Russian and German and two-score others. The three highest castes were allowed to read this so-called holy book. The Pariah, however, the despised member of the lowest caste, was not permitted to know its contents. Woe to the man of noble or priestly caste who should teach a Pariah to study the 'sacred' volume! "Brahman", the all-creator of this Indian Hindu religion, was regarded as the one God and supreme ruler of life and death and was worshipped as the highest ideal of perfection.

In its early form, brought in by the Aryan invaders, the Hindu religion consisted of ritual sacrifice of animals, and hymns of the Vedas to be sung as part of the ritual. Even in its early form, Hinduism was corrupted in that the understanding of Brahman was mired in darkness. The idea of the Triune God – one God in three persons – was perverted into many gods in one unknowable Brahman. But in many respects this early form of Hinduism reflects the true religion which no doubt was handed down from Noah to Japheth and to Japheth's descendants. There were no images or pictures of God in their religion, and the Vedic hymns suggest that the dead pass into heaven or hell, depending upon the life they had lived. There was even belief in the possibility of divine incarnation- the idea of the divine taking on the form of human flesh. And, of course, at that time in history animal sacrifices to God were appropriate, having been commanded by Him to prepare humanity for the great sacrificial atonement of Jesus Christ. But this early religion became more corrupted in India over the centuries.

More and more gods were added under the Brahman. And, sometime after 600 B.C., the belief in reincarnation was added. This strange, wicked belief taught that people's souls are in a seemingly endless cycle of birth and death, going from one creature to another on earth. From this point on, the emphasis of Hinduism moved from making offerings to please and pacify the Brahman to escaping the cycle of rebirths.

Sometime between 300 to 650 A.D. images and idols were added to Hindu worship, whereas before they had generally been absent. Stone temples with these idols were constructed. Also, female divinities were added, which had previously been absent. The Mother Goddess, called Shakti, was worshipped under various forms. Suttee, the burning of a widow on the funeral pyre of her dead husband, was incorporated into the religion. And later various animals, like the cow, were considered sacred. So, we see in all of this the slow but steady decline of true religion into greater and greater falsehood and wickedness.

In the sixth century BC, a notable personality came onto the stage in India. He was called by his followers 'Buddha'. His history is an interesting one. He was born within sight of the mighty Himalaya Mountains, where four hundred years before Zarathustra (or Zoroaster), one of the great leaders of the Aryan race, had taught his people to regard life as a continuous struggle between Ahriman, and Ormuzd, the Gods of Evil and Good. Buddha's father was Suddhodana, a mighty chief among the tribe of the Sakiyas. His mother, Maha Maya, was the daughter of a neighboring king. She had been married when she was a very young girl. But many moons had passed beyond the distant ridge of hills and still her husband was without an heir who should rule his lands after him. At last, when she was fifty years old, her day came, and she went forth that she might be among her own people when her baby should come into this world.

It was a long trip to the land of the Koliyans, where Maha Maya had spent her earliest years. One night she was resting among the cool trees of the garden of Lumbini. There her son was born. He was given the name of Siddhartha, but he is commonly known by the name Buddha. Buddha means the Enlightened One, but whoever first gave him this name must have been as blind as a bat. The doctrines of Siddhartha were hardly enlightened.

In due time, Siddhartha grew up to be a handsome young prince and when he was nineteen years old, he was married to his cousin Yasodhara. During the next ten years he lived far away from all pain and all suffering, behind the protecting walls of the royal palace, awaiting the day when he should succeed his father as King of the Sakiyas.

But it happened that, when he was thirty years old, he drove outside of the palace gates and saw a man who was old and worn out with labor and whose weak limbs could hardly carry the burden of life. Siddhartha pointed him out to his coachman, Channa, but Channa answered that there were lots of poor people in this world and that one more or less did not matter. The young prince was very sad but he did not say anything and went back to live with his wife and his father and his mother and tried to be happy. A little while later, he left the palace a second time. His carriage met a man who suffered from a terrible disease. Siddhartha asked Channa what had been the cause of this man's suffering, but the coachman answered that there were many sick people in this world and that such things could not be helped and did not matter very much. The young prince was very sad when he heard this but, again, he returned to his people.

A few weeks passed. One evening Siddhartha ordered his carriage in order to go to the river and bathe. Suddenly, his horses were frightened by the sight of a dead man whose rotting body lay sprawling in the ditch beside the road. The young prince, who had never been allowed to see such things, was frightened, but Channa told him not to mind such trifles. The world was full of dead people. It was the rule of life that all things must come to an end. Nothing was eternal. The grave awaited us all and there was no escape.

That evening, when Siddhartha returned to his home, he was received with music. While he was away his wife had given birth to a son. The people were delighted because now they knew that there was an heir to the throne, and they celebrated the event by the beating of many drums. Siddhartha, however, did not share their joy. The curtain of life had been lifted and he had learned the horror of man's existence. The sight of death and suffering followed him like a terrible dream.

That night the moon was shining brightly. Siddhartha woke up and began to think of many things. Never again could he be happy until he should have found a solution to the riddle of existence. He decided to find it far away from all those whom he loved. Softly he went into the room where Yasodhara was sleeping with her baby. Then he called for his faithful Channa and told him to follow.

Together the two men went into the darkness of the night, one to find rest for his soul, the other to be a faithful servant unto a beloved master.

Siddhartha, who had often observed these solitary wanderers who were seeking the truth far away from the turmoil of the cities and the villages, decided to follow their example. He cut his hair. He took his pearls and his rubies and sent them back to his family with a message of farewell, which the ever faithful Channa carried. Without a single follower, the young prince then moved into the wilderness.

Soon the fame of his conduct spread among the mountains. Five young men came to him and asked that they might be allowed to listen to his words of wisdom. For all the wisdom they got out of the Enlightened One, however, these five young men would have been better off staying home. But he, of course, agreed to be their master if they would follow him. They consented, and he took them into the hills and for six years he taught them all he knew amidst the lonely peaks of the Vindhya Mountains. But at the end of this period of study, he felt that he was still far from perfection. The world that he had left continued to tempt him. He now asked that his pupils leave him and then he fasted for forty-nine days and nights, sitting upon the roots of an old tree. At last he realized how hard it was to sit on the root of an old tree for forty-nine days. After all, how would you like it? Anyway, in a state of what surely was delirium, he thought he met Brahma. From that moment on, Siddhartha was called Buddha by his followers. They were actually gullible enough to believe the "Enlightened One" and his salvation from their unhappy mortal fate.

Buddha's religion can perhaps best be described by the phrase 'mind over matter.' No matter how bad things really are, if we just are happy with the way things are, well then, we'll be happy. So Buddha taught that human desires are the source of pain, and by overcoming desires, pain can be eliminated. So, son, just enjoy that tooth ache you now have, and pretty soon you won't mind it- right? Buddha can teach you how to overcome it in 8 lessons, or what he calls the Eightfold Path. It allowed people to ignore the real cause of man's pain and suffering in the world – man's sin and rebellion against God – by pretending that pain and suffering are only illusions created by human desires.

The last forty-five years of his life, Buddha spent within the valley of the Ganges River, teaching his 8 lessons. In the year 488 before our era, he died, full of years and beloved by millions of gullible people. He had not preached his doctrines for the benefit of a single class. Even the lowest Pariah might call himself a disciple of Buddha. The door to foolishness was wide open to every class.

This, however, did not please the nobles and the priests and the merchants who did their best to destroy a creed which recognized that everyone had an equal right to partake of the foolishness the Buddha offered. As soon as they could, they encouraged the people of India to return to the ancient doctrines of the Brahmin creed with its fasting and its tortures of the sinful body. But Buddhism could not be destroyed. Slowly the disciples of the 'Enlightened One' wandered across the valleys of the Himalayas and moved into China. They crossed the Yellow Sea and preached the message of their master unto the people of Japan, and they faithfully obeyed the will of their great master. But it really never caught on in India; the caste structure was too entrenched and Hinduism (which evolved from Vedism) remained the dominant religion.

Between the time of Buddha to the time our European discoverers first started arriving by ship in India, many dynasties and many waves of immigration had passed through India. Perhaps the most famous was the Gupta dynasty from around 300 to 550 AD. This dynasty marked the peak of classical Indian civilization. A succession of invaders penetrated India in the centuries following the Gupta dynasty. These included the Kushans, Sakas, and Ephthalites, or White Huns. Even the Mongols (who you will recall conquered China after invading from northern and western China) made raids into India. It seems as if every race has wanted its turn with the great Indian sub-continent, which is why there is such a mixture of racial features represented in India even to this day. As we shall see, the Indo-Europeans of Europe thought it was now their turn starting in the 16th century and lasting well into the 20th century.

CHAPTER 35: The Reformation

We often think that only a minister can be useful in igniting a religious reformation or revival. But in world history men of other occupations have done great things towards that end as well. One such example was a German who resided in the city of Mainz, named Johann zum Gänsefleisch. He is commonly known as Johann Gutenberg.

LET ME TELL YOU THE REAL STORY OF MANKIND

I have already told you how the Chinese had invented printing many years before. In Europe before the time of Gutenberg printing was only used to reproduce pictures and designs on cloth. However, books in Europe were copied by the laborious method of monks doing it by hand.

Gutenberg believed movable type could be used to copy books. He had studied the old woodcuts and had perfected a system by which individual letters of soft lead could be placed in such a way that they formed words and whole pages. His method of printing endured almost unchanged for five centuries, a testimony to its genius. In Mainz he went into partnership with a wealthy financier. They set up a printing press shop, and their masterpiece product was the famous 'Gutenberg Bible.' Sadly, Gutenberg soon lost all his money in a lawsuit which had to do with the original invention of the press.

Gutenberg died in poverty, but his invention and, more importantly, the spread of God's word made easier by his invention, did not die. Only two years after the printing of the Gutenberg Bible, a magnificent Psalter, printed in 1457 by Fust and Schoffer, resulted from the intricate work left by Gutenberg.

It would be another German to take this word and to faithfully proclaim what it meant, and to explain how the Romish Church had corrupted its meaning. But before I tell you about this German, let's first consider the state of affairs in 1500 when this German lived.

1500 was the year in which the Holy Roman Emperor Charles V was born. The feudal disorder of the Middle Ages had given way before the order of a number of highly centralized kingdoms. The most powerful of all sovereigns is the great Charles, then a baby in a cradle. He is the grandson of Ferdinand and Isabella and of Maximilian of Habsburg, the last of the mediæval knights, and of his wife Mary, the daughter of Charles the Bold, the ambitious Burgundian duke who had made successful war upon France but had been killed by the independent Swiss peasants. The child Charles, therefore, has fallen heir to the greater part of the map, to all the lands of his parents, grandparents, uncles, cousins and aunts in Germany, in

Austria, in Holland, in Belgium, in Italy, and in Spain, together with all their colonies in Asia, Africa and America. By a strange irony of providence, he has been born in Ghent, in that same castle of the counts of Flanders, which the Germans used as a prison during their recent occupation of Belgium, and although a Spanish king and a German emperor, he receives the training of a Fleming.

As his father is dead (poisoned, so people say, but this is never proved), and his mother has lost her mind (she is travelling through her domains with the coffin containing the body of her departed husband), the child is left to the strict discipline of his Aunt Margaret. Forced to rule Germans and Italians and Spaniards and a hundred strange ethnicities, Charles grows up a Fleming, a faithful son of the Roman Catholic Church, and one who would prove an archenemy of the Protestant Reformation. He wanted to see unity and peace throughout Europe, under the control of the Pope and the Holy Roman Emperor, but he was always at war to try to achieve those ends. At the age of fifty-five, we see him turn his back upon the human race in utter disgust. Three years later he dies, a very disappointed man.

So much for Charles the Emperor. How about the Catholic Church? The Church had changed greatly since the early days of the Middle Ages, when it started out to proclaim the gospel of Jesus Christ and show how we ought to serve Him in gratitude by a righteous life. In the first place, power in the Church had been taken by the Roman Papacy. Over time, the Papacy grew more powerful and richer. The Pope is no longer the shepherd of a flock of humble Christians. He lives in a vast palace and surrounds himself with artists and musicians and famous literary men. He is more humanist than Christian. His churches and chapels are covered with new pictures in which the saints look more like Greek gods. He divides his time unevenly between affairs of state and art. The affairs of state take ten percent of his time. The other ninety percent goes to an active interest in Roman statues, recently discovered Greek vases, plans for a new summer home, the rehearsal of a new play. The Archbishops and the Cardinals follow the example of their Pope. The Bishops try to imitate the Archbishops. Many of the village priests, however, have remained faithful to their duties. They keep themselves aloof from the worldliness and the heathenish love of beauty and pleasure. They stay away from the monasteries where the monks seem to have forgotten their ancient vows of simplicity and poverty and live as happily as they dare without causing too much of a public scandal. The Romish Church had corrupted the true Christian religion and worship.

Finally, there are the common people. They are more materially better off than centuries previous. They are more prosperous, they live in better houses, their children go to better schools, their cities are more beautiful than before, their firearms have made them the equal of their old enemies, the robber-barons, who for centuries have levied such heavy taxes upon their trade. But spiritually many are weighed down by the superstitions propagated by Rome. The bright light, however, was the rising spread of the printed word of God, and the faithful endurance of those who loved this word, like the English Lollards, the Bohemian Hussites, and the Piedmont Waldensians.

The people of northern Europe at the time had an outlook upon life which contrasted with that of their southern neighbors. The Germans, the Dutch, the English, and the Swedes did not like to be funny about matters holy and sacred. The "humanistic" part of the Renaissance, the books, the studies of ancient authors, the grammar and the text-books, interested them greatly. But the general return to the old pagan civilization of Greece and Rome, which was one of the chief results of the Renaissance in Italy and permeated the Papacy, filled their hearts with horror.

But the Papacy and the College of Cardinals was almost entirely composed of Italians and they had turned the Roman Catholic Church into a club where people discussed art and music and the theater, but rarely mentioned religion. Hence the split between the serious north and the indifferent south was growing wider and wider all the time.

There were a few minor reasons which might explain why the Reformation found such fertile soil in Germany to begin in full force, rather than in Sweden or England. The Germans bore an ancient grudge against Rome. The endless quarrels between Emperor and Pope had caused much mutual bitterness. In the other European countries where the government rested in the hands of a strong king, the ruler had often been able to protect his subjects against the greed of the Pope and his priests. In Germany, where a shadowy emperor ruled a turbulent crowd of little princelings, the good burghers were more directly at the mercy of their bishops and prelates. These dignitaries were trying to collect large sums of money for the benefit of those enormous churches which were a hobby of the Popes of the Renaissance. The Germans were being mulcted and quite naturally they did not like it.

And then there is the rarely mentioned fact that Germany was the home of the printing press. In northern Europe books were cheap and the Bible was no longer a mysterious manuscript owned and explained by the priest. It was a household book of many families where Latin was understood by the father and by the children. Whole families began to read it, which was against the law of the Romish Church. The Pope knew the reading of the Bible endangered his false gospel and his unrighteous position. As people began to read the Bible, they discovered that the Pope and his priests were telling them many things which, according to the original text of the Holy Scriptures, were different. This caused doubt. People began to ask questions. And questions, when they cannot be answered, often cause a great deal of trouble.

The attack began when some in the North opened fire upon the monks. In their heart of hearts, they still had too much respect and reverence for the Pope to direct their sallies against "his Holiness". But the lazy, ignorant monks, living behind the sheltering walls of their rich monasteries, offered rare sport.

The leader in this warfare, curiously enough, was a very faithful son of the church. Gerard Gerardzoon, or Desiderius Erasmus, as he is usually called, was a poor boy, born in Rotterdam in Holland, and educated at the same Latin school of Deventer from which Thomas à Kempis had graduated. He had become a priest and for a time he had lived in a monastery. He had travelled a great deal and knew whereof he wrote.

When he began his career as a public pamphleteer (he would have been called an editorial writer in our day) the world was greatly amused at an anonymous series of letters which had just appeared under the title of "Letters of Obscure Men." In these letters, the general stupidity and arrogance of the monks of the late Middle Ages was exposed in a strange German-Latin doggerel which reminds one of our modern limericks. Erasmus himself was a very learned and serious scholar, who knew both Latin and Greek and gave us the first reliable version of the New Testament, which he translated into Latin together with a corrected edition of the original Greek text. But he believed with Sallust, the Roman poet, that nothing prevents us from "stating the truth with a smile upon our lips."

In the year 1500, while visiting Sir Thomas More in England, he took a few weeks off and wrote a funny little book, called the "Praise of Folly," in which he attacked the monks and their credulous followers with that most dangerous of all weapons, humor. The booklet was the best seller of the sixteenth century. It was translated into almost every language and it made people pay attention to those other books of Erasmus in which he advocated reform of the many abuses of the church and appealed to his fellow humanists to help him in his task of bringing about a great rebirth of the Christian faith.

But nothing came of these plans. They were waiting for a leader of a more robust nature and one wholly committed to Christ.

He came from Germany, and his name was Martin Luther. Luther was a North-German peasant with a first-class brain and possessed of great personal courage, a man blessed by God to do a great task. He was a university man, a Master of Arts of the University of Erfurt; afterwards he joined an Augustinian monastery. Then he became a college professor at the theological school of Wittenberg and began to explain the scriptures to the indifferent ploughboys of his Saxon home. He had a lot of spare time and this he used to study the original texts of the Old and New Testaments.

The seriousness with which Luther took religious matters and God's word led him into a severe personal crisis. Realizing the great demand of God's law, yet his own sinfulness, Luther fell into despair. But in reading the Bible, especially the book of Romans, Luther came to understand that the Christian's salvation is totally a matter of God's grace bestowed through the person and work of Jesus Christ. He came to understand that Christ had fulfilled the law and died on the Cross as a substitutionary sacrifice on behalf of Christians. Luther understood now that Christians appropriate this justifying salvation by faith, which even itself is a gift of God. So Luther came to understand that great doctrine of the Reformation: justification by grace alone through faith alone.

Soon Luther also began to see the great difference which existed between the words of Christ and those that were preached by the Popes and the Bishops. In the year 1511, he visited Rome on official business. Alexander VI, of the family of Borgia, who had enriched himself for the benefit of his son and daughter, was dead. But his successor, Julius II, was spending most of his time fighting and building. Luther returned to Wittenberg a very disappointed man.

The gigantic church of St. Peter which Pope Julius had wished upon his successors, although only half begun, was already in need of repair. Alexander VI had spent every penny of the Papal treasury.

Leo X, who succeeded Julius in the year 1513, was on the verge of bankruptcy. He reverted to an old method of raising ready cash. He began to sell indulgences. An indulgence was a piece of parchment which in return for a certain sum of money or work, promised a sinner a decrease of the time which he would have to spend in purgatory. The Romish Church had claimed for itself the ability to forgive sins, and the right to shorten, through its intercession with the saints, the time during which the soul must be purified in the shadowy realms of Purgatory. Purgatory was an invention of man not taught in the holy scriptures.

These indulgences were sold for money, in order for the Papacy to raise money for its wicked imperial rule. They thus offered an easy form of revenue.

Now it happened, in the year 1517, that the exclusive territory for the sale of indulgences in Saxony was given to a Dominican monk by the name of Johan Tetzel. Brother Johan was a hustling salesman and shyster. His business methods outraged the pious people of the little duchy. And Luther took the bold and courageous step to stand against this wicked enterprise with its false gospel of how men may be saved. On the 31st of October of the year 1517, he went to the court church and upon the doors thereof he posted a sheet of paper with ninety-five statements (or theses), attacking the sale of indulgences. These statements had been written in Latin. Luther had no intention of starting a riot. He was not a revolutionist.

He objected to the institution of the Indulgences and he wanted his fellow professors to know what he thought about them. But this was still a private affair of the clerical and professorial world and there was no appeal to the prejudices of the community of laymen.

But in less than two months, all Europe was discussing the ninety-five theses of the Saxon monk. Everyone must take sides. Every obscure little theologian must print his own opinion. The papal authorities began to be alarmed. They ordered the Wittenberg professor to proceed to Rome and give an account of his action. Luther wisely remembered what had happened to Huss. He stayed in Germany and he was punished with excommunication. Luther burned the papal bull in the presence of an admiring multitude and from that moment, peace between himself and the Pope was no longer possible. Luther saw the Pope for what he was: the wicked anti-Christian man of sin who had unlawfully usurped the rule of Christ. Furthermore, he saw through Rome's false gospel and false worship. He repudiated the works which Rome said were necessary to attain salvation.

Without any desire on his part, Luther had become the leader of a vast army of Christians who by God's grace recognized these Biblical truths as well. German patriots like Ulrich von Hutten, rushed to his defense. The students of Wittenberg and Erfurt and Leipzig offered to defend him should the authorities try to imprison him. The Elector of Saxony reassured the eager young men. No harm would befall Luther as long as he stayed on Saxon ground.

All this happened in the year 1520. Charles V was twenty years old. As the ruler of half the world, he was forced to remain on pleasant terms with the Pope. He sent out calls for a Diet or general assembly in the good city of Worms on the Rhine and commanded Luther to be present and give an account of his behavior. Luther, who now was the national hero of the Germans, went.

At the Diet, Luther refused to take back a single word of what he had ever written or said. His conscience was controlled only by the word of God. He would live and die for what the word of God said. Thus, he held his ground for the truth of the Word of God.

The Diet of Worms, after due deliberation, declared Luther an outlaw before God and man, and forbade all Germans to give him shelter or food or drink, or to read a word of the books which the dastardly 'heretic' had written. But the great reformer was in no danger. By the majority of the Germans of the north the edict was denounced as a most unjust and outrageous document. For greater safety, Luther was hidden in the Wartburg, a castle belonging to the Elector of Saxony, and there he defied all papal authority by translating the entire Bible into the German language, that all the people might read and know the word of God for themselves.

Now princes began to take sides. Some princes became Protestants (as the "protesting" adherents of Luther were called). Others remained Roman Catholic. The Diet of Speyer of the year 1526 tried to settle this difficult question of allegiance by ordering that "the subjects should all be of the same religious denomination as their princes." This turned Germany into a checkerboard of a thousand hostile little duchies and principalities.

In February of the year 1546 Luther died and was put to rest in the same church where twenty-nine years before he had proclaimed his famous objections to the sale of Indulgences. In less than thirty years, the universal spiritual empire of the Popes came to a sudden end. Luther had completed his masterpiece, *The Bondage of the Will,* in which he set forth man's total depravity and God's electing grace through Jesus Christ. The countries of Scandinavia (such as Denmark and Sweden) declared themselves Lutheran and Protestant. The Protestant Reformation had by this time spread far and wide, much expanded from what John Wycliffe had initiated in the 14th century.

CHAPTER 36: The Further Spread of the Reformation in Continental Europe

One place the Reformation quickly got off the ground was in Switzerland, and there its early leader was Huldrych Zwingli. Zwingli was a Catholic minister turned Protestant Reformer in Zurich during roughly the same period of time that Luther was serving God in Germany. Like Luther, Zwingli proclaimed the great doctrine of *sola scriptura,* or scripture alone. He, along with the other Protestant Reformers, proclaimed that the Bible alone is the authoritative source for all religious faith and practice. He also preached the doctrine of justification by faith alone and the need for reformation of church and state.

Zwingli's preaching created an uproar in Switzerland, and especially in Zurich. It was clear Zurich would have to decide whether to remain in the Romish Church or join the Protestant cause. Zurich opted for Protestantism, along with several other cantons in Switzerland, but many cantons remained Roman Catholic.

One doctrine in which Zwingli and Luther could not agree, however, regarded the Lord's Supper. You may remember that I told you John Wycliffe had criticized the Romish doctrine of transubstantiation, which taught that in the Lord's Supper Christ is actually sacrificed, since the bread and wine in this rite actually became Christ's body and blood. Luther realized that there could not be a re-sacrifice of Christ in the Lord's Supper (for scripture teaches that Christ's sacrifice on Calvary was complete and sufficient), but he was never willing to admit that the bread and wine did not actually become Christ's body and blood. Zwingli did, however, and said that the bread and wine were just emblematically Christ's body and blood. This doctrinal difference kept the Lutherans and Zwinglians (later referred to as the Reformed) from ever fully uniting.

Switzerland is an interesting place. I have mentioned the term 'cantons' already. These are the self-governing units, not much larger than the size of a city, of which Switzerland is made. Some Swiss cantons are German-speaking, some are French-speaking, and some are Italian-speaking. The Swiss cantons joined together for mutual defense and commerce in a confederation arrangement. But each canton retained its separate governing authority. Anyway, Zwingli's Zurich was an example of a German-speaking canton that became Protestant. But there was a very famous French-speaking canton that became Protestant as well: Geneva.

As the reformation was preached in France, and strongly persecuted there, many of its French Protestant members had to flee for safety. One powerful preacher that landed in Switzerland was William Farel. He arrived in Geneva and boldly proclaimed the gospel. More and more people started to believe Farel, although opposition was fierce. Finally, the tide turned, and it was becoming clear that Geneva would declare itself Protestant.

Just at this time another French Protestant wandered into the city, with no idea of what was in store for him. His name was John Calvin.

J. Parnell McCarter

Calvin was more of a scholar than anything else. He was born in Noyon, France in 1509. He studied for the occupation that his father intended for him: law. But Calvin's career plans were interrupted when he came under conviction of the Protestant gospel which was circulating in France. He left the Roman Catholic Church and embraced the Protestant faith. He wrote a book that became the rallying point for Protestants all across Europe, his *Institutes of the Christian Religion*. In its first edition in the 1530s it was a summary of the Protestant faith, but Calvin expanded it in later editions in future years, so that it became a more detailed explanation and tome of the doctrines of the Protestant faith, especially among the Reformed. But as Calvin became known as a Protestant in France, he was forced to flee in 1536.

Farel got hold of Calvin as he was passing through Geneva. Farel wanted Calvin to help him lead the Protestant Reformation in Geneva. Now Farel was not a man you would want to disagree with. He was vehement. He was bold. He was energetic. And there was Calvin the scholar, looking incredulous at such an offer. Calvin just wanted to be a scholar, and here was a man who was going to thrust him in the thick of religious and political struggle in Geneva. But Calvin realized that this was not only Farel's call, but also God's, so he acceded.

Calvin laid out plans for how the model reformed Christian community should be organized, based upon scriptural principles. It called for certain powers and functions to be under the civil government of Geneva, and others to be under the church government of Geneva, but for both to be in submission to the rule of Christ. Both tables of the Ten Commandments would be enforced by the civil government, just as scripture dictates. But certain powers, like the power of excommunication, were to be retained by the Church. Calvin and Farel had the city and people of Geneva covenant to follow Christ as dictated in scripture and summarized in the written reformed confession. For a brief interlude Calvin and Farel were kicked out of the city, the opposition was so great. But later Calvin was invited back, and over time Geneva literally became the model 'city of God' on earth.

There were many elements to Geneva's reformation. In terms of the State, idols were destroyed, and idolatry outlawed. The Christian Sabbath was enforced. Adultery was punished by law. Promoters of flagrant heresy – be they Socinians who denied the Trinity (like Servetus), Roman Catholics who rejected justification through faith alone, Libertines who rejected God's moral law, or Anabaptists who rejected the principle of covenant headship and infant baptism – were punished. In terms of the Church, preaching was made central to the worship. A metrical Psalter of the book of Psalms was composed and made the hymnal of the Church's worship. Idols and musical instruments were removed from the Church's worship as well. Catechism in the reformed faith was stressed, and admission to the Lord's Table required affirmation with the reformed confession and catechism. Church government was reformed, and un-scriptural positions like pope and archbishop were not recognized.

Protestants came from all over Europe to learn how Geneva was organized, so they could replicate it in their countries and their communities. It was not perfect, but it was an excellent working model of how State and Church should work together to glorify God in Christ, like Israel had done in the days of King David or Judah had done in the days of King Hezekiah. Geneva was a excellent example of how a State and Church should 'kiss the Son.'

Following the example of Geneva, areas in Germany, eastern Europe, and the Netherlands became reformed. Let me briefly tell you about how it happened in the Netherlands.

Holy Roman Emperor Charles V was dead. Germany and Austria had been left to his brother Ferdinand. All his other possessions, Spain and the Netherlands and the Indies and America had gone to his son Philip. Philip was the son of Charles and a Portuguese princess who had been first cousin to her own husband. The children that are born of such a union are apt to be rather queer. The son of Philip, the unfortunate Don Carlos, (murdered afterwards with his own father's consent,) was crazy. Philip was not quite crazy, but his zeal bordered closely upon insanity. He believed that God had appointed him as one of the saviors of mankind, to preserve Romanism in the world. Therefore, whosoever was obstinate and refused to share his Majesty's views and love for Romanism, proclaimed himself an enemy of the human race and must be exterminated lest his example corrupt the souls of his pious neighbors.

Spain, of course, was a very rich country. All the gold and silver of the new world flowed into the Castilian and Aragonian treasuries. But Spain suffered from a curious economic disease. Her peasants were hard working men and even harder working women. But the better classes maintained a supreme contempt for any form of labor, outside of employment in the army or navy or the civil service. As for the Moors, who had been artisans, they had been driven out of the country long before. As a result, Spain, the treasure chest of the world, remained a poor country because all her money had to be sent abroad in exchange for the wheat and the other necessities of life which the Spaniards neglected to raise for themselves. It was a country very much corrupted by Romish theology.

Philip, ruler of the most powerful nation of the sixteenth century, depended for his revenue upon the taxes which were gathered in the busy commercial beehive of the Netherlands. But these Flemings and Dutchmen were devoted followers of the doctrines of Luther and Calvin and they had cleansed their churches of all images and idolatrous paintings and they had informed the Pope that they no longer regarded him as their shepherd but intended to follow the true gospel of Jesus Christ and the commands of their newly translated Bible.

This placed the king in a precarious position. He would not tolerate the reformed Protestant faith of his Dutch subjects, but he wanted their money. Being a man of uncertain will power, he hesitated a long time. He tried kindness and sternness and promises and threats. The Hollanders remained firm and continued to sing psalms and listen to the sermons of their reformed preachers. Philip in his despair sent his "man of iron," the Duke of Alba, to bring these Protestants around. Alba began by decapitating those leaders who had not left the country before his arrival. In the year 1572 (the same year that the French Protestant leaders were all killed during the terrible night of Saint Bartholomew), he attacked a number of Dutch cities and massacred the inhabitants as an example for the others. The next year he laid siege to the town of Leyden, the manufacturing center of Holland.

Meanwhile, the seven small provinces of the northern Netherlands had formed a defensive union, the so-called union of Utrecht, and had recognized William of Orange, a German prince who had been the private secretary of the Emperor Charles V, as the leader of their army and as commander of their freebooting sailors, who were known as the Beggars of the Sea. William, to save Leyden, cut the dykes, created a shallow inland sea, and delivered the town with the help of a strangely equipped navy consisting of scows and flat-bottomed barges which were rowed and pushed and pulled through the mud until they reached the city walls.

It was the first time that an army of the invincible Spanish king had suffered such a humiliating defeat. It surprised the world. The Protestant powers took fresh courage and Philip devised new means for the purpose of conquering his rebellious subjects. He hired a poor half-witted fanatic to go and murder William of Orange. But the sight of their dead leader did not bring the Seven Provinces to their knees. On the contrary it made them furiously angry. In the year 1581, the Estates General (the meeting of the representatives of the Seven Provinces) came together at the Hague and most solemnly abjured their "wicked king Philip" and themselves assumed the burden of sovereignty which thus far had been invested in their "King by the Grace of God." Eventually a republic was formed of the United Provinces of the Netherlands, independent of Spanish rule.

This is a very important event in history. It re-affirmed the reformed principle that a lower level civil magistrate has a right and responsibility to enforce God's law even if a higher-level magistrate refuses, protecting 'political liberty' in the true Biblical sense of the term. This law of God, summarized in the Ten Commandments, protects the interests of God and man alike. When a higher-level civil ruler refuses to enforce God's moral law, the lower level civil ruler must seek to do it at least within the sphere of his responsibility, even if this means overturning the power of the higher magistrate in the lower magistrate's realm. It was a step which reached even further than the uprising of the nobles which ended with the signing of the Magna Carta in England, protecting the rights of Englishmen. A similar principle was urged by Edward Coke in his Petition of Right in England, defending the powers of the Parliament and the liberties of the English people, as well as the interests of God. And it was used by the English and Scottish Parliaments in the 1640s in their Civil War with King Charles I of England. The American subjects of King George III in the year 1776 came to a similar conclusion. But the Americans had three thousand miles of ocean between themselves and their ruler and the Estates General took their decision (which meant a slow death in case of defeat) within hearing of the Spanish guns and although in constant fear of an avenging Spanish fleet. (Sadly, in the American case too, enforcement of God's law came to mean protection of man's interests as found in the second table of the Ten Commandments, but much less protection of God's interests as found in the first table of the Ten Commandments.)

King Philip of Spain did not see things the way the Dutch and the English (who we will explain more fully later also had become Protestant) did. He continued to wage war against these upstart Protestant territories. He sent a powerful Armada of ships to defeat them, but this effort failed dismally. He also continued land battles against the Netherlands.

J. Parnell McCarter

The Dutch Protestants, along with the British, thought it only fair to reciprocate. So, they now carried the war into the territory of the Spanish enemy. Before the end of the century, Houtman, with the help of a booklet written by Linschoten (a Hollander who had been in the Portuguese service), had at last discovered the route to the Indies. As a result, the great Dutch East India Company was founded and a systematic war upon the Portuguese and Spanish colonies in Asia and Africa was begun in all seriousness.

It was during this early era of colonial conquest that a curious lawsuit was fought out in the Dutch courts. Early in the seventeenth century a Dutch Captain by the name of van Heemskerk, a man who had made himself famous as the head of an expedition which had tried to discover the North Eastern Passage to the Indies and who had spent a winter on the frozen shores of the island of Nova Zembla, had captured a Portuguese ship in the straits of Malacca. You will remember that the Pope had divided the world into two equal shares, one of which had been given to the Spaniards and the other to the Portuguese. The Portuguese quite naturally regarded the water which surrounded their Indian islands as part of their own property and since, for the moment, they were not at war with the United Seven Netherlands, they claimed that the captain of a private Dutch trading company had no right to enter their private domain and steal their ships. And they brought suit. The directors of the Dutch East India Company hired a bright young lawyer, by the name of De Groot or Grotius, to defend their case. He made the astonishing plea that the ocean is free to all comers. Once outside the distance which a cannon ball fired from the land can reach, the sea is or (according to Grotius) ought to be, a free and open highway to all the ships of all nations. It was the first time that this startling doctrine had been publicly pronounced in a court of law. It was opposed by all the other seafaring people. To counteract the effect of Grotius' famous plea for the "Mare Liberum," or "Open Sea," John Selden, the Englishman, wrote his famous treatise upon the "Mare Clausum" or "Closed Sea" which treated of the natural right of a sovereign to regard the seas which surrounded his country as belonging to his territory.

To return to the warfare between Spaniard and Hollander and Englishman, before twenty years were over the most valuable colonies of the Indies and the Cape of Good Hope and Ceylon and those along the coast of China and even Japan were in Protestant hands. In 1621 a West Indian Company was founded which conquered Brazil and in North America built a fortress called Nieuw Amsterdam at the mouth of the river which Henry Hudson had discovered in the year 1609. These new colonies enriched both England and the Dutch Republic to such an extent that they could hire foreign soldiers to do their fighting on land while they devoted themselves to commerce and trade. God blessed both the Netherlands and England with great prosperity.

But the independent Dutch republic not only faced the continued external threat from Roman Catholic Spain (which had not relinquished its right to rule the Netherlands), but it also faced an internal religious controversy regarding the 'doctrines of grace.' The Dutch republic had an established reformed church, which the State rightly recognized and supported. Within this Church Arminius and his followers (the Arminians) denied the doctrines of grace, such as the total depravity of man and unconditional election. The true Calvinists in the Church knew this was no area in which there could be compromise. Led by the theologian Gomarus within the Church and the politician Maurice in the State, they argued against the Arminians, who were also known as the Remonstrants. Eventually a national synod was convened at Dort - to which reformed representatives from around the world were invited. They issued the famous Canons of Dort in 1619, defending the Calvinistic doctrines of grace, or otherwise known as the Five Points of Calvinism. The leading Remonstrants had to leave the country. And the reformed faith was maintained in the

Netherlands, at least for a time. During the Dutch efforts for independence, their English neighbors across the waters had aided in their cause. Let me now tell you about the reformation across the water in England and Scotland.

LET ME TELL YOU THE REAL STORY OF MANKIND

CHAPTER 37: The Protestant Reformation Reaches England, Scotland and Beyond

The history of what we know of today as Great Britain is fascinating. It is important to understand its history because God has used this island nation in such a remarkable way over history to spread the gospel of Jesus Christ and Biblical Christianity. In previous chapters I have given you hints of this even as I told you about men such as Boniface and John Wycliffe. But now let me give you a brief summary of its history and then its part in the Reformation.

Julius Caesar, the earliest explorer of north-western Europe, had crossed the Channel in the year 55 B.C. and had conquered England. During four centuries the country then remained a Roman province. But when the Barbarians began to threaten Rome, the garrisons were called back from the frontier that they might defend the home country and Britannia was left without a Roman government and without Roman protection. But even before the Romans had to evacuate, the Britons as a nation were won to Christ.

As soon as Rome's evacuation became known among the pagan Saxon tribes of northern Germany, they sailed across the North Sea and made themselves at home in the prosperous island. They founded a number of independent Anglo-Saxon kingdoms (so called after the original Angles or English and the Saxon invaders) but these small states were forever quarrelling with each other and no King was strong enough to establish himself as the head of a united country. For more than five hundred years, Mercia and Northumbria and Wessex and Sussex and Kent and East Anglia, or whatever their names, were exposed to attacks from various Scandinavian pirates. Over time even these Saxons were converted to Christianity.

One of the most notable Christian Anglo-Saxon kings was King Alfred the Great.

Alfred compiled the law into written form, showing its basis in the Ten Commandments. He translated the Psalms into the Anglo-Saxon tongue, he began the inscripturation of the *Anglo-Saxon Chronicles*, and he started an academy that became Oxford University later in history. He also successfully fought off the pagan Danish Viking invaders during his day.

But later in the island's history, the Danes got the better of the resident Saxons. In the eleventh century, England, together with

Norway and northern Germany became part of the large Danish Empire of Canute the Great and the last vestiges of independence disappeared. The Danes, in the course of time, were finally driven away.

But no sooner was England free, than it was conquered for the fourth time. The new enemies were the descendants of another tribe of Norsemen who early in the tenth century had invaded France and had founded the Duchy of Normandy. William, Duke of Normandy, who for a long time had looked across the water with an envious eye, crossed the Channel in October of the year 1066. At the battle of Hastings, on October the fourteenth of that year, he destroyed the weak forces of Harold of Wessex, the last of the Anglo-Saxon Kings and established himself as King of England. But neither William nor his successors of the House of Anjou and Plantagenet regarded England as their true home. To them the island was merely a part of their great inheritance on the continent – a sort of colony inhabited by rather backward people upon whom they forced their own language and civilization. Gradually however the "colony" of England gained upon the "Mother country" of Normandy. It was at this time that John Wycliffe lived, urging a return to the primitive doctrines and practices of the Christian Church, and away from Papal Tyranny. At the same time the Kings of France were trying desperately to get rid of the powerful Norman-English neighbors who were in truth no more than disobedient servants of the French crown. After a century of warfare, the French people, under the leadership of a young girl by the name of Joan of Arc, drove the "foreigners" from their soil. Joan herself, taken a prisoner at the battle of Compiègne in the year 1430 and sold by her Burgundian captors to the English soldiers, was burned as a witch. But the English never gained foothold upon the continent and their Kings were at last able to devote all their time to their British possessions. As the feudal nobility of the island had been engaged in one of those strange feuds which were as common in the middle ages as measles and small-pox, and as the greater part of the old landed proprietors had been killed during these so-called Wars of the Roses, it was quite easy for the Kings to increase their royal power. And by the end of the fifteenth century, England was a strongly centralized country, ruled by Henry VII of the House of Tudor, whose famous Court of Justice, the "Star Chamber" of terrible memory, suppressed all attempts on the part of the surviving nobles to regain their old influence upon the government of the country with the utmost severity.

In the year 1509, Henry VII was succeeded by his son Henry VIII, and from that moment on the history of England gained a new importance. The country ceased to be a mediæval island and became a modern state.

During Henry VIII's reign the Protestant Reformation was spreading throughout Europe, including England. Henry VIII opposed it at first, but a matter altogether separate was to lead him to separate his nation from Romanism. Henry VIII wanted the Pope to agree to the nullification of his marriage to Katherine of Aragon, on grounds that the marriage was not legally entered into. The Pope would not.

King Henry had already consulted the Archbishop of Canterbury and required him to procure the opinions of the bishops of England on the subject. All, with the exception of Fisher, Bishop of Rochester, declared that in their judgment it was an unlawful marriage. At length Cranmer, till then a comparatively unknown man, suggested that instead of a long and fruitless negotiation at Rome, Henry would be better to consult all the learned men and universities of Christendom, to ascertain whether the marriage was unlawful in itself.

Cranmer prosecuted the scheme which he had suggested so successfully, that he procured, both from the English universities, and from nearly all the learned men in Europe, answers to the effect, that the king's marriage was contrary to the law of God. These answers were laid before the English Parliament, and assented to by both its Houses, as also by the the Clergy, which met at the same time. Still the Pope had not consented, and the hostility between him and Henry was necessarily increased. Henry was not disposed to pause now, till he should have secured his power over the clergy. A petition was agreed upon by the English clergy to be offered to the king, in which he was styled, "The Protector and Supreme Head of the Church and the Clergy of England."

The question respecting the Pope's supremacy was now the subject of discussion throughout the kingdom; and at length it was formally brought before Parliament, and a bill was passed, abolishing papal supremacy in England, and declaring the king to be the Supreme Head of the Church of England.

Almost the first public use made by the king of his acknowledged supremacy in religion, was to send Cranmer, now Archbishop of Canterbury, on a visitation of the monasteries throughout the kingdom of England. It was no difficult matter to convict these Popish institutions of such crimes as are not fit to be mentioned, "equal," says Burnet, "to any that were in Sodom." It served, at the same time, as a measure by which the king's coffers were replenished, some of his favorites enriched, and the better part of the nation gratified by the removal of the system. About the same time, it was resolved that the Bible should be translated into English, and published for the instruction of the community; though this was strenuously resisted by a large proportion of the clergy, and carried only by the influence of Cranmer and the queen, Henry's second wife, Ann Boleyn. But, alas, like so many wives of Henry, he was not satisfied with poor Ann Boleyn. The fall of the queen, which took place soon after, threatened to retard the progress of reformation, and the Pope attempted a reconciliation with the king. But Henry had no inclination to subject himself again to papal control; and, following Cranmer's advice, he proceeded to make further changes. A Convocation was then induced to agree to certain articles of religion, which were accordingly promulgated on the royal authority. In these articles, the standards of faith were declared to be - the Bible, the Apostolic, Nicene, and Athanasian Creeds, and the decrees of the first four general Councils, without regard to tradition or the decrees of the Church; and the doctrine of justification was declared to "signify remission of sins, and acceptation into the favor of God, that is to say, a perfect renovation in Christ;" but many Romish doctrines and practices remained.

In 1547, Henry died and his son, young King Edward VI took his place. But Edward was only nine years old, so a regent administered the kingdom on behalf of Edward. No sooner had a suitable arrangement of civil affairs been effected by the regency, than Cranmer, supported by the Protector Somerset, and countenanced by the young king, Edward VI, resumed the important duty of reforming the Church. These reforms included instruction of the clergy in the Biblical reformed faith, permitting the communion to be received in both kinds (so that the people could partake both the bread and wine in communion, and not just bread like in the Romish Church), the prohibiting of private masses, preparation of a catechism for Biblical instruction of the people, and a new and more reformed liturgy was adopted for the Church's worship services. About the same time, there were several severe proceedings against Anabaptists and other sectaries.

In the year 1552, the alterations which had been made in the Book of Common Prayer by the reformers during the course of the preceding year, were ratified by act of Parliament, and ordered to be universally employed. In the same year the Articles of Religion were prepared, chiefly by Cranmer and Ridley, and published by the king's authority, a short time before King Edwards' sad death.

Mary, the daughter of Henry's first wife and a staunch Roman Catholic, became queen in the place of Edward. Mary returned the Popish bishops to their offices in the Church and removed the reformed bishops. She made sure the laws passed by King Edward concerning religion were repealed; and a negotiation commenced for procuring a reconciliation with the Pope. The Roman Catholic Mass was everywhere resumed, and every step taken for bringing the nation once more under the degrading thralldom of Popery.

She did not earn the title of "The Bloody Mary" for nothing. She had many of the Protestants put to death and in other ways followed the example of her royal Spanish husband. Providentially, Mary died, in the year 1558, and was succeeded by Elizabeth, the daughter of Henry VIII and Anne Boleyn, the second of his six wives, whom he had decapitated when she no longer pleased him.

Elizabeth, who had spent some time in prison, and who had been released only at the request of the Holy Roman Emperor, was a most cordial enemy of everything Catholic and Spanish. Although Elizabeth was by no means as open to Biblical reform as she should have been, she was a real improvement over Mary. The external policy of the Church was restored to almost the very same condition in which it had been at the death of King Edward.

Elizabeth, however, did not feel entirely safe upon her throne. She had a rival for the throne, and a very dangerous one at that. Mary, of the house of Stuart, daughter of a French duchess and a Scottish father, widow of king Francis II of France and daughter-in-law of Catherine of Medici (who had organized the murders of Saint Bartholomew's night), was the mother of a little boy who was afterwards to become the first Stuart king of England. (I'll tell you more about James and the history of Scotland later.) She was an ardent Catholic and a willing friend to those who were the enemies of Elizabeth. Her own lack of political ability and the violent methods which she employed to punish her Calvinistic subjects, caused a revolution in Scotland and forced Mary to take refuge on English territory. For eighteen years she remained in England, plotting forever and a day against the woman who had given her shelter and who was at last obliged to follow the advice of her trusted councilors "to cutte off the Scottish Queen's heade."

The head was duly "cutte off" in the year 1587 and caused a war with Spain. The stories about a mysterious Spanish fleet that was to conquer both Holland and England, when Protestant Queen Elizabeth had succeeded Catholic "Bloody Mary" was an old one. For years the sailors of the waterfront had talked about it. In the eighties of the sixteenth century, the rumor took a definite shape. According to pilots who had been in Lisbon, all the Spanish and Portuguese wharves were building ships. And in the southern Netherlands (in Belgium) the Duke of Parma was collecting a large expeditionary force to be carried from Ostend to London and Amsterdam as soon as the fleet should arrive.

In the year 1586 the Great Armada set sail for the north, as I mentioned to you in recounting the history of the Protestant Reformation in the Netherlands. The harbors of the Flemish coast were blockaded by a Dutch fleet and the Channel was guarded by the English, and the Spaniards, accustomed to the quieter seas of the south, did not know how to navigate in this squally and bleak northern climate.

J. Parnell McCarter

Attacked by ships and by storms of the Almighty, the Invincible Armada proved not so invincible after all. A few ships, by sailing around Ireland, escaped to tell the terrible story of defeat. The others perished and lie at the bottom of the North Sea. So, the combined navies of England and Holland defeated Philip's Invincible Armada, and the blow which had been meant to destroy the power of the two great anti-Catholic leaders was turned to their favor.

For now, at last, after many years of hesitation, the English as well as the Dutch thought it their good right to invade the Indies and America and avenge the ills which their Protestant brethren had suffered at the hands of the Spaniards. The English had been among the earliest successors of Columbus. British ships, commanded by the Venetian pilot Giovanni Caboto (or Cabot), had been the first to discover and explore the northern American continent in 1496. Labrador and Newfoundland were of little importance as a possible colony. But the banks of Newfoundland offered a rich reward to the English fishing fleet. A year later, in 1497, the same Cabot had explored the coast of Florida.

Then had come the busy years of Henry VII and Henry VIII when there had been no money for foreign explorations. But under Elizabeth, with the country at peace and Mary Stuart in prison (and later executed), the sailors could leave their harbor without fear for the fate of those whom they left behind. While Elizabeth was still a child, Willoughby had ventured to sail past the North Cape and one of his captains, Richard Chancellor, pushing further eastward in his quest of a possible road to the Indies, had reached Archangel, Russia, where he had established diplomatic and commercial relations with the mysterious rulers of this distant Muscovite Empire. During the first years of Elizabeth's rule this voyage had been followed up by many others. Merchant adventurers, working for the benefit of a "joint stock Company" had laid the foundations of trading companies which in later centuries were to become colonies. The sailors of Elizabeth had carried the English flag and the fame of their Virgin Queen to the four corners of the Seven Seas.

Over the course of Elizabeth's reign there emerged two distinct parties among the English Protestants. Those who wanted to retain many Romish practices, and those that wanted to discard them. Queen Elizabeth sided with those who wanted to retain many Romish practices, like the wearing of special vestments by the clergy, and the inclusion of various rites and ceremonies in worship which were not commanded in scripture. This party also wanted to retain an episcopal system of church government, with archbishops and other officers not found in scripture, but added later. The reforming party, which wanted church worship and government regulated by scripture alone, came to be called the Puritans. These Puritans regarded the Bible as the only standard; they believed in provincial and national synods of elders for Church government; and they believed the articles of religion of the Church should be approved and enforced by civil government.

Queen Elizabeth passed laws requiring that the Church practices conform to her wishes. When some ministers refused, they were removed from their offices. Thus, ejected from their churches and forbidden to preach anywhere else, the Puritans were driven to that extreme point where endurance ceases and active resistance begins. Accordingly, they met, and gravely and solemnly deliberated, whether it was not now both lawful and necessary to separate from the Established Church. After much earnest consultation, they came to the solemn and important conclusion, that since they could not have the word of God preached, nor the sacraments administered, without "idolatrous gear," as they termed the vestments and ceremonies, it was their duty, in the present circumstances, to separate from the public churches, and to assemble, as they had opportunity, in private houses or elsewhere, to worship God in a manner that might not offend. As a result, many of the Puritans suffered imprisonment.

The English Parliament tried to come to the aid of the Puritans, but Queen Elizabeth would have nothing of it. So, in response, a leading Puritan of the time, Thomas Cartwright, who is also called the 'father of English Presbyterianism', explained the duty of the English nation to adopt Puritan and Presbyterian principles in its church worship and government.

All hope of legislative assistance in prosecuting further reformation being cut off by the queen's arbitrary procedure, the Puritans resolved to take another step, still more daring and decisive than any on which they had previously ventured. Several of the ministers of London and its vicinity met together and determined to form themselves into a presbytery. In 1572 they formed the Presbyterian Church in England. Puritanism had thenceforward not only a vital principle, but also systematic organization, enabling it to live on, and increase in spite of any amount of persecution; for a system dies not with the individuals that held it, but draws into itself the fresh life of succeeding generations.

Ceasing to complain of Popish vestments and ceremonies, and to supplicate a further reformation, some radicals began to question whether the Church of England ought even to be regarded as a true Church, and her ministers true Christian ministers. They not only renounced communion with her in her forms of prayer and her ceremonies, but also in the dispensation of word and ordinance. The leader of these men of extreme and unfounded views was Robert Brown, a person who was a minister in the diocese of Norwich, whose family connections gave him considerable influence, and procured him protection, he being nearly related to Lord Treasurer Cecil. Brown appears to have been a man of hot and impetuous temper; rash and variable, except when opposed, and then headstrong and overbearing. Throwing himself headlong into the Puritan controversy, he traversed the country from place to place, pouring out the most fierce and bitter invectives against the whole Prelatic party, and also against all who could not concur with him in the rude violence of his mode of warfare. After repeated imprisonments, and many attempts to form a new party, he at last partially succeeded in collecting a small body of like-minded adherents; but was soon afterwards compelled to leave the kingdom, and to withdraw to Holland with a portion of his followers. There he formed a Church according to his own fancy; but it was soon torn to pieces with internal dissension, and Brown returned again to England, and exhibiting one of those recoils by no means rare with men of vehement temperament, he renounced his principles of separation, conformed to that worship which he had so violently assailed, and became rector of a parish in Northamptonshire.

The remainder of his life was by no means distinguished by purity of manners; and at length he terminated his dishonored days in the county jail, in the eighty-first year of his age. From this person the first form of what has since been termed the Independent, or Congregational system of Church government, appears to have had its origin, the great majority of the Puritans either retaining their connection with the Church of England in a species of constrained half conformity, or associating on the Presbyterian model. Brown not only renounced communion with the Church of England, but also with all others of the reformed Churches who would not adopt the model which he had constructed. The main principles of that model were, that every church ought to be confined within a single congregation;

that its government should be the most complete democracy; and. that there was no distinction in point of order between the office bearers and the ordinary members, so that a vote of the congregation was enough to constitute any man an office-bearer, and to entitle him to preach and to administer the sacraments. Those who adopted these opinions, and formed Congregational Churches on the same model, were at first termed Brownists, and were regarded by the main body of the Puritans with nearly as much dislike as they were by the Prelatists.

The struggle assumed a less serious aspect for a short time, in consequence of the publication of the famous Martin Mar-Prelate Tracts. Some of the Puritan party had procured a printing-press, – the liberty of the press having been taken away previously, – and commenced a series of pamphlets, containing attacks of wit, ridicule, and mockery, against the bishops and their supporters. Many of these tracts displayed very considerable power of sarcasm and invective; and as they were written intentionally for the mass of the nation, they were composed in a style not merely plain, but affectedly rude and vulgar. They were not, however, to be despised. Amidst much coarse vituperation, they contained statements of facts which could not be disputed, set forth with such home-thrusting vigor, as caused every direct and strong-aimed blow to tell upon the assailed prelates. Great was the indignation and dismay of the bishops and their friends, and every exertion was made to detect and seize the hidden armory of this unseen assailant. For a considerable time, these efforts were unsuccessful, and the Prelatic party were constrained to attempt their own defense in literary warfare. But, although they displayed considerable talent and activity in this attempt, they were not able to match their unknown antagonists, whose writings produced a deep and widespread. impression on the public mind. At length the Martin Mar-Prelate press was seized, with several unfinished tracts, and that aspect of the struggle terminated, but not till the Prelatic cause had sustained very considerable injury.

The Parliament again met, and the House of Commons once more attempted to rescue the suffering Puritans, by instituting an inquiry into the conduct of the High Commission, in imposing oaths and subscriptions not sanctioned by law. The queen was highly incensed, commanded them not to meddle with matters of state or causes ecclesiastical, and threw several of the members, and even the attorney-general, into prison. The Parliament, with a tameness unworthy of the spirit of free-born Englishmen, not merely yielded, but passed an act for the suppression of conventicles, by which was meant all religious meetings, except such as the queen and the bishops were pleased to permit, on pain of perpetual banishment. The principle of this act was of the most despotic nature, converting any difference from the religion of the sovereign into a crime against the State, and rendering the mere want of conformity equivalent to a proof of direct opposition. Great numbers were subjected to the most grievous sufferings through this enactment. Some went into voluntary exile, to escape the horrors of imprisonment; some endured a lengthened captivity, and then were banished; and some, chiefly of the Brownists, were condemned to death, and on the scaffold declared their loyalty to their sovereign, while they ceased not to testify against the tyranny of the prelates.

The controversy between the High Churchmen and the Puritans obtained the full development of all its main principles in the year 1595. At this time Dr. Bound published a treatise on the Sabbath; in which he maintained its perpetual sanctity, as a day of rest equally from business and recreation, that it might be devoted wholly to the worship of God. All the Puritans assented to this doctrine, while the Prelatists accused it as both an undue restraint of Christian liberty and an improper exalting of the Sabbath above the other festivals appointed by the Church.

About the same time, a controversy arose in Cambridge respecting those doctrinal points which form the leading distinctions between the Arminian and the Calvinistic systems of theology. Till this period there had existed no doubt in the minds of any of the English divines that the Thirty-nine Articles were decidedly and intentionally Calvinistic. Indeed, they could have no other opinion; because they were perfectly aware how much influence the writings of Calvin exercised over the minds of those by whom these Articles were framed. After the controversy had prevailed in the university a short time, an appeal was made to Whitgift, who, with the aid of other learned divines, prepared nine propositions, commonly called the Lambeth Articles, to which all the scholars in the university were strictly enjoined to conform their judgments. These Lambeth Articles were more strictly Calvinistic than Calvin himself would have desired, and certainly prove that, in its early period, the Church of England was anything but Arminian, whatever it may have since become. But though Whitgift was himself still a thorough Calvinist, considerable numbers of the Prelatic party were veering towards Arminianism; so that, partly on that account, and partly on account of their more strict observance of the Sabbath sanctity, the Puritans were now led to a more important field of conflict than that on which they had hitherto striven against their antagonists; and instead of contending about vestments and ceremonies, they now strove respecting the doctrines of grace, and began to be termed

Doctrinal Puritans. This led to two directly opposite results. It caused the Prelatists to swerve more and more widely from those doctrines which the Puritans maintained; and it impelled the Puritans to prosecute a profound study of those points, which had thus become the elements of controversy. This may account for the remarkable power and accuracy with which the Puritan divines of that and the succeeding generation state and explain the most solemn and profound truths of the Christian revelation.

At length, what may be termed a cessation of hostilities ensued. The queen was now evidently sinking under the infirmities of age, and both parties began to speculate upon the probable measures which might be adopted by her successor, James VI of Scotland. The Puritans hoped that his Presbyterian education might predispose him to be favorable to their views; and the Prelatic party were unwilling to exasperate, by continued severity, those who might possibly, ere long, be the ruling body in the Church. Both parties paused, at least in action; but there is no reason to suppose that their feelings of mutual jealousy and dislike were abated. Nor was it consistent with the usual policy, or king-craft of James, to declare his sentiments and intentions, but rather to hold out plausible grounds of expectation to both parties, thereby to secure the support of both, or at least to disarm the direct hostility of either.

Queen Elizabeth died in 1603. Her cousin, the great-grandson of her own grandfather Henry VII and son of Mary Stuart, her rival and enemy, succeeded her as James I. James left his native land of Scotland, commencing his journey to London to take possession of the English throne, to which he was now the direct heir, along with his reign over Scotland.

Let me pause here and tell you something about Scotland's history, which I think will help you better understand James and the other Stuart kings. In the first century A.D., when the Romans invaded Britain, they were unable to conquer what is present day Scotland. The people of Scotland they called 'Picts', meaning 'painted', because they painted their bodies. To keep the barbarian Picts from invading Romanized Britain, Roman Emperor Hadrian built a wall across the island, part of which still stands. During the days of Roman rule, many

Britons became Christian. One such Briton was a lad named Patrick, who was captured by pirates and taken to Ireland. Patrick later escaped back to Britain but returned to Ireland as a Christian missionary. He preached the gospel of Jesus Christ, and the people of Ireland embraced it. Not long afterwards in the fifth century, Celtic immigrants called Scots left Ireland for Scotland. The Scots were Christian, and Columba who was a Scot missionary took the gospel to the king of the Picts, who converted to Christianity, and with him all the Picts became professed Christians. In the 9th century the king of the Scots added the kingdom of the Picts to his own, and the whole first became known as Scotland.

In the 13th and 14th centuries the English made various efforts at conquering and controlling Scotland. The English captured Scotland's Stone of Scone, on which Scottish kings had long been crowned, and placed it in their own Westminster Abbey. But the fighting Scots did not appreciate this 'wee' bit of stone and nation thievery. Under William Wallace they fought back. But the English captured Wallace and hung his head from London Bridge. Not to be defeated, the Scots under Robert Bruce fought back and defeated superior English forces. Finally, Scotland's independence was recognized by England.

But union of the two kingdoms came by more peaceful means: marriage. King James IV of Scotland married the daughter of King Henry VII of England. This did not result in the immediate unification of the two kingdoms, but ultimately did. In the meantime, the Protestant Reformation was conquering Scotland. Scotland had long maintained purer doctrine and worship than Christians more enthralled under Roman influence, ever since the days of Columba. So, when men like John Knox preached Reformation, many of his reforms were a form of Christianity Scotland had experienced in its history. Knox had visited Calvin's Geneva, and he brought a similar reformation to Scotland. In 1560 Scotland's parliament adopted a reformed confession of faith and established the Church of Scotland on a Presbyterian basis. All of this did not sit well with Mary, Queen of Scots and daughter of deceased King James V. Mary was an ardent Roman Catholic and did everything she could to thwart this Protestant Reformation, but to no avail. Finally, Mary had to flee to England, after a series of intrigues back in Scotland, where Queen Elizabeth 'took care of her', so to speak. James VI, Mary's son, was brought up Presbyterian, and it is this James who also was entitled to the throne of England once Queen Elizabeth died.

King James, on his progress southward from Scotland to England to assume his throne over both kingdoms, met with English Puritan ministers. These Puritan ministers availed themselves of the opportunity to lay before James what is commonly termed the Millenary Petition. This Petition said, "That they [the Puritan ministers], to the number of more than a thousand ministers, groaned under the burden of human rites and ceremonies, and cast themselves at his majesty's feet for relief." They wanted a church reformed in England like James had grown up with in Scotland.

The Prelatic party in England, who did not want such reform for their Church, were at least equally strenuous in their endeavors to secure his majesty's favor. But as James had given a friendly reception to both parties, and as he was vain of his own acquirements in theology, and of his skill in polemical discussions, which he wished to exhibit to his new subjects, he thought proper to appoint a conference between the two parties, to be conducted in his own presence, as anal judge in all such matters. This gave occasion to the famous Hampton Court Conference. The place appointed for this conference was the drawing-room at Hampton Court. The king's response to the Puritans at this conference he stated thus: "No bishop, no king." So, the party opposing further Puritan reformation was firmly in power. James would make sure there would not be such thorough reform in England as he had grown up with in Scotland. And he would even do all in his power to undermine the quite reformed character of the Church of Scotland. But one notable gift he did bestow on the Puritans and mankind as a result of this Conference was sponsorship of a translation of the Bible into English which we know as the Authorized Version or King James Version Bible.

Within a few years of James' reign, the Puritans were removed from their Church offices in England, and some were persecuted by means of the infamous Star-Chamber. The king took upon himself broad powers in Church and State. It created a despotic climate, which was vigorously opposed by the Puritans who supported Parliamentary civil government and Presbyterian church government. By means of the authority thus acquired, the prelates urged on their persecuting career with double eagerness and severity; and the Puritans became, in consequence, so much the more determined in their adherence to their principles. Not merely suffering, but calumny of the grossest kind, was their portion; and ambitious churchmen found that the readiest road to preferment in the Church was to pour forth violent invectives and dark aspersions against the detested Puritans. As an answer to these reproaches, and to vindicate their character, the Puritans published a treatise entitled "English Puritanism," which Dr. Ames (better known by his Latinized name, Amesius) translated into Latin for the information of foreign Churches. It contains a very full and impartial statement of the peculiar opinions of the much-calumniated Puritans; and ought to be enough to vindicate them in the judgment of every candid and intelligent person.

During the reign of King James and his son Charles, successful efforts were made to establish Protestant English colonies in North America. Especially in New England, these colonies were Puritan. These North American colonies prospered, despite difficult beginnings. God was greatly expanding His kingdom on earth and His gospel message to peoples who had never heard it before.

Thus, the beginning of the 17th century was marked by circumstances in which the reformed Protestant religion was firmly in place in England and Scotland, but the opposition to more complete reform was strong and determined. I will resume the story of England and Scotland in the 17th century, but first let me explain to you the efforts of Rome to combat the Protestant Reformation both in continental Europe and the British Isles.

LET ME TELL YOU THE REAL STORY OF MANKIND

CHAPTER 38: Rome's Counter-Reformation

To say that Rome was dismayed by the Protestant Reformation would be a vast understatement. For centuries she had been able to maintain her authority over the Church by various forms of enticement and coercion. During the twenty years following the day Luther had hung his 95 Theses at Wittenberg, Papal Rome had seen her power, authority, and territory of control slip. Almost all of northern Europe had joined the Protestant fold, and significant portions of central Europe. Rome knew something significant had to be done to stop the Protestant tide. Rome's response was the Counter-Reformation.

The goals of the Counter-Reformation were to reform the Romish Church so as not to be as open to criticism, to combat the Protestant movement and reclaim lost territories, and to expand its missionary endeavors around the world. During the first twenty years of the Protestant Reformation Rome and its bureaucracy had resisted making any significant changes to address the Protestant threat. Only when there seemed no alternative did she adopt the goals of the Counter-Reformation.

One important tool of the Counter-Reformation was a Roman Catholic order founded in 1540 called the Society of Jesus, or Jesuits. The founder of this organization was a Spanish soldier who after a life of unholy adventures turned religious devotee. The name of this Spaniard was Ignatius de Loyola. He was born in the year before the discovery of America. He had been wounded and lamed for life, and while he was in the hospital, he thought he saw a vision of the Holy Virgin and her Son, who bade him give up the wickedness of his former life. He decided to go to the Holy Land and finish the task of the Crusades. But a visit to Jerusalem had shown him the impossibility of the task and he returned west to help in the warfare against the Protestants.

In the year 1534, he was studying in Paris at the Sorbonne. Together with seven other students he founded a fraternity. The eight men promised each other that they would lead holy lives, that they would not strive after riches but after righteousness (as defined by Rome and not by God's word), and would devote themselves, body and soul, to the service of the Romish Church. A few years later this small fraternity had grown into a regular organization and was recognized by Pope Paul III as the Society of Jesus.

Loyola had been a military man. He believed in discipline, and absolute obedience to the orders of the superior dignitaries became one of the main causes for the enormous success of the Jesuits. They specialized in education. They gave their teachers a most thorough-going education before they allowed them to talk to a single pupil. They lived with their students and they entered into their games. They watched them with tender care. And as a result, they raised a new generation of faithful Catholics who took their religious duties as seriously as the people of the early Middle Ages.

The shrewd Jesuits, however, did not waste all their efforts upon the education of the poor. They entered the palaces of the mighty and became the private tutors of future emperors and kings. And what this meant you will see for yourself when I tell you about the Thirty Years' War. But before this, a great many other things had happened.

The Jesuits founded colleges, seminaries, and other schools loyal to Romish orthodoxy, as well as conducting overseas missions. They wrote books, catechisms, and tracts presenting the Romish side of issues, and seeking to refute Protestant positions. Whether arguing against 'justification by faith alone' or against the view that the Pope was the Man of Sin and Anti-Christ, the Jesuits always remained focused on undermining the reformed Protestant faith. The Jesuits were devoted missionaries for the Romish Church. Jesuits were dispersed as far away as Asia and the Americas. And they were not above using deception and device in their efforts to protect and extend the power of the 'Holy See' of Rome.

Another major aspect of the Counter-Reformation was the infamous Council of Trent. Pope Paul III called this Council of Roman clerics (as well as some Jesuits) to respond to the theology and criticisms of the Protestants. Prior to the Reformation fairly great differences of view on many doctrines had been tolerated in the Church. This is indeed why there were even many adhering to what may be described as proto-Protestantism within the Roman Catholic Church up to the time of the Reformation. But in responding to the Reformation, the Roman Catholic Church narrowed the band of acceptable doctrines within the Church. All the tenets of Protestants were denounced as heresy. 'Justification by faith alone' was rejected, as well as the other doctrines of grace. The number of sacraments necessary was declared to be seven, and not just two (i.e., baptism and the Lord's Supper). Tradition, along with the Bible, was accepted as a source of faith. The Council even declared the right of the Church to add books to the Bible, which it did with the Apocryphal books.

But the Council did take certain actions to help 'clean up the act'. It required that bishops could have no more than one diocese and must reside in the one they were over. This meant no more absentee bishops. Education of priests was improved, and a goal was implemented to have a college or seminary in every diocese for their training.

The effect of the Council of Trent was to set the Romish Church in a very different direction from the Biblical Protestant churches. Hence forward, the Romish Church would be a formidable foe indeed.

Another tool of the Roman response to Protestantism was the Roman Inquisition. It was instituted in 1542 by Pope Paul III and was similar in design and operation to the medieval and Spanish inquisitions. The inquisition was spearheaded by a commission of six cardinals, called the Congregation of the Inquisition. The Roman inquisition was much freer from episcopal control than earlier inquisitions. Protestants were systematically rooted out and put to death. After Protestantism had been eliminated as a serious "danger" in places like Italy, the Roman Inquisition simply had to maintain the status quo. The Congregation of the Inquisition lasted in the Romish Church until 1908, when it was renamed the Holy Office. It was again renamed in 1965 the Congregation for the Doctrine of the Faith and re-organized then, as well.

These measures were quite effective in stopping the tide of growth of Protestantism, but Romanism also tried its hand at taking back lost territory by force. These efforts generally proved unsuccessful, as demonstrated in the case of the Spanish Armada. But Rome persevered in its course of tyranny even to the bloody Thirty Years War.

The Thirty Years War which broke out in the year 1618 and which ended with the famous treaty of Westphalia in 1648 was the result of Romish force employed to exterminate the Protestant faith. It did not work, but many lives were lost in the process.

The hostilities began almost as soon as Ferdinand II of the House of Habsburg had been elected Emperor. He was the product of a most careful Jesuit training and was a most obedient and devout son of the Romish Church. The vow which he had made as a young man, that he would eradicate opposed to Romanism from his domains, Ferdinand kept to the best of his ability. Two days before his election, his chief opponent, Frederick, the Protestant Elector of the Palatinate and a son-in-law of James I of England, had been made King of Bohemia, in direct violation of Ferdinand's wishes.

At once the Habsburg armies marched into Bohemia. The young king looked in vain for assistance against this formidable enemy. The Dutch Republic was willing to help, but, engaged in a desperate war of its own with the Spanish branch of the Habsburgs, it could do little. The Stuarts in England were more interested in strengthening their own absolute power at home than spending money and men upon a forlorn adventure in faraway Bohemia. After a struggle of a few months, the Elector of the Palatinate was driven away, and his domains were given to the Roman Catholic house of Bavaria. This was the beginning of the great war.

Then the Habsburg armies, under Tilly and Wallenstein, fought their way through the Protestant part of Germany until they had reached the shores of the Baltic. A Catholic neighbor meant serious danger to the Protestant king of Denmark. Christian IV tried to defend himself by attacking his enemies before they had become too strong for him. The Danish armies marched into Germany but were defeated. Wallenstein followed up his victory with such energy and violence that Denmark was forced to sue for peace. Only one town of the Baltic then remained in the hands of the Protestants. That was Stralsund.

There, in the early summer of the year 1630, landed King Gustavus Adolphus of the house of Vasa, king of Sweden, and famous as the man who had defended his country against the Russians. A Protestant prince of great skill and courage, Gustavus Adolphus was welcomed by the Protestant princes of Europe as the savior of the Lutheran cause.

He defeated Tilly, who had just successfully butchered the Protestant inhabitants of Magdeburg.

Then his troops began their great march through the heart of Germany in an attempt to reach the Habsburg possessions in Italy. Threatened in the rear by the Catholics, Gustavus suddenly veered around and defeated the main Habsburg army in the battle of Lützen. Unfortunately, the Swedish king was killed when he strayed away from his troops. But the Habsburg power had been broken.

Ferdinand, who was a suspicious sort of person, at once began to distrust his own servants.

Wallenstein, his commander-in-chief, was murdered at his instigation. When the Roman Catholic Bourbons, who ruled France and hated their Habsburg rivals, heard of this, they joined the Protestant Swedes. The armies of Louis XIII invaded the eastern part of Germany, and Turenne and Condé added their fame to that of Baner and Weimar, the Swedish generals, by murdering, pillaging and burning Habsburg property. The war took an extraordinary course when the Protestant Danes declared war upon the Protestant Swedes who were the allies of the Catholic French, whose political leader, the Cardinal de Richelieu, had just deprived the Huguenots (or French

Protestants) of those rights of public worship which the Edict of Nantes of the year 1598 had guaranteed them.

When this treacherous and winding war finally came to an end, Protestantism was preserved in most of the regions that it controlled before Roman attack. It came to an end with the treaty of Westphalia in 1648. The Roman Catholic powers remained Roman Catholic and the Protestant powers stayed faithful to the doctrines of Luther and Calvin and Zwingli. The Swiss and Dutch Protestants were recognized as independent republics. France kept the cities of Metz and Toul and Verdun and a part of the Alsace. The Holy Roman Empire continued to exist as a sort of scare-crow state, without men, without money, without hope and without courage. This would be the last major frontal attack by Romanism upon Protestantism for a very long time. Over time it learned to adopt more subtle means, which actually have proven far more effective as a tool of wickedness.

LET ME TELL YOU THE REAL STORY OF MANKIND

CHAPTER 39: England, Scotland, and the English Colonies in the 17th Century

For almost the entire 17th century the Stuarts ruled England and Scotland. The reign of the Stuarts in England and Scotland had seemed quite promising, at least at first. They could unite England and Scotland peacefully, which had not been successfully accomplished by war for centuries. But sadly, the Stuarts squandered their opportunity at successful and prosperous rule, due in no small measure to one trait they never could master: pride. The Stuart kings- from James I to Charles I to Charles II to James II- all firmly believed in the principle of their "divine right" to administer their realm as they thought fit without sufficiently consulting God's word or considering the advice of the Parliament. The idea was not new. The Popes, who in more than one way had been the successors of the Roman Emperors (or rather of the Roman Imperial ideal of a single and undivided state covering the entire known world), had always regarded themselves and had been publicly recognized by many as the "Vicar (or Vice-Regent) of Christ upon Earth." Christians did not question the right of God to rule the world as He saw fit. And the Papacy tricked most to believe that they should not doubt the right of the divine "Vicar" to do the same thing and to demand the obedience of the masses because he was the direct representative of the Absolute Ruler of the Universe and responsible only to Almighty God.

When the Reformation proved successful, those rights which formerly had been invested in the Papacy were in some cases taken over by European sovereigns who became Protestants. As head of their own national or dynastic churches they insisted upon being "Christ's Vice Regents" within the limit of their own territory. Many people in these countries did not question the right of their rulers to take such a step. England was one example that followed this pattern. But in nations where reformation was more thorough, like Geneva and Scotland, this pattern had been rejected. It was recognized that Christ and His law is above Church and State, and that these two institutions ordained by God must be kept separate. It was also recognized that a synod of elders was God's ordained Church government, and a council or parliament of elders should insure the enforcement of God's law in the civil realm.

The Netherlands was one of the first places where these two theories of government came into fierce collision. The "Divine Right" of sovereigns had been rejected in the Netherlands when the Estates General abjured their sovereign King Philip II of Spain, in the year 1581. "The King," so they said, "has broken God's law and the King therefore is dismissed like any other unfaithful servant." Since then, this particular idea of a king's responsibilities towards God and his subjects had spread among many of the nations who inhabited the shores of the North Sea. The next test case was England.

When the Stuarts began to annoy the people of England with their claim that they had a right to do what they pleased and never mind the responsibility, especially the English middle classes used the House of Commons as their first line of defense against this abuse of the Royal Power. Parliamentarians like Edward Coke put forth a bill of liberties for the English people- called the Petition of Right- and argued that even the King was not above the common law. But the Crown refused to give in and the King sent Parliament about its own business. Eleven long years, Charles I ruled alone. He levied taxes which was illegal for a King to do, and he managed his British kingdom as if it had been his own country estate. He had assistants in government to help him, and we must say that he had boldness even if he lacked wisdom.

Instead of assuring himself of the support of his faithful Scottish subjects, Charles became involved in a quarrel with the Scotch Presbyterians. He tried to force upon them worship rites not commanded in scripture, as well as episcopal church government in lieu of Biblical Presbyterian church government. The Scots rose up against this tyranny, engaging in a National Covenant to maintain the historic reformed faith in their realm. Charles fought to suppress this movement, and thus began a series of civil wars. Much against his will, but forced by his need for ready cash, Charles was at last obliged to call the English Parliament together once more. It met in April of 1640 and showed an ugly temper. It was dissolved a few weeks later. A new English Parliament convened in November. This one was even less pliable than the first one. The members understood that the question of "Divine Right of the King" or "Government by Law Protected by the Parliament" must be fought out for good and all. This Parliament was dominated by men of Presbyterian and Puritan persuasion. They attacked the King in his chief councilors and executed half a dozen of them. They announced that they would not allow themselves to be dissolved without their own approval. Finally, on December 1,

1641, they presented to the King a "Grand Remonstrance" which gave a detailed account of the many grievances of the people against their Ruler.

Charles, hoping to derive some support for his own policy in the country districts, left London in January of 1642. Each side organized an army and prepared for open warfare between the power of the crown and the power of Parliament. The English Parliament allied itself with the Scottish Parliament, and together they entered into a Solemn League and Covenant to govern the United Kingdom in accordance with the reformed faith. The regiments of "Godly men," commanded by Oliver Cromwell, with their iron discipline and their profound confidence in their aims, soon became the model for the entire army of the opposition. They were assisted in battle by the Scottish army. Twice Charles was defeated. After the battle of Naseby, in 1645, he fled to Scotland. The Scotch sold him to the English.

In the meantime, the famous Westminster Assembly had been convened by order of the English Parliament. Reformed ministers and elders from England and Scotland prepared the Westminster Standards. These were to be the confessional standards of the established church of England and Scotland. It was to be Presbyterian in church government and reformed in doctrine.

But Oliver Cromwell ultimately objected to Presbyterian church government and grew impatient with the English Parliament dominated by Presbyterian Puritans. He forced out the Presbyterians, and essentially set himself up as dictator of the Commonwealth. There followed a period of war with the Scotch Presbyterians, who were rightly upset with Cromwell's illegal actions and rejection of the aims of the Solemn League and Covenant, to which he himself had covenanted. In August of the year 1648 after the three-days' battle of Preston Pans, Cromwell made an end to this second civil war, and took Edinburgh. Meanwhile the English Parliament had been reduced to a "Rump Parliament", its Presbyterian members now evacuated. Thereupon the "Rump," which was what was left of the old Parliament, accused the King of high treason. The House of Lords refused to sit as a tribunal. A special tribunal was appointed, and it condemned the King to death. On the 30th of January of the year 1649, King Charles walked quietly out of a window of White Hall onto the scaffold. King Charles I was executed.

The period which followed the death of Charles is usually called after Oliver Cromwell. At first the unofficial Dictator of England, he was officially made Lord Protector in the year 1653.

Cromwell ruled five years. He used this period to continue the policies of Elizabeth. Spain once more became the arch enemy of England and war upon the Spaniard was made a national and sacred issue. Cromwell was a Puritan but adhering to independent church government and authoritarian civil government. He lacked the patience that Presbyterian and Parliamentary government require, and he was much too ready to assume more power that he rightfully should have. As a result, this program was destined for abandonment once Cromwell died. But despite the civil strife throughout the period, starting with Charles I's calling of Parliament, England prospered commercially. The Calvinistic and Puritan work ethic were good for business. In addition, the gospel of Jesus Christ spread, even as English commerce expanded around the world.

When Cromwell died in 1658, it was an easy matter for the Stuarts to return to their old kingdom. Indeed, they were welcomed as "deliverers" by the people. Provided the Stuarts were willing to forget about the Divine Right of their late and lamented father and were willing to recognize the superiority of Parliament, the people promised that they would be loyal and faithful subjects. Charles II had even signed onto the Solemn League and Covenant, so the Presbyterians were anticipating what Cromwell had foiled.

Two generations tried to make a success of this new arrangement. But the Stuarts apparently had not learned their lesson and were unable to drop their bad habits. Charles II, who came back in the year 1660, was an amiable but worthless person.

King Charles II's indolence and his constitutional insistence upon following the easiest course, together with his conspicuous success as a liar, prevented an open outbreak between himself and the mass of people. By the act of Uniformity in 1662 he broke the power of the Puritan clergy by banishing all dissenting clergymen from their parishes. By the so-called Conventicle Act of 1664, he tried to prevent the Presbyterian Dissenters from attending religious meetings by a threat of deportation to the West Indies.

Many Presbyterian dissenters – called Covenanters – lost their life for adhering to their Biblical principles. This looked too much like the "good old days" of Divine Right. People began to show the old and well-known signs of impatience with this dishonorable monarch, and Parliament suddenly experienced difficulty in providing the King with funds.

Since he could not get money from an unwilling Parliament, Charles borrowed it secretly from his neighbor and cousin King Louis of France. He betrayed his Protestant allies in return for 200,000 pounds per year and laughed at the poor simpletons of Parliament.

Economic independence suddenly gave the King great faith in his own strength. He had spent many years of exile among his Catholic relations and he had a secret liking for their religion.

Perhaps he could bring England back to Rome! He passed a Declaration of Indulgence which suspended the old laws against the Catholics and Dissenters. This happened just when Charles' younger brother James was said to have become a Catholic. All this looked suspicious to the man in the street, as a way ultimately to bring back Romanism to England. A new spirit of unrest entered the land. Many of the people wanted to prevent another outbreak of civil war. To them Royal Oppression and a Catholic King – yea, even Divine Right, – were preferable to a new struggle between members of the same race. Others however stood for principle above even life. These were the Scottish Covenanters and the English Puritan Dissenters.

For almost ten years, two great parties in England, the Whigs (the middle class element, called by this derisive name because in the year 1640 a lot of Scottish Whiggamores or horsedrovers headed by the Presbyterian clergy, had marched to Edinburgh to oppose the King) and the Tories (an epithet originally used against the Royalist Irish adherents but now applied to the supporters of the King) opposed each other, but neither wished to bring about a crisis. They allowed Charles to die peacefully in his bed and permitted the Catholic James II to succeed his brother in 1685.

But when James, after threatening the country with the terrible foreign invention of a "standing army" (which was to be commanded by Roman Catholic Frenchmen), issued a second Declaration of Indulgence in 1688 to increase toleration of Romanism (and thus ultimately to recover its lost position), and ordered it to be read in all Anglican churches, he went just a trifle beyond that line of sensible demarcation which can only be transgressed by the most popular of rulers under very exceptional circumstances. Seven Anglican bishops refused to comply with the Royal Command. They were accused of "seditious libel." They were brought before a court. The jury which pronounced the verdict of "not guilty" reaped a rich harvest of popular approval.

At this moment, James (who in a second marriage had taken to wife Maria of the Roman Catholic house of Modena-Este) became the father of a son. This meant that the throne was to go to a Roman Catholic boy rather than to his older sisters, Mary and Anne, who were Protestants. The man in the street again grew suspicious. It looked as if another civil war would break out. Then seven well-known men, both Whigs and Tories, wrote a letter asking the husband of James's oldest daughter Mary, William III the Stadtholder or head of the Dutch Republic, to come to England and deliver the country from its Romish sovereign.

On the fifth of November of the year 1688, William landed at Torbay. As he did not wish to make a martyr out of his father-in-law, he helped him to escape safely to France. On the 22nd of January of 1689 he summoned Parliament. On the 13th of February of the same year he and his wife Mary were proclaimed joint sovereigns of England and the country was saved for the Protestant cause.

Parliament, having undertaken to be something more than a mere advisory body to the King, made the best of its opportunities. The old Petition of Rights of the year 1628 was fished out of a forgotten nook of the archives. A second and more drastic Bill of Rights demanded that the sovereign of England should belong to the Anglican church. Furthermore, it stated that the king had no right to suspend the laws or permit certain privileged citizens to disobey certain laws. It stipulated that "without consent of Parliament no taxes could be levied, and no army could be maintained." Government by law was the realization of an aim of Presbyterian Puritans throughout the years of struggle.

In addition to these civil developments, it was confirmed that the established Church of England would be Anglican and adhere to the reformed Thirty-Nine Articles of Faith dating back to the 16th century, while the established Church of Scotland would be Presbyterian and adhere to the Westminster Standards. This settlement was less than what had been envisioned and committed to in the Solemn League and Covenant, a weakness that over time would undermine the United Kingdom's spiritual vitality and lessen God's blessing upon the society. In truth William was more concerned about the pocketbook than upon establishing a thorough Biblically reformed nation. He even maintained a personal mistress, in his personal life. But on the positive side, these developments did work to secure Protestantism for many years among the English-speaking peoples- albeit in a form which was weaker than it should have been.

During this eventful century in the Mother Country, the English were developing commerce and establishing colonies in far-flung locations around the globe, especially in North America and the Caribbean Islands, but even to territories in and around the Pacific Ocean. With this expansion the English brought their reformed Christian faith. Sometimes the reformed faith was according to the Anglican model (as in the southern colonies of what later became the United States), and sometimes it was according to the Puritan model (as in the northeastern colonies of what later became the United States).

In each case the gospel of Christ was brought to the native Americans with whom they came in contact. And these colonies became great outposts of the gospel, each generally having its established reformed church. Puritanism had a peculiarly great influence in the colonies of North America. The Puritans were the first to institute schools, colleges, printing presses, colonial constitutions, and many other advances- all in order to glorify Christ through the building up of His kingdom on earth. So, Protestantism greatly expanded westward, even though the Romish Counter-Reformation had brought its expansion to a halt in continental Europe. Protestant England was rapidly on its way to becoming the dominant nation in the world, a feat God blessed it with by the 19th century.

LET ME TELL YOU THE REAL STORY OF MANKIND

CHAPTER 40: The Balance of Power

As a contrast to the previous chapter, let me tell you what happened in France during the years when the English people were struggling to secure the reformed Protestant faith. A King came to the throne who rivaled his predecessors for wickedness: King Louis XIV. If you want to know what life becomes in a country following the Romish course, here is a good specimen.

The country over which the young king was called to rule was the most populous nation of that day. Louis came to the throne when Mazarin and Richelieu, the two powerful Roman Catholic Cardinals, had just hammered the ancient French Kingdom into the most strongly centralized state of the seventeenth century and thoroughly suppressed and undermined Huguenot Protestantism. He was himself a man of extraordinary ability. The present world is still surrounded by the memories of this age of the "Sun King." Its humanistic social life – which is what Romanism produces in defiance of Christ's rule – is based upon the manners of this court of Louis. In international and diplomatic relations, French became the official language of diplomacy and international gatherings. The theater of the King set the stage for its expansion worldwide, corrupting the morals of many peoples. During his reign the French Academy (an invention of Cardinal Richelieu) came to occupy a position in the world of letters which other countries have flattered by their imitation, thus inspiring and promoting ungodly humanistic education. We might continue this list for many pages. It is no matter of mere chance that our modern bill-of-fare is printed in French. The art of cooking was first perfected for the benefit of the great Monarch, but sadly the Monarch fed his belly but not his soul. The age of Louis XIV was a time of humanistic splendor, which has served as a stumbling block for many nations and many peoples. The

Stuarts of England did their best to imitate it in England, and unquestionably corrupted many thereby. The French society under the "Sun King" maintained the facade of Christianity, while thoroughly undermining it with false religion and false worship.

But the splendor of French society was only gilded gold. It was, to use Christ's words, a white-washed sepulcher. King Louis XIV succeeded his father in the year 1643. He died in the year 1715. That means that the government of France was in the hands of one single man for seventy-two years, almost two whole generations. It will be well to get a firm grasp of this idea, "one single man." Louis was the first of a long list of monarchs who in many countries established that particular form of highly efficient and despotic autocracy. He did not like kings who merely played at being rulers. He considered it his "divine right" to rule without consulting his subjects. He rejected the idea of a Parliamentary system which had been promoted by the reformed of continental Europe and the Puritans and Presbyterians of Great Britain.

Of course, the king could not attend to everything in person. He was obliged to surround himself with a few helpers and councilors. One or two generals, some experts upon foreign politics, a few clever financiers and economists would do for this purpose. But these dignitaries could act only through their Sovereign. They had no individual existence. To the mass of the people, the Sovereign actually represented in his own sacred person the government of their country. The glory of the common fatherland became the glory of a single dynasty. It meant the exact opposite of the system of the Protestant reformed nations. France was ruled of and by and for the House of Bourbon.

The disadvantages of such a system are clear. The King grew to be everything. Everybody else grew to be nothing at all. The old and useful nobility was gradually forced to give up its former shares in the government of the provinces. A little Royal bureaucrat, his fingers splashed with ink, sitting behind the greenish windows of a government building in faraway Paris, now performed the task which a hundred years before had been the duty of the feudal Lord. The feudal Lord, deprived of all work, moved to Paris to amuse himself as best he could at the court. Soon his estates began to suffer from that very dangerous economic sickness, known as "Absentee Landlordism." Within a single generation, the industrious and useful feudal administrators had become the well-mannered but quite useless loafers of the court of Versailles. And the best elements of French society – the reformed Protestant Huguenots – had been mostly chased out of the country or killed.

Louis was ten years old when the peace of Westphalia was concluded and the House of Habsburg, as a result of the Thirty Years War, lost its predominant position in Europe. It was inevitable that a man with his ambition should use so favorable a moment to gain for his own dynasty the honors which had formerly been held by the Habsburgs. In the year 1660 Louis had married Maria Theresa, daughter of the King of Spain. Soon afterward, his father-in-law, Philip IV, one of the half-witted Spanish Habsburgs, died. At once Louis claimed the Spanish Netherlands (Belgium) as part of his wife's dowry. Such an acquisition would have been disastrous to the peace of Europe and would have threatened the safety of the Protestant states. Under the leadership of Jan de Witt, Raadpensionaris or Foreign Minister of the United Seven Netherlands, the first great international alliance, the Triple Alliance of Sweden, England and Holland, of the year 1661, was concluded. It did not last long. With money and fair promises Louis bought up both King Charles and the Swedish Estates. Holland was betrayed by her allies and was left to her own fate. In the year 1672 the French invaded the low countries. They marched to the heart of the country. For a second time the dikes were opened, and the Royal Sun of France set amidst the mud of the Dutch marshes. The peace of Nimwegen which was concluded in 1678 settled nothing but merely anticipated another war.

A second war of aggression from 1689 to 1697, ending with the Peace of Ryswick, also failed to give Louis that position in the affairs of Europe to which he aspired. His old enemy, Jan de Witt, had been murdered by the Dutch rabble, but his successor, William III (whom you met in the last chapter), had checkmated all efforts of Louis to make France the ruler of Europe.

The great war for the Spanish succession, begun in the year 1701, immediately after the death of Charles II, the last of the Spanish Habsburgs, and ended in 1713 by the Peace of Utrecht, remained equally undecided, but it had ruined the treasury of Louis. On land the French king had been victorious, but the navies of England and Holland had spoiled all hope for an ultimate French victory; besides the long struggle had given birth to a new and fundamental principle of international politics, which thereafter made it impossible for one single nation to rule the whole of Europe or the whole of the world for any length of time.

That was the so-called "balance of power." It was not a written law but for three centuries it has been obeyed as closely as are the laws of nature. The people who originated the idea maintained that Europe, in its nationalistic stage of development, could only survive when there should be an absolute balance of the many conflicting interests of the entire continent. No single power or single dynasty must ever be allowed to dominate the others. In the aftermath of the Thirty Years War, the Habsburgs had been the victims of the application of this law. They, however, had been unconscious victims.

In order to preserve economic peace and the survival of smaller, less powerful states, "balance of power" politics became an operating principle. While this principle is not bad in and of itself- and indeed is very wise and necessary- it was sadly accompanied by a growing lack of spiritual vitality in many of the Protestant nations. They were attracted to some aspects of the humanism which Roman Catholic countries like France had to offer. Thus, politics was becoming not a means to glorify God, but to accumulate material possessions and to strive towards humanistic ends. Cold, economic considerations and calculations began to prevail in matters of international importance, instead of glorification of God through building up Christ's kingdom on earth and establishing conformity to the Ten Commandments. We discover the development of a new type of statesman, the statesman with the personal feelings of the slide rule and the cash-register.

Jan de Witt of the Netherlands was in many respects the first successful exponent of this new school of politics. William III was in many respects his pupil. And Louis XIV with all his fame and glory, was the first conscious victim. There have been many others since.

LET ME TELL YOU THE REAL STORY OF MANKIND

CHAPTER 41: The Rise of Russia

In the year 1492, as you know, Columbus discovered America. Early in the year, a Tyrolese by the name of Schnups, travelling as the head of a scientific expedition for the Archbishop of Tyrol, and provided with the best letters of introduction and excellent credit tried to reach the mythical town of Moscow. He did not succeed. When he reached the frontiers of this vast Moscovite state which was vaguely supposed to exist in the extreme Eastern part of Europe, he was firmly turned back. No foreigners were wanted. And Schnups went to visit the heathen Turk in Constantinople, in order that he might have something to report to his clerical master when he came back from his explorations.

Sixty-one years later, Richard Chancellor, trying to discover the North-eastern passage to the Indies, and blown by an ill wind into the White Sea, reached the mouth of the Dwina and found the Moscovite village of Kholmogory, a few hours from the spot where in 1584 the town of Archangel was founded. This time the foreign visitors were requested to come to Moscow and show themselves to the Grand Duke. They went and returned to England with the first commercial treaty ever concluded between Russia and the western world. Other nations soon followed, and something became known of this mysterious land.

Geographically, Russia is a vast plain. The Ural Mountains are low and form no barrier against invaders. The rivers are broad but often shallow. It was an ideal territory for nomads.

While the Roman Empire was founded, grew in power and disappeared again, Slavic tribes, who had long since left their homes in Central Asia, wandered aimlessly through the forests and plains of the region between the Dniester and Dnieper rivers. They were descendants of their ancient ancestor Japhet. The Greeks had sometimes met these Slavs and a few travellers of the third and fourth centuries mention them. Otherwise they were as little known as were the Nevada Indians in the year 1800.

Unfortunately for the peace of these primitive peoples, a very convenient trade-route ran through their country. This was the main road from northern Europe to Constantinople. It followed the coast of the Baltic until the Neva was reached. Then it crossed Lake Ladoga and went southward along the Volkhov river. Then through Lake Ilmen and up the small Lovat river. Then there was a short portage until the Dnieper was reached. Then down the Dnieper into the Black Sea.

The Norsemen knew of this road at a very early date. In the ninth century they began to settle in northern Russia, just as other Norsemen were laying the foundation for independent states in Germany and France. But in the year 862, three Norsemen, brothers, crossed the Baltic and founded three small dynasties. Of the three brothers, only one, Rurik, lived for a number of years. He took possession of the territory of his brothers, and twenty years after the arrival of this first Norseman, a Slavic state had been established with Kiev as its capital.

From Kiev to the Black Sea is a short distance. Soon the existence of an organized Slavic State became known in Constantinople. This meant a new field for the zealous missionaries of the Christian faith. Byzantine monks followed the Dnieper on their way northward and soon reached the heart of Russia. They found the people worshipping strange gods who were supposed to dwell in woods and rivers and in mountain caves. They taught them the Christian faith. There was no competition from the side of Roman missionaries or from proto-Protestant missionaries of Ireland and Scotland. These western missionaries were too busy educating the heathen Teutons or evangelizing northwestern Europe to bother about the distant Slavs. Hence

Russia received its religion and its alphabet and its first ideas of art and architecture from the Byzantine monks and as the Byzantine empire (a relic of the eastern Roman empire) had become very oriental and had lost many of its European traits, the Russians acquired these in consequence.

Politically speaking, these new states of the great Russian plains did not fare well. It was the Norse habit to divide every inheritance equally among all the sons. No sooner had a small state been founded but it was broken up among eight or nine heirs who in turn left their territory to an ever-increasing number of descendants. It was inevitable that these small competing states should quarrel among themselves. Anarchy was the order of the day. And when the red glow of the eastern horizon told the people of the threatened invasion of a savage Asiatic tribe, the little states were too weak and too divided to render any sort of defense against this terrible enemy.

It was in the year 1224 that the first great Tartar invasion took place and that the hordes of Jenghiz Khan, the conqueror of China, Bokhara, Tashkent and Turkestan made their first appearance in the west. The Slavic armies were beaten near the Kalka river and Russia was at the mercy of the Mongolians. Just as suddenly as they had come, they disappeared. Thirteen years later, in 1237, however, they returned. In less than five years they conquered every part of the vast Russian plains. Until the year 1380 when Dmitry Donskoi, Grand Duke of Moscow, beat them on the plains of Kulikovo, the Tartars were the masters of the Russian people.

All in all, it took the Russians two centuries to deliver themselves from this yoke. For a yoke it was a most offensive and objectionable one. It turned the Slavic peasants into miserable slaves. No Russian could hope to survive unless he was willing to creep before a dirty little yellow man who sat in a tent somewhere in the heart of the steppes of southern Russia and spat at him. It deprived the mass of the people of all feeling of honor and independence. It made hunger and misery and maltreatment and personal abuse the normal state of human existence. Until at last the average Russian, were he peasant or nobleman, went about his business like a neglected dog who has been beaten so often that his spirit has been broken and he dare not wag his tail without permission.

There was no escape. The horsemen of the Tartar Khan were fast and merciless. The endless prairie did not give a man a chance to cross into the safe territory of his neighbor. He must keep quiet and bear what his yellow master decided to inflict upon him or run the risk of death. Of course, Europe might have interfered. But Europe was engaged upon business of its own, fighting the quarrels between the Romish Pope and the emperor or suppressing this or that or the other proto-Protestant movement. And so, Europe left the Slav to his fate.

The final savior of Russia from this Mongolian oppression was one of the many small states, founded by the early Norse rulers. It was situated in the heart of the Russian plain. Its capital, Moscow, was upon a steep hill on the banks of the Moskwa river. This little principality, by dint of pleasing the Tartar (when it was necessary to please) and opposing him (when it was safe to do so), had, during the middle of the fourteenth century made itself the leader of a new national life. It must be remembered that the Tartars were wholly deficient in constructive political ability. They could only destroy. Their chief aim in conquering new territories was to obtain revenue. To get this revenue in the form of taxes, it was necessary to allow certain remnants of the old political organization to continue. Hence there were many little towns, surviving by the grace of the Great Khan, that they might act as tax-gatherers and rob their neighbors for the benefit of the Tartar treasury. These were thorough-going pagans, who had no desire to create a nation that would respect the rights of God and men.

The state of Moscow, growing fat at the expense of the surrounding territory, finally became strong enough to risk open rebellion against its masters, the Tartars. It was successful and its fame as the leader in the cause of Russian independence made Moscow the natural center for all those who still believed in a better future for the Slavic race. In the year 1458, Constantinople was taken by the Turks. Ten years later, under the rule of Ivan III, Moscow informed the western world that the Slavic state laid claim to the worldly and spiritual inheritance of the lost Byzantine Empire, and such traditions of the Roman empire as had survived in Constantinople. A generation afterwards, under Ivan the Terrible, the grand dukes of Moscow were strong enough to adopt the title of Cæsar, or Tsar, and to demand recognition by the western powers of Europe.

LET ME TELL YOU THE REAL STORY OF MANKIND

In the year 1598, with Feodor the First, the old Muscovite dynasty, descendants of the original Norseman Rurik, came to an end. For the next seven years, a Tartar half-breed, by the name of Boris Godunow, reigned as Tsar. It was during this period that the future destiny of the large masses of the Russian people was decided. This Empire was rich in land but very poor in money. There was no trade and there were no factories. Its few cities were dirty villages. It was composed of a strong central government and a vast number of illiterate peasants. This government, a mixture of Slavic, Norse, Byzantine and Tartar influences, recognized nothing beyond the interest of the state. To defend this state, it needed an army. To gather the taxes, which were necessary to pay the soldiers, it needed civil servants. To pay these many officials it needed land. In the vast wilderness on the east and west there was a sufficient supply of this commodity. But land without a few laborers to till the fields and tend the cattle, has no value. Therefore, the old nomadic peasants were robbed of one privilege after the other, until finally, during the first year of the sixteenth century, they were formally made a part of the soil upon which they lived. The Russian peasants ceased to be free men. They became serfs or slaves and they remained serfs until the year 1861, when their fate had become so terrible that they were beginning to die out. In the seventeenth century, this new state with its growing territory, which was spreading quickly into Siberia, had become a force with which the rest of Europe was obliged to reckon. In 1618, after the death of Boris Godunow, the Russian nobles had elected one of their own number to be Tsar. He was Michael, the son of Feodor, of the Moscow family of Romanow who lived in a little house just outside the Kremlin.

In the year 1672 his great-grandson, Peter, the son of another Feodor, was born. When the child was ten years old, his stepsister Sophia took possession of the Russian throne. The little boy was allowed to spend his days in the suburbs of the national capital, where the foreigners lived. Surrounded by Scotch barkeepers, Dutch traders, Swiss apothecaries, Italian barbers, French dancing teachers and German schoolmasters, the young prince obtained a first but rather extraordinary impression of that far away and mysterious Europe where things were done differently.

When he was seventeen years old, he suddenly pushed Sister Sophia from the throne. Peter himself became the ruler of Russia. He was not contented with being the Tsar of a semi-barbarous and half-Asiatic people. He must be the sovereign head of a civilized nation. To change Russia overnight from a Byzantine-Tartar state into a European empire was no small undertaking. It needed strong hands and a capable head. Peter possessed both.

In the year 1698, the great operation of grafting Modern Europe upon Ancient Russia was performed. The patient did not die. But he never got over the shock. And ever since Russia has been grappling between its half-European, half-Oriental existence.

LET ME TELL YOU THE REAL STORY OF MANKIND

CHAPTER 42: Russia *vs.* Sweden

In the year 1698, Tsar Peter set forth upon his first voyage to western Europe. He travelled by way of Berlin and went to Holland and to England. As a child he had almost been drowned sailing a homemade boat in the duck pond of his father's country home. This passion for water remained with him to the end of his life. In a practical way it showed itself in his wish to give his land-locked domains access to the open sea.

While the unpopular and harsh young ruler was away from home, the friends of the old Russian ways in Moscow set to work to undo all his reforms. A sudden rebellion among his lifeguards, the Streltsi regiment, forced Peter to hasten home by the fast mail. He appointed himself executioner-in-chief and the Streltsi were hanged and quartered and killed to the last man. Sister Sophia, who had been the head of the rebellion, was locked up in a cloister and the rule of Peter began in earnest. This scene was repeated in the year 1716 when Peter had gone on his second western trip. That time the reactionaries followed the leadership of Peter's half-witted son, Alexis. Again, the Tsar returned in great haste. Alexis was beaten to death in his prison cell and the friends of the old-fashioned Byzantine ways marched thousands of dreary miles to their final destination in the Siberian lead mines. After that, no further outbreaks of popular discontent took place. Until the time of his death, Peter could reform in peace.

It is not easy to give you a list of his reforms in chronological order. The Tsar worked with furious haste. He followed no system. He issued his decrees with such rapidity that it is difficult to keep count. Peter seemed to feel that everything that had ever happened before was entirely wrong. The whole of Russia therefore must be changed within the shortest possible time. When he died, he left behind a well-trained army of

200,000 men and a navy of fifty ships. The old system of government had been abolished overnight. The Duma, or convention of Nobles, had been dismissed and in its stead, the Tsar had surrounded himself with an advisory board of state officials, called the Senate.

Russia was divided into eight large "governments" or provinces. Roads were constructed. Towns were built. Industries were created wherever it pleased the Tsar, without any regard for the presence of raw material. Canals were dug and mines were opened in the mountains of the east. In this land of illiterates, schools were founded and establishments of higher learning, together with Universities and hospitals and professional schools. Dutch naval engineers and tradesmen and artisans from all over the world were encouraged to move to Russia. Printing shops were established, but all books must be first read by the imperial censors. The duties of each class of society were carefully written down in a new law and the entire system of civil and criminal laws was gathered into a series of printed volumes. The old Russian costumes were abolished by Imperial decree, and policemen, armed with scissors, watching all the country roads, changed the long-haired Russian moujiks suddenly into a pleasing imitation of smooth-shaven west-Europeans.

In religious matters, the Tsar tolerated no division of power. There must be no chance of a rivalry between an Emperor and a Pope as had happened in Europe. In the year 1721, Peter made himself head of the Russian Church. The Patriarchate of Moscow was abolished, and the Holy Synod made its appearance as the highest source of authority in all matters of the Established Church of Russia.

Since, however, these many reforms could not be successful while the old Russian elements had a rallying point in the town of Moscow, Peter decided to move his government to a new capital. Amidst the unhealthy marshes of the Baltic Sea the Tsar built this new city. He began to reclaim the land in the year 1703. Forty thousand peasants worked for years to lay the foundations for this Imperial city. The Swedes attacked Peter and tried to destroy his town and illness and misery killed tens of thousands of the peasants. But the work was continued, winter and summer, and the ready-made town soon began to grow. In the year 1712, it was officially declared to be the "Imperial Residence." A dozen years later it had 75,000 inhabitants and beautiful buildings.

Twice a year, the whole city was flooded by the Neva. But the terrific willpower of the Tsar created dykes and canals and the floods ceased to do harm. When Peter died in 1725, he was the owner of the largest city in northern Europe: St. Petersburg.

Of course, this sudden growth of so dangerous a rival had been a source of great worry to all the neighbors. From his side, Peter had watched with interest the many adventures of his Baltic rival, the kingdom of Sweden. In the year 1654, Christina, the only daughter of Gustavus Adolphus, the hero of the Thirty Years War, had renounced the throne and had gone to Rome to end her days as a devout Roman Catholic. A Protestant nephew of Gustavus Adolphus had succeeded the last Queen of the House of Vasa. Under Charles X and Charles XI, the new dynasty had brought Sweden to its highest point of development. But in 1697, Charles XI died suddenly and was succeeded by a boy of fifteen, Charles XII.

This was the moment for which many of the northern states had waited. During the great religious wars of the seventeenth century, Sweden had grown at the expense of her neighbors. The time had come, so the owners thought, to balance the account. At once war broke out between Russia, Poland,

Denmark and Saxony on the one side, and Sweden on the other. The raw and untrained armies of Peter were disastrously beaten by Charles in the famous battle of Narva in November of the year 1700. Then Charles, one of the most interesting military geniuses of that century, turned against his other enemies and for nine years he hacked and burned his way through the villages and cities of Poland, Saxony, Denmark and the Baltic provinces, while Peter drilled and trained his soldiers in distant Russia.

As a result, in the year 1709, in the battle of Poltawa, the Moscovites destroyed the exhausted armies of Sweden. Charles continued to be a highly picturesque figure, a wonderful hero of romance, but in his vain attempt to have his revenge, he ruined his own country. In the year 1718, he was accidentally killed or assassinated (we do not know which) and when peace was made in 1721, in the town of Nystadt, Sweden had lost all of her former Baltic possessions except Finland. The new Russian state, created by Peter, had become the leading power of northern Europe. But already a new rival was on the way. The Prussian state was taking shape.

CHAPTER 43: The Rise of Prussia

The history of Prussia is the history of a frontier district. In the ninth century, Charlemagne had transferred the old center of civilization from the Mediterranean to the wild regions of northwestern Europe. His Frankish soldiers had pushed the frontier of Europe further and further towards the east. They had conquered many lands from the heathenish Slavs and Lithuanians who were living in the plain between the Baltic Sea and the Carpathian Mountains, and the Franks administered those outlying districts just as the United States used to administer her territories before they achieved the dignity of statehood.

The frontier state of Brandenburg had been originally founded by Charlemagne to defend his eastern possessions against raids of the wild Saxon tribes. The Wends, a Slavic tribe which inhabited that region, were subjugated during the tenth century and their marketplace, by the name of Brennabor, became the center of and gave its name to the new province of Brandenburg.

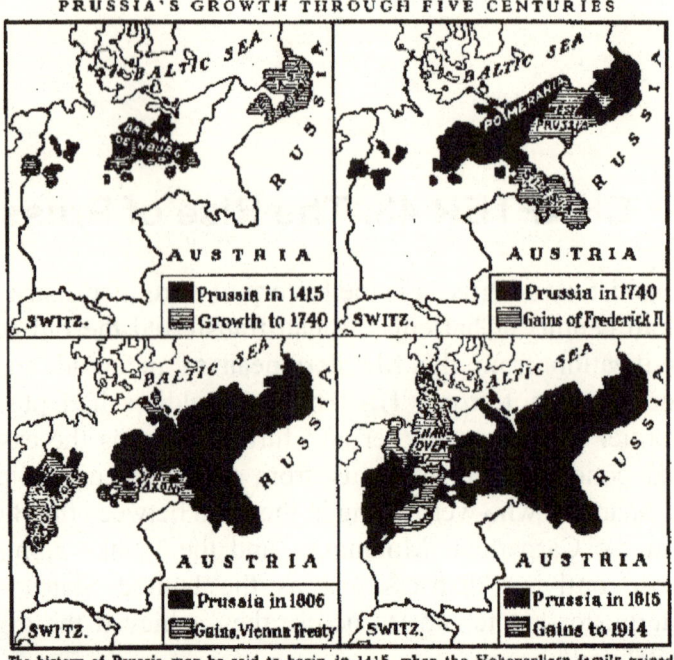

PRUSSIA'S GROWTH THROUGH FIVE CENTURIES

The history of Prussia may be said to begin in 1415, when the Hohenzollern family gained possession of the little electorate of Brandenburg. For two centuries there was no indication that this poor flat country was destined to be the nucleus of the greatest of the German states, but after the Hohenzollerns acquired East Prussia in 1618, their dominions steadily grew until they included two thirds of the territory and three fourths of the population of all Germany.

During the eleventh, twelfth, thirteenth and fourteenth centuries, a succession of noble families exercised the functions of imperial governor in this frontier state. Finally, in the fifteenth century the House of Hohenzollern made its appearance, and as Electors of Brandenburg commenced to change a sandy and forlorn frontier territory into one of the most efficient empires of the modern world.

These Hohenzollerns, who remained rulers until the conclusion of World War I in the twentieth century, came originally from southern Germany. They were of very humble origin. In the twelfth century a certain Frederick of Hohenzollern had made a providential marriage and had been appointed keeper of the castle of Nuremberg. His descendants had used every chance and every opportunity to improve their power and after several centuries of watchful grabbing, they had been appointed to the dignity of Elector, the name given to those sovereign princes who were supposed to elect the

Emperors of the old German Empire. During the Reformation, they had taken the side of the Protestants, at first becoming Lutheran.

The Hohenzollerns obtained rule over Prussia by the marriage in 1594 of John Sigismund, elector of Brandenburg, to the eldest daughter of the duke of Prussia. John Sigismund became Calvinist, but most of the people in his realm remained Lutheran. Henceforth his realm would remain bi-confessional, part Reformed and part Lutheran. Not only so, the early seventeenth century found the Hohenzollerns among the most powerful of the north German princes.

During the Thirty Years War in the 17th century, both Protestants and Catholics had sadly plundered Brandenburg and Prussia. But under Protestant Frederick William, the Great Elector, the damage was quickly repaired and by a wise and careful use of all the economic and intellectual forces of the country, a state was founded in which there was practically no waste.

Modern Prussia, a state in which the individual and his wishes and aspirations have been absorbed by the interests of the community as a whole, dates back to the father of Frederick the Great. Frederick William I. He was a hardworking, parsimonious Prussian sergeant, with a great love for bar-room stories and strong Dutch tobacco, an intense dislike of all frills and feathers, (especially if they were of French origin,) and possessed of but one idea. That idea was Duty. Severe with himself, he tolerated no weakness in his subjects, whether they be generals or common soldiers. The relation between himself and his son Frederick II was never cordial, to say the least. The son considered the father to have boorish stereotypical German manners. The son's love for French humanistic manners, literature, philosophy and music was rejected by father as a manifestation of sissy-ness. The father was more in the mold of his conservative Protestant heritage; but the son was in the mold of Romish French humanism. There followed a terrible outbreak between these two different temperaments. Frederick tried to escape to England. He was caught and court-martialed and forced to witness the decapitation of his best friend who had tried to help him. Thereupon as part of his punishment, the young prince was sent to a little fortress somewhere in the provinces to be taught the details of his future business of being a king. It proved a blessing in disguise. When Frederick came to the throne in 1740, he knew how his country was managed from the birth certificate of a pauper's son to the minutest detail of a complicated annual Budget. His father left him a regime with the best trained army in Europe, a large financial reserve, and an efficient government bureaucracy.

As an author, especially in his essay called the "Anti-Machiavel," Frederick had expressed his contempt for the political creed of the ancient Florentine historian, who had advised his princely pupils to lie and cheat whenever it was necessary to do so for the benefit of their country. The ideal ruler in Frederick's volume was the first servant of his people, the enlightened despot after the example of King Louis XIV of France. In practice, however, Frederick, while working for his people twenty hours a day, tolerated no one to be near him as a counsellor. His ministers were superior clerks. Prussia was his private possession, to be treated according to his own wishes. And nothing was allowed to interfere with the interest of the state. My son, this is forever the fruit of Romanist humanism. Neither God's nor man's interests are rightly protected when men refuse to submit to Christ as Lord.

Frederick II (also known as Frederick the Great), who lived from 1740 to 1786, undermined the Christian Evangelical Establishment of his realm. The Enlightenment humanist Voltaire of France praised him. Since the reformation, this establishment was Protestant and evangelical. He relaxed the standards, allowing greater freedom to Romanism to corrupt the nation. And this conveniently allowed him to amass more territory and more power for the State apparatus he controlled.

In the year 1740, the Emperor Charles VI of Austria died. He had tried to make the position of his only daughter, Maria Theresa, secure through a solemn treaty, written black on white, upon a large piece of parchment. But no sooner had the old emperor been deposited in the ancestral crypt of the Habsburg family, than the armies of Frederick were marching towards the Austrian frontier to occupy that part of Silesia for which (together with almost everything else in central Europe) Prussia clamored, on account of some ancient and doubtful rights of claim. In a number of wars, Frederick conquered all of Silesia, and although he was often very near defeat, he maintained himself in his newly acquired territories against all Austrian counterattacks.

Europe took due notice of this sudden appearance of a very powerful new state. In the eighteenth century the Germans were a people who had been ruined by the great religious wars and who were not held in high esteem by anyone. Frederick, by an effort as sudden and quite as terrific as that of Peter of Russia, changed this attitude of contempt into one of fear. The internal affairs of Prussia were arranged so skillfully that the subjects had less reason for complaint than elsewhere. The treasury showed an annual surplus instead of a deficit. Everything was quite efficient: from the judiciary system to the roads to the schools and universities. The government bureaucracy was scrupulously honest, a characteristic Protestantism reinforced. This made the people feel that whatever services were demanded of them, they (to speak the vernacular) got their money's worth.

After having been for several centuries the battlefield of the French and the Austrians and the Swedes and the Danes and the Poles, Germany, encouraged by the example of Prussia, began to regain self-confidence. And this was the work of the little old man, with his hook-nose and his old uniforms covered with snuff, who said very unpleasant things about his neighbors, and who played the scandalous game of eighteenth century diplomacy without any regard for the truth, provided he could gain something by his lies. This is in spite of his essay, "Anti-Machiavel" In the year 1786 the end came. His friends were all gone. Children he had never had. He died alone, tended by a single servant and his faithful dogs, whom he loved better than human beings because, as he said, they were never ungrateful and remained true to their friends.

Such is always the tragic end of a man or a people that lives for self instead of for God. That is a good lesson you will want to remember.

CHAPTER 44: The Mercantile System

We have seen how, during the sixteenth and the seventeenth centuries, the states of our modern world began to take shape. Their origins were different in almost every case. Some had been the result of the deliberate effort of a single king. Others had happened by an unusual set of historical circumstances. Still others had been the result of favorable natural geographic boundaries. But once they had been founded, they had all of them tried to strengthen their internal administration and to exert the greatest possible influence upon foreign affairs. All this of course had cost a great deal of money. The medieval state with its lack of centralized power did not depend upon a rich treasury. The king got his revenues from the crown domains and his civil service paid for itself. The modern centralized state was a more complicated affair. The old knights disappeared and hired government officials or bureaucrats took their place. Army, navy, and internal administration demanded millions. The question then became where was this money to be found?

Gold and silver had been a rare commodity in the middle ages. The average man, as I have told you, never saw a gold piece as long as he lived. Only the inhabitants of the large cities were familiar with silver coin. The discovery of America and the exploitation of the Peruvian mines changed all this. The center of trade was transferred from the Mediterranean to the Atlantic seaboard. The old "commercial cities" of Italy lost their financial importance. New "commercial nations" took their place and gold and silver were no longer a curiosity.

Through Spain and Portugal and Holland and England, precious metals began to find their way to Europe. The sixteenth century had its own writers on the subject of political economy, and they evolved a theory of national wealth which made sense in many ways and of the greatest possible benefit to their respective countries. They reasoned that both gold and silver were actual wealth. Therefore, they believed that the country with the largest supply of actual cash in the vaults of its treasury and its banks was at the same time the richest country. And since money meant armies, it followed that the richest country was also the most powerful and could rule the rest of the world.

We call this system the "mercantile system," and it was widely accepted. In practice, the Mercantile system worked out as follows: To get the largest surplus of precious metals a country must have a favorable balance of export trade. If you can export more to your neighbor than he exports to your own country, he will owe you money and will be obliged to send you some of his gold. Hence you gain and he loses. As a result of this creed, the economic program of almost every seventeenth century state was as follows:

1. Try to get possession of as many precious metals as you can.
2. Encourage foreign trade in preference to domestic trade.
3. Encourage those industries which change raw materials into exportable finished products.
4. Encourage a large population, for you will need workmen for your factories and an agricultural community does not raise enough workmen.
5. Let the State watch this process and interfere whenever it is necessary to do so.

Instead of leaving International Trade to market forces, the people of the sixteenth and seventeenth centuries tried to regulate their commerce by the help of official decrees and royal laws and financial help on the part of the government. And once one country's government engaged in the Mercantilist strategy, it was difficult for other countries not to follow suit.

In the sixteenth century Charles V adopted this Mercantile System (which was then something entirely new) and introduced it into his many possessions. Elizabeth of England flattered him by her imitation. The Bourbons, especially King Louis XIV, were fanatical adherents of this doctrine and Colbert, his great minister of finance, became the prophet of Mercantilism to whom all Europe looked for guidance.

The entire foreign policy of Cromwell was a practical application of the Mercantile System. It was invariably directed against the rich rival Republic of Holland. For the Dutch shippers, as the common-carriers of the merchandise of Europe, had certain leanings towards free-trade and therefore had to be destroyed at all cost.

It will be easily understood how such a system must affect the colonies. A colony under the Mercantile System became merely a reservoir of gold and silver and spices, which was to be tapped for the benefit of the home country. The Asiatic, American and African supply of precious metals and the raw materials of these tropical countries became a monopoly of the state which happened to own that particular colony. No outsider was ever allowed within the precincts and no native was permitted to trade with a merchant whose ship flew a foreign flag.

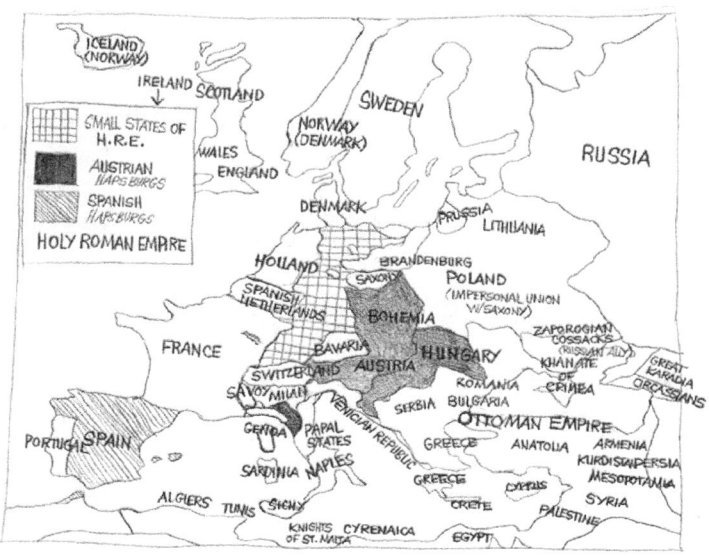

Undoubtedly, the Mercantile System encouraged the development of young industries in certain countries where there never had been any manufacturing before. It built roads and dug canals and made for better means of transportation. It demanded greater skill among the workmen and gave the merchant a better social position, while it weakened the power of the landed aristocracy.

On the other hand, it caused misery as well. It made the natives in the colonies the victims of what could too often be described as a most shameless exploitation. It exposed the citizens of the home country to an even more terrible fate. It helped in a great measure to turn every land into an armed camp and divided the world into little bits of territory, each working for its own direct benefit, while striving at all times to destroy the power of its neighbors and get hold of their treasures. It laid so much stress upon the importance of owning wealth that "being rich" came to be regarded as the sole virtue of the average citizen. Economic systems come and go like the fashions in surgery and in the clothes of women, and during the nineteenth century the Mercantile System was discarded by some leading countries at the time in favor of a system of free and open competition. But there has continued to this day a debate between free trade and protectionism, as well as those who advocate for free trade among similar allies but protectionism with enemies and dissimilar nations.

CHAPTER 45: The Enlightenment

"Heresy" has, throughout most of Christian history, been rightly regarded as a disease, but our modern era – especially in the West – has to a great degree lost an appropriate understanding of this, so let me explain it to you. Nowadays, when we see a man neglecting the personal cleanliness of his body and his home and exposing himself and his children to the dangers of typhoid fever or another preventable disease, we send for the board-of-health and the health officer calls upon the police to aid him in removing this person who is a danger to the safety of the entire community. In previous centuries, when men were more clear-headed about reality, a heretic, a man or a woman who openly doubted the fundamental principles of religion, was considered a more terrible menace than a typhoid carrier. Typhoid fever might (very likely would) destroy the body. But heresy would positively destroy the immortal soul. And the heresy has the power to corrupt a society and bring the judgment of God down upon it. A little leaven can easily end up leavening the whole lump.

In the years to come, you will hear a great deal about preventive medicine. Preventive medicine simply means that our doctors do not wait until their patients are sick, then step forward and cure them. On the contrary, they study the patient and the conditions under which he lives when he (the patient) is perfectly well and they remove every possible cause of illness by cleaning up rubbish, by teaching him what to eat and what to avoid, and by giving him a few simple ideas of personal hygiene. They go even further than that, and these good doctors enter the schools and teach the children how to use toothbrushes and how to avoid catching colds.

In the previous centuries, when this was more widely recognized in Christian society, which regarded (as I have tried to show you) bodily illness as much less important than sickness which threatened the soul, there was organized a system of spiritual preventive medicine. As soon as a child was old enough to spell his first words, he was educated in the true principles of the Christian faith. Indirectly, this proved to be a good thing for the general progress of the people of Europe. The Protestant lands were soon dotted with schools. They used a great deal of very valuable time to explain the Catechism, but they gave instruction in other things besides theology. They encouraged reading and they were responsible for the great prosperity of the printing trade.

But by the latter half of the 17th century and into the 18th century, a general spiritual fatigue began to settle into Britain and its American colonies, as well as throughout most of Europe. Along with this fatigue, Romish humanism was looking a lot more attractive than it had when Protestants had left the Romish yoke.

First, there was a fatigue with religious war, strife, and persecution. For example, the Thirty Years' War, with its great destruction in the battle pitting Romanists against Protestants, had exhausted Europeans. Also, the English civil wars of the 1640s followed later by the Stuarts' persecutions of Presbyterian and other dissenters made people desirous of peace.

Second, there was a fatigue with the seeming inability of the branches within Protestantism to unite. First there was the division between Lutheranism and Reformed. And within the reformed churches of the United Kingdom there were these three branches:

- Episcopal (the Anglican Church of England) – adhering to the Thirty-Nine Articles
- Presbyterian – adhering to the Westminster Standards
- Congregational – adhering to the Westminster Standards except regarding church government

The primary difference among these three concerned the form of church government. In addition, Presbyterianism and congregationalism were clearer and more emphatic that the elements of worship be limited to that which is prescribed in scripture, so as to remain pure of corruption and invention (hence the name 'puritan' to describe them).

Since the differences which separated them could not readily be ironed out, the intermediate measure had been to give each certain territory within the United Kingdom to be the established church. England, Wales, Ireland and the southern American colonies were Anglican; Scotland and effectively many colonial frontier settlements were Presbyterian; and New England was Congregational. While this led to a measure of peace, it nevertheless represented a disappointment that reformed Christians and the kingdom could not unite upon a common confession. And throughout Europe a similar development occurred, with Lutheran and Reformed each having its own territories. A united visible church with a common confession was not able to be forged at the time, though efforts were made. The closest thing to it was the great Synod of Dort among the Reformed. And there was even an effort to get the reformed of Europe to embrace the Westminster Standards, but local civil strife prevented its accomplishment.

Third, there was fatigue with controlling and containing the rising swell of non-reformed factions and sects, including Anabaptists, Baptists and Quakers, as well as others. Then there were the Roman Catholics, who never had entirely left most of the Protestant nations. One way to suppress them seemed to be by civil force, by the use typically of banishment from the territory, but many people were growing fatigued by this method of suppression. This was part of an even broader fatigue with the imposition of authority concerning religion by the state, church and family.

Fourth, there was fatigue, especially among many intellectuals, with the reformed view of man's incapacity to attain knowledge apart from divine revelation (i.e., scripture) due to man's depraved sinful nature. (And as I have previously mentioned, Lutheranism early on became weak in this area.) Some viewed this proposition as a hindrance and not a help to intellectual, societal and cultural development. It was becoming more fashionable to believe only that which could be deduced by reason (the rationalism of Descartes) or by observation in experience (the empiricism of Bacon and Locke), and to abandon a pre-suppositional approach to knowledge according to Augustine's dictum, "I believe in order that I may understand."

Fifth, there was fatigue among many, especially the more economically prosperous, with seeking to obey the regimen of the historic reformed faith, as summarized in the Ten Commandments. This fatigue compounded as many Britons enjoyed increasing prosperity with international commerce and colonization. Much of the prosperity which England and its American colonies enjoyed was a fruit of the Protestant work ethic, but this same prosperity tended towards more materialistic concerns and away from religious strictures. It also made time for more worldly entertainments.

Sixth, there was fatigue among many people within reformed churches, especially in the middle- and lower-class ranks, at a growing prevalence of lukewarm religion in the established reformed churches, especially arising from the spiritual fatigue among the economically prosperous. Many saw people just going through the motions of the reformed and Protestant religion, but with very little heart for Christ. Even in places like Puritan New England, Increase Mather observed that "clear, sound conversions are not frequent. Many of the rising generation are profane Drunkards, Swearers, Licentious and Scoffers at the power of Godliness."

Out of this milieu of fatigue, two great movements swept through the English-speaking world: the Enlightenment- which I will explain to you in this chapter- and the Great Awakening- which I will explain to you in the next.

The Enlightenment was a philosophical movement arising out of the 17th century which advocated a rational and scientific approach to religious, social, political, and economic issues, as opposed to an approach based upon divine revelation. As such, it promoted a secular view of the world and a general sense of progress and perfectibility. And it attacked religious authority, dogmatism, intolerance, censorship, and economic and social restraints. It sought to usher in an Age of Reason that it was believed would rid mankind of the ills it faced.

J. Parnell McCarter

Paving the way for the Enlightenment was a French-born philosopher named Descartes (1596-1650). Descartes sought to prove how, starting from a position of universal doubt, he could through reason arrive at a system of truth. This methodology has earned him the title of the 'father of modern philosophy.' As we have noted, this methodology directly contradicted the historic reformed, Biblical view of theologians like Augustine and Calvin whose methodology was instead: 'I believe in order that I may understand' (or as worded in scripture, 'the fear of the Lord is the beginning of wisdom'). Reformed Christianity stresses man's inability to attain true knowledge about the fundamental nature of God and man apart from divine revelation, due to man's sinful corruption.

Not surprisingly, Descartes rejected this reformed principle, for he was Roman Catholic, educated in the Jesuit College at La Flèche and the University of Poitiers. Romanist humanism had rejected the doctrine of the total depravity of fallen man, long before even Descartes. Descartes had significant influence even in Protestant countries, residing much of his life in Holland. Descartes' credibility was certainly enhanced by his significant achievements in mathematics and science.

It is not hard to see how the Enlightenment answered the general fatigue of the age, especially among the more economically prosperous and educated ranks. It promised a way to maintain social stability through reasonable approaches, while offering the prospect of avoiding the bloodshed and strife that had come with centuries of society based in religion. It offered the prospect of healing sectarian division. It offered the opportunity of more freedom of expression and thought, outside the confines of Biblical dogma.

The philosopher who arguably most popularized the Enlightenment among the English-speaking peoples was John Locke (1632-1704). Locke argued that people had the gift of reason, or the ability to think.

In the "Essay Concerning Human Understanding" Locke proposed that the mind is born blank, a tabula rasa upon which the world describes itself through the experience of the five senses. Knowledge arising from sensation is perfected by reflection, thus enabling humans to arrive at such ideas as space, time, and infinity.

Based upon man's presumed native ability to reason, Locke thought men had the natural ability to govern themselves and to look after the well-being of society. He wrote, "The state of nature has a law of nature to govern it, which [treats] everyone [equally]. Reason, which is that law, teaches all mankind... that being all equal and independent, no one ought to harm another in his life, health or possessions." Locke did not believe that

God had chosen a group or family of people to rule countries. He rejected the Divine Right of Kings, which many kings and queens used to justify their right to rule.

Instead, he argued that governments should only operate with the consent of the people they are governing. In this way, Locke supported democracy as a form of government. Locke wrote, "We have learned from] history we have reason to conclude that all peaceful beginnings of government have been laid in the consent of the people." Governments were formed, according to Locke, to protect the right to life, the right to freedom, and the right to property. Their rights were absolute, belonging to all the people. Locke also believed that government power should be divided equally into three branches of government so that politicians will not face the "temptation... to grasp at [absolute] power." If any government abused these rights instead of protecting them, then the people had the right to rebel and form a new government.

John Locke spoke out against the control of any man against his will. This control was acceptable neither in the form of an unfair government, nor in slavery. Locke wrote, "The natural liberty of man is to be free from any superior power on earth, and not to be under the will or legislative authority of man, but only have the law of nature for his rule."

Consonant with this opinion, Locke asserted in "A Letter Concerning Toleration" that "the toleration of those that differ from others in matters of religion is so agreeable to the Gospel of Jesus Christ, and to the genuine reason of mankind, that it seems monstrous for men to be so blind as not to perceive the necessity and advantage of it in so clear a light."

Locke's ideas were becoming increasingly embraced in the 18th century, in the American colonies as well as throughout much of Europe. Among those influenced was a young man that many have contended is the foremost theologian of the 18th century in America, if not the world: Jonathan Edwards. Edwards was born in Connecticut in 1703 and educated at home and at Yale University. As a youth, he had a keen interest in natural science, and wrote treatises "On Insects" and "On the Rainbow". When he was fourteen, he discovered the just-published writings of John Locke, doing so, as he said, "with greater pleasure than the greediest miser uncovering a rich hoard of gold and silver coins." Locke heavily influenced Edwards' philosophy, especially in the areas of psychology (how the human mind works) and epistemology (how we know things).

The Enlightenment was to have a profound influence in the United Kingdom and throughout Europe.

CHAPTER 46: England, Scotland, and the English Colonies in the 18th Century

We had our journey through English history with William as king at the conclusion of the seventeenth century. During William's reign the nature of the King's Cabinet evolved. No king of course can rule alone. He needs a few trusted advisors. The Tudors had their Great Council which was composed of Nobles and Clergy. This body grew too large. It was restricted to the small "Privy Council." In the course of time it became the custom of these councilors to meet the king in a cabinet in the palace. Hence, they were called the "Cabinet Council." After a short while they were known as the "Cabinet."

William, like most English sovereigns before him, had chosen his advisors from among all parties. But with the increased strength of Parliament, he had found it impossible to direct the politics of the country with the help of the Tories while the Whigs had a majority in the house of Commons. Therefore, the Tories had been dismissed and the Cabinet Council had been composed entirely of Whigs. A few years later when the Whigs lost their power in the House of Commons, the king, for the sake of convenience, was obliged to look for his support among the leading Tories. Until his death in 1702, William was too busy fighting Louis of France to bother much about the government of England. Practically all important affairs had been left to his Cabinet Council. When William's sister-in-law, Anne, succeeded him in 1702 this condition of affairs continued. When she died in 1714 (and not a single one of her seventeen children survived her) the throne went to George I of the House of Hanover, the son of Sophie, granddaughter of James I.

This somewhat rustic monarch, who never learned a word of English, was entirely lost in the complicated mazes of England's political arrangements. He left everything to his Cabinet Council and kept away from their meetings, which bored him as he did not understand a single sentence. In this way the Cabinet got into the habit of ruling England and Scotland (whose Parliament had been joined to that of England in 1707) without bothering the King, who was apt to spend a great deal of his time on the continent.

During the reign of George I and George II, a succession of great Whigs (of whom one, Sir Robert Walpole, held office for twenty-one years) formed the Cabinet Council of the King. Their leader was finally recognized as the official leader not only of the actual Cabinet but also of the majority party in power in Parliament. The attempts of George III to take matters into his own hands and not to leave the actual business of government to his Cabinet were so disastrous that they were never repeated. And from the earliest years of the eighteenth century on, England enjoyed representative government, with a responsible ministry which conducted the affairs of the land.

To be quite true, this government did not represent all classes of society. Less than one man in a dozen had the right to vote. But it was the foundation for the modern representative form of government. In a quiet and orderly fashion, it took the power away from the King and placed it in the hands of an ever-increasing number of popular representatives. It saved England from most of the revolutionary outbreaks which proved so disastrous to the European continent in the eighteenth and nineteenth centuries. And at least in respect of constitutional parliamentary government which was professedly Protestant, this fulfilled the aspirations of the Presbyterian Puritans of England and Scotland of the previous century.

On the other hand, there was much that a seventeenth century Presbyterian Puritan would be profoundly disappointed with regarding the eighteenth-century United Kingdom. For one, the Enlightenment which we have already described was making greater and greater inroads into the life and culture of society. The established church of England - the Anglican Church - was becoming ever more worldly. And the established church of Scotland- the Presbyterian Church - was battling a similar tendency, which there was called 'moderatism.' Moderatism downplayed the tenets of the reformed faith and emphasized instead just living a decent life. A similar situation was faced in many of the Protestant nations of Europe.

There were different responses to this state of spiritual declension. In Scotland the Established Church suffered through a variety of church splits, led by such men as the Erskines who wanted to see a revival of the course which had been begun by John Knox two centuries before. The reformed and Presbyterian faith had profoundly affected Scotland, so that there was a large contingent of the population who wanted to continue and revive what was begun during the Reformation. But in most other places Protestants wanted a revival different in character from the original Protestant Reformation. On continental Europe this took the form of the Pietistic movement, and in England and the English colonies of North America this took the form of the Great Awakening.

Pietism was a Protestant religious movement stressing the importance of personal godliness. At its best, it stressed personal godliness, without compromising doctrinal orthodoxy and Christianity's claim upon societies as well as individuals. Quite often though it tended to diminish the importance of confessional orthodoxy and move towards a sort of subjective mysticism. In these forms it also tended to undermine the Establishment Principle, which recognized the importance of Christian civil governments in support of true Biblical churches. The Pietistic movement was especially pronounced in Germany and the Netherlands, primarily in Lutheranism, but also in reformed circles.

The Great Awakening was similar to Pietism, and in some cases was influenced by it. This revival movement within English and North American Protestantism was led by men like the Anglicans George Whitefield and John Wesley, the New England Puritan Jonathan Edwards, and the Presbyterian Gilbert Tennent. It especially emphasized the need for a conversion experience and tended to de-emphasize strict confessional orthodoxy.

The movement reached its peak during the 1740s and 1750s, with George Whitefield as its central figure. Whitefield engaged in itinerant ministry in Great Britain and North America, which often included open air preaching, instead of at the invitation and in the setting of local churches. Large crowds gathered in cities, towns, and rural areas to hear the stirring sermons of George Whitefield.

Whitefield's visit to Williamsburg in 1739 was one stop on a journey through the colonies that ignited a movement that brought about personal religious renewal for many people. His visit helped to mold and redefine a new American culture- a culture which on the positive side stressed personal piety and the need for heart religion, yet on the negative side leaned against the imposition of authority, even where scripture requires it, and tended to undermine principles for maintaining an established church. Revivalists such as Whitefield and Tennant would denounce as unconverted those ministers who disapproved of various aspects of this revival movement.

During its time the Great Awakening thus encountered strong opposition, even as it generated mass appeal as well. Within New England Congregationalism, it created a rift between "New Lights" and "Old Lights". The revival movement itself died down in New England by the 1750s, but this rift would persist. The "Old Lights", led by Charles Chauncy, a Boston clergyman, opposed the revivalist movement as extravagant and impermanent. The theology of the "New Lights", a slightly modified Calvinism, crystallized into the Edwardian, or New England, theology that became dominant in western New England, whereas the liberal doctrines of the "Old Lights", strong in Boston and the vicinity, would develop into the Universalist or Unitarian positions. Even among the "New Lights" strict (or full) subscriptionism to the church confession was not required of ministers. But within New England congregationalism, strict confessional subscriptionism had died off even before the Great Awakening, perhaps forstered by Congregationalist church government itself.

Within Presbyterianism, the Great Awakening brought about a rift between the "New Side" which supported the Great Awakening and the "Old Side" which opposed it. The Presbyterian establishment was centered in Philadelphia and was "Old Side". It was sometimes referred to as the "Old Synod". Old Siders insisted that the call of men to the ordained gospel ministry must be carried out by the duly constituted officers of the church. They began to challenge the legitimacy of men trained under Tennent's supervision by the so called "Log College" in New Jersey. They were especially wary of Tennent's looser subscriptionism to the Westminster Confession. They were also concerned that the Tennents laid claim to supernatural discernment, which the Presbyterian anti-revivalists regarded as superstitious and pretentious. One likened the Tennents to astrologers and fortunetellers: Could Tennent really ascertain "Men's inward feelings?" If so, "Must not Mr. Tennent have some cunning beyond what is common to man?" In sum, the Old Side critique of the Tennents was that they claimed possession of that which Presbyterian orthodoxy reserved for the work of the Holy Spirit. On the other hand, the "New Siders" argued that subscription matters were judgments that belonged to the Presbyteries and not the synod, that American Presbyterians needed their own indigenous training school and not one in Scotland, and that, ultimately, Old Siders really opposed the "experiential Calvinism" of the revivalists. The rift led to denominational schism in 1741.

This schism lasted 17 years. The New Side Presbyterians grew substantially during the years of division, while the Old Side fought for survival. From 1741 to 1758, the numbers of New Side ministers increased from 22 to 73, while the ministerial members of the Old Side decreased from 27 to 23. Further, the New Side largely won over the respect and enthusiasm of most American Presbyterians. The congregations of the New Side grew to more than three times the size of the Old Side. A reunion of the Old Side and New Side eventually took place in 1758, and largely on New Side terms. Among the compromises of the Old Side were an endorsement of the Great Awakening, an affirmation of the necessity of experiential piety of ministers, a looser form of subscription to the Westminster Confession (only requiring agreement with it as a system of doctrine, and not in its details), and the power of ordination of presbyteries. But despite this reunion, there remained tensions within the Presbyterian synod for many years.

In the aftermath of the Great Awakening, the denominations which stressed a "religious experience" grew rapidly, at the expense of the established churches. There was significant growth of New Side Presbyterians, Baptists, and Arminian Methodists in the decades immediately preceding the American Revolution. From 1740 to 1760 the number of Presbyterian ministers in American Colonies had increased from 45 to over 100. Especially on the frontier of the American colonies, Baptists and Arminian Methodists grew faster than New Side Presbyterians. In New England alone the Baptist churches increased from 21 to 79 between 1740 and 1760. One of the things that made the Baptists so popular with the masses was their novel type of preaching, appealing primarily to the emotions. And one eyewitness Methodist recorded of the Methodist revivals: "In almost every assembly might be seen signal instances of divine power; more especially in the meetings of the classes . . . Many who had long neglected the means of grace now flocked to hear . . . This outpouring of the spirit extended itself more or less, through most of the circuits, which takes in a circumference of between four and five hundred miles."

The results of the Methodist movement are reflected in the statistics of the Virginia and North Carolina circuits. In 1774 there were only two circuits in the region, with a combined membership of 291; in 1776 the number of circuits had increased tremendously, with one circuit alone reporting 1,611 members. The following year there were six circuits with a combined membership of 4,379.

Christianity thus took a major turn in the aftermath of the Enlightenment and the Great Awakening. On the one side, those who questioned the authority of scriptures grew in numbers. The Enlightenment led men to believe they could really do without scriptures. On the other side, those who still believed in the authority of scriptures tended to emphasize the personal, emotional, and subjective aspects of the Christian faith, and to de-emphasize the need for doctrinal precision. They also tended to diminish the importance of the Establishment Principle, since personal salvation (and not societal reformation as well) became the preeminent concern. This was quite a departure from what Protestant reformers like John Calvin and John Knox had envisioned. That is not to say there were not those who still agreed with the earlier

Reformation views, but they became the minority in the Protestant community and Protestant nations.

The Enlightenment and the Great Awakening worked a cultural revolution in the English-speaking countries, a revolution which was to greatly influence a political revolution in the English colonies of North America.

CHAPTER 47: The American Revolution

Before taking up the American Revolution itself, let me explain its context by reviewing some history we have already covered before, but is worth rehearsing again.

During and immediately after the Thirty Years War, the rulers of the European nations, backed up by the capital of their merchants and the ships of their trading companies, fought for territory in Asia, Africa and America.

The Spaniards and the Portuguese had been exploring the Indian Sea and the Pacific Ocean for more than a century ere Holland and England appeared upon the stage. This proved an advantage to the latter. The first rough work had already been done. What is more, the earliest navigators had so often made themselves unpopular with the Asiatic and American and African natives- in no small measure due to their tyrannical Romish ways- that both the English and the Dutch were welcomed as friends and deliverers. During their first relations with other races, all European nations have behaved with some degree of injustice, which is not at all new in human history given the sinfulness of man. The English and the Dutch, however, knew better where to draw the line than the Spanish and Portuguese. Protestantism had made the former more just towards their fellow man. Provided they got their spices and their gold and silver in trade, and their taxes as excise, they were willing to let the native enjoy a certain measure of self-government and to afford them justice. Christian missions also came to these native territories, and in many cases, God blessed the natives with greater prosperity than they had known before.

It was not very difficult for them therefore to establish themselves in the richest parts of the world. But as soon as this had been accomplished, they began to fight each other for still further possessions. Strangely enough, the colonial wars were never settled in the colonies themselves. They were decided three thousand miles away by the navies of the contending countries. It is one of the most interesting principles of ancient and modern warfare that "the nation which commands the sea is also the nation which commands the land." So far, this law has never failed to work, but the modern airplane has changed it so that nations need to control the sea and the air. In the eighteenth century, however, there were no flying machines and it was the British navy which gained for England her vast American and Indian and African colonies.

The series of naval wars between England and Holland in the seventeenth century does not interest us here. It ended as all such encounters between hopelessly ill-matched powers will end. But the warfare between England and France (her other rival) is of greater importance to us, for while the superior British fleet in the end defeated the French navy, a great deal of the preliminary fighting was done on our own American continent. In this vast country both France and England claimed everything which had been discovered and a lot more which the eye of no white man had ever seen. In 1497 Cabot had landed in the northern part of America and twenty-seven years later, Giovanni Verrazano had visited these coasts. Cabot had flown the English flag. Verrazano had sailed under the French flag. Hence both England and France proclaimed themselves the owners of the entire continent.

During the seventeenth century, some ten small English colonies had been founded between Maine and the Carolinas. In New England they were an opportunity to establish a 'city upon a hill', based upon the model of the Puritans of England. In the South they were an extension of an Anglican culture of the Mother Country of England, albeit with definite "Low Church" tendencies not far distant from Puritanism. And in some of the Middle Colonies like Pennsylvania they were a foothold of an un-Biblical Quaker experiment, but which many Scot-Irish Presbyterians would move into and make their mark upon. These colonies generally consisted of small frontier communities, nestling close to the shores of the ocean, where people had gathered to make a new home and begin life among happier surroundings, far away from royal interference.

The French colonies, on the other hand, always remained a possession of the crown. No Huguenots or Protestants were allowed in these colonies for fear that they might contaminate the Indians with their "dangerous" Protestant doctrines and would perhaps interfere with the missionary work of the Jesuit fathers. The English colonies, therefore, had been founded upon a much healthier basis than their French neighbors and rivals. They were an expression of both Protestant ideals as well as commercial energy of the English middle classes, while the French settlements were inhabited by people who had crossed the ocean as servants of the king and who expected to return to Paris at the first possible chance.

Politically, however, the position of the English colonies was far from satisfactory. The French had discovered the mouth of the Saint Lawrence in the sixteenth century. From the region of the Great Lakes they had worked their way southward, had descended the Mississippi and had built several fortifications along the Gulf of Mexico. After a century of exploration, a line of sixty French forts cut off the English settlements along the Atlantic seaboard from the interior. The English land grants made to the different colonial companies had given them "all land from sea to sea." This sounded well on paper, but in practice British territory ended where the line of French fortifications began. To break through this barrier was possible but it took both men and money and caused a series of horrible border wars in which both sides murdered their white neighbors, with the help of the Indian tribes.

As long as the Stuarts had ruled England there had been no danger of war with France. The Stuarts needed the Bourbons in their attempt to establish an autocratic form of government and to break the power of Parliament and Puritanism in Britain. But in 1689 the last of the Stuarts had disappeared from British soil and Dutch William, the great enemy of Louis XIV, succeeded him. From that time on, until the Treaty of Paris of 1763, France and England fought for the possession of India and North America.

During these wars, as I have said before, the English navies invariably beat the French. Cut off from her colonies, France lost most of her possessions, and when peace was declared, the entire North American continent had fallen into British hands and the great work of exploration of Cartier, Champlain, La Salle, Marquette and a score of others was lost to France.

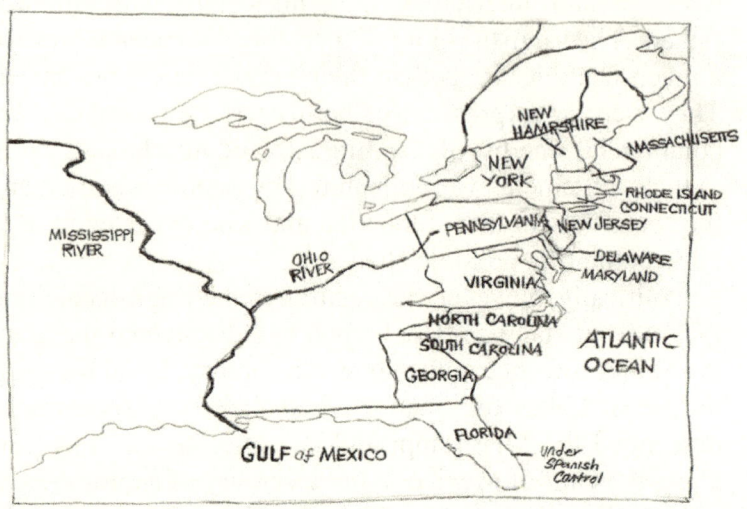

Only a very small part of this vast domain was inhabited. From Massachusetts in the north, where the Pilgrims had first landed in the year 1620 (and later the Puritans), to the Carolinas and Virginia (the tobacco-raising provinces), stretched a thin line of sparsely populated territory. But the men who lived in this new land of fresh air and high skies were very different from their brethren of the mother country. In the wilderness they had learned more independence and self-reliance. They were the sons of hardy and energetic ancestors. Few lazy and timorous people crossed the ocean in those days. The American colonists grew accustomed to self-government with their own colonial and local governments, separated by miles of ocean from English central government. This the ruling classes of England did not seem to understand. The central English government annoyed the colonists and the colonists, who hated to be bothered in this way, began to annoy the British government.

Bad feeling caused more bad feeling. It is not necessary to repeat here in detail what actually happened and what might have been avoided if the British king George III and his minister, Lord North, had taken a different tact. The British colonists took to arms. From being loyal subjects, they turned rebels, who exposed themselves to the punishment of death when they were captured by the German soldiers, whom George hired to do his fighting after the custom of that day, when Teutonic princes sold whole regiments to the highest bidder.

The war between England and her American colonies lasted seven years. During most of that time, the final success of the rebels seemed very doubtful. A great number of the people, especially in the cities, had remained loyal to their king. They were in favor of a compromise and would have been willing to sue for peace. But the great figure of Washington led the cause of the colonists who called themselves "patriots".

Ably assisted by a handful of brave men, he used his steadfast but badly equipped armies to weaken the forces of the king. Time and again when defeat seemed unavoidable, his strategy turned the tide of battle. Often his men were ill-fed. During the winter they lacked shoes and coats and were forced to live in unhealthy dugouts. But they stuck it out until the final hour of victory.

But more interesting than the campaigns of Washington or the diplomatic triumphs of Benjamin Franklin who was in Europe getting money from the French government and the Amsterdam bankers, was an event which occurred early in the revolution. The representatives of the different colonies had gathered in Philadelphia to discuss matters of common importance. It was the first year of the Revolution. Most of the big towns of the seacoast were still in the hands of the British. Reinforcements from England were arriving by the ship load. Only men who were deeply convinced of their cause would have found the courage to take the momentous decision of the months of June and July of the year 1776.

In June, Richard Henry Lee of Virginia proposed a motion to the Continental Congress that "these united colonies are, and of right ought to be, free and independent states, that they are absolved from all allegiance to the British crown, and that all political connection between them and the state of Great Britain is and ought to be, totally dissolved."

The motion was seconded by John Adams of Massachusetts. It was carried on July the second and on July fourth, it was followed by an official Declaration of Independence, which was the work of Thomas Jefferson, a student of both politics and government and destined to be one of the most famous of the American presidents.

There were both good and bad reasons for severing the rule of England over the American colonies. But in any case, it is to be regretted that the Revolutionary War and its aftermath ultimately took on the character of being in part an expression of the Enlightenment alongside a holy and righteous cause. A number of its leaders like Franklin and Jefferson were Deists who wanted to overthrow the Establishment Principle, which had maintained most of the colonies as reformed Protestant territories. They wanted a government and a society far more secularized and "based upon human reason instead of divine revelation." As time went on, they seemed to prevail more and more. So in the federal Constitution of this newly formed nation, adopted in 1787, which replaced the original constitution of the Articles of Confederation, there is hardly mention of God, the federal government is given supreme power, and the Establishment Principle for the federal government was strictly prohibited as well as any religious test oath for holding federal office. Furthermore, most of the colonies, which became states in the Union, severed their established Protestant churches, as well as their requirements that only Protestants could vote or hold office. For many years after this the States and localities would preserve the reformed Christian character of their laws and practices from the colonial days (as exhibited, for example, in the Sabbath laws), but a dangerous pattern was established which would over time thoroughly erode reformed Christianity. Roman Catholic France and the Pope were all too happy to undermine Protestant Britain and dislodge English America from established Protestantism.

When news of the Revolution reached Europe and was followed by the final victory of the colonists, it caused great interest. The dynastic system of the highly centralized states which had been developed after the great religious wars of the seventeenth century had reached the height of its power. Everywhere the palace of the king had grown to enormous proportions, while the cities of the royal realm were being surrounded by rapidly growing acres of slums. The success of the American colonists showed them that many things were possible which had been held impossible only a short time before. And the fever of the Enlightenment was given a great boost.

According to the poet, the shot which opened the battle of Lexington was "heard around the world." That was a bit of an exaggeration. The Chinese and the Japanese and the Russians (not to speak of the Australians, who had just been re-discovered by Captain Cook, whom they killed for his trouble,) never heard of it at all. But it carried across the Atlantic Ocean. It landed in the powder house of European discontent and in France it caused an explosion which rocked the entire continent from Petrograd to Madrid and buried the representatives of the old statecraft and the old diplomacy under several tons of bricks. "Human reason" divorced from Biblical revelation ultimately means depravity and destruction let loose. France, which unlike England and America, had little Biblical Protestant base (remember, the Roman Catholics there had forced most of the reformed Huguenots to flee for their life) to quell its ferocity, felt the full blast of this depravity and destruction.

CHAPTER 48: The French Revolution

Before we talk about a revolution it is just as well that we explain just what this word means. In the terms of a great Russian writer (and Russians ought to know what they are talking about in this field) a revolution is "a swift overthrow, in a few years, of institutions which have taken centuries to root in the soil, and seem so fixed and immovable that even the most ardent reformers hardly dare to attack them in their writings. It is the fall, the crumbling away in a brief period, of all that up to that time has composed the essence of social, religious, political and economic life in a nation."

Such a revolution took place in France in the eighteenth century when the old civilization of the country had grown stale. The king in the days of Louis XIV had become EVERYTHING and was the state. The Nobility, formerly the civil servant of the federal state, found itself without any duties and became a social ornament of the royal court.

This French state of the eighteenth century, however, cost incredible sums of money. This money had to be produced in the form of taxes. Unfortunately, the kings of France had not been strong enough to force the nobility and the clergy to pay their share of these taxes. Hence the taxes were paid entirely by the agricultural population. But the peasants living in dreary hovels, no longer in intimate contact with their former landlords, but victims of cruel and incompetent land agents, were going from bad to worse. Why should they work and exert themselves? Increased returns upon their land merely meant more taxes and nothing for themselves and therefore they neglected their fields as much as they dared.

Hence, we have a king who wanders in empty splendor through the vast halls of his palaces, habitually followed by hungry office seekers, all of whom live upon the revenue obtained from peasants who are no better than the beasts of the fields. It is not a pleasant picture, but it is not exaggerated. There was, however, another side to the so-called "Ancien Régime" which we must keep in mind.

A wealthy middle class, closely connected with the nobility (by the usual process of the rich banker's daughter marrying the poor baron's son) and a court composed of all the most vain people of France, had brought the polite art of this vanity to its highest expression. As the best brains of the country were not allowed to occupy themselves with questions of political economics, they spent their idle hours upon the discussion of abstract and wicked ideas; ideas which were quite contrary to Biblical principles and firmly rooted in the Enlightenment.

As fashions in modes of thought and personal behavior are quite as likely to run to extremes as fashion in dress, it was natural that the most artificial society of that day should take a tremendous interest in what they considered "the simple life." The king and the queen, the absolute and unquestioned proprietors of this country called France, together with all its colonies and dependencies, went to live in funny little country houses all dressed up as milkmaids and stable-boys and played at being shepherds in a happy vale of ancient Hellas. Around them, their courtiers danced attendance, their court-musicians composed lovely minuets, their court barbers devised more and more elaborate and costly headgear, until from sheer boredom and lack of real jobs, this whole artificial world of Versailles (the great show place which Louis XIV had built far away from his noisy and restless city) talked of nothing but those subjects which were furthest removed from their own lives, just as a man who is starving will talk of nothing except food.

When Voltaire, the atheistic old philosopher, playwright, historian and novelist, and the great enemy of all true religion, began to throw his bombs of criticism at everything connected with the Established Order of Things, the whole French world applauded him and his theatrical pieces played to standing room only.

When Jean Jacques Rousseau waxed sentimental about primitive man and gave his contemporaries delightful descriptions of the happiness of the original inhabitants of this planet, (about whom he knew as little as he did about the children, upon whose education he was the recognized authority,) all France read his "Social Contract" and this society in which the king and the state were one, wept bitter tears when they heard Rousseau's appeal for a return to the blessed days when the real sovereignty had lain in the hands of the people and when the king had been merely the servant of his people.

When Montesquieu published his "Persian Letters" in which two distinguished Persian travelers turn the whole existing society of France topsy-turvy and poke fun at everything from the king down to the lowest of his six hundred pastry cooks, the book immediately went through four editions and assured the writer thousands of readers for his famous discussion of the "Spirit of the Laws" in which the noble Baron compared the excellent English system with the backward system of France and advocated instead of an absolute monarchy the establishment of a state in which the Executive, the Legislative and the Judicial powers should be in separate hands and should work independently of each other. When Lebreton, the Parisian book-seller, announced that Messieurs Diderot, d'Alembert, Turgot and a score of other distinguished writers were going to publish an encyclopædia which was to contain "all the new ideas and the new science and the new knowledge," the response from the side of the public was most satisfactory, and when after twenty-two years the last of the twenty-eight volumes had been finished, the somewhat belated interference of the police could not repress the enthusiasm with which French society received this most important but very dangerous contribution to the discussions of the day.

Here, let me give you a little warning. When you read most books about the French revolution, you will easily get the impression that the Revolution was the work of the rabble from the Paris slums. It was nothing of the kind. The mob appears often upon the revolutionary stage, but invariably at the instigation and under the leadership of those middle-class professional men who used the hungry multitude as an efficient ally in their warfare upon the king and his court. But the fundamental ideas which caused the revolution were invented by a few brilliant if wicked minds, and they were at first introduced into the charming drawing-rooms of the "Ancien Régime" to provide amiable diversion for the much-bored ladies and gentlemen of his Majesty's court. These pleasant but careless people played with the dangerous fireworks of social criticism until the sparks fell through the cracks of the floor, which was old and rotten just like the rest of the building. Those sparks unfortunately landed in the basement where age-old rubbish lay in great confusion. Then there was a cry of fire. But the owner of the house who was interested in everything except the management of his property, did not know how to put the small blaze out. The flame spread rapidly, and the entire edifice was consumed by the conflagration, which we call the Great French Revolution.

For the sake of convenience, we can divide the French Revolution into two parts. From 1789 to 1791 there was a more or less orderly attempt to introduce a constitutional monarchy. This failed, ostensibly because of lack of good faith and stupidity on the part of the monarch himself, but ultimately because God had determined to judge a wicked society based upon Romanism, hedonism, and humanism.

From 1792 to 1799 there was a Republic and a first effort to establish a democratic form of government. But the actual outbreak of violence had been preceded by many years of unrest and many ineffectual attempts at reform.

When France had a debt of 4000 million francs and the treasury was always empty and there was not a single thing upon which new taxes could be levied, even King Louis (who was an expert locksmith and a great hunter but a very poor statesman) felt vaguely that something ought to be done. Therefore, he called for Turgot to be his Minister of Finance. Anne Robert Jacques Turgot, Baron de l'Aulne, a man in the early sixties, a splendid representative of the fast disappearing class of landed gentry, had been a successful governor of a province and was an amateur political economist of great ability. He did his best. Unfortunately, he could not perform miracles. As it was impossible to squeeze more taxes out of the ragged peasants, it was necessary to get the necessary funds from the nobility and clergy who had never paid a cent. This made Turgot the best hated man at the court of Versailles. Furthermore, he was obliged to face the enmity of Marie Antoinette, the queen, who was against everybody who dared to mention the word "economy" within her hearing. Soon Turgot was called an "unpractical visionary" and a "theoretical-professor" and then of course his position became untenable. In the year 1776 he was forced to resign.

After the "professor" there came a man of Practical Business Sense. He was an industrious Swiss by the name of Necker who had made himself rich as a grain speculator and the partner in an international banking house. His ambitious wife had pushed him into the government service that she might establish a position for her daughter who afterwards as the wife of the Swedish minister in Paris, Baron de Staël, became a famous literary figure of the early nineteenth century.

Necker set to work with a fine display of zeal just as Turgot had done. In 1781 he published a careful review of the French finances. The king understood nothing of this "Compte Rendu." He had just sent troops to America to help the colonists against their common enemies, the English. This expedition proved to be unexpectedly expensive and Necker was asked to find the necessary funds. When instead of producing revenue, he published more figures and made statistics and began to use the dreary warning about "necessary economies" his days were numbered. In the year 1781 he was dismissed as an incompetent servant.

After the Professor and the Practical Businessman came the delightful type of financier who will guarantee everybody 100 per cent per month on their money if only they will trust his own infallible system. He was Charles Alexandre de Calonne, a pushing official, who had made his career both by his industry and his complete lack of honesty and scruples. He found the country heavily indebted, but he was a clever man, willing to oblige everybody, and he invented a quick remedy. He paid the old debts by contracting new ones. This method is not new. The result since time immemorial has been disastrous. In less than three years more than 800,000,000 francs had been added to the French debt by this charming Minister of Finance who never worried and smilingly signed his name to every demand that was made by His Majesty and by his lovely Queen, who had learned the habit of spending during the days of her youth in Vienna.

At last even the Parliament of Paris (a high court of justice and not a legislative body) although by no means lacking in loyalty to their sovereign, decided that something must be done. Calonne wanted to borrow another 80,000,000 francs. It had been a bad year for the crops and the misery and hunger in the country districts were terrible. Unless something sensible were done, France would go bankrupt. The King as always was unaware of the seriousness of the situation. Would it not be a good idea to consult the representatives of the people? Since 1614 no Estates General had been called together. In view of the threatening panic there was a demand that the Estates be convened. Louis XVI however, who never could take a decision, refused to go as far as that.

To pacify the popular clamor, he called together a meeting of the Notables in the year 1787. This merely meant a gathering of the best families who discussed what could and should be done, without touching their feudal and clerical privilege of tax-exemption. It is unreasonable to expect that a certain class of society shall commit political and economic suicide for the benefit of another group of fellow citizens. The 127 Notables obstinately refused to surrender a single one of their ancient rights. The crowd in the street, being now exceedingly hungry, demanded that Necker, in whom they had confidence, be reappointed. The Notables said "No." The crowd in the street began to smash windows and do other unseemly things. The Notables fled. Calonne was dismissed.

A new colorless Minister of Finance, the Romanist Cardinal Loménie de Brienne, was appointed and Louis, driven by the violent threats of his starving subjects, agreed to call together the old Estates General as "soon as practicable." This vague promise of course satisfied no one.

No such severe winter had been experienced for almost a century. The crops had been either destroyed by floods or had been frozen to death in the fields. All the olive trees of the Provence had been killed. Private charity tried to do something but could accomplish little for eighteen million starving people. Everywhere bread riots occurred. A generation before these would have been put down by the army. But the work of the new philosophical school had begun to bear fruit. People began to understand that a shotgun is no effective remedy for a hungry stomach and even the soldiers (who came from among the people) were no longer to be depended upon. It was absolutely necessary that the king should do something definite to regain the popular goodwill, but again he hesitated.

Here and there in the provinces, little independent Republics were established by followers of the new "Enlightenment" school. The cry of "no taxation without representation" (the slogan of the American rebels a quarter of a century before) was heard among the faithful middle classes. France was threatened with general anarchy. To appease the people and to increase the royal popularity, the government unexpectedly suspended the former very strict form of censorship of books. At once a flood of ink descended upon France. Everybody, high or low, criticized and was criticized. More than 2000 pamphlets were published. Loménie de Brienne was swept away by a storm of abuse. Necker was hastily called back to placate, as best he could, the nation-wide unrest. Immediately the stock market went up thirty per cent. And by common consent, people suspended judgment for a little while longer. In May of 1789 the Estates General were to assemble and then the wisdom of the entire nation would speedily solve the difficult problem of recreating the kingdom of France into a healthy and happy state.

This prevailing idea, that the combined wisdom of the people would be able to solve all difficulties, proved disastrous. (Never underestimate the folly of wicked men in rebellion against true religion.) It lamed all personal effort during many important months. Instead of keeping the government in his own hands at this critical moment, Necker allowed everything to drift. Hence there was a new outbreak of the acrimonious debate upon the best ways to reform the old kingdom. Everywhere the power of the police weakened. The people of the Paris suburbs, under the leadership of professional agitators, gradually began to discover their strength, and commenced to play the rôle which was to be theirs all through the years of the great unrest, when they acted as the brute force which was used by the actual leaders of the Revolution to secure those things which could not be obtained in a legitimate fashion.

As a sop to the peasants and the middle class, Necker decided that they should be allowed a double representation in the Estates General. Upon this subject, the Abbé Siéyès then wrote a famous pamphlet, "To what does the Third Estate Amount?" in which he came to the conclusion that the Third Estate (a name given to the middle class) ought to amount to everything, that it had not amounted to anything in the past, and that it now desired to amount to something. He expressed the sentiment of the great majority of the people.

Finally, the elections took place under the worst conditions imaginable. When they were over, 308 clergymen, 285 noblemen and 621 representatives of the Third Estate packed their trunks to go to Versailles. The Third Estate was obliged to carry additional luggage. This consisted of voluminous reports called "cahiers" in which the many complaints and grievances of their constituents had been written down. The stage was set for the great final act that was to "save" France.

The Estates General came together on May 5th, 1789. The king was in a bad humor. The Romanist Clergy and the Nobility let it be known that they were unwilling to give up a single one of their privileges. The king ordered the three groups of representatives to meet in different rooms and discuss their grievances separately. The Third Estate refused to obey the royal command. They took a solemn oath to that effect in a squash court (hastily put in order for the purpose of this illegal meeting) on the 20th of June 1789. They insisted that all three Estates, Nobility, Clergy and Third Estate, should meet together and so informed His Majesty. The king gave in.

As the "National Assembly," the Estates General began to discuss the state of the French kingdom. The King got angry. Then again he hesitated. He said that he would never surrender his absolute power. Then he went hunting, forgot all about the cares of the state and when he returned from the chase, he gave in. For it was the royal habit to do the right thing at the wrong time in the wrong way. When the people clamored for A, the king scolded them and gave them nothing. Then, when the Palace was surrounded by a howling multitude of poor people, the king surrendered and gave his subjects what they had asked for. By this time, however, the people wanted A plus B. The comedy was repeated. When the king signed his name to the

Royal Decree which granted his beloved subjects A and B they were threatening to kill the entire royal family unless they received A plus B plus C. And so on, through the whole alphabet and up to the scaffold.

Unfortunately, the king was always just one letter behind. He never understood this. Even when he laid his head under the guillotine, he felt that he was a much-abused man who had received a most unwarrantable treatment at the hands of people whom he had loved to the best of his limited ability.

Historical "ifs," as I have often warned you, are never of any value. It is very easy for us to say that the monarchy might have been saved "if" Louis had been a man of greater energy and more wisdom. But the king was not alone. Even "if" he had possessed the ruthless strength of Napoleon, his career during these difficult days might have been easily ruined by his wife who was the daughter of Maria Theresa of Austria and who possessed all the characteristic virtues and vices of a young girl who had been brought up at the most autocratic and mediæval court of that age and trained in Romanist humanism: Marie Antoinette.

She decided that some action must be taken and planned a counter-revolution. Necker was suddenly dismissed, and loyal troops were called to Paris. The people, when they heard of this, stormed the fortress of the Bastille prison, and on the fourteenth of July of the year 1789, they destroyed this familiar but much-hated symbol of Autocratic Power which had long since ceased to be a political prison and was now used as the city lock-up for pickpockets and second-story men. Many of the nobles took the hint and left the country. But the king as usual did nothing. He had been hunting on the day of the fall of the Bastille and he had shot several deer and felt very much pleased.

The National Assembly now set to work and on the 4th of August, with the noise of the Parisian multitude in their ears, they abolished all privileges. This was followed on the 27th of August by the "Declaration of the Rights of Man," the famous preamble to the first French constitution. So far so good, but the court had apparently not yet learned its lesson. There was a wide-spread suspicion that the king was again trying to interfere with these reforms and as a result, on the 5th of October, there was a second riot in Paris. It spread to Versailles and the people were not pacified until they had brought the king back to his palace in Paris. They did not trust him in Versailles. They liked to have him where they could watch him and control his correspondence with his relatives in Vienna and Madrid and the other courts of Europe.

In the Assembly, meanwhile, Mirabeau, a nobleman who had become leader of the Third Estate, was beginning to put order into chaos. But before he could save the position of the king he died, on the 2nd of April of the year 1791. The king, who now began to fear for his own life, tried to escape on the 21st of June. He was recognized from his picture on a coin, was stopped near the village of Varennes by members of the National Guard, and was brought back to Paris,

In September of 1791, the first constitution of France was accepted, and the members of the National Assembly went home. On the first of October of 1791, the legislative assembly came together to continue the work of the National Assembly. In this new gathering of popular representatives there were many extremely revolutionary elements. The boldest among these were known as the Jacobins, after the old Jacobin cloister in which they held their political meetings. These young men (most of them belonging to the professional classes) made very violent speeches and when the newspapers carried these orations to Berlin and Vienna, the King of Prussia and the Emperor decided that they must do something to save their good brother and sister. They were very busy just then dividing the kingdom of Poland, where rival political factions had caused such a state of disorder that the country was at the mercy of anybody who wanted to take a couple of provinces. But they managed to send an army to invade France and deliver the king.

Then a terrible panic of fear swept throughout the land of France. All the pent-up hatred of years of hunger and suffering came to a horrible climax. The mob of Paris stormed the palace of the Tuileries. The faithful Swiss bodyguards tried to defend their master, but Louis, unable to make up his mind, gave order to "cease firing" just when the crowd was retiring. The people, drunk with blood and noise and cheap wine, murdered the Swiss to the last man, then invaded the palace, and went after Louis who had escaped into the meeting hall of the Assembly, where he was immediately suspended of his office, and from where he was taken as a prisoner to the old castle of the Temple.

But the armies of Austria and Prussia continued their advance and the panic changed into hysteria and turned men and women into wild beasts. In the first week of September of the year 1792, the crowd broke into the jails and murdered all the prisoners. The government did not interfere. The Jacobins, headed by Danton, knew that this crisis meant either the success or the failure of the revolution, and that only the most brutal audacity could save them.

The Legislative Assembly was closed and on the 21st of September of the year 1792, a new National Convention came together. It was a body composed almost entirely of extreme revolutionists. The king was formally accused of high treason and was brought before the Convention. He was found guilty and by a vote of 361 to 360 (the extra vote being that of his cousin the Duke of Orleans) he was condemned to death.

LET ME TELL YOU THE REAL STORY OF MANKIND

On the 21st of January of the year 1793, he quietly and with much dignity suffered himself to be taken to the scaffold. He had never understood what all the shooting and the fuss had been about. And he had been too proud to ask questions.

Then the Jacobins turned against the more moderate element in the convention, the Girondists, called after their southern district, the Gironde. A special revolutionary tribunal was instituted and twenty-one of the leading Girondists were condemned to death. The others committed suicide. They were too moderate to survive during these frightful years.

In October of the year 1793, the Constitution was suspended by the Jacobins "until peace should have been declared." All power was placed in the hands of a small committee of Public Safety, with Danton and Robespierre as its leaders. The Christian religion and the old chronology were abolished. The "Age of Reason" (of which Thomas Paine had written so eloquently during the American Revolution) had come and with it the "Terror" which for more than a year killed good and bad and indifferent people at the rate of seventy or eighty a day. (Always remember, such human reason is a facade for human depravity.)

The autocratic rule of the King had been destroyed. It was succeeded by the tyranny of a few people who had such a passionate love for democracy so-called that they felt compelled to kill all those who disagreed with them. France was turned into a slaughterhouse. Everybody suspected everybody else. No one felt safe. Out of sheer fear, a few members of the old Convention, who knew that they were the next candidates for the scaffold, finally turned against Robespierre, who had already decapitated most of his former colleagues. Robespierre, "the only true and pure Democrat," tried to kill himself but failed. His shattered jaw was hastily bandaged, and he was dragged to the guillotine. On the 27th of July, of the year 1794 (the 9th Thermidor of the year II, according to the strange chronology of the revolution which had tried to totally overturn all vestiges of Christianity), the reign of Terror came to an end, and all Paris danced with joy.

The dangerous position of France, however, made it necessary that the government remain in the hands of a few strong men, until the many enemies of the revolution should have been driven from the soil of the French fatherland. While the half-clad and half-starved revolutionary armies fought their desperate battles of the Rhine and Italy and Belgium and Egypt and defeated every one of the enemies of the Great Revolution, five Directors were appointed, and they ruled France for four years. Then the power was vested in the hands of a successful general by the name of Napoleon Bonaparte, who became "First Consul" of France in the year 1799. And during the next fifteen years, the old European continent became the laboratory of a number of political experiments, the like of which the world had never seen before. It was sheer madness run wild.

LET ME TELL YOU THE REAL STORY OF MANKIND

CHAPTER 49: Napoleon

Napoleon was born in the year 1769, the third son of Carlo Maria Buonaparte, a notary public of the city of Ajaccio in the island of Corsica, and his wife, Letizia Ramolino. He therefore was not a Frenchman, but an Italian whose native island (an old Greek, Carthaginian and Roman colony in the Mediterranean Sea) had for years been struggling to regain its independence, first of all from the Genoese, and after the middle of the eighteenth century from the French, who had kindly offered to help the Corsicans in their struggle for freedom and had then occupied the island for their own benefit.

During the first twenty years of his life, young Napoleon was a professional Corsican patriot – a Corsican Sinn Feiner, who hoped to deliver his beloved country from the yoke of the bitterly hated French enemy. But the French revolution had unexpectedly recognized the claims of the Corsicans and gradually Napoleon, who had received a good training at the military school of Brienne, drifted into the service of his adopted country. Although he never learned to spell French correctly or to speak it without a broad Italian accent, he became a Frenchman. In due time he came to stand as the highest expression of all French virtues (which is not saying much about modern French virtues). At present he is regarded as the symbol of the Gallic genius.

Napoleon was what is called a fast worker. His career does not cover more than twenty years. In that short span of time he fought more wars and gained more victories and marched more miles and conquered more square kilometers and killed more people and brought about more reforms and generally upset Europe to a greater extent than anybody (including Alexander the Great and Genghis Khan) had ever managed to do.

He was a little fellow and during the first years of his life his health was not very good. He never impressed anybody by his good looks, and he remained to the end of his days very clumsy whenever he was obliged to appear at a social function. He did not enjoy a single advantage of breeding or birth or riches. For the greater part of his youth he was desperately poor and often he had to go without a meal or was obliged to make a few extra pennies in curious ways.

He gave little promise as a literary genius. When he competed for a prize offered by the Academy of Lyons, his essay was found to be next to the last and he was number 15 out of 16 candidates. But he overcame all these difficulties through his absolute and unshakable belief in his own destiny, and in his own glorious future. Ambition was the main spring of his life. The thought of self, the worship of that capital letter "N" with which he signed all his letters, and which recurred forever in the ornaments of his hastily constructed palaces, the absolute will to make the name Napoleon the most important thing in the world next to the name of God, these desires carried Napoleon to a pinnacle of fame (or more accurately, infamy).

When he was a half-pay lieutenant, young Bonaparte was very fond of the "Lives of Famous Men" which Plutarch, the Roman historian, had written. But he never tried to live up to the high standard of character set by these heroes of the older days. Napoleon seems to have been devoid of all those considerate and thoughtful sentiments which make men different from the animals. It will be very difficult to decide with any degree of accuracy whether he ever loved anyone besides himself. He kept a civil tongue to his mother, but Letizia had the air and manners of a great lady and after the fashion of Italian mothers, she knew how to rule her brood of children and command their respect. For a few years he was fond of Josephine, his pretty Creole wife, who was the daughter of a French officer of Martinique and the widow of the Vicomte de Beauharnais, who had been executed by Robespierre when he lost a battle against the Prussians. But the Emperor divorced her when she failed to give him a son and heir and married the daughter of the Austrian Emperor, because it seemed good policy.

During the siege of Toulon, where he gained great fame as commander of a battery, Napoleon studied Machiavelli with industrious care. He followed the advice of the Florentine statesman and never kept his word when it was to his advantage to break it. The word "gratitude" did not occur in his personal dictionary. Neither, to be quite fair, did he expect it from others. He was totally indifferent to human suffering. He executed prisoners of war (in Egypt in 1798) who had been promised their lives, and he quietly allowed his wounded in Syria to be chloroformed when he found it impossible to transport them to his ships. He ordered the Duke of Enghien to be condemned to death by a prejudiced court-martial and to be shot contrary to all law on the sole ground that the "Bourbons needed a warning." He decreed that those German officers who were made prisoner while fighting for their country's independence should be shot against the nearest wall, and when Andreas Hofer, the Tyrolese hero, fell into his hands after a most heroic resistance, he was executed like a common traitor.

In short, when we study the character of the Emperor, we begin to understand those anxious British mothers who used to drive their children to bed with the threat that "Bonaparte, who ate little boys and girls for breakfast, would come and get them if they were not very good." And yet, having said these many unpleasant things about this strange tyrant, who looked after every other department of his army with the utmost care, but neglected the medical service, and who ruined his uniforms with Eau de Cologne because he could not stand the smell of his poor sweating soldiers.

Millions of men gave their lives to serve this wretch. They received no reward, but they expected none. They cheerfully gave legs and arms and lives to serve this foreigner, who took them a thousand miles away from their homes and marched them into a barrage of Russian or English or Spanish or Italian or Austrian cannon and stared quietly into space while they were rolling in the agony of death. They would do all of this to serve the wretch but were completely unwilling to serve the Lord Jesus Christ who died for His people. It makes no sense, but the fool will always play the fool.

Napoleon was the greatest of actors and the whole European continent was his stage. At all times and under all circumstances, he knew the precise attitude that would impress the spectators most and he understood what words would make the deepest impression. Whether he spoke in the Egyptian desert, before the backdrop of the Sphinx and the pyramids, or addressed his shivering men on the dew-soaked plains of Italy, made no difference. At all times, he was master of the situation. Even at the end, an exile on a little rock in the middle of the Atlantic, a sick man at the mercy of a dull and intolerable British governor, he held the center of the stage.

After the defeat of Waterloo, no one outside of a few trusted friends ever saw the great Emperor. The people of Europe knew that he was living on the island of St. Helena – they knew that a British garrison guarded him day and night – they knew that the British fleet guarded the garrison which guarded the Emperor on his farm at Longwood. But he was never out of the mind of either friend or enemy. When illness and despair had at last taken him away, his silent eyes continued to haunt the world. Even today he is as much of a force in the life of France as years ago when people fainted at the mere sight of this sallow-faced man who stabled his horses in the holiest temples of the Russian Kremlin, and who treated the Pope and the mighty ones of this earth as if they were his lackeys.

To give you a mere outline of his life would demand couple of volumes. To tell you of his great political reform of the French state, of his new codes of laws which were adopted in most European countries, of his activities in every field of public activity, would take thousands of pages. But I can explain in a few words why he was so successful during the first part of his career and why he failed during the last ten years. From the year 1789 until the year 1804, Napoleon was the great leader of the French revolution. He was not merely fighting for the glory of his own name. He defeated Austria and Italy and England and Russia because he, himself, and his soldiers were the apostles of the new creed of "Liberty, Fraternity and Equality" and were the enemies of the courts while they were the friends of the people.

But in the year 1804, Napoleon made himself Hereditary Emperor of the French and sent for Pope Pius VII to come and crown him, even as Leo III, in the year 800 had crowned that other great King of the Franks, Charlemagne, whose example was constantly before Napoleon's eyes.

Once upon the throne, the old revolutionary chieftain became an unsuccessful imitation of a Habsburg monarch. He forgot his spiritual Mother, the Political Club of the Jacobins. He ceased to be the defender of the oppressed. He became the chief of all the oppressors and kept his shooting squads ready to execute those who dared to oppose his imperial will. No one had shed a tear when in the year 1806 the sad remains of the Holy Roman Empire were carted to the historical dustbin and when the last relic of ancient Roman glory was destroyed by the grandson of an Italian peasant. But when the Napoleonic armies had invaded Spain, had forced the Spaniards to recognize a king whom they detested, had massacred the poor Madrilenes who remained faithful to their old rulers, then public opinion turned against the former hero of Marengo and Austerlitz and a hundred other revolutionary battles. Then and only then, when Napoleon was no longer the hero of the revolution but the personification of all the bad traits of the Old Régime, was it possible for England to give direction to the fast-spreading sentiment of hatred which was turning all honest men into enemies of the French Emperor.

The Protestant people of England from the very beginning had felt deeply disgusted when their newspapers told them the gruesome details of the Terror. They had staged their own great revolution (during the reign of Charles I) a century before. It had been a very simple affair compared to the upheaval of Paris. In the eyes of the average Englishman a Jacobin was a monster to be shot at sight and Napoleon was the Chief Devil. The British fleet had blockaded France ever since the year 1798. It had spoiled Napoleon's plan to invade India by way of Egypt and had forced him to beat an ignominious retreat, after his victories along the banks of the Nile. And finally, in the year 1805, England got the chance it had waited for so long.

Near Cape Trafalgar, on the southwestern coast of Spain, Nelson annihilated the Napoleonic fleet, beyond a possible chance of recovery. From that moment on, the Emperor was landlocked. Even so, he would have been able to maintain himself as the recognized ruler of the continent had he understood the signs of the times and accepted the honorable peace which the powers offered him. But Napoleon had been blinded by the blaze of his own glory. He would recognize no equals. He could tolerate no rivals. And his hatred turned against Russia, the mysterious land of the endless plains with its inexhaustible supply of cannon-fodder.

As long as Russia was ruled by Paul I, the half-witted son of Catherine the Great, Napoleon had known how to deal with the situation. But Paul grew more and more irresponsible until his exasperated subjects were obliged to murder him (lest they all be sent to the Siberian lead mines) and the son of Paul, the Emperor Alexander, did not share his father's affection for the usurper whom he regarded as the enemy of mankind, the eternal disturber of the peace. He was a pious man who believed that he had been chosen by God to deliver the world from the Corsican curse. He joined Prussia, England, and Austria, and he was defeated. He tried five times and five times he failed. In the year 1812 he once more taunted Napoleon until the French Emperor, in a blind rage, vowed that he would dictate peace in Moscow. Then, from far and wide, from Spain and Germany and Holland and Italy and Portugal, unwilling regiments were driven northward, that the wounded pride of the great Emperor might be duly avenged. The rest of the story is common knowledge. After a march of two months, Napoleon reached the Russian capital and established his headquarters in the holy Kremlin. On the night of September 15 of the year 1812, Moscow caught fire. The town burned four days. When the evening of the fifth day came, Napoleon gave the order for the retreat. Two weeks later it began to snow. The army trudged through mud and sleet until November the 26th when the river Berezina was reached. Then the Russian attacks began in all seriousness. The Cossacks swarmed around the "Grande Armée" which was no longer an army but a mob. In the middle of December, the first of the survivors began to be seen in the German cities of the East.

Then there were many rumors of an impending revolt. "The time has come," the people of Europe said, "to free ourselves from this insufferable yoke." And they began to look for old shotguns which had escaped the eye of the ever-present French spies. But ere they knew what had happened, Napoleon was back with a new army. He had left his defeated soldiers and in his little sleigh had rushed ahead to Paris, making a final appeal for more troops that he might defend the sacred soil of France against foreign invasion.

Children of sixteen and seventeen followed him when he moved eastward to meet the allied powers. On October 16, 18, and 19 of the year 1813, the terrible battle of Leipzig took place where for three days boys in green and boys in blue fought each other until the Elbe ran red with blood. On the afternoon of the 17th of October, the massed reserves of Russian infantry broke through the French lines and Napoleon fled.

Back to Paris he went. He abdicated in favor of his small son, but the allied powers insisted that Louis XVIII, the brother of the late king Louis XVI, should occupy the French throne, and surrounded by Cossacks and Uhlans, the dull-eyed Bourbon prince made his triumphal entry into Paris.

As for Napoleon, he was made the sovereign ruler of the little island of Elba in the Mediterranean where he organized his stable boys into a miniature army and fought battles on a chess board.

But no sooner had he left France than the people began to realize what they had lost. The last twenty years, however costly, had been a period of great glory. Paris had been the capital of the world. The fat Bourbon king who had learned nothing and had forgotten nothing during the days of his exile disgusted everybody by his indolence.

On the first of March of the year 1815, when the representatives of the allies were ready to begin the work of unscrambling the map of Europe, Napoleon suddenly landed near Cannes. In less than a week the French army had deserted the Bourbons and had rushed southward to offer their swords and bayonets to the "little Corporal." Napoleon marched straight to Paris where he arrived on the twentieth of March. This time he was more cautious. He offered peace, but the allies insisted upon war. The whole of Europe arose against the "perfidious Corsican." Rapidly the Emperor marched northward that he might crush his enemies before they should be able to unite their forces. But Napoleon was no longer his old self. He felt sick. He got tired easily. He slept when he ought to have been up directing the attack of his advance-guard. Besides, he missed many of his faithful old generals. They were dead.

Early in June, his armies entered Belgium. On the 16th of that month he defeated the Prussians under Blücher. But a subordinate commander failed to destroy the retreating army as he had been ordered to do. Two days later, Napoleon met Wellington near Waterloo.

It was the 18th of June, a Sunday. At two o'clock of the afternoon, the battle seemed won for the French. At three a speck of dust appeared upon the eastern horizon. Napoleon believed that this meant the approach of his own cavalry who would now turn the English defeat into a rout. At four o'clock he knew better. Cursing and swearing, old Blucher drove his deathly tired troops into the heart of the fray. The shock broke the ranks of the guards. Napoleon had no further reserves. He told his men to save themselves as best they could, and he fled.

For a second time, he abdicated in favor of his son. Just one hundred days after his escape from Elba, he was making for the coast. He intended to go to America. In the year 1803, for a mere song, he had sold the French colony of Louisiana (which was in great danger of being captured by the English) to the young American Republic. "The Americans," so he said, "will be grateful and will give me a little bit of land and a house where I may spend the last days of my life in peace and quiet." But the English fleet was watching all French harbors. Caught between the armies of the Allies and the ships of the British, Napoleon had no choice. The Prussians intended to shoot him. The English might be more generous. At Rochefort he waited in the hope that something might turn up. One month after Waterloo, he received orders from the new French government to leave French soil inside of twenty-four hours. Always the tragedian, he wrote a letter to the Prince Regent of England (George IV, the king, was in an insane asylum) informing His Royal Highness of his intention to "throw himself upon the mercy of his enemies and like Themistocles, to look for a welcome at the fireside of his foes.

On the 15th of July, he went on board the "*Bellerophon*," and surrendered his sword to Admiral Hotham. At Plymouth he was transferred to the "Northumberland" which carried him to St. Helena. There he spent the last seven years of his life. He tried to write his memoirs, he quarreled with his keepers and he dreamed of past times. Curiously enough he returned (at least in his imagination) to his original point of departure. He remembered the days when he had fought the battles of the Revolution. He tried to convince himself that he had always been the true friend of those great principles of "Liberty, Fraternity and Equality" which the ragged soldiers of the convention had carried to the ends of the earth. He liked to dwell upon his career as Commander-in-Chief and Consul. He rarely spoke of the Empire. Sometimes he thought of his son, the Duke of Reichstadt, the little eagle, who lived in Vienna, where he was treated as a "poor relation" by his young Habsburg cousins, whose fathers had trembled at the very mention of the name of Him. When the end came, he was leading his troops to victory. He ordered Ney to attack with the guards. Then he died.

The French Revolution and Napoleon thus came to an end. But the Enlightenment and Age of Reason- which promised to rid the world of war, injustice, and brutality, but delivered just the opposite- have survived many more years and led to many more tragedies. In the meantime, the gospel of Jesus Christ continued to spread around the world through vigilant missionaries, in preparation for the day when Christ would destroy every Napoleonic usurper who dared to take the authority which He alone is due.

CHAPTER 50: The (Un) Holy Alliance

The Imperial Highnesses, the Royal Highnesses, their Graces the Dukes, the Ministers Extraordinary and Plenipotentiary, together with the plain Excellencies and their army of secretaries, servants and hangers-on, whose labors had been so rudely interrupted by the sudden return of the terrible Corsican (now sweltering under the hot sun of St. Helena) went back to their jobs. The victory was duly celebrated with dinners, garden parties and balls at which the new and very shocking "waltz" was danced to the great scandal of the ladies and gentlemen who remembered the minuet of the old Régime.

For almost a generation they had lived in retirement. At last the danger was over. They were very eloquent upon the subject of the terrible hardships which they had suffered. And they expected to be recompensed for every penny they had lost at the hands of the unspeakable Jacobins who had dared to kill their anointed king, who had abolished wigs and who had discarded the short trousers of the court of Versailles for the ragged pantaloons of the Parisian slums.

You may think it absurd that I should mention such a detail. But, if you please, the Congress of Vienna was one long succession of such absurdities and for many months the question of "short trousers vs. long trousers" interested the delegates more than the future settlement of the Saxon or Spanish problems. His Majesty the King of Prussia went so far as to order a pair of short ones, that he might give public evidence of his contempt for everything revolutionary.

Another German potentate, not to be outdone in this noble hatred for the revolution, decreed that all taxes which his subjects had paid to the French usurper should be paid a second time to the legitimate ruler who had loved his people from afar while they were at the mercy of the Corsican ogre. And so on. From one blunder to another, until one gasps and exclaims "but why did not the people object?" Why not indeed? Because the people were utterly exhausted, were desperate, did not care what happened or how or where or by whom they were ruled, provided there was peace. They were sick and tired of war and revolution and reform.

In the eighties of the previous century they had all danced around the tree of liberty. Princes had embraced their cooks and Duchesses had danced the Carmagnole with their lackeys in the honest belief that the Millennium of Equality and Fraternity had at last dawned upon this wicked world. Instead of the Millennium they had been visited by the Revolutionary commissary who had lodged a dozen dirty soldiers in their parlor and had stolen the family plate when he returned to Paris to report to his government upon the enthusiasm with which the "liberated country" had received the Constitution, which the French people had presented to their good neighbors.

When they had heard how the last outbreak of revolutionary disorder in Paris had been suppressed by a young officer, called Bonaparte, or Buonaparte, who had turned his guns upon the mob, they gave a sigh of relief. A little less liberty, fraternity and equality seemed a very desirable thing. But ere long, the young officer called Buonaparte or Bonaparte became one of the three consuls of the French Republic, then sole consul and finally Emperor. As he was much more efficient than any ruler that had ever been seen before, his hand pressed heavily upon his poor subjects. He showed them no mercy. He impressed their sons into his armies, he married their daughters to his generals, and he took their pictures and their statues to enrich his own museums. He turned the whole of Europe into an armed camp and killed almost an entire generation of men.

Now he was gone, and the people (except a few professional military men) had but one wish. They wanted to be let alone. For a while they had been allowed to rule themselves, to vote for mayors and aldermen and judges. The system had been a terrible failure. The new rulers had been inexperienced and extravagant. From sheer despair the people turned to the representative men of the old Régime. "You rule us," they said, "as you used to do. Tell us what we owe you for taxes and leave us alone. We are busy repairing the damage of the age of liberty."

The men who stage-managed the famous congress certainly did their best to satisfy this longing for rest and quiet. The Holy Alliance, the main result of the Congress, made the policeman the most important dignitary of the State and held out the most terrible punishment to those who dared criticize a single official act. This was surely the reward of a people who rejected God and the true Protestant reformed religion for a lie. Europe had peace, but it was the peace of the cemetery.

The three most important men at Vienna were the Emperor Alexander of Russia, Metternich, who represented the interests of the Austrian house of Habsburg, and Talleyrand, the erstwhile bishop of Autun, who had managed to live through the different changes in the French government by the sheer force of his cunning and his intelligence and who now travelled to the Austrian capital to save for his country whatever could be saved from the Napoleonic ruin. Like the gay young man of the limerick, who never knew when he was slighted, this unbidden guest came to the party and ate just as heartily as if he had been really invited. Indeed, before long, he was sitting at the head of the table entertaining everybody with his amusing stories and gaining the company's good will by the charm of his manner.

Before he had been in Vienna twenty-four hours, he knew that the allies were divided into two hostile camps. On the one side were Russia, who wanted to take Poland, and Prussia, who wanted to annex Saxony; and on the other side were Austria and England, who were trying to prevent this grab because it was against their own interest that either Prussia or Russia should be able to dominate Europe.

Talleyrand played the two sides against each other with great skill and it was due to his efforts that the French people were not made to suffer for the ten years of oppression which Europe had endured at the hands of the Imperial officials. He argued that the French people had been given no choice in the matter. Napoleon had forced them to act at his bidding.

But Napoleon was gone, and Louis XVIII was on the throne. "Give him a chance," Talleyrand pleaded. And the Allies, glad to see a legitimate king upon the throne of a revolutionary country, obligingly yielded and the

Bourbons were given their chance, of which they made such use that they were driven out after fifteen years.

The second man of the triumvirate of Vienna was Metternich, the Austrian prime minister, the leader of the foreign policy of the house of Habsburg. Wenzel Lothar, Prince of Metternich Winneburg, was exactly what the name suggests. He was a Grand Seigneur, a very handsome gentleman with very fine manners, immensely rich, and very able, but the product of a society which lived a thousand miles away from the sweating multitudes who worked and slaved in the cities and on the farms.

As a young man, Metternich had been studying at the University of Strassburg when the French Revolution broke out. Strassburg, the city which gave birth to the Marseillaise, had been a center of Jacobin activities. Metternich remembered that his pleasant social life had been sadly interrupted, that a lot of incompetent citizens had suddenly been called forth to perform tasks for which they were not fit, that the mob had celebrated the dawn of the new liberty by the murder of perfectly "innocent" persons. He had failed to see the honest enthusiasm of the masses, the ray of hope in the eyes of women and children who carried bread and water to the ragged troops of the Convention, marching through the city on their way to the front and a glorious death for the French Fatherland.

The whole thing had filled the young Austrian with disgust. It was uncivilized. If there were any fighting to be done it must be done by dashing young men in lovely uniforms, charging across the green fields on well-groomed horses. But to turn an entire country into an evil smelling armed camp where tramps were overnight promoted to be generals, that was both wicked and senseless in Metternich's eyes. "See what came of all your fine ideas," he would say to the French diplomats whom he met at a quiet little dinner given by one of the innumerable Austrian grand-dukes. "You wanted liberty, equality and fraternity and you got Napoleon. How much better it would have been if you had been contented with the existing order of things." And he would explain his system of "stability." He would advocate a return to the normalcy of the good old days before the war, when everybody was happy, and nobody talked nonsense about "everybody being as good as everybody else." In this attitude he was entirely sincere and as he was an able man of great strength of will and a tremendous power of persuasion, he was one of the most dangerous enemies of the Revolutionary ideas. He did not die until the year 1859, and he therefore lived long enough to see the complete failure of all his policies when they were swept aside by the revolution of the year 1848. He then found himself the most hated man of Europe and more than once ran the risk of being lynched by angry crowds of outraged citizens. But until the very last, he remained steadfast in his belief that he had done the right thing.

He had always been convinced that people preferred peace to liberty, and he had tried to give them what was best for them. And in all fairness, it ought to be said that his efforts to establish universal "peace" were fairly successful. (Of course, true peace only will exist when men are at peace with God and obedient to the Ten Commandments. All other "peace" is a poor imitation.) The great powers did not fly at each other's throat for almost forty years, indeed not until the Crimean war between Russia and England, France and Italy and Turkey, in the year 1854. That means a record for the European continent. But it was at a great price, as I will tell you about.

The third hero of this waltzing congress was the Emperor Alexander. He had been brought up at the court of his grandmother mother, the famous Catherine the Great. Between the lessons of this shrewd old woman, who taught him to regard the glory of Russia as the most important thing in life, and those of his private tutor, a Swiss admirer of Voltaire and Rousseau, who filled his mind with a general love of humanism, the boy grew up to be a strange mixture of a selfish tyrant and a sentimental revolutionist. He had suffered great indignities during the life of his crazy father, Paul I. He had been obliged to witness the wholesale slaughter of the Napoleonic battlefields. Then the tide had turned. His armies had won the day for the Allies. Russia had become the savior of Europe and the Tsar of this mighty people was acclaimed as a half-god who would cure the world of its many ills.

But Alexander was not very clever. He did not know men and women as Talleyrand and Metternich knew them. He did not understand the strange game of diplomacy. He was vain and loved to hear the applause of the multitude and soon he had become the main "attraction" of the Congress while Metternich and Talleyrand and Castlereagh (the very able British representative) sat around a table and drank a bottle of Tokay and decided what was actually going to be done. They needed Russia and therefore they were very polite to Alexander, but the less he had personally to do with the actual work of the Congress, the better they were pleased. They even encouraged his plans for a Holy Alliance that he might be fully occupied while they were engaged upon the work at hand.

Alexander was a sociable person who liked to go to parties and meet people. Upon such occasions he was happy and gay but there was a very different element in his character. He tried to forget something which he could not forget. On the night of the 23rd of March of the year 1801 he had been sitting in a room of the St. Michael Palace in Petersburg, waiting for the news of his father's abdication. But Paul had refused to sign the document which the drunken officers had placed before him on the table, and in their rage, they had put a scarf around his neck and had strangled him to death. Then they had gone downstairs to tell Alexander that he was Emperor of all the Russian lands.

The memory of this terrible night stayed with the Tsar, who was a very sensitive person. He had been educated in the school of the great French philosophers who did not believe in God but in Human Reason. But Reason alone could not satisfy the Emperor in his predicament. He began to hear voices and see things. He tried to find a way by which he could square himself with his conscience. He became very pious and began to take an interest in mysticism, that strange love of the mysterious and the unknown which is as old as the temples of Thebes and Babylon.

The tremendous emotion of the great revolutionary era had influenced the character of the people of that day in a strange way. Men and women who had lived through twenty years of anxiety and fear were no longer quite normal. They jumped whenever the doorbell rang. It might mean the news of the "death on the field of honor" of an only son. The phrases about "brotherly love" and "liberty" of the Revolution were hollow words in the ears of sorely stricken peasants. They clung to anything that might give them a new hold on the terrible problems of life. In their grief and misery, they were easily imposed upon by a large number of imposters who posed as prophets and preached a strange new doctrine which they dug out of the more obscure passages of the Book of Revelation.

In the year 1814, Alexander, who had already consulted a large number of wonder-doctors, heard of a new seeress who was foretelling the coming doom of the world and was exhorting people to repent ere it be too late. The Baroness von Krüdener, the lady in question, was a Russian woman of uncertain age and similar reputation who had been the wife of a Russian diplomat in the days of the Emperor Paul. She had squandered her husband's money and had disgraced him by her strange love affairs. She had lived a very dissolute life until her nerves had given way and for a while she was not in her right mind. Then she had been converted by the sight of the sudden death of a friend. Thereafter she despised all gaiety. She confessed her former sins to her shoemaker, a pious Moravian brother, a follower of the old reformer John Huss, who had been burned for his heresies by the Council of Constance in the year 1415.

The next ten years the Baroness spent in Germany making a specialty of the "conversion" of kings and princes. To convince Alexander, the Savior of Europe, of the error of his ways was the greatest ambition of her life. And as Alexander, in his misery, was willing to listen to anybody who brought him a ray of hope, the interview was easily arranged. On the evening of the fourth of June of the year 1815, she was admitted to the tent of the Emperor. She found him reading his Bible. We do not know what she said to Alexander, but when she left him three hours later, he was bathed in tears, and vowed that "at last his soul had found peace." From that day on the Baroness was his faithful companion and his spiritual adviser. She followed him to Paris and then to Vienna and the time which Alexander did not spend dancing he spent at the Krüdener prayer-meetings.

In many respects Alexander embodied the schizophrenia that is Russia itself. He was humanist, mystic, hedonist, communist, tyrant, Eastern orthodox, royalist, and many other things, all rolled into one. He read his Bible yet had his mistress. He had a love for piety, but he also had a love for party. He was superstitious, yet he avowed rational humanism. It is not coherent, but it is emblematic of the Russian enigma.

You may ask why I tell you this story in such great detail? Are not the social changes of the nineteenth century of greater importance than the career of an ill-balanced woman who had better be forgotten? Of course, they are, but there exist any number of books which will tell you of these other things with great accuracy and in great detail. I want you to learn something more from this history than a mere succession of facts. I want you to approach all historical events in a frame of mind that will take nothing for granted. Don't be satisfied with the mere statement that "such and such a thing happened then and there." Try to discover the hidden motives behind every action and then you will understand the world around you much better.

I do not want you to think of the Holy Alliance as a piece of paper which was signed in the year 1815 and lies dead and forgotten somewhere in the archives of state. It may be forgotten but it is by no means dead. The Holy Alliance was directly responsible for the promulgation of the Monroe Doctrine, and the Monroe Doctrine of America for the Americans has a very distinct bearing upon your own life. That is the reason why I want you to know exactly how this document happened to come into existence and what the real motives underlying this outward manifestation of piety and "Christian" devotion to duty.

The Holy Alliance was the joint labor of an unfortunate man who had suffered a terrible mental shock and who was trying to pacify his much-disturbed soul, and of an ambitious woman who after a wasted life had lost her beauty and her attraction and who satisfied her vanity and her desire for notoriety by assuming the rôle of self-appointed Messiah of a new and strange creed. I am not giving away any secrets when I tell you these details. Such sober minded people as Castlereagh, Metternich and Talleyrand fully understood the limited abilities of the sentimental Baroness. It would have been easy for Metternich to send her back to her German estates. A few lines to the almighty commander of the imperial police and the thing was done.

But France and England and Austria depended upon the good-will of Russia. They could not afford to offend Alexander. And they tolerated the silly old Baroness because they had to. And while they regarded the Holy Alliance as utter rubbish and not worth the paper upon which it was written, they listened patiently to the Tsar when he read them the first rough draft of this attempt to create the Brotherhood of Men upon a fanciful interpretation of the Holy Scriptures. For this is what the Holy Alliance tried to do, and the signers of the document solemnly declared that they would "in the administration of their respective states and in their political relations with every other government take for their sole guide the precepts of that Holy Religion, namely the precepts of Justice, Christian Charity and Peace, which far from being applicable only to private concerns must have an immediate influence on the councils of princes, and must guide all their steps as being the only means of consolidating human institutions and remedying their imperfections." They then proceeded to promise each other that they would remain united "by the bonds of a true and indissoluble fraternity, and considering each other as fellow-countrymen, they would on all occasions and in all places lend each other aid and assistance." And more words to the same effect.

Eventually the Holy Alliance was signed by the Emperor of Austria, who did not understand a word of it. It was signed by the Bourbons who needed the friendship of Napoleon's old enemies. It was signed by the King of Prussia, who hoped to gain Alexander for his plans for a "greater Prussia," and by all the little nations of Europe who were at the mercy of Russia. England never signed, because Castlereagh thought the whole thing buncombe. The Pope did not sign because he resented this interference in his business by a Greek-Orthodox and a Protestant. And the Sultan did not sign because he never heard of it.

The general mass of the European people, however, soon were forced to take notice. Behind the hollow phrases of the Holy Alliance stood the armies of the Quintuple Alliance which Metternich had created among the great powers. These armies meant business. They let it be known that the peace of Europe must not be disturbed by the so-called liberals who were in reality nothing but disguised Jacobins and hoped for a return of the revolutionary days. The enthusiasm for the great wars of liberation of the years 1812, 1818, 1814 and 1815 had begun to wear off. It had been followed by a sincere belief in the coming of a happier day. The soldiers who had borne the brunt of the battle wanted peace and they said so.

But they did not want the sort of peace which the Holy Alliance and the Council of the European powers had now bestowed upon them. They cried that they had been betrayed. But they were careful lest they be heard by a secret-police spy.

LET ME TELL YOU THE REAL STORY OF MANKIND

The reaction was victorious. It was a reaction caused by men who sincerely believed that their methods were necessary for the good of humanity. But it was just as hard to bear as if their intentions had been less kind. And it caused a great deal of unnecessary suffering. A satisfactory peace can never be achieved premised upon false religion, humanism, or pluralism.

CHAPTER 51: The Great Reaction

To undo the damage done by the great Napoleonic flood was almost impossible. Age-old fences had been washed away. The palaces of two score dynasties had been damaged to such an extent that they had to be condemned as uninhabitable. Other royal residences had been greatly enlarged at the expense of less fortunate neighbors. Strange odds and ends of revolutionary doctrine had been left behind by the receding waters and could not be dislodged without danger to the entire community. But the political engineers of the Congress did the best they could, and this is what they accomplished.

France had disturbed the peace of the world for so many years that people had come to fear that country almost instinctively. The Bourbons, through the mouth of Talleyrand, had promised to be good, but the Hundred Days had taught Europe what to expect should Napoleon manage to escape for a second time. The Dutch Republic, therefore, was changed into a Kingdom, and Belgium (which had not joined the Dutch struggle for independence in the sixteenth century and since then had been part of the Habsburg domains, first under Spanish rule and thereafter under Austrian rule) was made part of this new kingdom of the Netherlands. Nobody wanted this union either in the Protestant North or in the Catholic South, but no questions were asked. It seemed good for the peace of Europe and that was the main consideration. Poland had hoped for great things because a Pole, Prince Adam Czartoryski, was one of the most intimate friends of Tsar Alexander and had been his constant advisor during the war and at the Congress of Vienna. But Poland was made a semi-independent part of Russia with Alexander as her king. This solution pleased no one and caused much bitter feeling and three revolutions.

Denmark, which had remained a faithful ally of Napoleon until the end, was severely punished. Seven years before, an English fleet had sailed down the Kattegat and without a declaration of war or any warning had bombarded Copenhagen and had taken away the Danish fleet, lest it be of value to Napoleon. The Congress of Vienna went one step further. It took Norway (which since the union of Calmar of the year 1397 had been united with Denmark) away from Denmark and gave it to Charles XIV of Sweden as a reward for his betrayal of Napoleon, who had set him up in the king business. This Swedish king, curiously enough, was a former French general by the name of Bernadotte, who had come to Sweden as one of Napolean's adjutants, and had been invited to the throne of that country when the last of the rulers of the house of Hollstein-Gottorp had died without leaving either son or daughter. From 1815 until 1844 he ruled his adopted country (the language of which he never learned). He was a clever man and enjoyed the respect of both his Swedish and his Norwegian subjects, but he did not succeed in joining two countries which nature and history had put asunder. The dual Scandinavian state was never a success and in 1905, Norway, in a most peaceful and orderly manner, set up as an independent kingdom and the Swedes bade her "good speed" and very wisely let her go her own way.

The Italians, who since the days of the Renaissance had been at the mercy of a long series of invaders, also had put great hopes in General Bonaparte. The Emperor Napoleon, however, had grievously disappointed them. Instead of the United Italy which the people wanted, they had been divided into a number of little principalities, duchies, republics and the Papal State, which (next to Naples) was the worst governed and most miserable region of the entire peninsula. The Congress of Vienna abolished a few of the Napoleonic republics and in their place resurrected several old principalities which were given to deserving members, both male and female, of the Habsburg family.

The poor Spaniards, who had started the great nationalistic revolt against Napoleon, and who had sacrificed the best blood of the country for their king, were punished severely when the Congress allowed His Majesty to return to his domains. This vicious Romanist creature, known as Ferdinand VII, had spent the last four years of his life as a prisoner of Napoleon. He had improved his days by knitting garments for the statues of his favorite Romish patron saints. He celebrated his return by re-introducing the Inquisition and the torture-chamber, both of which had been abolished by the Revolution.

He was a disgusting person, despised as much by his subjects as by his four wives, but the Holy Alliance maintained him upon his throne and all efforts of the Spaniards to get rid of this curse and make Spain a constitutional kingdom ended in bloodshed and executions.

Portugal had been without a king since the year 1807 when the royal family had fled to the colonies in Brazil. The country had been used as a base of supply for the armies of Wellington during the Peninsula war, which lasted from 1808 until 1814. After 1815 Portugal continued to be a sort of British province until the house of Braganza returned to the throne, leaving one of its members behind in Rio de Janeiro as Emperor of Brazil, the only American Empire which lasted for more than a few years, and which came to an end in 1889 when the country became a republic.

In the east, nothing was done to improve the terrible conditions of both the Slavs and the Greeks who were still subjects of the Sultan. In the year 1804 Black George, a Serbian swineherd, (the founder of the Karageorgevich dynasty) had started a revolt against the Turks, but he had been defeated by his enemies and had been murdered by one of his supposed friends, the rival Serbian leader, called Milosh Obrenovich, (who became the founder of the Obrenovich dynasty) and the

Turks had continued to be the undisputed masters of the Balkans.

The Greeks, who since the loss of their independence, two thousand years before, had been subjects of the Macedonians, the Romans, the Venetians and the Turks, had hoped that their countryman, Capo d'Istria, a native of Corfu and together with Czartoryski, the most intimate personal friends of Alexander, would do something for them. But the Congress of Vienna was not interested in Greeks but was very much interested in keeping all "legitimate" monarchs, Christian, Moslem and otherwise, upon their respective thrones. Therefore, nothing was done.

The last, but perhaps the greatest blunder of the Congress was the treatment of Germany. Germany had been for several centuries quite politically divided, consisting of a couple of kingdoms, a few grand-duchies, a large number of duchies and hundreds of margraviates, principalities, baronies, electorates, free cities and free villages, ruled by the strangest assortment of potentates that was ever seen off the comic opera stage. Frederick the Great had changed this when he created a strong Prussia, but this state had not survived him by many years.

Napoleon had blue-penciled the demand for independence of most of these little countries, and only fifty-two out of a total of more than three hundred had survived the year 1806. During the years of the great struggle for independence, many a young soldier had dreamed of a new Fatherland that should be strong and united. But there can be no union without a strong leadership, and who was to be this leader?

There were five kingdoms in the German speaking lands. The rulers of two of these, Austria and Prussia, were hereditary kings. The rulers of three others, Bavaria, Saxony and Wurtemberg, were kings by Napoleon's appointment, and as they had been the faithful henchmen of the Emperor, their patriotic credit with the other Germans was therefore not very good.

The Congress had established a new German Confederation, a league of thirty-eight sovereign states, under the chairmanship of the King of Austria, who was now known as the Emperor of Austria. It was the sort of make-shift arrangement which satisfied no one. It is true that a German Diet, which met in the old coronation city of Frankfort, had been created to discuss matters of "common policy and importance." But in this Diet, thirty-eight delegates represented thirty-eight different interests and as no decision could be taken without a unanimous vote (a parliamentary rule which had in previous centuries ruined the mighty kingdom of Poland), the famous German Confederation became very soon the laughing stock of Europe and the politics of the old Empire began to resemble those of Central American countries in the 1840s and 1850s.

It was terribly humiliating to the people who had sacrificed everything for a national ideal. But the Congress was not interested in the private feelings of "subjects," and the debate was closed.

Did anybody object? Most assuredly. As soon as the first feeling of hatred against Napoleon had quieted down – as soon as the enthusiasm of the great war had subsided – as soon as the people came to a full realization of the crime that had been committed in the name of "peace and stability" they began to murmur. They even made threats of open revolt. But what could they do? They were powerless. They were at the mercy of the most pitiless and efficient police system the world had ever seen.

The members of the Congress of Vienna honestly and sincerely believed that "the Revolutionary Principle had led to the criminal usurpation of the throne by the former emperor Napoleon." They felt that they were called upon to eradicate the adherents of the so-called "French ideas" just as Philip II had only followed the voice of his conscience when he burned Protestants. In the beginning of the sixteenth century a man who did not believe in the divine right of the Pope to rule his subjects as he saw fit was a "heretic" and it was the "duty" of all loyal citizens to kill him. In the beginning of the nineteenth century, on the continent of Europe, a man who did not believe in the divine right of his king to rule him as he or his Prime Minister saw fit, was a "heretic," and it was the duty of all loyal citizens to denounce him to the nearest policeman and see that he got punished. It was tyrannical situation, designed primarily by Romanists with no true understanding of how to create a blessed civil state.

But the rulers of the year 1815 had learned efficiency in the school of Napoleon. The period between the year 1815 and the year 1860 was the great era of the political spy. Spies were everywhere. They lived in palaces and they were to be found in the lowest gin-shops. They peeped through the keyholes of the ministerial cabinet and they listened to the conversations of the people who were taking the air on the benches of the Municipal Park. They guarded the frontier so that no one might leave without a duly authorized passport and they inspected all packages, that no books with dangerous "French ideas" should enter the realm of their Royal masters. They sat among the students in the lecture hall and woe to the Professor who uttered a word against the existing order of things. They followed the little boys and girls on their way to church lest they play hooky.

In many of these tasks they were assisted by the Romish clergy. The Romish church had suffered greatly during the days of the revolution. The church property had been confiscated. Several priests had been killed and the generation that had learned its catechism from Voltaire and Rousseau and the other French philosophers had danced around the Altar of

Reason when the Committee of Public Safety had abolished the worship of God in October of the year 1793. The Romish priests had followed the "emigrés" into their long exile. Now they returned in the wake of the allied armies and they set to work with a vengeance.

Even the Jesuits came back in 1814 and resumed their former labors of educating the young. Their order had been a little too successful in its fight against the enemies of the church. It had established "provinces" in every part of the world, to teach the natives the blessings of Christianity, but soon it had developed into a regular trading company which was forever interfering with the civil authorities. During the reign of the Marquis de Pombal, the great reforming minister of Portugal, they had been driven out of the Portuguese lands and in the year 1773 at the request of most of the Roman Catholic powers of Europe, the order had been suppressed by Pope Clement XIV. Now they were back on the job and preached the principles of "obedience" and "love for the legitimate dynasty" to children whose parents had hired shop windows that they might laugh at Marie Antoinette driving to the scaffold which was to end her misery.

But in the Protestant countries like Prussia- which had undergone tremendous spiritual declension and widespread theological liberalism- things were not much better. The great patriotic leaders of the year 1812, the poets and the writers who had preached a holy war upon the usurper, were now branded as dangerous "demagogues." Their houses were searched. Their letters were read. They were obliged to report to the police at regular intervals and give an account of themselves. The Prussian drill master was let loose in all his fury upon the younger generation. When a party of students celebrated the tercentenary of the Reformation with noisy but harmless festivities on the old Wartburg, the Prussian bureaucrats had visions of an imminent revolution. When a theological student, more honest than intelligent, killed a Russian government spy who was operating in Germany, universities were placed under police supervision and professors were jailed or dismissed without any form of trial.

Russia, of course, was even more extreme in these anti-revolutionary activities. Alexander had recovered from his attack of piety. He was gradually drifting toward melancholia. He well knew his own limited abilities and understood how, at Vienna, he had been the victim both of Metternich and the Krüdener woman. More and more he turned his back upon the west and became a truly Russian ruler whose interests lay in Constantinople, the old holy city that had been the first teacher of the Slavs. The older he grew, the harder he worked and the less he was able to accomplish. And while he sat in his study, his ministers turned the whole of Russia into a land of military barracks.

It is not a pretty picture. Perhaps I might have shortened this description of the Great Reaction. But it is just as well that you should have a thorough knowledge of this era. It was a ticking time bomb.

CHAPTER 52: National Independence

It will serve no good purpose to say, "if only the Congress of Vienna had done such and such a thing instead of taking such and such a course, the history of Europe in the nineteenth century would have been different." The Congress of Vienna was a gathering of men who had just passed through a great revolution and through twenty years of terrible and almost continuous warfare. They came together for the purpose of giving Europe that "peace and stability" which they thought that the people needed and wanted. They were, as I have said, primarily Romanist reactionaries. They re-arranged the map of Europe in such a way as seemed to them to promise the greatest possibility of a lasting success. They failed. They were, for the greater part, men of their past who remembered the days of their quiet youth and ardently wished a return of that imperial period. They failed to recognize the strong hold which ethnic loyalty played upon the people of the European continent, even as it does upon all mankind. They forgot the aspiration of people to their own nation and nationality. Furthermore, the long history of successful representative government based upon law in the United Kingdom and the United States made it very difficult to explain to continental Europeans why they could not enjoy the same benefits as well.

Napoleon, who respected nothing and nobody, was utterly ruthless in his dealing with national and patriotic aspirations. But the early revolutionary generals had proclaimed the age-old principle that "nationality was not a matter of political frontiers or round skulls and broad noses, but a matter of the heart and soul." In reality, it is also a matter of God's design for mankind. While they were teaching the French children the greatness of the French nation, they encouraged Spaniards and Hollanders and Italians to do the same thing. Soon these people, who all shared Rousseau's belief in the superior virtues of Original Man (remember, humanism and the Age of Enlightenment remained alive and well; they did not die with Napoleon) began to dig into their past and found, buried beneath the ruins of the feudal system, the bones of the mighty races of which they supposed themselves the feeble descendants.

The first half of the nineteenth century was the era of the great historical discoveries. Everywhere historians were busy publishing medieval charters and early medieval chronicles and in every country the result was a new pride in the old fatherland. In practical politics, it too often does not matter what is true, but depends upon what the people believe to be true. And in most countries both the kings and their subjects firmly believed in the glory and fame of their ancestors.

The Congress of Vienna was not inclined to be sentimental. Their Excellencies divided the map of Europe according to the best interests of half a dozen dynasties and put "national aspirations" upon the Index, or list of forbidden books, together with all other dangerous "French doctrines."

But history is no respecter of Congresses. Divine law has set forth that nations are necessary for the orderly development of human society and the attempt to stem this tide was quite as unsuccessful as the Metternichian effort to prevent people from thinking.

Curiously enough the first trouble began in a very distant part of the world, in South America. The Spanish colonies of that continent had been enjoying a period of relative independence during the many years of the great Napoleonic wars. They had even remained faithful to their king when he was taken prisoner by the French Emperor and they had refused to recognize Joseph Bonaparte, who had in the year 1808 been made King of Spain by order of his brother.

Indeed, the only part of America to get very much upset by the Revolution was the island of Haiti, the Espagnola of Columbus' first trip. Here in the year 1791 the French Convention, in a sudden outburst of love and human brotherhood, had bestowed upon their black brethren all the privileges hitherto enjoyed by their white masters. Just as suddenly they had repented of this step, but the attempt to undo the original promise led to many years of terrible warfare between General Leclerc, the brother-in-law of Napoleon, and Toussaint l'Ouverture, the negro chieftain.

In the year 1801, Toussaint was asked to visit Leclerc and discuss terms of peace. He received the solemn promise that he would not be molested. He trusted his white adversaries, was put on board a ship and shortly afterwards died in a French prison. But the negroes gained their independence all the same and founded a Republic, in the process killing many of the white inhabitants, and forcing the rest to flee. White departure from the island led to precipitous economic decline and abject poverty, combined with long term political turmoil.

Simon Bolivar, a native of Caracas in Venezuela, born in the year 1783, had been educated in Spain, had visited Paris where he had seen the Revolutionary government at work, had lived for a while in the United States and had returned to his native land where the widespread discontent against Spain, the mother country, was beginning to take a definite form.

In the year 1811, Venezuela declared its independence and Bolivar became one of the revolutionary generals. Within two months, the rebels were defeated, and Bolivar fled.

For the next five years he was the leader of an apparently lost cause. He sacrificed all his wealth and he would not have been able to begin his final and successful expedition without the support of the President of Haiti. Thereafter the revolt spread all over South America and soon it appeared that Spain was not able to suppress the rebellion unaided. She asked for the support of the Holy Alliance.

This step greatly worried England. The British shippers had succeeded the Dutch as the Common Carriers of the world and they expected to reap heavy profits from a declaration of independence on the part of all South America. They had hopes that the United States of America would interfere, but the Senate had no such plans and, in the House, too, there were many voices which declared that Spain ought to be given a free hand.

Just then, there was a change of ministers in England. The Whigs went out and the Tories came in. George Canning became secretary of State. He dropped a hint that England would gladly back up the American government with all the might of her fleet, if said government would declare its disapproval of the plans of the Holy Alliance in regard to the rebellious colonies of the southern continent. President Monroe thereupon, on the 2nd of December of the year 1823, addressed Congress and stated that: "America would consider any attempt on the part of the allied powers to extend their system to any portion of this western hemisphere as dangerous to our peace and safety," and gave warning that "the American government would consider such action on the part of the Holy Alliance as a manifestation of an unfriendly disposition toward the United States." Four weeks later, the text of the "Monroe Doctrine" was printed in the English newspapers and the members of the Holy Alliance were forced to make their choice.

Metternich hesitated. Personally, he would have been willing to risk the displeasure of the United States (which had allowed both its army and navy to fall into neglect since the end of the Anglo-American war of the year 1812). But Canning's threatening attitude and trouble on the continent forced him to be careful. The expedition never took place and South America and Mexico gained their independence.

As for the troubles on the continent of Europe, they were coming fast and furious. The Holy Alliance had sent French troops to Spain to act as guardians of the peace in the year 1820. Austrian troops had been used for a similar purpose in Italy when the "Carbonari" (the secret society of the Charcoal Burners) were making propaganda for a united Italy and had caused a rebellion against the unspeakable Ferdinand of Naples.

Bad news also came from Russia where the death of Alexander had been the sign for a revolutionary outbreak in St. Petersburg, a short but bloody upheaval, the so-called Dekaberist revolt (because it took place in December,) which ended with the hanging of a large number of patriots who had been disgusted by the reaction of Alexander's last years and had tried to give Russia a constitutional form of government.

But worse was to follow. Metternich had tried to assure himself of the continued support of the European courts by a series of conferences at Aix-la-Chapelle at Troppau at Laibach and finally at Verona. The delegates from the different powers duly travelled to these agreeable watering places where the Austrian prime minister used to spend his summers. They always promised to do their best to suppress revolt, but they were none too certain of their success. The spirit of the people was beginning to be ugly and especially in France the position of the king was by no means satisfactory.

The real trouble, however, began in the Balkans, the gateway to western Europe through which the invaders of that continent had passed since the beginning of time. The first outbreak was in Moldavia, the ancient Roman province of Dacia which had been cut off from the Empire in the third century. Since then, it had been a lost land, a sort of Atlantis, where the people had continued to speak the old Roman tongue and still called themselves Romans and their country Romania.

Here in the year 1821, a young Greek, Prince Alexander Ypsilanti, began a revolt against the Turks.

He told his followers that they could count upon the support of Russia. But Metternich's fast couriers were soon on their way to St Petersburg and the Tsar, entirely persuaded by the Austrian arguments in favor of "peace and stability," refused to help. Ypsilanti was forced to flee to Austria where he spent the next seven years in prison.

In the same year, 1821, trouble began in Greece. Since 1815 a secret society of Greek patriots had been preparing the way for a revolt. Suddenly they hoisted the flag of independence in the Morea (the ancient Peloponnesus) and drove the Turkish garrisons away. The Turks answered in the usual fashion. They took the Greek Patriarch of Constantinople, who was regarded as their Pope both by the Greeks and by many Russians, and they hanged him on Easter Sunday of the year 1821, together with a number of his bishops. The Greeks came back with a massacre of all the Mohammedans in Tripolitsa, the capital of the Morea and the Turks retaliated by an attack upon the island of Chios, where they murdered 25,000 Christians and sold 45,000 others as slaves into Asia and Egypt.

Then the Greeks appealed to the European courts, but Metternich told them in so many words that they could "stew in their own grease," (I am not trying to make a pun, but I am quoting His Serene Highness who informed the Tsar that this "fire of revolt ought to burn itself out beyond the pale of civilization") and the frontiers were closed to those volunteers who wished to go to the rescue of the patriotic Hellenes. Their cause seemed lost. At the request of Turkey, an Egyptian army was landed in the Morea and soon the Turkish flag was again flying from the Acropolis, the ancient stronghold of Athens. The Egyptian army then pacified the country "à la Turque," and Metternich followed the proceedings with quiet interest, awaiting the day when this "attempt against the peace of Europe" should be a thing of the past.

Once more it was England which upset his plans. There never has been a cause, however unpopular or however distant, which has not counted a number of Englishmen among its staunchest adherents. The mass of the English people is not different from those in other lands. They stick to the business at hand and have no time for unpractical "sporting ventures." But they rather admire their eccentric neighbor who drops everything to go and fight for some obscure people in Asia or Africa and when he has been killed, they give him a fine public funeral and hold him up to their children as an example of valor and chivalry.

Even the police spies of the Holy Alliance were powerless against this national characteristic. In the year 1824, Lord Byron, a rich young Englishman who wrote the poetry over which all Europe wept, hoisted the sails of his yacht and started south to help the Greeks. Three months later the news spread through Europe that their hero lay dead in Missolonghi, the last of the Greek strongholds. His lonely death caught the imagination of the people. In all countries, societies were formed to help the Greeks. Lafayette, the grand old man of the American revolution, pleaded their cause in France. The king of Bavaria sent hundreds of his officers. Money and supplies poured in upon the starving men of Missolonghi.

In England, George Canning, who had defeated the plans of the Holy Alliance in South America, was now prime minister. He saw his chance to checkmate Metternich for a second time. The English and Russian fleets were already in the Mediterranean. They were sent by governments which dared no longer suppress the popular enthusiasm for the cause of the Greek patriots. The French navy appeared because France, since the end of the Crusades, had assumed the role of the defender of the Christian faith in Mohammedan lands. On October 20 of the year 1827, the ships of the three nations attacked the Turkish fleet in the bay of Navarino and destroyed it. Rarely has the news of a battle been received with such general rejoicing. The people of western Europe and Russia who enjoyed no freedom at home consoled themselves by fighting an imaginary war of liberty on behalf of the oppressed Greeks. In the year 1829 they had their reward. Greece became an independent nation and the policy of reaction and stability suffered its second great defeat.

It would be absurd were I to try, in this short volume, to give you a detailed account of the struggle for national independence in all other countries. There are a large number of excellent books devoted to such subjects. I have described the struggle for the independence of Greece because it was the first successful attack upon the bulwark of reaction which the Congress of Vienna had erected to "maintain the stability of Europe." That mighty fortress of suppression still held out and Metternich continued to be in command. But the end was near.

In France the Bourbons had established an almost unbearable rule of police officials who were trying to undo the work of the French revolution, with an absolute disregard of the regulations and laws of civilized warfare. When Louis XVIII died in the year 1824, the people had enjoyed nine years of "peace" which had proved even more unhappy than the ten years of war of the Empire. Louis was succeeded by his brother, Charles X.

Louis had belonged to that famous Bourbon family which, although it never learned anything, never forgot anything. The recollection of that morning in the town of Hamm, when news had reached him of the decapitation of his brother, remained a constant warning of what might happen to those kings who did not read the signs of the times aright. Charles, on the other hand, who had managed to run up private debts of fifty million francs before he was twenty years of age, knew nothing, remembered nothing and firmly intended to learn nothing. As soon as he had succeeded his brother, he established a government "by priests, through priests and for priests," and while the Duke of Wellington, who made this remark, cannot be called a violent liberal, Charles ruled in such a way that he disgusted even that trusted friend of law and order. When he tried to suppress the newspapers which dared to criticize his government, and dismissed the Parliament because it supported the Press, his days were numbered.

On the night of the 27th of July of the year 1830, a revolution took place in Paris. On the 30th of the same month, the king fled to the coast and set sail for England. In this way the "famous farce of fifteen years" came to an end and the Bourbons were at last removed from the throne of France. They were too hopelessly incompetent. France then might have returned to a Republican form of government, but such a step would not have been tolerated by Metternich.

The situation was dangerous enough. The spark of rebellion had leaped beyond the French frontier and had set fire to another powder house filled with national grievances. The new kingdom of the Netherlands had not been a success. The Belgian and the Dutch people had nothing in common and their king, William of Orange (the descendant of an uncle of William the Silent), while a hard worker and a good business man, was too much lacking in tact and pliability to keep the peace among his uncongenial subjects. Besides, the horde of Romish priests which had descended upon France, had at once found its way into Belgium and whatever Protestant William tried to do was howled down by large crowds of excited citizens as a fresh attempt upon the "freedom of the Catholic church." On the 25th of August there was a popular outbreak against the Dutch authorities in Brussels. Two months later, the Belgians declared themselves independent and elected Leopold of Coburg, the uncle of Queen Victoria of England, to the throne. The two countries, which never ought to have been united, parted their ways and thereafter lived in relative harmony, each leaving the other alone.

News in those days when there were only a few short railroads, travelled slowly, but when the success of the French and the Belgian revolutionists became known in Poland there was an immediate clash between the Poles and their Russian rulers which led to a year of terrible warfare and ended with a complete victory for the Russians who "established order along the banks of the Vistula" in the well-known Russian fashion. Nicholas the first, who had succeeded his brother Alexander in 1825, firmly believed in the Divine Right of his own family, and the thousands of Polish refugees who had found shelter in western Europe bore witness to the fact that the principles of the Holy Alliance were still more than a hollow phrase in Holy Russia.

In Italy too there was a moment of unrest. Marie Louise Duchess of Parma and wife of the former Emperor Napoleon, whom she had deserted after the defeat of Waterloo, was driven away from her country, and in the Papal state the exasperated people tried to establish an independent Republic. But the armies of Austria marched to Rome and soon everything was as of old. Metternich continued to reside at the Ball Platz, the home of the foreign minister of the Habsburg dynasty, the police spies returned to their job, and peace reigned supreme. Eighteen more years were to pass before a second and more successful attempt could be made to deliver Europe from the terrible inheritance of the Vienna Congress.

Again, it was France, the revolutionary weathercock of Europe, which gave the signal of revolt. Charles X had been succeeded by Louis Philippe, the son of that famous Duke of Orleans who had turned Jacobin, had voted for the death of his cousin the king, and had played a rôle during the early days of the revolution under the name of "Philippe Egalité" or "Equality Philip." Eventually he had been killed when Robespierre tried to purge the nation of all "traitors," (by which name he indicated those people who did not share his own views) and his son had been forced to run away from the revolutionary army. Young Louis Philippe thereupon had wandered far and wide. He had taught school in Switzerland and had spent a couple of years exploring the unknown "far west" of America. After the fall of Napoleon, he had returned to Paris. He was much more intelligent than his Bourbon cousins. He was a simple man who went about in the public parks with a red cotton umbrella under his arm, followed by a brood of children like any good housefather. But France had outgrown the king business and Louis did not know this until the morning of the 24th of February, of the year 1848, when a crowd stormed the Tuileries and drove his Majesty away and proclaimed the Republic.

When the news of this event reached Vienna, Metternich expressed the casual opinion that this was only a repetition of the year 1793 and that the Allies would once more be obliged to march upon Paris and make an end to this very unseemly democratic row. But two weeks later his own Austrian capital was in open revolt. Metternich escaped from the mob through the back door of his palace, and the Emperor Ferdinand was forced to give his subjects a constitution which embodied most of the revolutionary principles which his Prime Minister had tried to suppress for the last thirty-three years.

This time all Europe felt the shock. Hungary declared itself independent and commenced a war against the Habsburgs under the leadership of Louis Kossuth. The unequal struggle lasted more than a year. It was finally suppressed by the armies of Tsar Nicholas who marched across the Carpathian Mountains and made Hungary, once more, safe for autocracy. The Habsburgs thereupon established extraordinary court-martials and hanged the greater part of the Hungarian patriots whom they had not been able to defeat in open battle.

As for Italy, the island of Sicily declared itself independent from Naples and drove its Bourbon king away. In the Papal states the prime minister, Rossi, was murdered and the Pope was forced to flee.

He returned the next year at the head of a French army which remained in Rome to protect His "Holiness" against his subjects until the year 1870. Then it was called back to defend France against the Prussians, and Rome became the capital of Italy. In the north, Milan and Venice rose against their Austrian masters. They were supported by king Albert of Sardinia, but a strong Austrian army under old Radetzky marched into the valley of the Po, defeated the Sardinians near Custozza and Novara and forced Albert to abdicate in favour of his son, Victor Emanuel, who a few years later was to be the first king of a united Italy.

In Germany, the unrest of the year 1848 took the form of a great national demonstration in favor of political unity and a representative form of government. In Bavaria, the king who had wasted his time and money upon an Irish lady who posed as a Spanish dancer – (she was called Lola Montez and lies buried in New York's Potter's Field) – was driven away by the enraged students of the university. In Prussia, the king was forced to stand with uncovered head before the coffins of those who had been killed during the street fighting and to promise a constitutional form of government. And in March of the year 1849, a German parliament, consisting of 550 delegates from all parts of the country came together in Frankfort and proposed that king Frederick William of Prussia should be the Emperor of a United Germany.

Then, however, the tide began to turn. Incompetent Ferdinand had abdicated in favor of his nephew Francis Joseph. The well-drilled Austrian army had remained faithful to their warlord. The hangman was given plenty of work and the Habsburgs, after the nature of that strangely cat-like family, once more landed upon their feet and rapidly strengthened their position as the masters of eastern and western Europe. They played the game of politics very adroitly and used the jealousies of the other German states to prevent the elevation of the Prussian king to the Imperial dignity. Their long training in the art of suffering defeat had taught them the value of patience. They knew how to wait. They bided their time and while the liberals, utterly untrained in practical politics, talked and talked and talked and got intoxicated by their own fine speeches, the Austrians quietly gathered their forces, dismissed the Parliament of Frankfort and reestablished the old and impossible German confederation which the Congress of Vienna had wished upon an unsuspecting world.

But among the men who had attended this strange Parliament of unpractical enthusiasts, there was a Prussian country squire by the name of Bismarck, who had made good use of his eyes and ears. He had a deep contempt for oratory. In his own way he was a sincere patriot. He had been trained in the old school of diplomacy and he could outlie his opponents just as he could outwalk them and outdrink them and outride them.

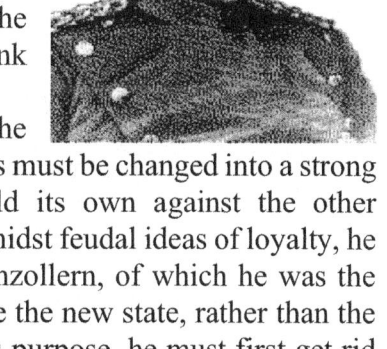

Bismarck felt convinced that the loose confederation of little states must be changed into a strong united country if it would hold its own against the other European powers. Brought up amidst feudal ideas of loyalty, he decided that the house of Hohenzollern, of which he was the most faithful servant, should rule the new state, rather than the incompetent Habsburgs. For this purpose, he must first get rid of the Austrian influence, and he began to make the necessary preparations for this painful operation.

LET ME TELL YOU THE REAL STORY OF MANKIND

Italy in the meantime had solved her own problem and had rid herself of her hated Austrian master. The unity of Italy was the work of three men, Cavour, Mazzini and Garibaldi. Of these three, Cavour, the civil-engineer with the short-sighted eyes and the steel-rimmed glasses, played the part of the careful political pilot. Mazzini, who had spent most of his days in different European garrets, hiding from the Austrian police, was the public agitator, while Garibaldi, with his band of red-shirted rough-riders, appealed to the popular imagination.

Mazzini and Garibaldi were both believers in the Republican form of government. Cavour, however, was a monarchist, and the others who recognized his superior ability in such matters of practical statecraft, accepted his decision and sacrificed their own ambitions for the greater good of their beloved Fatherland.

Cavour felt towards the House of Sardinia as Bismarck did towards the Hohenzollern family. With great care and shrewdness, he set to work to jockey the Sardinian King into a position from which His Majesty would be able to assume the leadership of the entire Italian people. The unsettled political conditions in the rest of Europe greatly helped him in his plans and no country contributed more to the independence of Italy than her old and trusted (and often distrusted) neighbor, France.

In that turbulent country, in November of the year 1852, the Republic had come to a sudden but not unexpected end. Napoleon III the son of Louis Bonaparte the former King of Holland, and the small nephew of a great uncle, had reestablished an Empire and had made himself Emperor "by the Grace of God and the Will of the People."

This young man, who had been educated in Germany and who mixed his French with harsh Teutonic gutturals (just as the first Napoleon had always spoken the language of his adopted country with a strong Italian accent) was trying very hard to use the Napoleonic tradition for his own benefit. But he had many enemies and did not feel very certain of his hold upon his ready-made throne.

He had gained the friendship of Queen Victoria, but this had not been a difficult task, as the Queen was not particularly brilliant and was very susceptible to flattery.

As for the other European sovereigns, they treated the French Emperor with insulting haughtiness and sat up nights devising new ways in which they could show their upstart "Good Brother" how sincerely they despised him.

Napoleon was obliged to find a way in which he could break this opposition, either through love or through fear. He well knew the fascination which the word "glory" still held for his subjects. Since he was forced to gamble for his throne, he decided to play the game of Empire for high stakes. He used an attack of Russia upon Turkey as an excuse for bringing about the Crimean war in which England and France combined against the Tsar on behalf of the Sultan. It was a very costly and exceedingly unprofitable enterprise. Neither France nor England nor Russia reaped much glory.

But the Crimean war did one good thing. It gave Sardinia a chance to volunteer on the winning side and when peace was declared it gave Cavour the opportunity to lay claim to the gratitude of both England and France.

Having made use of the international situation to get Sardinia recognized as one of the more important powers of Europe, the clever Italian then provoked a war between Sardinia and Austria in June of the year 1859. He assured himself of the support of Napoleon in exchange for the provinces of Savoy and the city of Nice, which was really an Italian town. The Franco-Italian armies defeated the Austrians at Magenta and Solferino, and the former Austrian provinces and duchies were united into a single Italian kingdom. Florence became the capital of this new Italy until the year 1870 when the French recalled their troops from Home to defend France against the Germans. As soon as they were gone, the Italian troops entered the eternal city and the House of Sardinia took up its residence in the old Palace of the Quirinal which an ancient Pope had built on the ruins of the baths of the Emperor Constantine.

The Pope, however, moved across the river Tiber and hid behind the walls of the Vatican, which had been the home of many of his predecessors since their return from the exile of Avignon in the year 1377. He protested loudly against this high-handed theft of his domains and addressed letters of appeal to those Roman Catholics who were inclined to sympathize with him in his loss. Their number, however, was small, and it has been steadily decreasing. So nothing came of the Papacy's protests.

In this way, the attempt of the Congress of Vienna to settle the Italian question by making the peninsula an Austrian province was at last undone.

The German problem, however, remained as yet unsolved. It proved the most difficult of all. The failure of the revolution of the year 1848 had led to the wholesale migration of the more energetic and liberal elements among the German people. These young fellows had moved to the United States of America, to Brazil, to the new colonies in Asia and America. Their work was continued in Germany but by a different sort of men.

In the new Diet which met at Frankfort, after the collapse of the German Parliament and the failure of the Liberals to establish a united country, the Kingdom of Prussia was represented by that same Otto von Bismarck from whom we parted a few pages ago. Bismarck by now had managed to gain the complete confidence of the king of Prussia.

That was all he asked for. The opinion of the Prussian parliament or of the Prussian people interested him not at all. With his own eyes he had seen the defeat of the Liberals. He knew that he would not be able to get rid of Austria without a war and he began by strengthening the Prussian army. The Landtag, exasperated at his high-handed methods, refused to give him the necessary credits. Bismarck did not even bother to discuss the matter. He went ahead and increased his army with the help of funds which the Prussian house of Peers and the king placed at his disposal. Then he looked for a national cause which could be used for the purpose of creating a great wave of patriotism among all the German people.

In the north of Germany there were the Duchies of Schleswig and Holstein which, ever since the middle ages, had been a source of trouble. Both countries were inhabited by a certain number of Danes and a certain number of Germans, but although they were governed by the King of Denmark, they were not an integral part of the Danish State and this led to endless difficulties. The Germans in Holstein were very loud in their abuse of the Danes and the Danes in Schleswig made a great ado of their Danishness, and all Europe was discussing the problem and German Mannerchors and Turnvereins listened to sentimental speeches about the "lost brethren" and the different chancelleries were trying to discover what it was all about, when Prussia mobilized her armies to "save the lost provinces." As Austria, the official head of the German Confederation, could not allow Prussia to act alone in such an important matter, the Habsburg troops were mobilized too and the combined armies of the two great powers crossed the Danish frontiers and after a very brave resistance on the part of the Danes, occupied the two duchies. The Danes appealed to Europe, but Europe was otherwise engaged, and the poor Danes were left to their fate.

Bismarck then prepared the scene for the second number upon his Imperial program. He used the division of the spoils to pick a quarrel with Austria. The Habsburgs fell into the trap. The new Prussian army, the creation of Bismarck and his faithful generals, invaded Bohemia and in less than six weeks, the last of the Austrian troops had been destroyed at Königgratz and Sadowa and the road to Vienna lay open. But Bismarck did not want to go too far. He knew that he would need a few friends in Europe. He offered the defeated Habsburgs very decent terms of peace, provided they would resign their chairmanship of the Confederation. He was less merciful to many of the smaller German states who had taken the side of the Austrians and annexed them to Prussia. The greater part of the northern states then formed a new organization, the so-called North German Confederacy, and victorious Prussia assumed the unofficial leadership of the German people.

Europe stood aghast at the rapidity with which the work of consolidation had been done. England was quite indifferent, but France showed signs of disapproval. Napoleon's hold upon the French people was steadily diminishing. The Crimean war had been costly and had accomplished nothing.

A second adventure in the year 1863, when a French army had tried to force an Austrian Grand-Duke by the name of Maximilian upon the Mexican people as their Emperor, had come to a disastrous end as soon as the American Civil War had been won by the North. For the Government at Washington had forced the French to withdraw their troops and this had given the Mexicans a chance to clear their country of the enemy and shoot the unwelcome Emperor.

It was necessary to give the Napoleonic throne a new coat of glory-paint. Within a few years the North German Confederation would be a serious rival of France. Napoleon decided that a war with Germany would be a good thing for his dynasty. He looked for an excuse and Spain, the poor victim of endless revolutions, gave him one. Just then the Spanish throne happened to be vacant. It had been offered to the Roman Catholic branch of the house of Hohenzollern. The French government had objected, and the Hohenzollerns had politely refused to accept the crown. But Napoleon, who was showing signs of illness, was very much under the influence of his beautiful wife, Eugénie de Montijo, the daughter of a Spanish gentleman and the granddaughter of William Kirkpatrick, an American consul at Malaga, where the grapes come from. Eugénie, although shrewd enough, was as badly educated as most Spanish women of that day. She was at the mercy of her spiritual advisers and these worthy gentlemen felt no love for the Protestant King of Prussia. "Be bold," was the advice of the Empress to her husband, but she omitted to add the second half of that famous Persian proverb which admonishes the hero to "be bold but not too bold." Napoleon, convinced of the strength of his army, addressed himself to the king of Prussia and insisted that the king give him assurances that "he would never permit another candidature of a Hohenzollern prince to the Spanish crown." As the Hohenzollerns had just declined the honor, the demand was superfluous, and Bismarck so informed the French government. But Napoleon was not satisfied.

It was the year 1870 and King William was taking the waters at Ems. There one day he was approached by the French minister who tried to re-open the discussion. The king answered very pleasantly that it was a fine day and that the Spanish question was now closed and that nothing more remained to be said upon the subject. As a matter of routine, a report of this interview was telegraphed to Bismarck, who handled all foreign affairs. Bismarck edited the dispatch for the benefit of the Prussian and French press. Many people have called him names for doing this. Bismarck however could plead the excuse that the doctoring of official news, since time immemorial, had been one of the privileges of all "civilized" (albeit corrupt) governments. When the "edited" telegram was printed, the good people in Berlin felt that their old and venerable king with his nice white whiskers had been insulted by an arrogant little Frenchman and the equally good people of Paris flew into a rage because their perfectly courteous minister had been shown the door by a Royal Prussian flunkey.

And so, they both went to war and in less than two months, Napoleon and the greater part of his army were prisoners of the Germans. The Second Empire had come to an end and the Third Republic was making ready to defend Paris against the German invaders. Paris held out for five long months. Ten days before the surrender of the city, in the nearby palace of Versailles, built by that same King Louis XIV who had been such a dangerous enemy to the Germans, the King of Prussia was publicly proclaimed German Emperor and a loud booming of guns told the hungry Parisians that a new German Empire had taken the place of the old harmless Confederation of Teutonic states and stateless.

In this rough way, the German question was finally settled. By the end of the year 1871, fifty-six years after the memorable gathering at Vienna, the work of the Congress had been entirely undone. Metternich and Alexander and Talleyrand had tried to give the people of Europe a lasting peace. The methods they had employed had caused endless wars and revolutions and the feeling of a common brotherhood of the eighteenth century was followed by an era of nationalism.

LET ME TELL YOU THE REAL STORY OF MANKIND

CHAPTER 53: The Age of the Engine and the Industrial Revolution

In Washington, the story is told of a director of the Patent Office who in the early thirties of the last century suggested that the Patent Office be abolished, because "everything that possibly could be invented had been invented." Indeed one of the most interesting chapters of history is the effort of man to let someone else or something else do his work for him, while he enjoyed his leisure, sitting in the sun or painting pictures on rocks, or training young wolves and little tigers to behave like peaceful domestic animals.

Of course, in the very olden days it was always possible to enslave a weaker neighbor and force him to do the unpleasant tasks of life. One of the reasons why the Greeks and Romans, who were quite as intelligent as we are, failed to devise more interesting machinery, was to be found in the widespread existence of slavery. Why should a great mathematician waste his time upon wires and pulleys and cogs and fill the air with noise and smoke when he could go to the marketplace and buy all the slaves he needed at a very small expense?

And during the Middle Ages, although slavery had been abolished and only a mild form of serfdom survived, the guilds discouraged the idea of using machinery because they thought this would throw a large number of their brethren out of work. Besides, the Middle-Ages were not at all interested in producing large quantities of goods. Their tailors and butchers and carpenters worked for the immediate needs of the small community in which they lived and had no desire to compete with their neighbors, or to produce more than was strictly necessary. But towards the latter stages of the Middle Ages trade began to increase. And the Protestant Reformation had the tendency of greatly enhancing the climate for economic enterprise and innovation.

So, following the Reformation, a large number of people began to devote their lives to mathematics and astronomy and physics and chemistry. Two years before the beginning of the Thirty Years War, John Napier, a Scotchman, had published his little book which described the new invention of logarithms. During the war itself, Gottfried Leibnitz of Leipzig had perfected the system of infinitesimal calculus. Eight years before the peace of Westphalia, Newton, the great English natural philosopher, was born, and in that same year Galileo, the Italian astronomer, died.

The work of all these people provided the world with a solid scientific foundation upon which it was possible to build even the most complicated of engines, and a number of practical people made good use of it. The Middle Ages had used wood for the few bits of necessary machinery. But wood wore out easily. Iron was a much better material, but iron was scarce except in England. In England therefore most of the smelting was done. To smelt iron, huge fires were needed. In the beginning, these fires had been made of wood, but gradually the forests had been used up. Then "stone coal" (the petrified trees of ancient times) was used. But coal as you know has to be dug out of the ground and it has to be transported to the smelting ovens and the mines have to be kept dry from the ever-invading waters.

These were two problems which had to be solved at once. For the time being, horses could still be used to haul the coal-wagons, but the pumping question demanded the application of special machinery. Several inventors were busy trying to solve the difficulty. They all knew that steam would have to be used in their new engine. The idea of the steam engine was very old. Hero of Alexandria, who lived in the first century before Christ, has described to us several bits of machinery which were driven by steam. The people of the Renaissance and Reformation had played with the notion of steam-driven war chariots. The Marquis of Worcester, a contemporary of Newton, in his book of inventions, tells of a steam engine. A little later, in the year 1698, Thomas Savery of London applied for a patent for a pumping engine. At the same time, a Hollander, Christian Huygens, was trying to perfect an engine in which gunpowder was used to cause regular explosions in much the same way as we use gasoline in our motors.

All over Europe, people were busy with the idea. Denis Papin, a Frenchman, friend and assistant of Huygens, was making experiments with steam engines in several countries. He invented a little wagon that was driven by steam, and a paddle-wheel boat. But when he tried to take a trip in his vessel, it was confiscated by the authorities on a complaint of the boatmen's union, who feared that such a craft would deprive them of their livelihood. Papin finally died in London in great poverty, having wasted all his money on his inventions. But at the time of his death, another mechanical enthusiast, Thomas Newcomen, was working on the problem of a new steam-pump.

Fifty years later, his engine was improved upon by James Watt, a Glasgow instrument maker. In the year 1777, he gave the world the first steam engine that proved of real practical value.

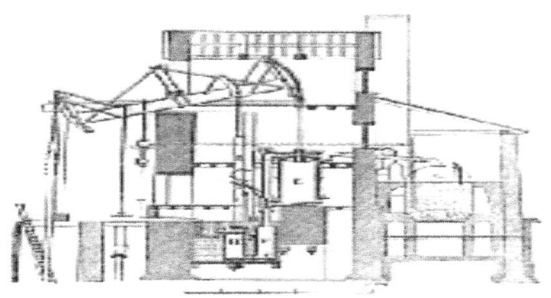

But during the centuries of experiments with a "heat-engine," the political world had greatly changed. The British people had succeeded the Dutch as the common carriers of the world's trade. They had opened up new colonies. They took the raw materials which the colonies produced to England, and there they turned them into finished products, and then they exported the finished goods to the four corners of the world. During the seventeenth century, the people of Georgia and the Carolinas had begun to grow a new shrub which gave a strange sort of woolly substance, the so-called "cotton wool." After this had been plucked, it was sent to England and there the people of Lancastershire wove it into cloth. This weaving was done by hand and in the homes of the workmen. Very soon, a number of improvements were made in the process of weaving. In the year 1730, John Kay invented the "fly shuttle." In 1770, James Hargreaves got a patent on his "spinning jenny." Eli Whitney, an American, invented the cotton-gin, which separated the cotton from its seeds, a job which had previously been done by hand at the rate of only a pound a day. Finally, Richard Arkwright and the Reverend Edmund Cartwright invented large weaving machines, which were driven by waterpower. And then, in the eighties of the eighteenth century, just when the Estates General of France had begun those infamous meetings which were to revolutionize the political system of Europe, the engines of Watt were arranged in such a way that they could drive the weaving machines of Arkwright, and this created an economic and social revolution which has changed human relationship in almost every part of the world.

As soon as the stationary engine had proved a success, the inventors turned their attention to the problem of propelling boats and carts with the help of a mechanical contrivance. Watt himself designed plans for a "steam locomotive," but ere he had perfected his ideas, in the year 1804, a locomotive made by Richard Trevithick carried a load of twenty tons at Pen-y-darran in the Wales mining district.

At the same time, an American jeweler and portrait-painter by the name of Robert Fulton was in Paris, trying to convince Napoleon that with the use of his submarine boat, the

"Nautilus," and his "steam-boat," the French might be able to destroy the naval supremacy of England.

Fulton's idea of a steamboat was not original. He had undoubtedly copied it from John Fitch, a mechanical genius of Connecticut whose cleverly constructed steamer had first navigated the Delaware river as early as the year 1787. But Napoleon and his scientific advisers did not believe in the practical possibility of a self-propelled boat, and although the Scotch-built engine of the little craft puffed merrily on the Seine, the great Emperor neglected to avail himself of this formidable weapon which might have given him his revenge for Trafalgar.

As for Fulton, he returned to the United States and, being a practical man of business, he organized a successful steamboat company together with Robert R. Livingston, a signer of the Declaration of Independence, who was American Minister to France when Fulton was in Paris, trying to sell his invention. The first steamer of this new company, the "Clermont," which was given a monopoly of all the waters of New York State, equipped with an engine built by Boulton and Watt of Birmingham in England, began a regular service between New York and Albany in the year 1807.

As for poor John Fitch, the man who long before anyone else had used the "steam-boat" for commercial purposes, he came to a sad death. Broken in health and empty of purse, he had come to the end of his resources when his fifth boat, which was propelled by means of a screw propeller, had been destroyed. His neighbors jeered at him as they were to laugh a hundred years later when Professor Langley constructed his funny flying machines. Fitch had hoped to give his country an easy access to the broad rivers of the west and his countrymen preferred to travel in flat-boats or go on foot. In the year 1798, in utter despair and misery, Fitch killed himself by taking poison.

But twenty years later, the "Savannah," a steamer of 1850 tons and making six knots an hour, crossed the ocean from Savannah to Liverpool in the record time of twenty-five days. Then there was an end to the derision of the multitude and in their enthusiasm the people gave the credit for the invention to the wrong man.

Six years later, George Stephenson, a Scotchman, who had been building locomotives for the purpose of hauling coal from the mine-pit to smelting ovens and cotton factories, built his famous "traveling engine" which reduced the price of coal by almost seventy per cent and which made it possible to establish the first regular passenger service between Manchester and Liverpool, when people were whisked from city to city at the unheard-of speed of fifteen miles per hour. A dozen years later, this speed had been increased to twenty miles per hour.   But while these practically-minded engineers were improving upon their rattling "heat engines," a group of "pure" scientists (men who devote fourteen hours of each day to the study of those "theoretical" scientific phenomena without which no mechanical progress would be possible) were following a new scent.

Two thousand years ago, a number of Greek and Roman philosophers (notably Thales of Miletus and Pliny who was killed while trying to study the eruption of Vesuvius of the year 79 when Pompeii and Herculaneum were buried beneath the ashes) had noticed the strange antics of bits of straw and of feather which were held near a piece of amber which was being rubbed with a bit of wool. The schoolmen of the Middle Ages had not been interested in this mysterious "electric" power. But immediately after the Renaissance, William Gilbert, the private physician of Queen Elizabeth, wrote his famous treatise on the character and behavior of Magnets. During the Thirty Years War Otto von Guericke, the burgomaster of Magdeburg and the inventor of the air-pump, constructed the first electrical machine. During the next century a large number of scientists devoted themselves to the study of electricity. Not less than three professors invented the famous Leyden Jar in the year 1795. At the same time, Benjamin Franklin was devoting his attention to this subject. He discovered that lightning and the electric spark were manifestations of the same electric power and continued his electric studies until the end of his busy and useful life. Then came Volta with his famous "electric pile" and Galvani and Day and the Danish professor Hans Christian Oersted and Ampère and Arago and Faraday, all of them diligent searchers after the true nature of the electric forces.

They freely gave their discoveries to the world and Samuel Morse (who like Fulton began his career as an artist) thought that he could use this new electric current to transmit messages from one city to another. He intended to use copper wire and a little machine which he had invented. People laughed at him. Morse therefore was obliged to finance his own experiments and soon he had spent all his money and then he was very poor, and people laughed even louder. He then asked Congress to help him and a special Committee on Commerce promised him their support. But the members of Congress were not at all interested and Morse had to wait twelve years before he was given a small congressional appropriation.

He then built a "telegraph" between Baltimore and Washington. In the year 1887 he had shown his first successful "telegraph" in one of the lecture halls of New York University. Finally, on the 24th of May of the year 1844 the first long-distance message was sent from Washington to Baltimore. Twenty-three years later Alexander Graham Bell used the electric current for his telephone. And half a century afterwards Marconi improved upon these ideas by inventing a system of sending messages which did away entirely with the old-fashioned wires with the radio. And, of course, this was followed up in the twentieth century by the television.

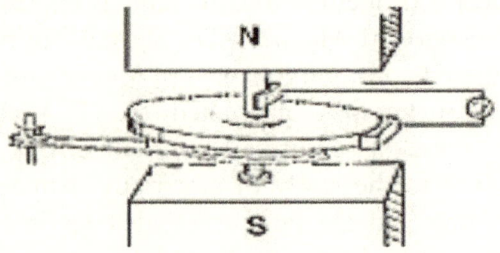

While Morse, the New Englander, was working on his "telegraph," Michael Faraday, the Yorkshireman, had constructed the first "dynamo."

This tiny little machine was completed in the year 1881 when Europe was still trembling as a result of the great July revolutions which had so severely upset the plans of the Congress of Vienna.

The first dynamo grew and grew and grew and today it provides us with heat and with light (you know the little incandescent bulbs which Thomas Edison, building upon French and English experiments of the forties and fifties, first made in 1878) and with power for all sorts of machines.

Edison's inventive genius did not stop there though. His laboratory churned out a remarkable array of new products and devices. For example, he invented the phonograph by which people could play back recorded sound.

And after that invention he said in 1888: "I am experimenting upon an instrument which does for the eye what the phonograph does for the ear, which is the recording and reproduction of things in motion." Edison's laboratory was responsible for the invention of the Kinetograph (a motion picture camera) and the Kinetoscope (a peephole motion picture viewer). Communication was further enhanced in the twentieth century with the invention of the television.

At the same time communication was being revolutionized, travel was as well. The invention of the automobile revolutionized travel over land. Henry Ford engineered the mass production of the automobile for the general public with his famous Model T.

The revolution in travel continued with the invention of the airplane by the Wright Brothers. The story of Orville and Wilbur Wright is one of two Christian bicycle mechanics who used their knowledge, ingenuity, daring, and drive to create the plane, which they first flew at Kitty Hawk, North Carolina.

God ordained this industrial revolution in technology to accomplish His own sovereign ends. The industrial revolution has given wicked humanity the capability to destroy itself physically and spiritually as never before, but it has also brought all humanity closer to one another so that the gospel of Jesus Christ can be more readily proclaimed. The same airplane that can deliver an atomic bomb to an enemy nation can transport a missionary to a distant land. And the same radio and television which can bring pornography into virtually every living room can also supply it with Biblical truth. The industrial revolution has increased the necessity of human repentance and obedience to Christ.

CHAPTER 54: The Social Revolution that Accompanied the Industrial Revolution

In the olden days, the work of the world was done by independent workmen who sat in their own little workshops in the front of their houses, who owned their tools, who boxed the ears of their own apprentices and who, within the limits prescribed by their guilds, conducted their business as it pleased them. They lived simple lives and were obliged to work very long hours, but they were their own masters. If they got up and saw that it was a fine day to go fishing, they went fishing and there was no one to say "no."

But the introduction of machinery changed this. A machine is really nothing but a greatly enlarged tool. A  railroad train which carries you at the speed of a mile a minute is, in reality, a pair of very fast legs, and a steam hammer which flattens heavy plates of iron is just a terrible big fist, made of steel.

But whereas we can all afford a pair of good legs and a good strong fist, a railroad train and a steam hammer and a cotton factory and a steel plant and an oil refinery are very expensive pieces of machinery and they are not generally owned by a single man, but usually by a company of people who all contribute a certain sum and then divide the profits of their railroad or cotton mill according to the amount of money which they have invested. When machines had been improved until they were really practicable and profitable, the builders of those large tools, the machine manufacturers, began to look for customers who could afford to pay for them in cash.

During the early middle ages, when land had been almost the only form of wealth, the nobility were the only people who were considered wealthy. But as I have told you in a previous chapter, the gold and silver which they possessed was quite insignificant and they used the old system of barter, exchanging cows for horses and eggs for honey. During the crusades, the burghers of the cities had been able to gather riches from the reviving trade between the east and the west, and they had been serious rivals of the lords and the knights.

The French revolution had entirely destroyed the wealth of the nobility and had enormously increased that of the middle class or "bourgeoisie." The years of unrest which followed the Great Revolution had offered many middle-class people a chance to get more than their share of this world's goods. The estates of the church had been confiscated by the French Convention and had been sold at auction. There had been a terrific amount of graft. Land speculators had stolen thousands of square miles of valuable land, and during the Napoleonic wars, they had used their capital to "profiteer" in grain and gunpowder, and now they possessed more wealth than they needed for the actual expenses of their households, and they could afford to build themselves factories and to hire men and women to work the machines.

This caused a very abrupt change in the lives of hundreds of thousands of people. Within a few years, many cities doubled the number of their inhabitants and the old civic center which had been the real "home" of the citizens was surrounded with ugly and cheaply built suburbs where the workmen slept after their eleven or twelve hours, or thirteen hours, spent in the factories and from where they returned to the factory as soon as the whistle blew.

Far and wide through the countryside there was talk of the fabulous sums of money that could be made in the towns. The peasant boy, accustomed to a life in the open, went to the city. He rapidly lost his old health amidst the smoke and dust and dirt of those early and badly ventilated workshops, and the end, very often, was death in the poorhouse or in the hospital.

Of course, the change from the farm to the factory on the part of so many people was not accomplished without a certain amount of opposition. Since one engine could do as much work as a hundred men, the ninety-nine others who were thrown out of employment did not like it. Sometimes they even attacked the factory-buildings and set fire to the machines, but Insurance Companies had been organized as early as the 17th century and as a rule the owners were well protected against loss.

Soon, newer and better machines were installed, the factory was surrounded with a high wall and then there was an end to the rioting. The ancient guilds could not possibly survive in this new world of steam and iron. They went out of existence and then in many cases the workmen tried to organize regular labor unions. But the factory-owners, who through their wealth could exercise great influence upon the politicians of the different countries, went to the Legislature and had laws passed which forbade the forming of such trade unions because they interfered with the "liberty of action" of the working man. Since these considered "liberty" to be the foremost virtue of man, they believed it was not right that labor unions should dictate to their members the hours during which they could work and the wages which they must demand. The workman must at all times, be "free to sell his services in the open market," and the employer must be equally "free" to conduct his business as he saw fit. The days of the Mercantile System, when the state had regulated the industrial life of the entire community, were coming to an end. The new idea of "freedom" insisted that the state stand entirely aside and let commerce take its course.

Many Christian people of all classes opposed these unions as well because of their generally atheistic leanings and inappropriate conduct in relation to management.

The last half of the 18th century had not merely been a time of intellectual and political doubt, but the old economic ideas, too, had been replaced by new ones. Several years before the French revolution, Turgot, who had been one of the unsuccessful ministers of finance of Louis XVI, had preached the novel doctrine of "economic liberty." Turgot

lived in a country which had suffered from too much red-tape, too many regulations, too many officials trying to enforce too many laws. "Remove this official supervision," he wrote, "let the people do as they please, and everything will be all right." Soon his famous advice of "laissez faire" became the battle cry around which the economists of that period rallied. So civil libertarianism and economic libertarianism were alike promoted.

At the same time in England, Adam Smith was working on his mighty volumes on the "Wealth of Nations," which made another plea for "liberty" and the "natural rights of trade." Thirty years later, after the fall of Napoleon, when the reactionary powers of Europe had gained their victory at Vienna, that same freedom which was denied to the people in their political relations was forced upon them in their industrial life.

The general use of machinery, as I have said at the beginning of this chapter, proved to be of great advantage to the state. Wealth increased rapidly. The machine made it possible for a single country, like England, to carry all the burdens of the great Napoleonic wars. The capitalists (the people who provided the money with which machines were bought) reaped enormous profits. They became ambitious and began to take an interest in politics. They tried to compete with the landed aristocracy which still exercised great influence upon the government of most European countries.

In England, where the members of Parliament were still elected according to a Royal Decree of the year 1265, and where a large number of recently created industrial centers were without representation, they brought about the passing of the Reform Bill of the year 1882, which changed the electoral system and gave the class of the factory-owners more influence upon the legislative body. This however caused great discontent among the millions of factory workers, who were left without any voice in the government. They too began an agitation for the right to vote. They put their demands down in a document which came to be known as the "People's Charter." The debates about this charter grew more and more violent. They had not yet come to an end when the revolutions of the year 1848 broke out. Frightened by the threat of a new outbreak or Jacobinism and violence, the English government placed the Duke of Wellington, who was now in his eightieth year, at the head of the army, and called for Volunteers. London was placed in a state of siege and preparations were made to suppress the coming revolution.

But the Chartist movement killed itself through bad leadership, and no acts of violence took place. The new class of wealthy factory owners (I dislike the word "bourgeoisie" which has been used to death by the apostles of the Marxist social order,) slowly increased its hold upon the government. In many cases these were unaccompanied by appropriate legislation to protect a safe and healthy environment and to more fully promote reformed Biblical belief and practice. These conditions of industrial life in the large cities continued to transform vast acres of pasture and wheat-land into smog-filled slums with many poor prone to embrace the siren song of Marxism in desperation. There was also a growing urban middle class that resulted from the initial stages of the industrial revolution, which tended to have a stabilizing influence upon society. But the situation became volatile not only in England, but throughout Europe.

Capitalist investors and businessmen like Vanderbilt in railroads, Rockefeller in oil, Morgan in banking, and Carnagie in steel amassed great fortunes through their shrewd investments and control over large business enterprises.

Those who looked upon these capitalists with especial suspicion and even disdain coined the name 'robber baron' to describe them. In many cases they acquired their wealth through just and legal means, but in some cases, they used their clout to secure monopolies illegally and to the detriment of the public. Wealth tempered by Christian charity is a blessing, but wealth absent Christianity can lead to great vice. The Gilded Age of wealth resulting from the Industrial Revolution was not sufficiently tempered by Biblical Christianity, but the "cures" that some were to propose (like Marxists and socialists) were worse than the "disease" itself.

CHAPTER 55: Abolition of Slavery, States' Rights, and the American Civil War

I have already told you how the Enlightenment led to a degeneration in the dominant political philosophy throughout the Protestant West. The notion of a distinctively reformed Christian government informed by scripture and enforcing the Ten Commandments was discarded, at least in part. But much of the English common law system rooted in Biblical Christianity, which Blackstone had so ably described and defended in his commentaries, remained intact in the early 19th century in the English-speaking world. So, the blessings of Christianity continued to be enjoyed, even as the method which had produced it was ridiculed. The Enlightenment had declared human reason could arrive at the same just laws, without reference to scripture. But as I have already noted, the fallacy of the Enlightenment was its failure to take into account the depraved nature of man's reason after the Fall, and his dependence upon scripture to attain true understanding. It was only a matter of time before the legal system itself would be changed with the Enlightenment fallacy.

One early prominent advocate for change was Jeremy Bentham. Unlike Enlightenment philosophers such as John Locke, he believed the law should be completely divorced from a notion of rights and responsibilities given by God. According to Bentham, no longer must we conceive of law as ensuring the rights and responsibilities God has bestowed upon man. Rather, we should conceive of it in merely human terms as what the government required its people to do. He, and later John Stuart Mill, developed a utilitarian philosophy which said laws should be instituted which result in the most happiness for the people. So, the question became, according to this thoroughly humanistic framework: which political and economic system best produces this result?

For many years capitalism and libertarianism were clearly in vogue as answers to this question. The philosophy of Adam Smith was widely embraced. But the ideal of "economic freedom" (the "laissez faire" of Turgot) and "liberty of action" which had been the highest law of the land had seemed to lead to some unjust conditions. The hours in the factory were limited only by the physical strength of the workers. As long as a woman could sit before her loom, without fainting from fatigue, she was supposed to work. Children of five and six were taken to the cotton mills, to save them from the dangers of the street and a life of idleness. A law had been passed which forced the children of paupers to go to work or be punished by being chained to their machines. In return for their services they got enough bad food to keep them alive and a sort of pigsty in which they could rest at night. Often, they were so tired that they fell asleep at their job. To keep them awake a foreman with a whip made the rounds and beat them on the knuckles when it was necessary to bring them back to their duties. Of course, under these circumstances thousands of little children died. This was regrettable and the employers, who after all were human beings and not without a heart, sincerely wished that they could abolish "child labor." But since man was "free" it followed that children were "free" too. Besides, if Mr. Jones had tried to work his factory without the use of children of five and six, his rival, Mr. Stone, would have hired an extra supply of little boys and Jones would have been forced into bankruptcy. It was therefore impossible for Jones to do without child labor until such time as an act of Parliament should forbid it for all employers.

But the options which would have altered this situation in a proper way had seemingly been closed off. Libertarianism had replaced Biblical law as an operating principle. And Parliament was no longer dominated by the old landed aristocracy (which had despised the upstart factory owners with their money bags and had treated them with open contempt) but was under control of the representatives from the industrial centers. Money had been made the avenue into political power, instead of moral character.

J. Parnell McCarter

Curiously enough, at the very time when political reform was needed to address these realities of the Industrial Revolution, a movement was underway to address the condition of slave labor primarily concentrated in agriculture. The abolitionist movement was made on behalf of the black slaves of Africa and America. Slavery had been introduced into the American continent by the Spaniards. They had tried to use the Indians as laborers in the fields and in the mines, but the Indians, when taken away from a life in the open, either died or fled. A Roman Catholic priest had suggested that negroes be brought from Africa to do the work. The negroes were strong and could stand rough treatment. Besides, association with the white man would give them a chance to learn Roman Catholicism. The use of slave labor spread to the English colonies of North America and continued past the formation of the United States.

Stories of cruelty found their way to Europe and in all countries men and women began to agitate for the abolition of slavery. The slavery practiced often times lacked the protections which Biblical law had provided to slaves. In England, William Wilberforce and Zachary Macaulay, (the father of a famous English historian) organized a society for the suppression of slavery. First of all, they got a law passed which made "slave trading" illegal. And after the year 1840 there was not a single slave in any of the British colonies. The revolution of 1848 put an end to slavery in the French possessions. The Portuguese passed a law in the year 1858 which promised all slaves their liberty in twenty years from date. The Dutch abolished slavery in 1863 and in the same year Tsar Alexander II returned to his serfs that liberty which had been taken away from them more than two centuries before. In the United States of America, the question led to grave difficulties and a prolonged Civil War. The founders of the United States were perplexed by what to do about the slave question. In their Declaration of Independence, they had laid down the principle that "all men were created free and equal," but an exception was made for black slaves. As time went on, the dislike of the people of the North for the institution of slavery increased and they made no secret of their feelings. There was no longer any economic advantage to them from slavery, like the period before slave trade from Africa was prohibited. Before it had been primarily New England ships which transported the slaves to the South. The southerners claimed that they could not grow their cotton without slave-labor, and for almost fifty years a mighty debate raged in both the Congress and the Senate.

The North remained obdurate and the South would not give in, and neither side was sufficiently in the mood to consult scripture for how the matter should be handled. When it appeared impossible to reach a compromise, the southern states threatened to leave the Union. It was a most dangerous point in the history of the Union. Many things "might" have happened.

On the sixth of November of the year 1860, Abraham Lincoln, an Illinois lawyer, and a man who had made his own intellectual fortune, had been elected president by the Republicans who were very strong in the anti-slavery states.

When a number of southern states seceded and formed the "Confederate States of America," Lincoln accepted the challenge. The Northern states were called upon for volunteers.

Hundreds of thousands of young men responded with eager enthusiasm and there followed four years of bitter civil war. The South, better prepared and following the brilliant leadership of Lee and Jackson, repeatedly defeated the armies of the North.

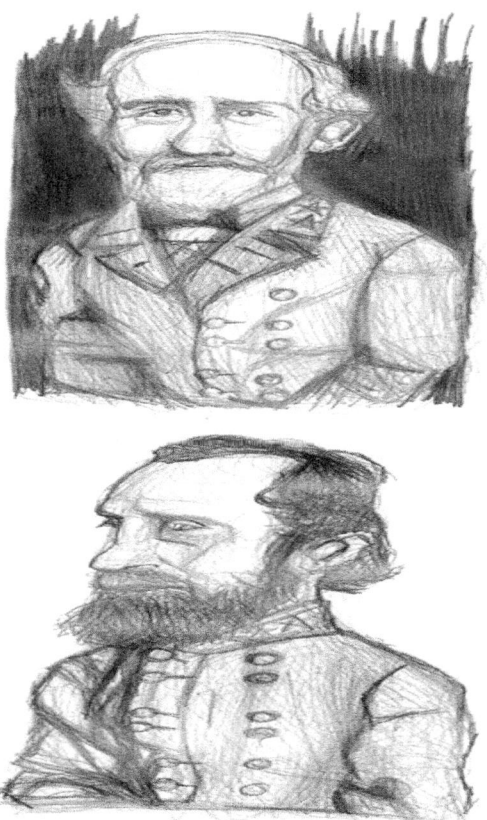

Then the economic strength of New England and the West began to tell. An unknown officer by the name of Grant arose from obscurity and became the Charles Martel of the great slave war. Without interruption he hammered his mighty blows upon the crumbling defenses of the South. Early in the year 1863, President Lincoln issued his "Emancipation Proclamation" which set all slaves free. In April of the year 1865 Lee surrendered the last of his brave armies at Appomattox. A few days later, President Lincoln was murdered. But his work was done. With the exception of Cuba which was still under Spanish domination, slavery had come to an end in every part of the civilized world. It would be later that labor unrest in the industrial centers would arise and cause social upheaval.

CHAPTER 56: Science and Pseudo-science

"Pride goeth before destruction." So saith the ancient wise man. And so history demonstrates. Like the men who had built the great edifice at Babel millennia before, Western men by the 19th century had accomplished great technological and scientific feats. Galileo observed the movements of the planets and other astronomical bodies with his telescope and provided Isaac Newton with a mass of practical observations, which greatly helped the English mathematician when he discovered the existence of that interesting law established by the Creator of falling objects which came to be known as the Law of Gravitation.

The invention of a workable microscope, (a strange and clumsy little thing,) by Anthony van Leeuwenhoek during the last half of the 17th century, gave man a chance to study the "microscopic" creatures who are responsible for so many of his ailments. It laid the foundations of the science of "bacteriology" which in the last forty years has delivered the world from a great number of diseases by discovering the tiny organisms which cause the complaint. There were inventions ranging from trains to steamboats to the machine gun. Add to this the notion that had continued and developed since the Enlightenment, regarding the elevated status of man's innate reason and an absence of innate depravity that warps that reason, and these were the ingredients for a human pride which swelled as great as that of the builders of the Tower of Babel.

"If man is this smart and this unbiased in his thought and reason, who needs divine revelation anyway? We can determine who we are and where we came from and what we should do without God." So thought men. And the results were inevitable: "Because that, when they knew God, they glorified [him] not as God, neither were thankful; but became vain in their imaginations, and their foolish heart was darkened. Professing themselves to be wise, they became fools."

They denied that God had supernaturally created the universe according to his revealed word, and they proposed fantastic theories of how the universe and everything in it is here by mere chance, due to the working of 'natural forces.' So, in the year 1830, Sir Charles Lyell published his "Principles of Geology" which denied the story of creation as related in the Bible and gave a description of slow growth and gradual development by these 'natural forces.' At the same time, the Marquis de Laplace was working on a new theory of creation, which made the earth a little blotch in the nebulous sea out of which the planetary system had been formed. And biologists such as Lamarck and Charles Darwin proposed that the human race had evolved from a long series of ancestors who could trace the family-tree back to the little jellyfishes who were the first inhabitants of our planet. Incredibly, they said all these things happened by the chance movement of particles and the forces between them. They reduced all reality to the material, or so they thought. Seemingly overnight much of the academic community embraced the theories Darwin proposed in his book "Origin of Species" when it was published in 1859.

J. Parnell McCarter

Never mind that Darwin had really not proved the mechanism for this upwardly evolving variety from which natural selection would cull out only the best. Never mind that he was unable to provide the fossil evidence for all the transitional forms that would be necessary if all plants and animals evolved by small degrees from lower forms. Never mind that many of the underlying assumptions of his theory were unobserved hypotheses rather than observed facts. In the mad rush to embrace his form of modern science (which came to be understood as precluding God in any explanation), centuries of Western Christian scholarship were literally swept under the rug and everyone who was "reasonable" recognized its "obvious" correctness.

By the time of the American Scopes Monkey Trial in 1925 – pitting pro-evolutionist attorney Darrow against antievolutionist Bryan – in a court case intended by the American Civil Liberties Union (ACLU) to rid the country of antievolutionist laws, most of academia trumpeted that only monkeys would deny evolution.

[11] "The Proposition Would Get a Lot of Support If the Monkeys Could Vote on It." (Orr in the *Chicago Tribune*)

Now man thought he was completely emancipated from the 'chains' of God. In the Enlightenment they had declared their independence from His word; and with materialistic Evolution they declared their independence from His person. These men found the tree of the knowledge of good and evil, quickly ate the fruit and –lo and behold- believed they were now free to create their own world and reality totally apart from God. Most of the rest of this book will be taken up with describing the world that foolish, depraved modern man created in his ignorance.

CHAPTER 57: Socialism and Marxism

Two factors then combined to produce what became the socialist and Marxist movements. First, the atheistic materialism of evolution was embraced by many men in academic circles. Second, an abhorrence of the mistreatment and poor working conditions of many people in the industrial centers grew. Many of these workmen (the so-called proletariat) did indeed live in wretched conditions. They lived in dirty houses situated in miserable parts of the slums. They ate bad food. They received just enough schooling to fit them for their tasks. In case of death or an accident, their families were not provided for. But the brewery and distillery interests, (who could exercise great influence upon the Legislature,) encouraged them to forget their woes by offering them unlimited quantities of whisky and gin at very cheap rates.

There were men who contemplated the sight of all the belching smoke-stacks, who heard the rattle of the railroad trains, who saw the store-houses filled with a surplus of all sorts of materials, and who wondered to what ultimate goal this tremendous activity would lead in the years to come. They sought a solution divorced from Biblical revelation. Could they change the existing order of things and do away with a system of rivalry which so often sacrificed human happiness to profits?

This idea – this vague hope for a better day – was not restricted to a single country. In England, Robert Owen, the owner of many cotton mills, established a so-called "socialistic community" which was a success. But when he died, the prosperity of New Lanark came to an end and an attempt of Louis Blanc, a French journalist, to establish "social workshops" all over France fared no better. Indeed, the increasing number of socialistic writers soon began to see that little individual communities which remained outside of the regular industrial life, would never be able to accomplish anything at all. It was necessary to study the fundamental principles underlying the whole industrial and capitalistic society before useful remedies could be suggested.

The practical socialists like Robert Owen and Louis Blanc and François Fournier were succeeded by theoretical students of socialism like Karl Marx and Friedrich Engels. Of these two, Marx is the best known. He was a very intelligent but wicked person, a secular Jew, whose family had, for a long time, lived in Germany. He had heard of the experiments of Owen and Blanc and he began to interest himself in questions of labor and wages and unemployment. He also had embraced the materialistic atheism of evolution and incorporated this into his notions of how society and economics should be considered.

In the 'Manifesto of the Communist Party' published by Marx and Engels in 1848, they espoused the belief that the course of history is determined primarily by the operation of economic forces, what is known as historical materialism. Many of their ideas were borrowed from the writings of men in the French Revolution like Babeuf, who proclaimed that the key to social justice was the abolition of private property altogether.

But these liberal views made Marx very unpopular with the police authorities of Germany, and he was forced to flee to Brussels and then to London, where he lived a poor and shabby life as the correspondent of the New York Tribune.

No one, thus far, had paid much attention to his books on economic subjects. But in the year 1864 he organized the first international association of working men and three years later in 1867, he published the first volume of his well-known treatise called "Capital." Marx believed that all history was a long struggle between those who "have" and those who "don't have." The introduction and general use of machinery had created a new class in society, that of the capitalists who used their surplus wealth to buy the tools which were then used by the laborers to produce still more wealth, which was again used to build more factories and so on, until the end of time. Meanwhile, according to Marx, the third estate (the bourgeoisie) was growing richer and richer and the fourth estate (the proletariat) was growing poorer and poorer, and he predicted that in the end, one man would possess all the wealth of the world while the others would be his employees and dependent upon his good will.

To prevent such a state of affairs, Marx advised working men of all countries to unite and to fight for a number of political and economic measures which he had enumerated in a Manifesto in the year 1848, the year of the last great European revolution. Marx called for a revolution of the proletariat which would put all wealth in the hands of the government and enforce economic equality.

He scorned religion as "the opiate of the people". He thought it prevented men from engaging in his revolution, and he considered it a waste of time since he denied Jesus Christ and even the existence of God. Marx thought that history would inevitably move in this direction, because this is where economic forces would naturally lead it.

These views, especially regarding proletariat revolution, of course were very unpopular with the governments of Europe. Many countries, especially Prussia, passed severe laws against the Socialists and policemen were ordered to break up the Socialist meetings and to arrest the speakers. In Europe the number of socialists steadily increased.

Some of these Socialists, however, disavowed the violent methods advocated by Marx. They were willing to work with others, including Christians, who were also concerned about working and living conditions and the plight of children. They were willing to work through the Parliaments and Congresses of the various countries to pass legislative reforms. They endeavored to introduce a number of laws which regulated the relations between the factory owners and the factory workers. Their legislative efforts paid off, resulting in legislation which set limits on work hours, regulated working conditions, and required that children be sent to the schools instead of to the mine pit and to the carding-room of the cotton mills. While some of this legislation went overboard, some of it was indeed necessary. And in many countries like the United States, especially where Protestantism had a great historic hold upon the people, the Marxist movement became an insignificant threat. But in some other countries, Marxism was a disaster waiting to happen.

CHAPTER 58: Art, Architecture, and Literature Through the Centuries

As soon as the Egyptians and the Babylonians and the Persians and all the other people of the east had founded their little countries along the Nile and the Euphrates, they began to build magnificent palaces for their kings, invented bright pieces of jewelry for their women and planted gardens which sang songs of color with their many bright flowers.

The descendants of Japheth composed songs which celebrated the mighty deeds of their great leaders and invented a form of poetry which has survived until our own day. A thousand years later, when they had established themselves on the Greek mainland, and had built their "city-states," they expressed their joy (and their sorrows) in temples, in statues, in comedies and in tragedies, and in every conceivable form of art.

The Romans, like their Carthaginian rivals, were too busy administering other people and making money to have much love for "useless and unprofitable" adventures of the spirit. They conquered the world and built roads and bridges, but they borrowed their art wholesale from the Greeks. They invented certain practical forms of architecture which answered the demands of their day and age. But their statues and their histories and their mosaics and their poems were mere Latin imitations of Greek originals. The business of writing poetry or making pictures was left to foreigners.

With the rise of Christianity among the Gentiles in the early Church, Christians recognized how literature and architecture could be used to glorify God. But they condemned art and drama which led to moral degeneracy. And they rejected the use of icons in their religious worship, but instead insisted upon that simplicity of worship which the Bible had prescribed. The Middle Ages continued this early Church practice, but increasingly idolatry was introduced into worship. Also, there was lost some of that knowledge for building which had been possessed during the Roman Empire.

In northern Europe (especially among the Germanic peoples) during the Middle Ages there developed Gothic art. You have all heard the word 'Gothic.' You probably associate it with the picture of a grand old cathedral, lifting its slender spires towards heaven. But what does the word really mean? It means something "uncouth" and "barbaric" – something which one might expect from an "uncivilized Goth," a rough backwoodsman who had no respect for the established rules of classical art. And yet for several centuries this form of Gothic architecture was the highest expression of the sincere feeling for art which inspired the whole northern continent. From a previous chapter, you will remember how the people of the late Middle Ages lived. Unless they were peasants and dwelt in villages, they were citizens of a "city" or "civitas," the old Latin name for a tribe. And indeed, behind their high walls and their deep moats, these burghers were true tribesmen who shared the common dangers and enjoyed the common safety and prosperity which they derived from their system of mutual protection.

In the old Greek and Roman cities, the marketplace, where the temple stood, had been the center of civic life. During the Middle Ages, the Church, the House of God, became such a center. Modern Western society hardly knows what a medieval church meant to the community. Then, before you were a week old, you were taken to the Church to be baptized. As a child, you visited the Church to learn the holy Scriptures. Later on, you became a member of the congregation. (Of course, as the Middle Ages passed, Romish additions were added. If a person were rich enough, he built himself a separate little chapel sacred to the memory of the Patron Saint of his own family. In the twelfth century musical instruments began to be added in the churches and worship, as I will tell you about shortly.) In the church you very likely caught a first glimpse of the girl who was to become your bride at a service. And finally, when the end of the journey had come, you were buried beneath the stones of this familiar building, that all your children and their grandchildren might pass over your grave until the Day of Judgement. It was the center of community life, as it really should be.

Because the Church was not only the House of God but also the true center of all common life, the building had to be different from anything that had ever been constructed by the hands of man. The temples of the Egyptians and the Greeks and the Romans had been merely the shrine of a local divinity. As no sermons were preached before the images of Osiris or Zeus or Jupiter, it was not necessary that the interior offer space for a great multitude. All the religious processions of the old Mediterranean peoples took place in the open. But in the north, where the weather was usually bad, most functions were held under the roof of the church.

During many centuries the architects struggled with this problem of constructing a building that was large enough. The Roman tradition taught them how to build heavy stone walls with very small windows lest the walls lose their strength. On the top of this they then placed a heavy stone roof. But in the twelfth century, after the beginning of the Crusades, when the architects had seen the pointed arches of the Mohammedan builders, the western builders discovered a new style which gave them their first chance to make the sort of building which an intense religious life demanded. And then they developed this strange style upon which the Italians bestowed the contemptuous name of "Gothic" or barbaric. They achieved their purpose by inventing a vaulted roof which was supported by "ribs." But such a roof, if it became too heavy, was apt to break the walls, just as a man of three hundred pounds sitting down upon a child's chair will force it to collapse. To overcome this difficulty, certain French architects then began to re-enforce the walls with "buttresses" which were merely heavy masses of stone against which the walls could lean while they supported the roof. And to assure the further safety of the roof they supported the ribs of the roof by so-called "flying buttresses."

This new method of construction allowed the introduction of enormous windows. In the twelfth century, glass was still an expensive curiosity, and very few private buildings possessed glass windows. Even the castles of the nobles were without protection and this accounts for the eternal drafts and explains why people of that day wore furs in-doors as well as out.

The art of making colored glass, with which the ancient people of the Mediterranean had been familiar, had not been entirely lost. There was a revival of stained glassmaking and soon the windows of the Gothic churches told the stories of the Holy Book in little bits of brilliantly colored windowpane, which were caught in a long framework of lead. It should be remembered by this time that most iconoclastic Christians had been killed, and it would not be until the Protestant Reformation that pictures of the Father, Son, and Holy Spirit would again be removed.

The Romans of the early Christian period had covered the floors and the walls of their temples and houses with mosaics; pictures made of colored bits of glass. But this art had been exceedingly difficult. It gave the painter no chance to express all he wanted to say, as all children know who have ever tried to make figures out of colored blocks of wood. The art of mosaic painting therefore died out during the late Middle Ages except in Russia, where the Byzantine mosaic painters had found a refuge after the fall of Constantinople and continued to ornament the walls of the orthodox churches until the day of the Bolsheviks, when there was an end to the building of churches.

Of course, the medieval painter could mix his colors with the water of the wet plaster which was put upon the walls of the churches. This method of painting upon "fresh plaster" (which was generally called "fresco" or "fresh" painting) was very popular for many centuries. Today, it is as rare as the art of painting miniatures in manuscripts and among the hundreds of artists of our modern cities there is perhaps one who can handle this medium successfully. But during the Middle Ages there was no other way and the artists were "fresco" workers for lack of something better. The method however had certain great disadvantages. Very often the plaster came off the walls after only a few years, or dampness spoiled the pictures, just as dampness will spoil the pattern of our wallpaper. People tried every imaginable expedient to get away from this plaster background. They tried to mix their colors with wine and vinegar and with honey and with the sticky white of egg, but none of these methods were satisfactory. For more than a thousand years these experiments continued. In painting pictures upon the parchment leaves of manuscripts the medieval artists were very successful. But when it came to covering large spaces of wood or stone with paint which would stick, they did not succeed very well.

At last, during the first half of the fifteenth century, the problem was solved in the southern Netherlands by Jan and Hubert van Eyck. The famous Flemish brothers mixed their paint with specially prepared oils and this allowed them to use wood and canvas or stone or anything else as a background for their pictures.

But by this time the rich burghers of the cities were succeeding the bishops as the primary patrons of the arts, especially in Protestant countries. And as art invariably follows the full dinner-pail, the artists now began to work for these employers and painted pictures for kings, for grand-dukes and for rich bankers. Within a very short time, the new method of painting with oil spread through Europe and in every country, there developed a school of special painting which showed the characteristic tastes of the people for whom these portraits and landscapes were made.

In Spain, for example, Velasquez painted court-dwarfs and the weavers of the royal tapestry factories, and all sorts of persons and subjects connected with the king and his court. But in Holland, Rembrandt and Frans Hals and Vermeer painted the barnyard of the merchant's house, and they painted his rather dowdy wife and his healthy but bumptious children and the ships which had brought him his wealth.

In Italy on the other hand, where the Pope remained the largest patron of the arts, Michelangelo and Correggio continued to paint Madonnas and Saints, while in England, where the aristocracy was very rich and powerful and in France where the kings had become uppermost in the state, the artists painted distinguished gentlemen who were members of the government, and very lovely ladies who were friends of His Majesty.

The invention of printing had made it possible for authors to win fame and reputation by writing books for the multitudes. The Protestant Reformation was stimulated by the writing of books and tracts by the Reformers. The first book from the first printing press in North America was the Bay Psalm Book of the Puritans. And then there developed the rise of allegories like John Bunyan's "Pilgrim's Progress" and later the rise of novels like Daniel Defoe's "Robinson Crusoe."

But regrettably art was also beginning to be used to promote immorality and amusement. For the first time since the early Greek city-states of two thousand years before, the professional playwright had a chance to ply his trade. The Middle Ages had known the theater merely as part of certain church celebrations, and even here it was inappropriate. The tragedies of the thirteenth and fourteenth centuries had told the story of the suffering of our Lord. But during the sixteenth century the worldly theater made its reappearance.

The playwright William Shakespeare during the reign of Elizabeth and James I became quite famous.

William's contemporary, Lope de Vega, the Spaniard who wrote no less than 1800 worldly and 400 religious plays, was a person of rank who received the papal approval upon his work.

A century later, Molière, the Frenchman, was deemed worthy of the companionship of none less than King Louis XIV.

Since then, the theater has enjoyed an ever-increasing affection on the part of the people. Today a "theater" is part of every city, and movies and television dramas permeate social life and entertainment. These generally promote moral degeneracy.

The art of music has in all ages been popular. The Egyptians and the Babylonians and the ancient Jews had all been great lovers of music. They had even combined different instruments into regular orchestras. But the Greeks had frowned upon this barbaric foreign noise. They liked to hear a man recite the stately poetry of Homer and Pindar. They allowed him to accompany himself upon the lyre (the poorest of all stringed instruments). That was as far as anyone could go without incurring the risk of popular disapproval. The Romans, on the other hand, had loved orchestral music at their dinners and parties and they had invented most of the instruments which (in *very* modified form) we use to-day. The Jews had their music accompanied by instruments in the Temple but unaccompanied by such instruments in the synagogues.

The early church followed the pattern of the Jewish synagogues, singing the inspired Psalms in their public worship, unaccompanied by musical instruments. But in the twelfth century the Romish church had allowed the use of an organ, an invention of the second century of our era which consisted of a combination of the old pipes of Pan and a pair of bellows. But in the Eastern churches such musical instruments were not so soon added, and in the reformed churches during the Reformation they were generally removed.

In the late Middle Ages, there developed a new demand for musicians. Instruments like the horn, which had been used only as signal-instruments for hunting and fighting, were remodeled until they could reproduce sounds which were agreeable in the dancehall and in the banqueting room. A bow strung with horse-hair was used to play the old-fashioned guitar and before the end of the Middle Ages this six-stringed instrument (the most ancient of all string-instruments which dates back to Egypt and

Assyria) had grown into our modern four-stringed fiddle which Stradivarius and the other Italian violin-makers of the eighteenth century brought to the height of perfection.

And finally, the modern piano was invented, the most widespread of all musical instruments, which has followed man into the wilderness of the jungle and the icefields of Greenland. The organ had been the first of all keyed instruments, but the performer always depended upon the co-operation of someone who worked the bellows, a job which nowadays is done by electricity. The musicians therefore looked for a handier and less circumstantial instrument to assist them in training the pupils of the many church choirs. During the great eleventh century, Guido, a Benedictine monk of the town of Arezzo (the birthplace of the poet Petrarch) gave us our modern system of musical annotation. Sometime during that century, when there was a great deal of popular interest in music, the first instrument with both keys and strings was built. It must have sounded as tinkly as one of those tiny children's pianos which you can buy at every toyshop. In the city of Vienna, the town where the strolling musicians of the Middle Ages (who had been classed with jugglers and card sharps) had formed the first separate Guild of Musicians in the year 1288, the little monochord was developed into something which we can recognize as the direct ancestor of our modern Steinway. From Austria the "clavichord" as it was usually called in those days (because it had "craves" or keys) went to Italy. There it was perfected into the "spinet" which was so called after the inventor, Giovanni Spinetti, of Venice. At last during the eighteenth century, sometime between 1709 and 1720, Bartolomeo Cristofori made a "clavier" which allowed the performer to play both loudly and softly or as it was said in Italian, "piano" and "forte." This instrument with certain changes became our "pianoforte" or piano.

Then for the first time the world possessed an easy and convenient instrument which could be mastered in a couple of years and did not need the eternal tuning of harps and fiddles and was much pleasanter to the ears than the mediæval tubas, clarinets, trombones and oboes. The early "pianoforte" carried the knowledge of music into much wider circles. Music became part of the education of every well-bred man and woman. Princes and rich merchants maintained private orchestras. The musician ceased to be a wandering "jongleur" and became a highly valued member of the community. Music was added to the dramatic performances of the theater and out of this practice, grew the modern Opera. Originally only a few very rich princes could afford the expenses of an "opera troupe." But as the taste for this sort of entertainment grew, many cities built their own theaters where Italian and afterwards German operas were given to the whole community. But reformed Christians rightly spurned these operatic dramas which entertained the people by immorality.

By the middle of the eighteenth century the musical life of Europe was in full swing. Then there came forward a man who was a greater musician than all others, a simple organist of the Thomas Church of Leipzig, by the name of Johann Sebastian Bach.

In his compositions for every known instrument, from comic songs and popular dances to the most stately of sacred hymns and oratorios, he laid the foundation for all our modern music. When he died in the year 1750, he was succeeded by Mozart, who created musical fabrics of sheer loveliness which remind us of lace that has been woven out of harmony and rhythm. Then came Ludwig van Beethoven, the most tragic of men, who gave us our modern orchestra, yet heard none of his greatest compositions because he was deaf, as the result of a cold contracted during his years of poverty.

Beethoven lived through the period of the great French Revolution. Full of hope for a new and glorious day, he had dedicated one of his symphonies to Napoleon. But he lived to regret the hour. When he died in the year 1827, Napoleon was gone and the French Revolution was gone, but the steam engine had come and was filling the world with a sound that had nothing in common with the dreams of the Third Symphony.

Art in the twentieth century took an especially degenerate turn, even as did Western society at large. Modern art, whether in paintings, sculpture, or music, came to see beauty in disorder, inaccuracy, and unrefinement. It is exemplified in the *livre d'artiste*, a genre of art which was developed in France during the first quarter of the twentieth century and then spread throughout Europe. Artists working in this genre included such names as Chagall, Clair, Cocteau, Derain, Duchamp, Dufy, Matisse, Picasso, Rouault, Toulouse-Lautrec, Utrillo, and de Vlaminck.

We must look forward to the day when society is reformed, and the beauty of order and refinement is reflected in art. Art, rightly employed, can glorify God and can be consistent with morality.

LET ME TELL YOU THE REAL STORY OF MANKIND

CHAPTER 59: Colonial Expansion and War

In the latter nineteenth and early twentieth century, the majority of the greater powers ceased to be mere political agencies and became large business enterprises. They built railroads. They founded and subsidized steam-ship lines to all parts of the world. They connected their different possessions with telegraph wires. And they steadily increased their holdings in other continents. Every available bit of African or Asiatic territory was claimed by one of the rival powers. France became a colonial nation with interests in Algiers and Madagascar and Annam and Tonkin (in eastern Asia). Germany claimed parts of southwest and east Africa, built settlements in Cameroon on the west coast of Africa and in New Guinea and many of the islands of the Pacific, and used the murder of a few missionaries as a welcome excuse to take the harbor of Kisochau on the Yellow Sea in China. Italy tried her luck in Abyssinia, was disastrously defeated by the soldiers of the Negus, and consoled herself by occupying the Turkish possessions in Tripoli in northern Africa. Russia, having occupied all of Siberia, took Port Arthur away from China. Japan, having defeated China in the war of 1895, occupied the island of Formosa and in the year 1905 began to lay claim to the entire empire of Corea.

In the year 1883, England, the largest colonial empire the world has ever seen, undertook to "protect" Egypt. She performed this task most efficiently and to the great material benefit of that much neglected country, which ever since the opening of the Suez Canal in 1868 had been threatened with a foreign invasion. During the next thirty years she fought a number of colonial wars in different parts of the world and in 1902 (after three years of bitter fighting) she conquered the independent Boer republics of the Transvaal and the Orange Free State. Meanwhile she had encouraged Cecil Rhodes to lay the foundations for a great African state, which reached from the Cape almost to the mouth of the Nile and had faithfully picked up such islands or provinces as had been left without a European owner. In Rhodes' 1877 "Confession of Faith," he stated, "I contend that we are the finest race in the world and that the more of the world we inhabit the better it is for the human race. Rhodes applied the popular view of Darwinism that "dog eat dog," the bigger dog consumes the smaller, to humanity.

He believed that it was only right and proper that the more advanced races should displace or destroy the less advanced. And he bequeathed his estate upon death to Rhodes' Scholarships, that young scholars from around the world could study at England's Oxford University.

While we must reject various aspects of British imperialism, like the Darwinian lie that permeated its impetus in its latter stages, still we must acknowledge how God wonderfully used the spread of the British Empire to spread the gospel of Jesus Christ. John G. Patton in the New Hebrides, Dr. David Livingstone in Africa, and William Carey in India are just some of the noteworthy missionaries which brought the gospel to far flung lands.

In contrast, some used colonialism as a mere tool for their material gain. The shrewd king of Belgium, by name Leopold, used the discoveries of Henry Stanley to found the Congo Free

State in the year 1885. Stanley worked on behalf of Belgium to establish Leopold's "possession", after having successfully located the British missionary and explorer of Africa, Dr. David Livingstone. (Stanley himself had been born in Great Britain, so it is fitting that he greeted his fellow Brit upon discovery in a most polite British fashion: "Dr. Livingston, I presume.") Originally this gigantic tropical empire was an "absolute monarchy." But after many years of scandalous mismanagement, it was annexed by the Belgian people who made it a colony (in the year 1908) and abolished the terrible abuses which had been tolerated by this very unscrupulous Roman Catholic Majesty, who cared nothing for the fate of the natives as long as he got his ivory and rubber.

As for the United States, they had so much land that they desired no further territory. But the terrible Spanish misrule of Cuba, one of the last of the Spanish possessions in the western hemisphere, practically "forced" the Washington government to take action. After a short and rather uneventful Spanish-American War, the Spaniards were driven out of Cuba and Puerto Rico and the Philippines, and the two latter became colonies of the United States. The sinking of the ship USS *Maine* was the ostensible reason for the war. But I suspect that more lies below the surface than just that sunken warship.

This economic development of the world was perfectly natural. The increasing number of factories in England and France and Germany needed an ever-increasing amount of raw materials and the equally increasing number of European workers needed an ever-increasing amount of food. Everywhere the cry was for more and for richer markets, for more easily accessible coal mines and iron mines and rubber plantations and oil-wells, for greater supplies of wheat and grain.

The purely political events of the European continent dwindled to mere insignificance in the eyes of men who were making plans for steamboat lines on Victoria Nyanza or for railroads through the interior of Shantung. They knew that many European questions still remained to be settled, but they did not bother, and through sheer indifference and carelessness they bestowed upon their descendants a terrible inheritance of hate and misery. For untold centuries the southeastern corner of Europe had been the scene of rebellion and bloodshed. During the 1870s the people of Serbia and Bulgaria and Montenegro and Roumania were once more trying to gain their freedom and the Turks (with the support of many of the western powers), were trying to prevent this, often using the most brutal of means.

After a period of particularly atrocious massacres in Bulgaria in the year 1876, the Russian people lost all patience. The Government was forced to intervene just as President McKinley was obliged to go to Cuba and stop the shooting-squads of General Weyler in Havana. In April of the year 1877 the Russian armies crossed the Danube, stormed the Shipka pass, and after the capture of Plevna, marched southward until they reached the gates of Constantinople. Turkey appealed for help to England. There were many English people who denounced their government when it took the side of the Sultan. But the British Prime Minister Disraeli, who was Jewish, (and who had just made Queen Victoria Empress of India and who loved the picturesque Turks while he hated the Russians who were brutally cruel to the Jewish people within their frontiers) decided to interfere. Russia was forced to conclude the peace of San Stefano (1878) and the question of the Balkans was left to a Congress which convened at Berlin in June and July of the same year.

This famous conference was entirely dominated by the personality of Disraeli. Even Bismarck feared the clever old man with his well-oiled curly hair and his supreme arrogance, tempered by a cynical sense of humor and a marvelous gift for flattery. At Berlin, the British prime minister carefully watched over the fate of his friends the Turks. Montenegro, Serbia and Romania were recognized as independent kingdoms. The principality of Bulgaria was given a semi-independent status under Prince Alexander of Battenberg, a nephew of Tsar Alexander II. But none of those countries were given the chance to develop their powers and their resources as they would have been able to do, had England been less anxious about the fate of the Sultan, whose domains were necessary to the safety of the British Empire as a bulwark against further Russian aggression.

To make matters worse, the congress allowed Austria to take Bosnia and Herzegovina away from the Turks to be "administered" as part of the Habsburg domains. It is true that Austria administered it quite efficiently. The neglected provinces were as well managed as the best of the British colonies, and that is saying a great deal. But they were inhabited by many Serbians. In older days they had been part of the great Serbian empire of Stephan Dushan, who early in the fourteenth century had defended western Europe against the invasions of the Turks and whose capital of Uskub had been a center of civilization one hundred and fifty years before Columbus discovered the new lands of the west. The Serbians remembered their ancient glory as who would not? They resented the presence of the Austrians in two provinces, which, so they felt, were theirs by every right of tradition.

And it was in Sarajevo, the capital of Bosnia, that the archduke Ferdinand, heir to the Austrian throne, was murdered on June 28 of the year 1914. The assassin was a Serbian student who had acted from patriotic motives.

But the blame for this terrible catastrophe, which was the immediate, though not the only cause of World War I, did not lie with the half-crazy Serbian boy or his Austrian victim. It must be traced back to the days of the famous Berlin Conference when Europe was too busy building a material civilization to care about the aspirations and the dreams of a forgotten race in a dreary corner of the old Balkan peninsula. And it must ultimately be traced back to a continued unwillingness of mankind to repent of its rebellion against God and to conduct itself in accordance with the divinely revealed principles of scripture.

LET ME TELL YOU THE REAL STORY OF MANKIND

CHAPTER 60: World War I

So began World War I in 1914. The world passed through an agony of pain compared to which the French Revolution was a mere incident. The shock was so great that it almost killed the last spark of hope in the breasts of millions of men. They were chanting a hymn of progress based upon their Enlightenment dream of 'human reason', and four years of slaughter followed their prayers for peace. "Is it worthwhile," so they asked, "to work and slave for the benefit of creatures who have not yet passed beyond the stage of the earliest cave men?" They had embraced the notion that man was a mere descendant of an ape-like animal, and they thoroughly behaved like it. They lived up to the myth they created.

You will gradually begin to understand what I am driving at. The engineer and the scientist and the chemist, within a single generation, filled Europe and America and Asia with their vast machines, with their telegraphs, their flying machines, their coal-tar products. They created a new world in which time and space were reduced to complete insignificance. They invented new products and they made these so cheap that almost everyone could buy them. I have told you all this before, but it certainly will bear repeating.

To keep the ever-increasing number of factories going, the owners, who had also become the rulers of the land, needed raw materials and coal. Especially coal. Meanwhile the mass of the people was still thinking in terms of the sixteenth and seventeenth centuries and clinging to the old notions of the state as a dynastic or political organization. This clumsy medieval institution was then suddenly called upon to handle the highly modern problems of a mechanical and industrial world. It did its best, according to the rules of the game which had been laid down centuries before. The different states created enormous armies and gigantic navies which were used for the purpose of acquiring new possessions in distant lands. Wherever there was a tiny bit of land left, there arose an English or a French or a German or a Russian colony. If the natives objected, they were killed. In most cases they did not object, and were allowed to live peacefully, provided they did not interfere with the diamond mines or the coal mines or the oil mines or the gold mines or the rubber plantations, and they derived many benefits from the foreign occupation.

Sometimes it happened that two states in search of raw materials wanted the same piece of land at the same time. Then there was a war. This occurred in the early twentieth century when Russia and Japan fought for the possession of certain territories which belonged to the Chinese people. Such conflicts, however, were the exception. No one really desired to fight. Indeed, the idea of fighting with armies and battleships and submarines began to seem absurd to the men of the early 20th century. They naively associated the idea of violence with the long-ago age of unlimited monarchies and intriguing dynasties. Every day they read in their papers of still further inventions, of groups of English and American and German scientists who were working together in perfect friendship for the purpose of an advance in medicine or in astronomy. They lived in a busy world of trade and of commerce and factories. But too few noticed that the nature of man had really never changed since the earlier wars, and "Enlightenment" was a dismal failure in preventing war.

But unlike previous wars, the inventions of the Industrial Revolution were to be fully employed by nations in the world wars of the twentieth century. This reality was about to hit with deadly force.

The nations of Europe had built such an array of alliances that a war between any two of them must ultimately involve all of them. So, when Austria-Hungary declared war on Serbia, it could count on support from its fellow Triple Alliance member, Germany. Likewise, the Eastern Orthodox, Slavic Serbians could count on aid and protection from Russia, a fellow Eastern Orthodox, Slavic nation. But since Russia was part of a Triple Entente with England and France, it could count on them to side with it. And since Russia saw this as a grand opportunity to seize various possessions from Turkey, especially Constantinople which would give Russia free passage from the Black Sea to the Aegean Sea, Turkey was also dragged into the war. And since these European nations had colonies worldwide, they too were brought in. This was truly a world war like none before.

But it was not only a world war, it was a total war. In this war, nations did not simply hire some mercenary soldiers to fight on their behalf. Rather, all the resources of each nation involved were employed to try to defeat the enemy. This meant the war touched many, many lives.

This war was surely a display of God's great indignation upon mankind, for this World War, and the next one, were not only widespread but ruthless. The Germans had attempted a quick conquest of France by a massive attack through Belgium and then heading south to Paris. But this attack was repulsed by the French outside Paris, and the war settled down to trench warfare. The British in turn utilized naval blockades upon Germany to weaken it, while Germany responded with the use of submarines to destroy English vessels.

Other innovative yet destructive methods were utilized in this war. Chemical and biological weapons, such as deadly chlorine gas, were used.

The airplane and the armored tank were added as instruments of war as well. Meanwhile the war on the 'eastern front' was especially deadly. Lacking the sophistication of war of its neighbors to the west, Russia sought to compensate by sacrificing thousands of Russian troops in quite deadly combat.

Amidst carnage and economic collapse, Russia succumbed to an internal revolution, which led to the abdication of its Czar. I will tell you in the next chapter about the details of the sad consequence in Russia. But for now, suffice it to say that the devastation of Russia forced it to sue for peace with the Germans.

What finally brought this horrible war to a temporary conclusion (I say temporary, because in many respects it was only a pause until the next world war) was the entry of America into the war in 1917, with its huge supply of fresh soldiers and industrial backbone, on the side of the Allies. This was simply too great a factor not to tip the balance in a conflict involving the war-weary states of Europe.

The 'man of the hour' at this stage of world events – Woodrow Wilson – was born into a family of Presbyterian ministers and teachers. He did not begin attending school until the age of 13, because his father – a Presbyterian minister – taught him at home. He taught him how to write especially well, which would serve him well later as a college professor at Princeton University. From Wilson's youth he took great interest in parliamentary law and government, an interest he exercised in politics first as governor in New Jersey and later as President of the United States. Wilson was a man of high political ideals, but he had abandoned the conservative Presbyterianism of his forefathers, basing his ideals upon humanism instead. He promised that his plan for concluding the Great War would make it a "war to end war." He offered a Fourteen Point program that he said would lead to this result. Borrowing from some ideas from the Solemn League and Covenant of his Presbyterian forefathers in the United Kingdom, he proposed for the nations of the world a Covenant of the League of

Nations. This League of Nations, which later evolved into the United Nations, was meant to adjudicate disputes so war would not erupt.

But Wilson's ideals, built on a shaky foundation, did not fulfill his promises, and Wilson died a very disappointed man. It rested not upon the sound Biblical principles of the Solemn League and Covenant, but upon the humanistic principles which had captured the imagination of the West since the Age of Enlightenment. The Treaty of Versailles, which concluded World War I, was quite severe on Germany, requiring exorbitant reparations on an already collapsed economy. The Germans signed it only under duress in 1919. Though many nations joined the newly formed League of Nations, the United States did not. Wars quickly erupted in various parts of the world, from the area of Turkey and Greece to Syria. Most devastating to the prospects of peace were the totalitarian regimes that formed in the aftermath of World War I.

Another World War was imminent.

CHAPTER 61: Communism, Fascism, World War II, and a Cold War

Karl Marx's 'Manifesto of the Communist Party' began with these words: "a specter is haunting Europe- the specter of Communism." It called for the forcible overthrow of all existing social institutions, concluding with words as ominous as its beginning: "Let the ruling classes tremble at a Communist revolution. The proletarians have nothing to lose but their chains. They have a world to win. Workingmen of all countries, unite!"

Socialist parties espousing this wicked philosophy formed in many countries of the world, but as of the beginning of World War I communists had been unable to gain power in any major country. Ironically, communism first gained a foothold in the nation of Russia which Marx had anticipated would be one of the last to embrace it, owing to its backward economic conditions. The collapse of social and economic conditions in Russia owing to World War I made it ripe for communist revolution.

The Bolshevik communists, led by Lenin, seized control of Russia.

Lenin was succeeded by Stalin, and Russia and its territories became known as the Soviet Union. Stalin established in the Soviet Union one of the most repressive totalitarian regimes that the world has ever known. Literally millions were killed in Communist purges, and religion was outlawed. The specter of Communism had truly arrived, and mankind had another taste of life without God, steered by human depravity.

But an equally ruthless specter was arising in Italy, Germany, and Japan following World War I: fascism. Like communism, its philosophical foundations are to be found in evolutionary theory and atheistic materialism. It drew from the philosophy of the nineteenth century German Friedrich Nietzsche, who derided Christianity as a refuge for the weak and base and exalted the superhero who overcomes opposition in this world and attains power. It had little compassion for the weak, but lauded strength and prowess based upon a Darwinian 'survival of the fittest.' It stressed nationalism, strong central authority, uniformity, and subordination of the individual to the good of the state. Hitler in Germany, Mussolini in Italy, and

Tojo in Japan all incorporated these themes in the governments they led.

Their objective was to conquer weaker states, just as they had gained personal power in their respective countries by coercion.

Even before World War II officially began, the fascist countries had made provocative moves. Japan conquered Manchuria, Italy conquered Ethiopia, and Germany conquered Austria and Czechoslovakia. They became known as the Axis powers, and their opponents were the Allied forces. The war began in earnest when Germany invaded Poland on September 1, 1939.

England and France had no choice but to declare war against this rising menace. The Soviet Union signed a pact with Germany in which they divided control over Poland and promised not to fight each other. (But never trust the promise of a scoundrel.)

Like World War I, World War II inevitably dragged most of the nations of the world into it. The nations of the British Empire and Commonwealth rallied behind it, while the colonies of the other European powers supported them. Meanwhile, Japan was busily seeking to conquer lands and territory in East Asia, with China as its formidable opponent.

At first, it was dubbed the "phony war", because on the Western front there was no fighting between the Allies of Great Britain and France versus the Axis powers of Germany and Italy. But in 1940, it became obvious this was no phony war. In 1940 Fascist Germany invaded and quickly conquered the Low Countries of Belgium, The Netherlands, and Luxembourg. The Allied forces had to perform a massive evacuation of troops and material from Dunkirk, Belgium. Then with lightning speed Germany invaded France, conquering it. In the same rail car where Germany had signed an armistice of surrender, France signed one to Germany.

A fascist French government, called the Vichy government, was established with Petain as its premier.

The Vichy government agreed to collaborate with Germany, but a Free French government under Charles de Gaulle continued to fight while in exile. In what was surely the darkest hour of the war, the Battle of Britain ensued. Germany ferociously bombed Britain, but Britain- now under Sir Winston Churchill- refused to cave in. *"I offer nothing but blood, sweat, toil, and tears,"* he had told the British people. *"We will fight them on the beaches, on the landing places, on the farms and in the cities. We will never surrender."*

In 1941, Germany invaded the Soviet Union. (Remember what I said about trusting scoundrels.) Now Germany was again forced to fight on two fronts, the Eastern Front against the Soviet Union and the Western Front against Britain. Surely it was God's mercy upon unworthy humanity that led Adolf Hitler to begin such a foolish enterprise, for this was the very strategy that led to Germany's defeat in World War I and Napoleon's defeat decades earlier. The Eastern Front extended for miles, and Germany quickly became bogged down as it tried to march further inward into the Soviet Union, especially during treacherous winter conditions.

In the meantime, the United States, under Franklin Roosevelt, was providing to Great Britain all the supplies it could, while yet technically remaining out of the war. Roosevelt also pursued a policy of blocking Japan's ability to obtain needed oil from southeast Asia. This placed Japan in an especially difficult bind, for it needed the oil to conduct its military operations in the Far East. In what was another foolish move by the Axis powers of Germany, Italy, and Japan, on December 7, 1941 Japan attacked the United States at its military installation of Pearl Harbor in Hawaii. The United States immediately and officially entered World War II.

Despite the initial success and advances of the Axis powers, over the course of the next several years they were forced to retreat by the Allied forces. The Soviet Union advanced towards Germany from the East, after deadly and bruising battles in the heart of Russia. The United States and Great Britain engaged in a massive invasion from the West, landing on the beaches of Normandy in France, under the command of General Dwight Eisenhower. They advanced towards Germany through France and the Low Countries, as well as moving up the peninsula of Italy. Finally, in early 1945 the Germans surrendered.

Meanwhile, in the Pacific theater, the United States had been regaining islands from the Japanese, under the command of General Douglas MacArthur.

In 1945, the United States dropped atomic bombs upon two Japanese cities. Never before had mankind the ability to deliver such destructive force against an enemy.

This new method of deadly warfare was based upon the theoretical predictions of physicist Albert Einstein, as one part of his theory of relativity. Scientists had been working since the early decades of the twentieth century to harness the energy of splitting an atom, and this was fully achieved in the atomic bomb.

This bomb led to the final surrender of Japan in 1945, and World War II thus came to an end.

Even during the war most people did not recognize the full extent of the death and destruction which had been wrought by man. For after the war people came to learn of the cruel genocide perpetrated by the Nazi regime in Germany, and the utter brutality of the Japanese occupying force in China. Man's total depravity was on full display, yet remarkably men still refused to repent. And men continued to entertain the naïve hope that humanism could solve our problems.

Incredibly, almost as soon as World War II was completed, however, a new and more subtle war was begun: The Cold War. The Soviet Union, while advancing towards Germany in World War II, had gained a firm grip on all of Eastern Europe. There it installed communist regimes loyal to the Soviet Union and separated from communication with the West. Winston Churchill, the great leader of Great Britain during World War II, described this as an "Iron Curtain" which had descended upon Europe, dividing it almost in half. Germany itself was divided into communist Eastern Germany and democratic Western Germany, and its former capital of Berlin was later divided by the Berlin Wall erected by the communists.

Having learned its lesson from the aftermath of World War I, in which totalitarian regimes gained power amidst economic collapse, the United States sought to economically rebuild Europe under what was called the Marshall Plan. Tremendous amounts of aid flowed there from the United States, and the economies of Western Europe quickly began to prosper, unlike communist Eastern Europe.

On the heels of World War II, the communists achieved a major victory in the conquest of China, following years of foreign intervention and intrigue in Chinese affairs. The Portuguese had been the first Europeans since Marco Polo to arrive and engage in trade with China, during the Ming dynasty. They established a trading post in Macao that lasted for centuries. In 1582 Matteo Ricci, an Italian Jesuit missionary arrived in Macao, and then moved to Peking. His relationship with the Ming emperors allowed other Jesuits to enter, and these Jesuits were able to garner several hundred thousand converts to Roman Catholicism. In 1644 the Manchus of the north began a dynasty in China that lasted until 1911. During this period Great Britain and other Western nations wanted access to engage in trade in China, against the resistance of the Chinese emperors and government. This conflict resulted in the Opium Wars, which led to Western victory and open trade. The nineteenth century was marked by a series of rebellions, and in 1900 there was the Boxer Rebellion aiming to expel all foreigners, including the Manchus themselves. Led by Sun Yat-sen, a Chinese doctor-turned-politician who was educated in Hawaii and converted to Christianity, the Republic of China replaced the dynasty of the Manchus. This Republic, ruled by the Nationalist Party, tried tirelessly to rid itself of foreign domination, even as it was battling a burgeoning communist movement. When attacked by Japan in 1937, it struggled in its war against Japanese aggression and communist guerrilla warfare, led by Mao Zedong.

At the conclusion of World War II, the communists were able to quickly take over territory which had been controlled by the Japanese during the war. Finally, in 1949 the Nationalists were forced to flee to Taiwan, and the communists proclaimed the establishment of the People's Republic of China for the mainland. Up until 1949 Protestant Christian missionaries had been able to proclaim the gospel throughout many areas of China, but in that year the door closed tight. The Communist government under Mao Zedong ruthlessly oppressed the people of China, especially Christians, yet Christianity grew despite the oppression. But communism has proved a formidable foe to truth and grace in China.

Other theaters of the Cold War following World War II included Korea and Vietnam. Japan had occupied Korea during World War II. But following Japan's defeat, the United States occupied the area south of the famous 38th parallel in Korea and the Soviet Union occupied the area north of this line. The United Nations had recommended a nationwide vote in Korea to determine its leadership, but the north refused. The elected government in the south formed the Republic of Korea, whereas the communist government in the north formed the People's Republic of Korea. In 1950 North Korea invaded the South, setting off the Korean War which lasted until 1953 when a truce was signed. During the war the Soviet Union and later China aided North Korea, while the United States was the principal party supporting South Korea. With the truce of 1953, the line of demarcation between North and South was approximately where it was at the beginning of the war. In the years following the war North Korea remained a repressive communist regime enforcing atheism, whereas South Korea has developed into a prosperous democratic republic. Presbyterian missions have long been active in Korea, and there are millions of Protestants in South Korea. But the division between North and South Korea have kept circumstances tense throughout the Korean peninsula ever since the truce.

Vietnam, like Korea, had been occupied by the Japanese during World War II. With Japanese evacuation, there was an over seven-year war for control between the French, who had held it as a colony for over a century, and communist

Vietnamese. In 1954, Vietnam was partitioned, with North Vietnam controlled by the communists, while South Vietnam was controlled by an elected (but corrupt) government. Communist guerrillas in the south, supported by North Vietnam, greatly destabilized the nation, so that gradually the United States was drawn in to support South Vietnam. The years under French Roman Catholic control had not provided a strong base for better government like Protestant missions in South Korea had provided. Opposition to the war grew in the U.S., so that eventually the U.S. exited from the war in humiliation. South Vietnam was overtaken and conquered by the communists to the north. Its neighbors, Laos and Cambodia also were conquered by the communists.

The theater of Cold War conflict quickly included other regions of the world, like the Caribbean, Africa, Central and South America, and central Asia. Just as France was losing control over its foreign colonies like Vietnam (formerly French Indochina), all of the European powers were losing control over their colonies Africa and Asia. Those which had been controlled by Roman Catholic countries like France and Portugal were especially vulnerable to becoming communist-controlled. In the 1960s communists led by Jesuit-educated Fidel Castro gained control over Cuba. And his regime along with the Soviet Union promoted communism in Central America and Africa. Accordingly, Nicaragua in Central America and Angola in Africa fell to Marxist insurgents. A large segment of the Roman Catholic Church in Africa and the Americas actually inspired Marxist revolutions, through teaching what became known as 'liberation theology.'

Former British and American colonies tended to fare better in resisting communism but were nevertheless plagued by monumental challenges. Following World War II India obtained its independence from Great Britain under the leadership of Mahatma Gandhi. It had been made a colony of Great Britain starting in 1757 through the enterprises of Robert Clive with the British East India Company. The gospel was preached in India for many years by British missionaries, although the vast majority of its citizens remained Hindu and

Muslim. In the years leading up to independence Britain gave the Indians experience in self-government, which gave it an advantage when independence was achieved. India maintained a parliamentary democracy following independence but was beset by internal conflicts between the Hindus and Muslims, which ended up issuing in the formation of the independent states of Pakistan and Bangladesh.

The American colony of the Philippines obtained their independence immediately following World War II as well, establishing a constitutional democracy patterned after America's. You will remember that the Philippines had become a colony of the United States as a result of the Spanish-American War, following centuries of Spanish rule. In the waning days of Spanish rule, the Jesuit orders became more influential in the Philippines and acquired great amounts of property. It was the opposition to the power of the clergy that in large measure brought about the rising sentiment for independence from Spain even before America took it over during the Spanish-American War. Just as Great Britain had given India some experience in self-government during its colonial days, likewise America had given the Philippines such experience. Similarly, Protestant American missionaries brought the gospel into the Philippines, but a considerable majority remained Roman Catholic. Former colonies of Great Britain and America like the Philippines and India in Asia, as well as Kenya and Nigeria in Africa, have been especially challenged by graft and corruption permeating society as well as political leadership, causing de-stabilization.

Although the difficulties in the West were great, the communist Soviet Union was experiencing mounting difficulties in its Cold War with the United States and the West by the 1980s. It had tried to invade and conquer Afghanistan in central Asia. The military quagmire in Afghanistan was unpopular in Russia and appeared to be a no-win situation. Also, the people of Eastern Europe were becoming increasingly restive as they saw the prosperity of their neighbors in the West, in comparison with their own flagging economies. There were protest movements in Poland and other Eastern European countries, and large numbers of Eastern Europeans seeking to flee the throes of communism. In addition, U.S. President Ronald Reagan threw down the gauntlet with the communist Soviet Union, challenging it to tear down the Berlin Wall, calling it the "Evil Empire", and spending billions of dollars in military capability to overcome it.

The Soviet Union simply did not have the economic resources or political will to beat this challenge, and eventually threw in the towel. It allowed the people of Eastern Europe to overthrow the communist regimes in their nations, and eventually the communist regime in the Soviet Union itself was overthrown under Boris Yeltsin.

By the end of the twentieth century the primary remaining Communist powers were China, North Korea, Vietnam, and Cuba. But even in these countries, and especially in China and Vietnam, there were significant modifications in the economic model. The People's Republic of China, following the death of Mao Zedong, opened its economy to certain capitalistic tendencies, while trying to maintain an essentially communistic political regime. The military capabilities of these Communist powers is such that a communist menace still persists, even though communism and Marxism have lost all credibility as political and economic theories. By the end of the twentieth century it has become even more obvious that communism remains only as an excuse for totalitarian and anti-Christian regimes.

LET ME TELL YOU THE REAL STORY OF MANKIND

CHAPTER 62: Zionism and Islamic Resurgence

From the time of the Enlightenment movement beginning in the late seventeenth century, anticipated even earlier by the Renaissance, the logical consequences of humanism have been played out. As I have reminded you before, humanistic philosophy is grounded upon the anti-Biblical and erroneous assumption that man is not totally depraved. This assumption well suited Romanism, with its denial of the doctrine of man's total depravity. Many Protestant denominations have also been infected. And most European Judaists readily embraced the error as well. This humanism is accompanied by secularism, as people became less inclined to depend upon divine revelation to shape life and culture, and more inclined to trust their own capability to reason and discover truth by observation of the material world. Jewish Zionism itself was part of this overall trend, and the rise of the Zionist movement in the late nineteenth century was influenced by nationalist currents in Europe, as well as by the secularization of Jewish life in Eastern Europe, which led many assimilated Jewish intellectuals to seek a new basis for a Jewish national life. By 1900 many European Jews were thoroughly secularized, and they wanted to see the formation of a Jewish state in which they could implement their generally humanistic and socialistic aspirations.

Theodor Herzl, an Austrian journalist who wrote *The Jewish State* (1896), called for the formation of a Jewish nation state. In 1897 Herzl called the first World Zionist Congress at Basel, which brought together diverse proto-Zionist groups into one movement. The meeting helped found Zionist organizations in most countries with large Jewish populations. The first great controversy in the Zionist movement was whether Palestine was essential to a Jewish state. A majority of the delegates to the 1903 congress felt that it was essential and rejected the British offer of a homeland in Uganda. And the Zionist movement remained a diverse mixture of secularized Jews who longed for a Marxist socialist state as well as components which held to more traditional Judaism.

The Zionist movement received special assistance with the Balfour Declaration. In 1917, Great Britain, then at war with Turkey during World War I, issued the Balfour Declaration, which promised to help establish a national home for the Jewish people in Palestine. Great Britain was given a mandate of Palestine in 1920 by the League of Nations, in part to implement the Balfour Declaration. Jewish colonization vastly increased in the early years of this mandate, but soon the British limited their interpretation of the declaration in the face of Arab pressure. However, the rise of Nazism in Europe during the 1930s led to a great increase in Jewish immigration.

After World War II, the Zionist movement intensified its activities. The persecutions of the European Jews by the Germans were used as a rationale for the opening of a refuge for the world's Jews. But Arab opposition intensified as well. In the period from the end of World War I to the end of World War II, the number of Jews in Palestine had increased tenfold, whereas the number of Muslims had less than doubled. And the number of Jews had surpassed the number of nominal Christians. Britain was unable to reconcile the competing claims of Jews and Muslims, so handed Palestine over to the newly formed United Nations (which had replaced the League of Nations) to try to solve.

But the United Nations was unable to solve the quandary, and so the Jews took matters into their own hands. In 1948, the Jews proclaimed the creation of the state of Israel in Palestine, and in 1949 they moved their capital to Jerusalem, much to the consternation of most Palestinians.

The formation of Israel, especially supported by the United States, galvanized Arab opposition. And the conflict at first became part of the larger Cold War, pitting the United States against the Soviet Union. A Palestinian Liberation Organization was supported by the Soviets, while Americans supplied Israel with billions of dollars in aid. Various attempts by neighboring Arab states to defeat Israel ended in failure, and even resulted in Israel controlling more territory. But as the communist Soviet Union was collapsing, the struggle over Palestine and Israel took on a very different character.

I have told you how secular humanism has been on the rise for the last several hundred years. But starting in the latter half of the twentieth century, there became a gradually building momentum away from secularism and towards building political life and culture upon religion (i.e., theocracy), especially in the Middle East, but even in the territory of the former Soviet Union. I will tell you more about that change in the next chapter, but I would simply mention here that the change in character of the Palestinian conflict was part of this broader, gradually occurring shift. The nation of Israel was not only an island of Jews in an Arab ocean; but it was also a Western secularist outpost in the midst of many Muslims who yearned for a Muslim state under Islamic law.

America's support for Israel corresponded with its support of a pro-western regime in Iran, under the absolute monarchy of the Shah of Iran. The Shah's pro-Western policies lasted into the 1970s. However, opposition to the growing Westernization and secularization was strongly denounced by the Islamic clergy, headed by the Ayatollah Khomeini. Such internal opposition within the country was regularly purged by the Shah's secret police force. But in 1979 opposition grew so great to the Shah's rule that he was overthrown in an Islamic Revolution creating the Islamic Republic of Iran under Ayatollah Khomeini.

Islamic militant groups supported by the Islamic Republic of Iran, as well as fundamentalist Muslims scattered throughout the Middle East, joined the fight against Israel in Palestine. They saw Israel not only as a beachhead for Jewish nationalism, but also as a beachhead of Western secularism in the Middle East. This Islamic Palestinian movement became a rallying point for the greater Islamic movement.

Adding to this Islamic movement was the Muslim war in Afghanistan, to rid it of the Soviet Union. Fundamentalist Muslims received support not only from Muslims throughout the Middle East, but even from the United States, in an effort to undermine the Soviet Union. Their successful effort in forcing the evacuation of the Soviet Union only strengthened their cause. It also created another state dedicated to radical Islamic rule.

J. Parnell McCarter

The movement to create states enforcing Muslim Sharia law spread ever further. In places like Sudan and Nigeria civil wars ensued over this very issue. And America's military presence in Saudi Arabia as a result of Iraqi aggression in the region, only intensified the effort by Muslims to fight against secularism, Israel, and the United States. In perhaps its most startling enterprise in the West, a Muslim terrorist group destroyed New York City's World Trade Towers and much of the Pentagon on September 11, 2001.

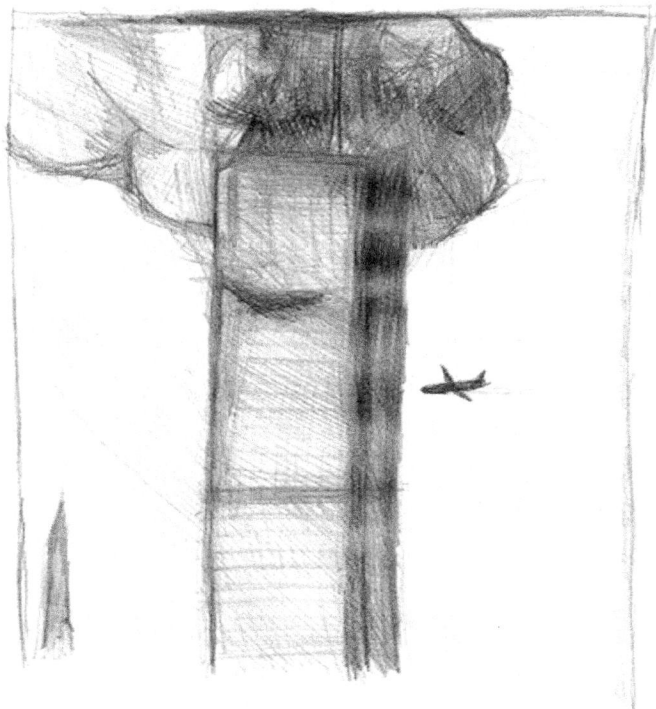

Throughout Christian history, God has employed the wicked Muslim scourge to discipline Christian societies when they have fallen from the Biblical path into deep sin. *"And there came out of the smoke locusts upon the earth: and unto them was given power, as the scorpions of the earth have power. And it was commanded them that they should not hurt the grass of the earth, neither any green thing, neither any tree; but only*

those men which have not the seal of God in their foreheads...And the shapes of the locusts [were] like unto horses prepared unto battle; and on their heads [were] as it were crowns like gold, and their faces [were] as the faces of men." It would seem this is but another incident of that same historical pattern. But we cannot expect that this chastisement by Muslims will be the primary factor leading to repentance, for *"the rest of the men which were not killed by these plagues yet repented not of the works of their hands, that they should not worship devils, and idols of gold, and silver, and brass, and stone, and of wood: which neither can see, nor hear, nor walk: Neither repented they of their murders, nor of their sorceries, nor of their fornication, nor of their thefts."* Rather, the primary instrument by which repentance will be effected is the preaching of the gospel, for *"out of his mouth goeth a sharp sword, that with it he should smite the nations: and he shall rule them with a rod of iron: and he treadeth the winepress of the fierceness and wrath of Almighty God."* And it is this topic which will occupy the final chapter in this history lesson.

CHAPTER 63: Secular Humanism and the Information Age

"The fool saith in his heart there is no God." This would be an appropriate motto for Western civilization as the "Age of Enlightenment" has come to its full fruition. Nothing happened overnight, but gradually over the decades Western society has become more secularized and based in humanistic principles. Just as the Roman harlot's power was being severely reduced in the Reformation, it passed its humanistic baton over to many daughter whores who have continued to run with it. These have generally promoted secular humanism.

The secularist trend started with an unwillingness to enforce and maintain the reformed and Protestant faith which had been so successfully planted in much of northern Europe, the American colonies, and beyond. Once heresy and idolatry were allowed to openly survive, it thrived. This scriptural saying is true for any society of man: *"A little leaven leavens the whole lump."* One-by-one Biblical standards were overturned, even as Romans chapter one implies will happen to those people who have abandoned true religion and true worship. God has given the Western societies over to all sorts of wicked sexual perversions, covenant-breaking divorce, murder and abortion, and the like. The Christian Sabbath has been thoroughly ignored and desecrated. The entertainment industry, with its capital in Hollywood in the United States, has promoted all manner of vices. The public schools removed Bible lessons and prayer and replaced it by teaching Darwin's evolutionary theory as fact. And after numerous civil and even world wars it became painfully obvious that secularism could not deliver humanity from war. Finally, the "sexual revolution" of the 1960s and the decades following saw the full flowering of humanism, promoting sodomy, feminism, and unrestrained sexual conduct.

But in adopting this secular humanist agenda, the West has laid the seeds for its own destruction. Margaret Sanger's feminist message promoting abortion and contraception, though it was formerly prohibited by law under the Comstock Law, became legally tolerated and finally promoted by the governments of the West beginning in the twentieth century. The end result, following World War II, has been a declining population in the West, even as the population in other parts of the world has been booming. By the end of the twentieth century, population statistics were revealing what one American political commentator has termed 'the death of the West.' This has been accompanied by growing immigration from the Third World into the Western nations. So called 'multiculturalism' has taken hold in the West, spawning a veritable modern Babel, with the USA as its shining example.

At the very time Western society in general was plunging deeper and deeper into secular humanism and multiculturalism, the information age has also been coming into full fruit, and with it, accessibility to informational resources which make knowledge and truth far more accessible to more people. As was prophesied in Daniel 12:4: "But thou, O Daniel, shut up the words, and seal the book, even to the time of the end: many shall run to and fro, and knowledge shall be increased." Modern telecommunications, publishing and the internet have all contributed towards this trend. The internet has sped up the dissemination of communications both bad and good, both pornographic and salutary. The Reformation that began around five centuries ago was greatly aided by Gutenberg's invention of a movable type printing press. It made possible the dissemination of the Bible and reformed literature at a fraction of the cost previously possible. As the twentieth century closed and the twenty first century dawned God has provided a new tool that even further stimulates the flow of communication and information: the internet. Combined with the computer technology which also developed during the twentieth century, reformed Christian books, tracts, and messages can be disseminated worldwide at a fraction of the cost previously possible. Transportation as well has been greatly simplified in the twentieth century, with the invention and sale of mass-produced automobiles and the airplane.

As wickedness has abounded, so too has accessible information contravening it. For instance, a growing body of scholars and scholarship began to dissent from the evolutionist "orthodoxy". With very few exceptions, until the 1960s, even most Christian leaders who claimed to hold to the inerrancy of scripture nevertheless allowed revelation to accommodate science at least insofar as the age of the earth. But the situation began to change dramatically with the publication in 1961 of *The Genesis Flood* by John C. Whitcomb, Jr., and Henry M. Morris, and the formation two years later of the Creation Research Society (CRS). Whitcomb, an Old Testament scholar, and Morris, a civil engineer, collaborated on an up-to-date presentation of flood geology that attracted considerable attention in conservative Christian circles. Their argument that science should accommodate revelation rather than vice versa resonated with the sentiments of many concerned Christians, who followed Whitcomb and Morris in jettisoning the gap and day-age theories as unholy compromises with naturalistic science. In 1963, Morris joined nine other creationists with scientific training to form the CRS, an organization committed to the propagation of young-earth creationism.

In the 1920s, antievolutionists had lacked a single scientist with so much as a master's degree in science. In contrast, five of the ten founding members of the CRS had earned Ph.D.'s in the biological sciences at reputable universities, and a sixth held a doctorate in biochemistry. Public-opinion polls, though failing to distinguish young- from old-earth creationists, showed that forty-seven percent of Americans, including a quarter of college graduates, professed belief in the recent special creation of the first humans within the past 10,000 years. (It just goes to show that you cannot fool all the people all of the time.) A hundred and forty years of evolutionist claptrap had left many Americans unconvinced. And the American creationist movement spawned creationist societies internationally.

On a different front, the Banner of Truth Trust originated in 1957 in London. The founders believed that much of the best literature of historic Christianity had been allowed to fall into oblivion and that its recovery under God could well lead not only to a strengthening of the Church today but to true revival. The origins of the work were closely connected with the prayer that God would be pleased to visit the land again in true awakening.

It was believed that former literature - particularly of the Reformation and Puritan eras - had become buried for two reasons. Firstly, that the emphasis of that literature was not congenial to much that passed for Biblical Christianity in the present century. Secondly that religious publishing had become far too market oriented, that is to say, a primary question with publishers was that a title was saleable and to what degree it could be expected to be popular. The publication of old reformed and Puritan literature began to awake a more widespread audience of Christians to the doctrines of the historic faith.

The first impact of the Puritan literature was to re-awaken a number of Protestant Christians to God's prescription for personal faith and piety, and then His will relating to worship, civil government and many other topics. The nineteenth and twentieth centuries had undermined the reformed perspective regarding personal faith and piety. On the one hand, liberal Protestantism had weakened the authority of scripture; whereas on the other hand, dispensational Protestantism had weakened the authority of God's law as summarized in the Ten Commandments and had clouded the doctrines of grace. The newly published literature from the past refreshed men's knowledge regarding the Biblical path on these subjects.

J. Parnell McCarter

The second impact of the reformed and Puritan literature, published by Banner of Truth Trust as well as by others like Free Presbyterian Publications, was to re-awaken Protestant Christians to God's prescription for church and civil life. Issues like church discipline and church government began to be discussed again more widely, and that not simply on the basis of pragmatic- but rather Biblical- grounds. As these issues have been further considered, the dust that had gathered on the historic reformed confessions has begun to be wiped away. Their vision for personal, ecclesiastical, and civil life and doctrine has been viewed with renewed appreciation. While at the beginning of the twenty first century this vision still enjoys only minority support; nevertheless, more resources are available to defend the Biblical doctrines summarized in the historic reformed confessions like the Westminster Confession of Faith and the Three Forms of Unity. And these resources are available worldwide via the internet, as well as more traditional publications. For example, the Trinitarian Bible Society has been distributing the Received Text of the Bible across the world in many different languages.

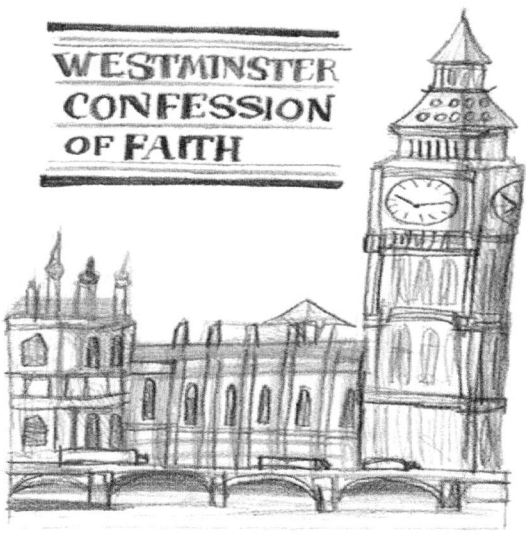

Even the multiculturalist agenda of the Western establishment has met with significant grassroots opposition that has made its presence felt. Ethnic nationalism, opposing modern Western multiculturalism and secularism, has been helped by the freer flow of information through the internet. The multiculturalist establishment has found it hard to maintain their ideological monopoly in a day when mass communication is possible on a shoe-string budget. Ironically, some of the strongest opposition to modern multiculturalism and open borders, in favor of more traditional Christian nationalism, has come from formerly communist Eastern European nations.

While true information is not reformation, long term it is an important means towards that end. The days of secularist humanist and false religionist hegemony are numbered. God will bring down the modern Babel even as He brought down the ancient one. Papal Rome too will likely have a last hurray, but her doom is sealed as well. There is good reason to believe God will convert the Jews en masse to Biblical Christianity, and that these will then lead the Gentile world away from the errors of Roman Catholicism and Islam. God has allowed us to wander in the wilderness to teach us a lesson about the vanity of life under the sun, apart from life based upon God's word. Now it is for us to embrace His promises in faith, even as the few like Joshua and Caleb embraced it in ancient days.

With the benefits that God has providentially bestowed in new technologies, lies as well great dangers. After the invention of the atomic bomb, came the invention of the hydrogen bomb. And in World War II Germany developed rocket technology, which has been greatly improved since then to deliver weapons of mass destruction. And newly developed technologies associated with genetic engineering hold out a promise of great benefits or catastrophic dangers. As the world has become closer tied together through modern technology, it is all the more important that mankind make peace with God through conformity to His revealed will in Jesus Christ, in order that there might be true peace on earth. The cost of war with God and with man is escalating. The rationale for Christian obedience is greater than it ever has been. Christians have the solution in Jesus Christ of how man can enjoy technology without destroying himself. And Christians must take this message of peace to the world.

The grand vision for the future- which Christians are to strive for, pray for, and trust in- is displayed in the second petition of the Lord's Prayer. As the Westminster Larger Catechism so eloquently elucidates it: in the second petition, (which is, *Thy kingdom come*) acknowledging ourselves and all mankind to be by nature under the dominion of sin and Satan, we pray, that the kingdom of sin and Satan may be destroyed, the gospel propagated throughout the world, the Jews called, the fullness of the Gentiles brought in; the church furnished with all gospel-officers and ordinances, purged from corruption, countenanced and maintained by the civil magistrate: that the ordinances of Christ may be purely dispensed, and made effectual to the converting of those that are yet in their sins, and the confirming, comforting, and building up of those that are already converted: that Christ would rule in our hearts here, and hasten the time of his second coming, and our reigning with him forever: and that he would be pleased so to exercise the kingdom of his power in all the world, as may best conduce to these ends."

So, my sons, I come now to the end of my story. It is a story that God has written and continues to write in His Providence. It is a story whose end is the glory of Jesus Christ, which He especially receives through the work of His redemption of a people from all nations unto Himself. It is a story which I hope you will take to heart while you are still young and have time and energy to labor for Christ's kingdom. I end where you must begin: *"Remember now thy Creator in the days of thy youth."*

LET ME TELL YOU THE REAL STORY OF MANKIND

BIBLIOGRAPHY

An Outline of American History, United States Department of State, Department of International Information, Editor: Howard Cincotta, 1994.

Compton's Encyclopedia, Compton's Learning Company, 1992.

Custance, Arthur C., *Noah's Three Sons: Human History in three Dimensions.* Doorway Publications, Ontario, Canada.

Encyclopedia Britannica, London, 1973.

Encyclopedia.com, Infonautics Corporation, 2001.

Numbers, Ronald L. *The Creationists.* New York: Alfred A. Knopf, 1992.

Van Loon, Hendrik Willem. *The Story of Mankind,* Boni and Liveright, 1921.

Yonge, Charlotte Mary. *The Chosen People: A Compendium of Sacred & Church History for School-children* . New York: Pott and Amery, 1868.

LET ME TELL YOU THE REAL STORY OF MANKIND

INDEX

A
Abraham, 14, 32, 36, 38–40, 50, 97, 155
Abyssinia, 260, 503
Achæans, 69, 93
ACLU (American Civil Liberties Union), 485
Adam, 2, 5–6, 11, 97, 127
Adams, John, 390
adultery, 29–30, 292
Afghanistan, 524, 530
Africa, 8, 19, 99, 114, 118, 158, 214, 259–60, 264, 266, 279, 297, 479–80, 504–5, 523–24
African Sea, 99–100, 107, 110, 114
Ægeans, 66–67, 69, 71, 85, 101, 267
Ægean Sea, 32, 65, 67–68, 86, 98, 212, 511
Alexander, 18, 27, 73, 93–95, 114, 120, 135, 179, 207, 260, 425–28, 431, 434, 438, 443
Alexandria, 27, 121, 207, 463
Alfred, King, 302
Allied forces, 517–19
Alps, 102, 108, 110, 118, 120, 165, 180, 182, 188, 225
America, 261, 269, 321, 323, 385–86, 392, 398, 440, 442–43, 449, 455, 479–80, 509, 513, 523–24
American colonies, 370, 372, 375, 382, 389–90, 523–24, 533
American government, 442–43
American Revolution, 382, 385, 406, 446
Anabaptists, 292, 306, 371
Ancien Régime, 394, 396
Anglican churches, 336–37
Anti-Christ, 143, 180–81, 208, 210, 323
apostles, 132–36, 229, 250, 413, 475
Apostles' Creed, 161
archbishops, 232, 237, 240, 279–80, 293, 310
aristocracy, 59, 495
Aristophanes, 82

Aristotle, 93, 207, 229
Armenia, 6–7, 11–12
artists, 279, 467, 494–95, 501
Aryans, 63–64, 269, 271
Asia, 55, 65, 86, 88, 98, 111, 118, 139, 151, 158, 185, 187, 445, 455, 523–24
Asia Minor, 8, 66, 71, 88, 103, 110, 115, 133, 147, 183, 185, 188, 212
Athens, 65, 68, 76, 86–88, 91–93, 104, 115, 138, 143, 147, 188, 213, 445; people of, 75, 86, 91
Augustine, 148–49, 239, 373
Augustus, 27, 124, 127–28, 163–64, 171
Austria, 293, 363, 402, 415, 422, 428, 435, 444, 454–56, 498, 507
authority, 120, 127, 136, 145, 161, 163, 207, 210, 229, 286, 290, 319, 321, 371, 380; papal, 211, 234, 239, 286–87
Axis powers, 517, 519

B

Babel, 8, 12, 14, 483
Babylon, 14–16, 29, 53, 68–69, 72, 94, 99, 127, 158, 426
Babylonians, 11, 52, 72, 95, 105, 141, 143, 491, 497
Balfour Declaration, 528
Balkans, 434, 444, 506
Baltic, 215–16, 325, 348
Baltic Sea, 356, 359
baptism, 132, 323
Baptists, 371, 382
barbarians, 58, 77, 105, 139–41, 146, 211–12, 215, 301
Barbarossa, 182–83
Bastille prison, 403
Bavaria, 325, 435, 446, 450
Beethoven, 500
Belgians, 447–48, 505
Belgium, 279, 308, 344, 407, 431, 447, 504–5, 512, 518
Bentham, Jeremy, 477
Berlin, 355, 404, 458, 506, 521
Bethlehem, 125, 127–28
Biblical Christianity, 219, 301, 476–77, 536, 538
bishops, 134, 145, 148–49, 172, 232, 234–35, 240, 280–81, 284, 304, 313–14, 323, 445, 495
Bismarck, 451–52, 455–56, 458, 506
Black Death, 262
Black Sea, 9, 33, 118, 214, 348–49, 511
Blanc, Louis, 487–88

blessings, 37, 40, 43, 45, 97, 131, 155, 193, 338, 362, 437, 476–77
Bloody Mary, 308
Bohemia, 238, 325
Boleyn, Anne, 305, 307
Bolivar, 442
Bologna, 223, 245
Bonaparte, Napoleon, 407
Boxer Rebellion, 521
Brahman, 270–71
Brandenburg, 359–61
Brazil, 259, 264, 266, 433, 455
Brownists, 313–14
Brussels, 448, 489
Buddha, 271–72, 274–75
Bulgaria, 506
Bunyan, John, 496
Byzantine Emperor, 150–51, 161
Byzantine Empire, 149–52, 349

C
Calvin, John, 290–92, 294, 315, 327, 373, 383;
Calvinistic doctrines, 298
Canaan, 7–8, 11, 29–30, 34–35, 37, 45, 53, 127, 266; land of, 29, 44
Canaanites, 29–30, 36, 45–46
Canary Islands, 259
Cannibal Islands, 228
Canterbury, archbishop of, 234, 236, 304–5

Cape Verde Islands, 259
cardinals, 181, 240, 279–80, 324
Carpathian Mountains, 171, 359, 449
Carthage, 31, 98–101, 106–7, 110–11, 114, 116
Carthaginian armies, 107
Carthaginians, 106–8, 110, 115, 267, 409
Cæsar, Julius, 27, 119–22, 124, 128, 171, 301, 351
Cathay, 14, 249, 258, 261, 263, 266
Catholics, 307, 326, 336, 361
Central Asia, 64, 348, 523–24
centuries: eighteenth, 14, 266, 363, 378, 386, 393, 409, 459, 464, 498–99; eleventh, 98, 169, 172, 180, 185, 261, 302; seventeenth, 256, 265, 297, 341, 352, 357, 361, 365–66, 377, 386, 391, 464, 509, 527; sixteenth, 215, 221, 267, 294, 308, 352, 365, 387, 431, 436, 496; thirteenth, 173, 192, 215–17, 220, 226, 249, 256–58; twelfth century, 207, 222, 259, 360, 492–

93, 497; twentieth, 360, 467, 469, 500–501, 510, 520, 525, 530, 534–36; early, 33, 152, 503, 510
Chaldeans, 12, 16–17
Charlemagne, 161, 163–65, 168, 171, 179, 203, 359, 413
Charles I, 329–30, 334, 414
Charles II, 329, 334, 344
Chartist movement, 475
children, 8–9, 35–36, 40, 42, 116, 118, 128, 130, 168–69, 280–81, 369, 411, 478, 490, 492
China, 55–60, 98, 249–53, 255, 257–58, 264, 266, 269, 275, 298, 349, 503, 518, 520–22, 525
Ch'in Dynasty, 58–60
Chou Dynasty, 56–58, 250
Christ, 40, 42–43, 127, 129, 131–34, 144, 149, 179–80, 205, 207–8, 247, 283–84, 292–93, 329–30, 539
Christian Church, 132–33, 147–50, 303
Christianity, 136, 141, 143–44, 155, 184–85, 301, 317, 342, 383, 406, 437, 477, 491, 521–22
Christian missionaries, 146, 165, 261, 317
Christian Sabbath, 292, 533
church, eastern, 149, 151–52, 497
church government, 42, 292–93, 310, 312, 332, 370, 537
Churchill, Winston, 520
Church of England, 305, 311–12, 315
Church of Rome, 149, 243–44, 246
Church of Scotland, 317–18
circumcision, 36, 40, 132
citizens, 71–72, 74, 76–77, 92, 100, 104–5, 113, 179, 196, 200, 213, 221, 368, 423, 472
city-states, 138, 194, 491
city walls, 72, 201, 295
civil government, 48, 292, 310, 334, 379, 536
civil wars, 296, 331, 336–37, 481, 531
Cleopatra, 27–28, 121, 123
Cold War, 520, 522–24, 529
colonies, 298, 303, 310, 319, 339, 367–68, 380, 386–87, 390–91, 394, 433, 505, 511, 518, 522–24
colonists, 229, 388–89, 391, 398
Columbus, Christopher, 14, 158, 252, 256, 263–64, 266, 309, 347, 440, 507;

Commandments, 41–42, 52, 129, 148, 153, 175, 209, 292, 296, 302, 345, 372, 424, 477, 536
communion, 130, 306; renounced, 312
communism, 152, 515–16, 522, 525
Confucianism, 252
Congo, 228
Congregational, 312, 370–71, 381
Congress of Vienna, 419, 431–32, 434, 436, 439–40, 446, 448, 451, 454, 468
Constantine, 139, 146–47
Constantinople, 139, 141, 147, 151–52, 164, 185, 187, 189–90, 228, 347–49, 351, 438, 444, 506, 511
Continental Europe, 238, 289, 319, 339, 342, 379
Corsicans, 165, 409
Cossacks, 415–16
cotton mills, 471, 478, 487, 490
Counter-Reformation, 246, 321, 323
Crete, 67, 188, 266
Crimean war, 424, 454, 457
Cromwell, Oliver, 332–34, 367

CRS (Creation Research Society), 535
Crusades, 176, 183, 188–89, 194–95, 198, 201, 211–12, 218, 249, 257–58, 321, 446, 472, 493; second, 183, 187
Cuba, 482, 505–6, 523, 525
culture, 25, 219, 378, 380, 527, 530

D

Darius, King, 65
Darwin, Charles, 484–85
Darwinian, 504, 516
David, King, 48–51, 97, 127–28, 293
Dead Sea, 45
democracy, 213, 313, 375, 406, 524
Denmark, 167, 216, 288, 325, 358, 432, 456
dictator, 119–21, 124, 250, 333
Dionysos, 80, 82
disciples, 131–32, 231, 275
Divine Right of Kings, 329–30, 334–36, 342, 375, 448
divorce, covenant-breaking, 533
Doctrine, Monroe, 427, 443
Dutch Protestants, 297, 327
Dutch Republic, 298, 325, 337, 431

E

East Asia, 518
Eastern Europe, 250, 293, 520, 524–25, 527
Eastern Europeans, 524
Eastern Orthodox Church, 151
Eastern Roman Empire, 149, 151, 185, 189, 349
Eden, 5
Edinburgh, 333, 336
Edward, King, 233, 306–7
Egypt, 8, 11, 19–20, 23–29, 38–40, 43–44, 46, 63, 65, 72, 95, 97–98, 114, 121–23, 266
Egyptian army, 121, 445
Egyptians, 19–20, 22–25, 27, 32, 39–40, 95, 105, 121, 141, 143, 173, 491, 493, 497
Elba, 416–17
Elizabeth, Queen, 310–11, 316, 318, 467
England, 296, 298–99, 301–5, 308–9, 311–12, 317–19, 329–30, 332–37, 377–79, 385–90, 413–15, 445–48, 464–65, 474–75, 505–6
English Colonies, 329, 377, 379, 384, 387, 479
English Parliament, 233, 305, 311, 331–33
English Puritanism, 319
Enlightenment, 369, 372–74, 376, 378, 383–84, 390–91, 394, 418, 440, 477, 483, 486, 510, 513
Epistles, 133–34, 235
Erasmus, 221, 282–83
Establishment Principle, 147, 379, 383, 390–91
Estates General, 295–96, 330, 399–401; old, 399
Ethiopia, 133
Etruscans, 102–3
Euphrates, 11, 158, 267, 491
Euripides, 78, 82
Europe, 63–65, 86, 171–74, 185–86, 278–79, 344–45, 350–52, 370–71, 415–16, 421–22, 424–26, 435–37, 439–40, 448–49, 456–57; history of, 163, 439
European countries, 281, 385, 413, 474, 511
European Jews, 527–28
Eve, 2, 5, 11
excommunication, 181, 236, 286, 292

F

factories, 78, 116, 352, 366, 472–73, 478, 489, 505, 509–10; cotton, 466, 471
faith, scriptural, 247
false religion, 147, 342, 430

false worship, 147, 151, 157, 161, 286, 342; suppressing, 150
families, 6–7, 36, 38, 40, 61, 77, 79, 116–17, 281, 284, 371, 375, 448, 450, 487–88
Far East, 55, 62, 98, 164, 253, 255, 519
fascism, 515–16
fever, typhoid, 256, 369
Finland, 358
Florence, 213, 225–26, 229, 245, 454
flying buttresses, 493
Ford, Henry, 469
France, 168, 186, 290–91, 341–45, 386–88, 391–95, 399–401, 404, 406–7, 446–50, 454, 457, 511–12, 518–20, 523
Frankfort, 435, 450–51, 455
freedom, 116, 185, 362, 374–75, 409, 446, 473–74, 506
French Emperor, 414–15, 440, 453
French government, 390, 421, 457–58, 519
French Protestant, 290, 294
French Revolution, 393, 396–97, 409, 413, 418, 423, 446, 472–73, 488, 500, 509
French society, 342–43, 396

G
Gauls, 105, 108, 164
Geneva, 290–93, 330
Genoa, 188, 211, 214, 216, 221, 266
German Diet, 435
Germanic tribes, 161, 165, 167, 171
German princes, 181, 295
Germans, 167, 223, 270, 277–81, 286–87, 363, 435, 454, 456, 458, 510, 512–13, 520, 528
Germany, 180, 182, 278, 280–81, 283, 286–87, 289, 293, 325–26, 434, 453, 455–57, 488–89, 511–13, 516–20
Gilead, 44–45
God, false, 25, 82, 103, 124, 144
gospel, 95, 113, 132–35, 138, 143–44, 146, 251, 255, 317, 334, 339, 504, 522–24, 532, 539; false, 208, 281, 285–86; true, 149, 208, 294
Gothic, 492–93
Gothic Kingdom, 141
Goths, 140, 149
Great Awakening, 379–84
Great Britain, 301, 342, 380, 390, 505, 518–20, 523–24, 528

Great Flood, 5, 55, 63, 68, 269
Greece, 55, 64–66, 71, 87, 92–93, 98, 101, 115–16, 121, 179, 188, 194, 197, 444, 446
Greek cities, 75, 77, 82, 86, 91, 104–5
Greek civilizations, 69, 71, 227
Greek colonies, 85, 107
Greek New Testament, 229
Greek philosophers, 207
Greeks, 20–21, 26, 65–68, 71–74, 76–81, 85–87, 93, 95, 98–99, 103–5, 114, 141, 206–7, 433–34, 445–46
Gutenberg Bible, 278

H

Habsburgs, 278, 325, 344–45, 421, 449–51, 456
Hagar, 153
Ham, descendants of, 8, 11–12, 19, 29, 269
Hamites, 7–8, 12
Hamitic cultures, 26, 72
Hammurabi, King, 94
Hannibal, 108–11, 114, 158
Hawaii, 519, 521
heaven, 5, 40, 42, 44, 49, 55–57, 128, 131–32, 145–46, 156, 204, 207–9, 226, 267, 270
Hebrews, 12, 22, 27, 30–31, 35, 38–39, 55–56, 68, 97, 206

Henry VII, 303, 309
Henry VIII, 303–4, 307, 309
heresy, 135, 147–48, 183, 237, 239, 323, 369, 426, 533
heretics, 135, 147, 287, 369, 436
Herod, 127–29
Hezekiah, King, 293
hieroglyphics, 20, 22, 32
Hinduism, 270–71, 275
Hindu religion, 270–71
Hindus, 523–24
Hitler, Adolph, 519
Hittites, 15, 29, 32–34
Hohenstaufens, 182–83
Hohenzollerns, 360–61, 457–58
Holland, 168, 279, 281, 294, 308–9, 312, 344, 355, 365, 367, 373, 386, 415, 452, 495
Hollanders, 294, 297–98, 439, 463
Holy Alliance, 419, 421, 425, 427–29, 433, 442–43, 445, 448
Holy Land, 183, 185–89, 198, 200, 212
Holy Roman Emperor, 171, 180, 279, 307
Holy Roman Empire, 161, 165, 171, 179, 327, 414
Holy Scriptures, 201, 247, 281, 285, 428, 492
Holy Spirit, 131–32, 144, 381, 494

Hsia Dynasty, 55–56, 62
humanist, 228, 279, 427
humanistic, 280, 341, 345, 527
Hungary, 187, 223, 449
Huns, 61, 139–40, 161, 171, 174
Hyksos, 27, 38–39

I
Iceland, 261–62
icon veneration, 151, 157, 161
idolatry, 29–30, 46, 52, 150, 292, 492, 533
immigration, 186, 269, 275
India, 9, 17, 55, 63, 179, 260, 269–71, 275–76, 387, 504, 506, 523–24
Indian Ocean, 265
Indies, 256, 261–64, 266, 293, 297–98, 309, 347
Indo-Europeans, 9, 12, 17, 34, 63, 65, 68, 98, 102, 153, 171, 270
indulgences, 239, 284–86, 335–36
industrial life, 473–75
infidels, 183, 186–87
institutions, 48, 104, 155, 194, 250, 286, 330, 393, 479
instruments, musical, 5, 25, 50, 293, 492, 497–98
invasions, 61, 102, 125, 140, 212, 507
Iran, 8, 64, 530
Ireland, 309, 317, 349, 371

Isaac, 36
Ishbosheth, 49
Ishmael, 36
Islam, 153, 155–58, 185, 538
Islamic Revolution, 530
Israel, 29, 38, 40, 42, 44, 46, 49, 51–52, 97, 293, 529–31
Israelites, 29–30, 38–41, 43–48, 269
Italy, 31–32, 101, 103, 105, 110–11, 118, 120, 182–83, 211, 245, 279–80, 412–13, 450, 452, 516–20

J
Jacobinism, 475
Jacobins, 404, 406, 413–14, 448
James, King, 318–19
Japheth, 7, 12, 17, 34, 63, 65, 68, 270; descendants of, 9, 17, 491
Japhethites, 7, 9, 12, 63
Jerusalem, 50, 53, 127–30, 132, 134, 183, 188–89, 194, 231, 321, 529
Jesuits, 246, 321–23, 437, 521
Jesus, 130, 144, 155, 185, 321–22
Jews, 53, 127–29, 132–34, 143, 187, 199, 497, 528–30, 538–39
jihad, 157

John, King, 233
Judah, 38, 45–46, 48–49, 52, 293

K
Khan, Jenghiz, 349
King James Version Bible, 318
knighthood, 173–74, 176
knights, 172–76, 186–87, 195, 198, 204, 206, 472
Knox, John, 317, 379, 383
Korea, 522

L
Latin, 13, 103, 105, 121, 206–7, 213, 221, 238, 270, 281–82, 285, 319
laws, 15, 32, 41, 46–47, 75–76, 283–84, 291–92, 296, 330, 337–38, 345, 446–47, 473–74, 477–79, 490
Lebanon, 29, 45
liberty, natural, 375
Lincoln, Abraham (President), 480
Locke, John, 374–76, 477
Lollards, 235–38, 240, 243
Lord, feudal, 195, 201, 343
Lord's Day, 132, 147
Lord's Prayer, 539
Lord's Supper, 130, 132, 236, 289–90, 323
Lord's Supper Roman Catholics, 236
Lord's Table, 293

Louis XIV, King, 341, 345, 387, 393–94
Lucifer, 226
Luther, Martin, 283–90, 294, 321, 327
Lutheran, 288, 290, 325, 361, 370–71, 379

M
Macedonia, 73, 93, 114–16, 207
Magellan, 255–56, 264–66
Magna Carta in England, 296
Mao Zedong, 521–22, 525
Marx, Karl, 488–90, 515
Marxism, 475, 487, 490, 525
mathematics, 16, 251, 261, 373, 462
mediæval world, 215, 256, 258
Medina, 154–55, 260
Mediterranean, 8, 26, 30, 101, 111, 115–16, 121, 258, 260, 266, 359, 365, 416, 446, 494
Mercantile System, 365–68, 473
Mesopotamia, 8, 11–12, 18–19, 32, 35–37, 56, 72, 97–98, 266, 269
Messiah, 48, 50, 53, 129
Mexico, 387, 443
Middle Ages, 173, 179, 193–94, 203, 207–8, 210, 212–13, 217–18, 220–22, 255–56, 266,

278–79, 461–62, 491–92, 496–98; early, 172, 179, 196–97, 322, 472; late, 211, 282, 492, 494, 497
middle class, 56, 400–401, 472
Middle East, 7, 185, 530
migrations, 7, 55, 69, 173, 195, 197, 455
miracles, 73, 125, 129, 397
missionaries, 141, 146, 162, 470, 503–4
missionary work, 321, 323, 349, 387, 418
Moabites, 50
Mohammedans, 156, 158, 161, 175, 183, 185, 207, 258, 445
monarchy: absolute, 395, 505, 530; constitutional, 397
monasteries, rich, 281
Moors, 163, 262–63, 294
moral degeneracy, 491, 497
moral law, 42, 147, 292, 296
Moscow, 14, 221, 347, 350–51, 356, 415
Moses, 39–44, 97, 129, 154, 186
Muslims, 154–58, 185, 187, 434, 524, 528, 530–32

N

Napoleon, 402, 410–18, 422, 424, 428, 431–36, 439–41, 449, 453–54, 457–58, 464–65, 474, 500
Napoleonic wars, great, 440, 474
National Assembly, 401, 403–4
Nazi regime in Germany, 520
Nazism, 528
Nebuchadnezzar, 16, 99
Netherlands, 293–98, 308, 330, 344–45, 379, 431, 447, 518
New England, 319, 371, 381–82, 386, 480–81
Newfoundland, 264, 309
newspapers, 20, 196, 404, 414, 447
Newton, Isaac, 483
Nicene Creed, 147, 161, 306
Nile, 19–21, 23, 26–27, 121, 217, 259, 267, 414, 491, 504
Noah, 6–7, 55, 63, 68, 97, 270, 541
Noah's Ark, 11
nobility, 104, 343, 393–94, 397, 401, 472
Normandy, 168–69, 187, 302–3, 520
Norsemen, 167, 174, 259, 302, 348

North America, 298, 319, 338–39, 379–80, 384, 387, 479, 496
North Korea, 522, 525
North Sea, 216, 301, 309, 330

O

Octavian, 123–25
Old Testament, 41, 127, 535
Orange Free State, 504

P

pagan, 19, 92–93, 147, 155, 206, 351
palaces, magnificent, 15, 491
Palestine, 157, 185–86, 188, 527–30
Papacy, 134, 149, 161, 163, 180–81, 183, 234, 243, 279–80, 285, 329
Paris, 222–23, 226, 387, 398, 403–4, 406, 414–16, 420, 427, 442, 447, 449, 458, 464–65, 512
peace, 86–87, 105, 107, 145–46, 370–71, 388–89, 415–17, 420–21, 424, 427–31, 441, 443, 446–48, 454, 538–39
Peace of Ryswick, 344
Peace of Utrecht, 344
Peace of Westphalia, 344, 462
Pentecostal gift, 132
Persian Empire, 17, 94
Persian Gulf, 11, 260
Persian Kings, 85–86
Persians, 18, 27, 63–64, 68, 85–88, 95, 127, 491
Philip, King, 259, 296
Philippines, 265, 505, 524
Philistines, 46–47, 50
Phoenicians, 29–32, 46, 85–86, 99, 105, 259, 267
pirates, 167, 216, 317
Plato, 147, 229
Pliny, 466
Poland, 357–58, 404, 422, 431, 435, 448, 518, 524
politicians, 71, 375, 473
Polo, Marco, 62, 247, 250, 252, 521
Pompey, 119–21
Pope Paul III, 322–24
pornography, 470, 534
Portugal, 258, 262, 266, 365, 415, 433, 437, 523
Portuguese, 258–59, 262–64, 266–67, 269, 297, 385, 479, 521
poverty, 278, 280, 500
power: absolute, 325, 401; divine, 128, 382; royal, 303, 330; western, 351, 506
Presbyterians, 318, 333–34, 338, 342, 370–71
priests, 24, 42, 47–51, 128, 145, 173, 181, 192,

213, 222, 238, 269, 275, 281–82, 447
principles, scriptural, 147, 149, 292
Promised Land, 30, 32, 37, 41, 43–44, 53
prophet, 44, 47, 51–52, 129–30, 154, 156–57, 229, 367, 426
Protestant Reformation, 201, 205–6, 279, 288, 301, 303, 308, 317–19, 321, 379, 461, 494, 496
Protestants, 287–91, 293–94, 296, 298, 307, 322–25, 329, 336–37, 343, 361–62, 370, 378–79, 387, 391, 429
Prussia, 359, 361–64, 404, 415, 419, 422, 428, 435, 450, 455–58, 490
Puritans, 310–16, 318–19, 334, 339, 342, 371, 388, 496; seventeenth century Presbyterian, 378
puritan work ethic, 334
Pyrenees, 107–8, 158, 163, 207

Q
Quakers, 371

R
races, 5, 18, 43, 63, 68, 115, 192, 276, 279, 293, 336, 385, 484, 504, 507
rebellion, 2, 51, 60–61, 275, 355, 400, 442–43, 447, 506–7, 521
redemption, 2, 98, 132, 136, 539
Red Sea, 38, 40, 260
reformation, 218–19, 229, 231, 240, 243, 247, 289–90, 299, 301, 311, 323, 329–30, 361–62, 462–63, 533–34; awakening, 241; puritan, 318; religious, 277; societal, 383
reformers, 118, 235, 306, 496
regime, 127, 362, 523
Rembrandt, 258, 495
Renaissance, 218–21, 226, 243–44, 266, 280–81, 432, 463, 466, 527; humanist, 229
revolution, 390–91, 393, 396, 405–7, 418, 420, 424, 426, 431, 433, 436–37, 447, 449, 468–69, 489; cultural, 384; industrial, 461, 470–71, 475–76, 479, 510; political, 384; proletariat, 490; sexual, 533; social, 464, 471
righteousness, 47, 144, 204, 322

Roman armies, 105, 107–8, 110, 113, 115
Roman Catholic Church, 150, 162, 199, 210, 237, 246, 279–80, 291, 323
Roman Catholics, 236, 287, 289, 292, 325, 327, 336, 345, 371, 373, 392, 437, 454, 457, 523–24
Roman Empire, 98, 111, 113, 127–28, 134, 136, 145, 149, 171, 191, 194, 203, 250, 348, 351
Romans, 17–18, 20, 102–7, 110–11, 113–17, 119, 124–25, 129–30, 134, 141, 143–44, 146, 161, 163–64, 493–94
Rome, 98–99, 101–7, 109–10, 113–16, 118–25, 133–34, 137–40, 143–44, 179–83, 208–9, 226–28, 243–46, 280–81, 286, 321–24; bishop of, 134, 145, 149, 171; early history of, 104, 106
Roosevelt, Franklin (President), 519
Rousseau, Jean Jacques, 424, 436
Rubicon River, 120
Russia, 151–52, 347–50, 353, 355–57, 413–14, 421–22, 424–25, 427–29, 431, 443–44, 446, 454, 503, 510–12, 515–16
Russians, 240, 270, 325, 349–50, 391, 393, 412, 445, 448, 506

S

Sabbath, 43, 131–32, 315
Sabbath assembly, 42
Sabbath laws, 391
Sabbath sanctity, 315
Sabbath worship, 50, 133
sacrifice, 6, 29, 41–42, 48, 130, 132
salvation: justifying, 284; personal, 383; planned, 6
Saudi Arabia, 531
scholars, 58, 60, 219, 226, 228, 231–32, 238, 282, 291, 315, 535
Scotland, 299, 301, 308, 316–19, 329–30, 332, 338, 349, 371, 377–79, 382
secular humanism, 530, 533–34; promoted, 533
secularism, 180, 372, 527, 530–31, 533, 538
self-government, 76–77, 85, 388, 524
Semitic peoples, 7, 12
Serbia, 506, 511
serfs, 138, 192, 204, 211, 352, 479
servants, 7, 29, 35–36, 44, 49, 175, 326, 387, 395, 398, 419

services, civil, 294, 365
Shakespeare, William, 81, 258
Shang Dynasty, 56
Shem, descendants of, 8, 269
ships, 87, 92, 100–101, 212, 216, 255–57, 261, 264–65, 267, 296–97, 309, 411, 417, 441, 446
Sicily, 92, 101, 106–7, 183, 450
Siddhartha, 272–74
slavery, 38, 78, 375, 461, 479–80, 482; abolition of, 477, 479
slaves, 56, 77–80, 111, 116, 138, 352, 445, 461, 479–81, 509
Smith, Adam, 474, 478
Solomon, 51–52, 97
South America, 263, 440, 442–43, 446, 523
South Korea, 522–23
South Vietnam, 523
Soviet Union, 516, 518–20, 522–23, 525, 529–30
Spain, 100, 107–8, 110, 116, 120, 258, 262–64, 266, 293–94, 296, 330, 334, 414–15, 440, 442–43
Sparta, 72, 86–88, 91–93
Spice Islands, 264–65
Stalin, 516
steam engine, 463, 500
St. Helena, 413, 418–19

Stuart, Mary, 309, 316
Stuarts, 307, 325, 329–30, 334, 387
Sudan, 531
Suez Canal, 503
Sumatra, 228
Sumeria, 14, 29, 63
Sumerians, 12–14, 31–32
Sun King, 341–42
suppression, 314, 371, 446, 479
Sweden, 167, 223, 281, 288, 325, 344, 355, 357–58, 432
Switzerland, 240, 289–90, 449
Syria, 29, 32, 114–16, 120, 157, 188, 411, 514

T

Tabernacle, 42, 45
T'ang dynasty, 252
Taoism, 251–52; favored, 251
Tartars, 171, 350–52
taxation, 138, 400
temples, 14, 19–20, 50–51, 56, 74, 128, 131, 135, 143–44, 149, 404, 426, 491–94, 497
Teutons, 118, 125, 146
Thebes, 27, 69, 426
Themistocles, 87–88, 418
Thermopylae, 87–88
Third Estate, 401, 403
Tiberius Gracchus, 117, 128

Troubadours, 173, 175, 220
Troy, 66, 71, 80
Turkey, 8, 29, 32–33, 424, 445, 454, 506, 511, 514, 528
Turks, 18, 151, 185–89, 198, 228, 240, 351, 433–34, 444–45, 506–7
tyranny, 234, 315, 324, 331, 406
tyrants, selfish, 225, 424

U
Uganda, 528
United Kingdom, 332, 338, 370–71, 376, 439, 513
United States, 143, 338, 359, 439, 442–43, 465, 479, 490, 505, 513–14, 519–24, 529–31, 533

V
Venezuela, 442
Venice, 188, 198, 211–14, 216, 249, 266, 450, 498
Versailles, 343, 394, 397, 401, 403, 419, 458, 513
Victoria, Queen, 448, 453
Vienna, 398, 403–4, 418–19, 421–22, 427, 431–32, 434, 436, 438–40, 446, 451, 454, 456, 458, 468
Vietnam, 59, 522–23, 525

Vineland, 261
Virgil, 225–27
Virginia, 383, 388, 390

W
Wales, 371
war, 77–78, 106–7, 111, 114–16, 118–19, 183, 326–27, 333–34, 387, 410–11, 454–55, 457–58, 503, 510–14, 517–23; holy, 157, 437; phony, 518; total, 511
Washington, 176, 389–90, 457, 461, 467
Waterloo, 413, 417–18, 448
weapons, biological, 512
Western society, 500, 533–34
Westminster Confession, 381–82
Westminster Standards, 332, 338, 370–71
Whitcomb, John C., 535
Whitney, Eli, 464
wickedness, 6, 271, 321, 327, 341, 535
World War I, 360, 507, 509, 513, 515, 518–19, 521, 528
World War II, 515, 517–18, 520–22, 528
Wyckliffe, John, 231–39, 288, 301, 303

X
Xerxes, 88, 93

Z
Zarathustra, 64, 271
Zeus, 78, 103, 493
Zionism, 527
Zurich, 289
Zwingli, 289–90, 327
Zwolle, 246–47

Made in the USA
Monee, IL
13 December 2020